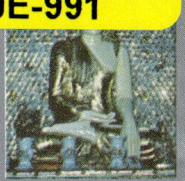
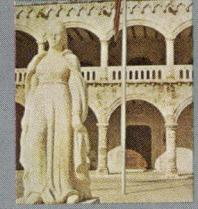

THE WORLD AND ITS PEOPLES

FRANCE

GREYSTONE PRESS/NEW YORK

PHOTO CREDITS: S.E.F./Istituto Geografico De Agostini/ Karquel/Veronese/Sun-Slides/Giancolombo/G. E. Piazzoli/ Regie Renault/P.A.H./EPS/P. Culmann/S.N.C.F./M. Rossi/ Farabola/Tourisme Monaco/C. Cisventi/French Government Tourist Office/French Embassy FACSEA/Magnum/Air France/ Cineriz/F. Fantini/D.G.A.C.T./M.A.T.P./Rigal/C.D.P.C./ G. Mairani/R. Jacques/Giraudon/Alinari/L. Laniepce/G. Marussi/F. A. Mella/Giancomelli/Astor Pictures, Inc./Janus Films/Films Around the World / *the Chrysler Corporation for the end papers that keynote "The World and Its Peoples" theme.*

Library of Congress Catalogue Card Number 63-20568.

Special contents of this edition copyright © GREYSTONE PRESS, 100 SIXTH AVENUE, NEW YORK, 1963. All rights reserved. No part of the contents of this book may be reproduced without the written permission of the publishers. The original copyright is held by ISTITUTO GEOGRAFICO DE AGOSTINI–Novara–publisher in Italy of the Encyclopaedia "Il Milione"–Chief Editor: Giuseppe Sormani.

Cover and Book Designed by Harold Franklin

MANUFACTURED IN THE UNITED STATES OF AMERICA

EDITORIAL CONSULTANT FOR FRANCE AND MONACO:

JOHN C. LAPP, PH.D.
Chairman, Department of French
University of California, Los Angeles

THE WORLD AND ITS PEOPLES—EDITORS AND CONTRIBUTORS

UMBERTO ALBINI
Lecturer in Greek Literature
University of Florence

JOHN JOSEPH BAUGHMAN
Ph.D., University of Michigan
Associate Professor of History
De Pauw University

PIERLUIGI BRACCO
Assistant Professor of History
of International Relations
University of Padua

LIMENTANI IDA CALABI
Associate Professor of
Greek and Roman Antiquities
University of Milan

BASILIO CIALDEA
Lecturer in History of
International Relations
University of Rome

FEDERICO CURATO
Professor of Modern History
University of Pavia

PIERO DAGRADI
Reader in Geography
University of Pavia

JOHN S. ERWIN
Composer, author and critic

JOHNSON E. FAIRCHILD
M.A., Clark University
Director, Adult Education,
Cooper Union
for the Advancement of
Science and Art;
Chairman, Cooper Union Forum

ELLEN HERSEY
B.A., Oberlin College

ROBERT HIGGINS
M.A., Cambridge University

PIERO LANDINI
Professor of Geography
University of Palermo

DWIGHT LEROY LING
Ph.D., University of Illinois
Associate Professor of History
De Pauw University

GEORGE B. MANHART
Ph.D., University of Pennsylvania
Professor Emeritus of History
De Pauw University

ELIO MIGLIORINI
Professor of Geography
University of Naples

GEORGE THORNTON MILLER
A.B., University of Arkansas
The New York Times

GUISEPPE MORELLI
Professor of Classic Philology
University of Rome

GERALD NEEDHAM
M.A., New York University
Lecturer in Art History
Brown University

WILLIAM NETHERCUT
M.A., Columbia University
Instructor of Greek and
Latin, Columbia University

JOSEPH NEWMAN
B.A., Williams College
Author; Editorial Board:
The New York Herald Tribune

RICCARDO PICCHIO
Professor of Polish
Literature and Language
University of Florence

CLARK V. POLING, JR.
B.A., Columbia University

MARCO ROSCI
Associate Professor
University of Milan

RUGGERI JOLE SCUDIERI
Associate Professor of
Spanish Literature
University of Rome

ASHLEY TALBOT
B.A., University of Michigan
Senior Editor
C. S. Hammond and Company

JOSEPH THAN
Film producer, writer and critic

LEONE TRAVERSO
Professor
University of Urbino

GIORGIO VALUSSI
Professor of Geography
University of Trieste

ROBERT VAN NUFFEL
Professor of French Literature
University of Brussels

EUGENIO VILLICAÑA
Ph.D., Cambridge University

HELMUT WOHL
Ph.D., Institute of Fine Arts, N.Y.U.
Assistant Professor of Fine Arts
Yale University

ROBERT WORTH
Ph.D., University of Chicago

RENÉ WELLEK
Ph.D., Charles University, Prague
Professor of Comparative Literature
Yale University

MONACO

FRANCE

Table of Contents

FRANCE:	**PAGE**
A Prologue	6
The Land	30
The People	105
The History	190
In the succeeding volume:	
The History *(Continued)*	217
The Fine Arts	239
The Louvre	330
The Literature	352
The Theater	396
The Music	405
The Film	416

MONACO:	
The Land	427
The History	427
The People	430

Maps and Reference Material

32-33	**MAP: FRANCE & MONACO**
38	Geological map
39	Dimensions of major rivers
46	Profile of the Paris Basin
52	Profile of the Massif Central
52	Profile of the Alpine chain
52	Profile of the Vosges Mountains
58	Population distribution map
64	Population chart
97	Map of grape-growing regions
100	Mineral resource map
100	Map of major industries
180	Map of Paris
191	Map of Gaul in 476 A.D.
192	Map of Carolingian Empire
196	Map of France in 1154
212	Genealogical Table: Bourbon and Bourbon – Orléans kings
214	Growth of France: 17th & 18th centuries
224	Map of Napoleon's Empire in 1810
233	Genealogical Table: House of Bonaparte
237	Fundamental dates in French history
238	Rulers and Governments of France

Château de Chenonceaux

FRANCE:
a prologue

THE CELTIC TRIBESMEN WHO BUILT THEIR huts on an island in the middle of the Seine more than 2000 years ago had no intention of founding a great nation. Down through the centuries, the Romans seized the land from the original settlers, Germanic tribes invaded it, and then the French Kings attempted to widen their power.

Île de la Cité, from which Paris grew

Despite the monarchs' efforts, ambitious nobles carved out huge estates for themselves and built walled cities where the king's arm could not reach. Gradually, the terror of incessant warfare subsided. Throughout the Middle Ages magnificent cathedrals rose in testimony to the new faith that the world was good, their spires reaching toward the heavens.

Left: *Strasbourg, the cathedral*
Below: *The walled city of Carcassonne*

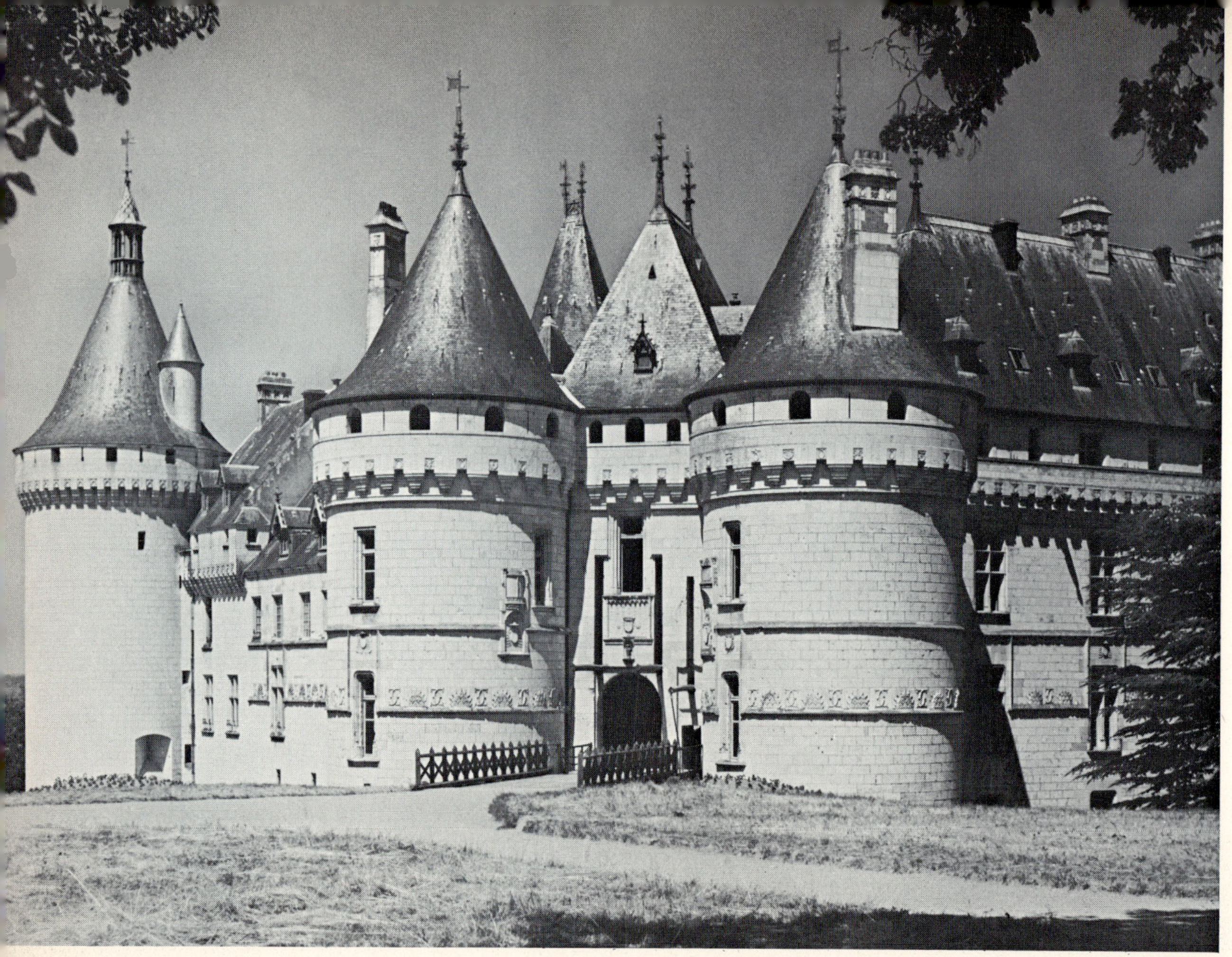

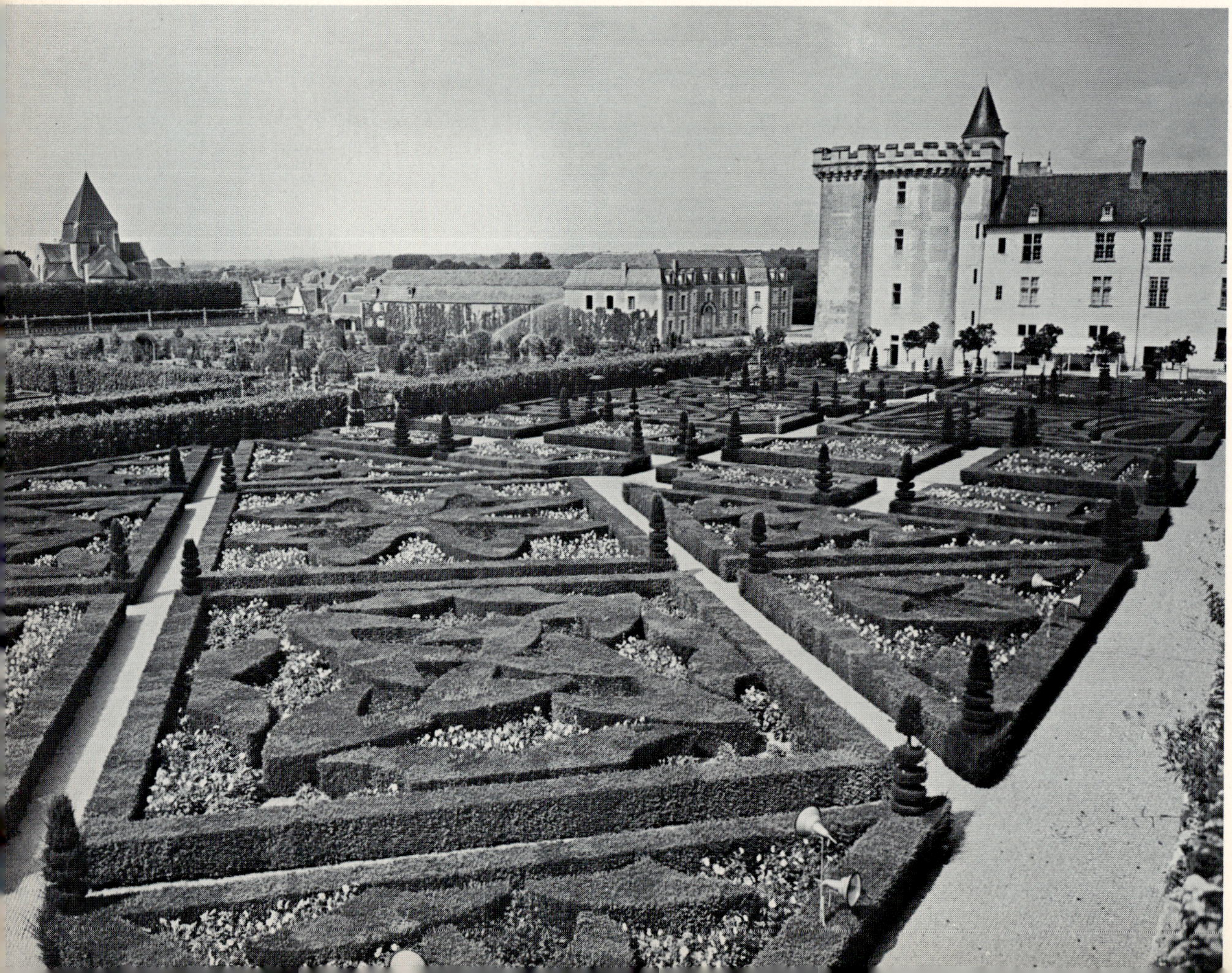

The massive stone castles of the rich and powerful grew less forbidding as the spread of artillery made such strongholds obsolete. Drill fields were turned into gardens as the king's peace spread throughout the land.

Left, top: *Château de Chaumont, Loir-et-Cher department*

Left, bottom: *Château de Villandry, Indre-et-Loire department*

Above: *Château de Valençay, Indre department*

But the artistic traditions of older times remained, abiding inspirations to the generations that came after. The great legacies in stone challenged each succeeding age, resulting in buildings that met changing needs and aspirations.

Left: *Arles, the 12th-century cloister of St. Trophîme*

Above: *The new UNESCO building in Paris*

PARIS CONTINUED TO GROW ABOUT THE SMALL ISLAND IN the middle of the Seine, and became the most cosmopolitan city in Europe. Artists from every part of France and Europe came to learn and to teach, and created more beautiful buildings, statues and paintings to adorn the nation's capital.

Right: *Montmartre café, Paris*
Above: *Place de la Concorde, Paris*

16 / FRANCE · *A Prologue*

Gilles, by Antoine Watteau

Thus Paris was a magnet which attracted the greatest talents of each age, turning the city into a thriving workshop that provided art masterpieces for the world.

From the time of Louis XIV on, French painters were the most elegant and admired portrayers of court life and amusements. In modern times French artists have been the avant garde, creating new techniques and media, constantly experimenting, and producing new challenges to the art world.

Woman Dancing, by Toulouse-Lautrec

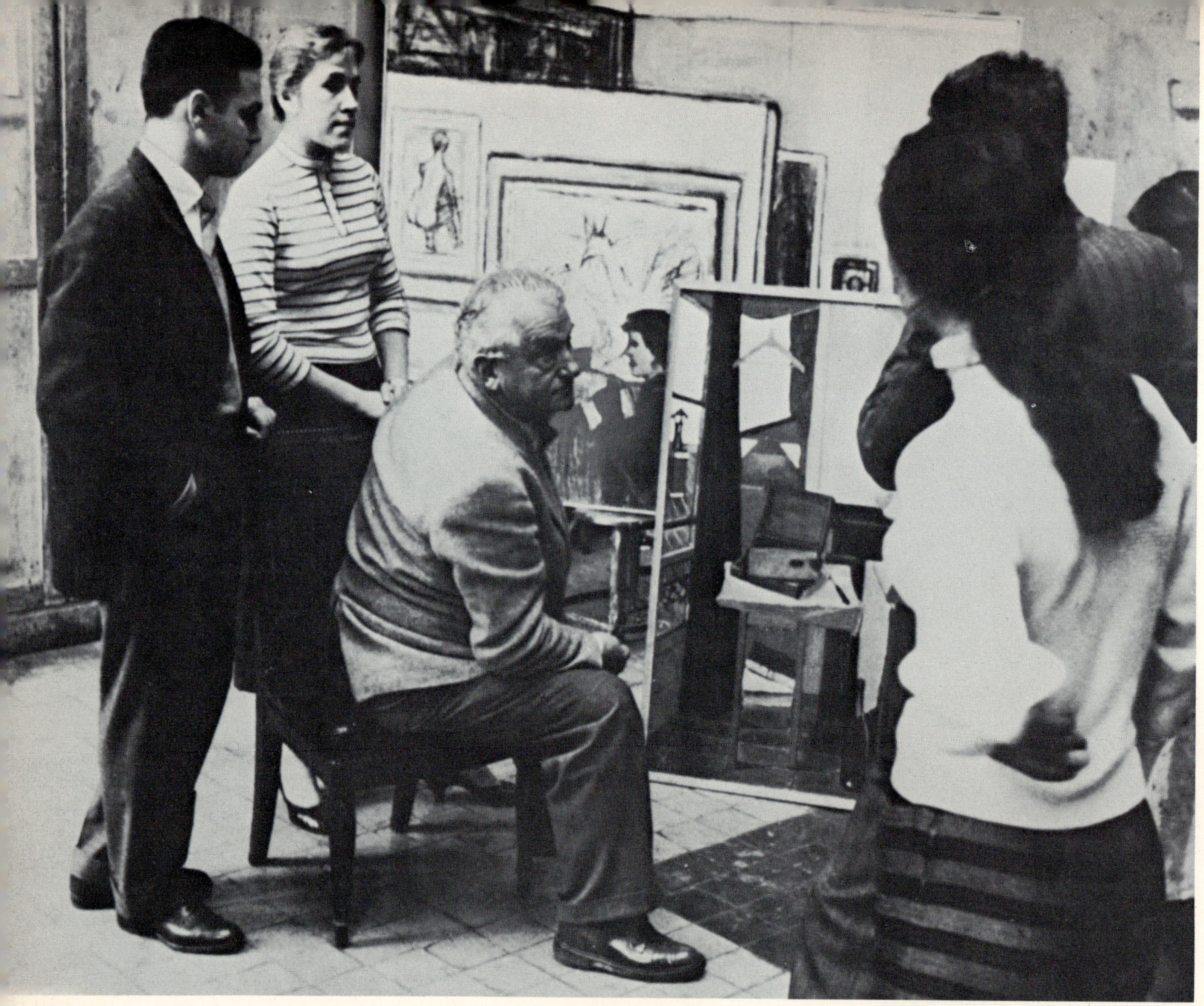

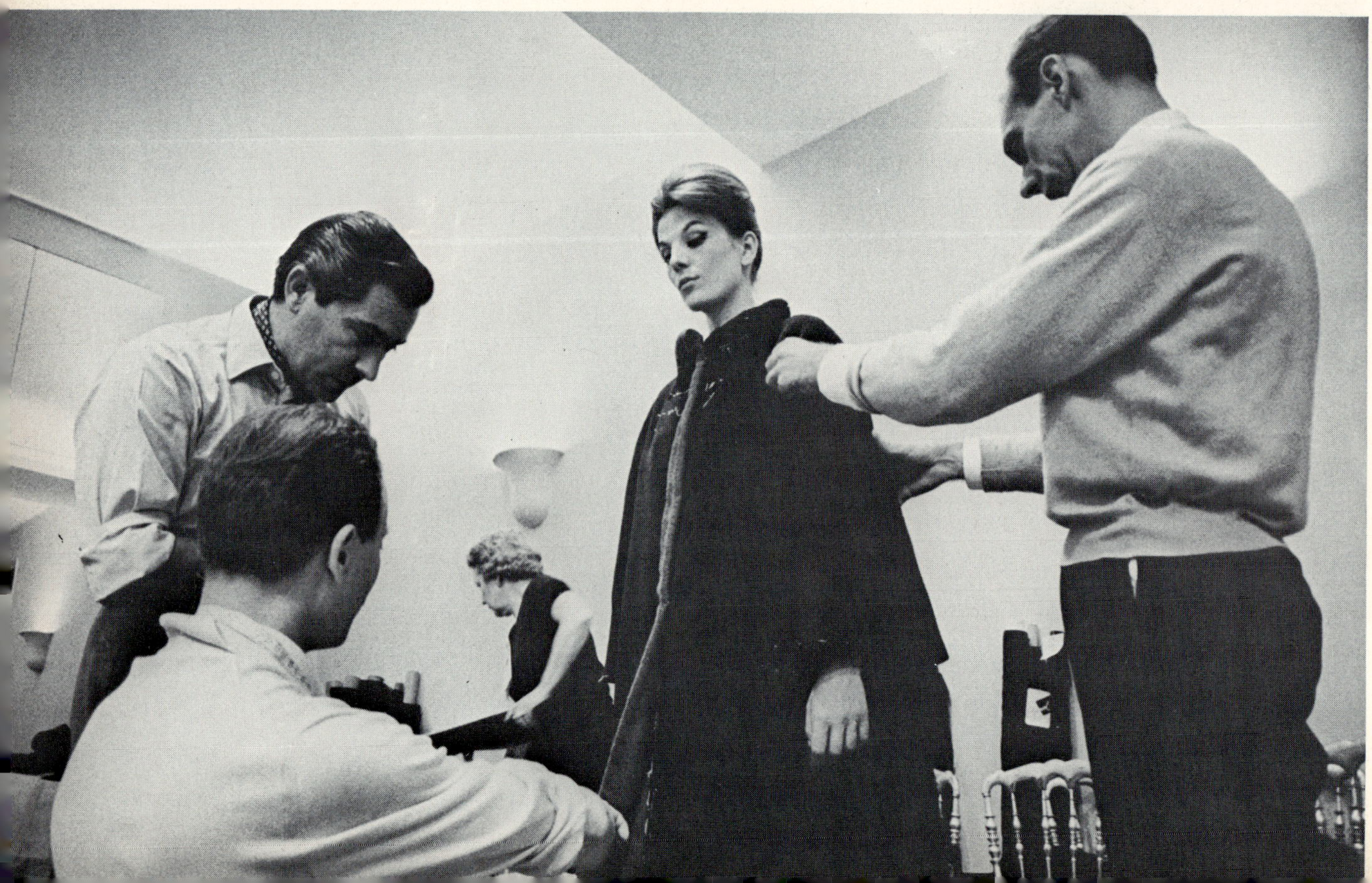

FRANCE · *A Prologue* / 19

The people of Paris, long influenced by this artistic excellence, have achieved international acclaim in other endeavors, making France a world leader in high fashion and fine food.

Left, top: *École des Beaux Arts, Paris*
Left, bottom: *A fashion designer's atelier, Paris*
Below: *School for chefs, Paris*

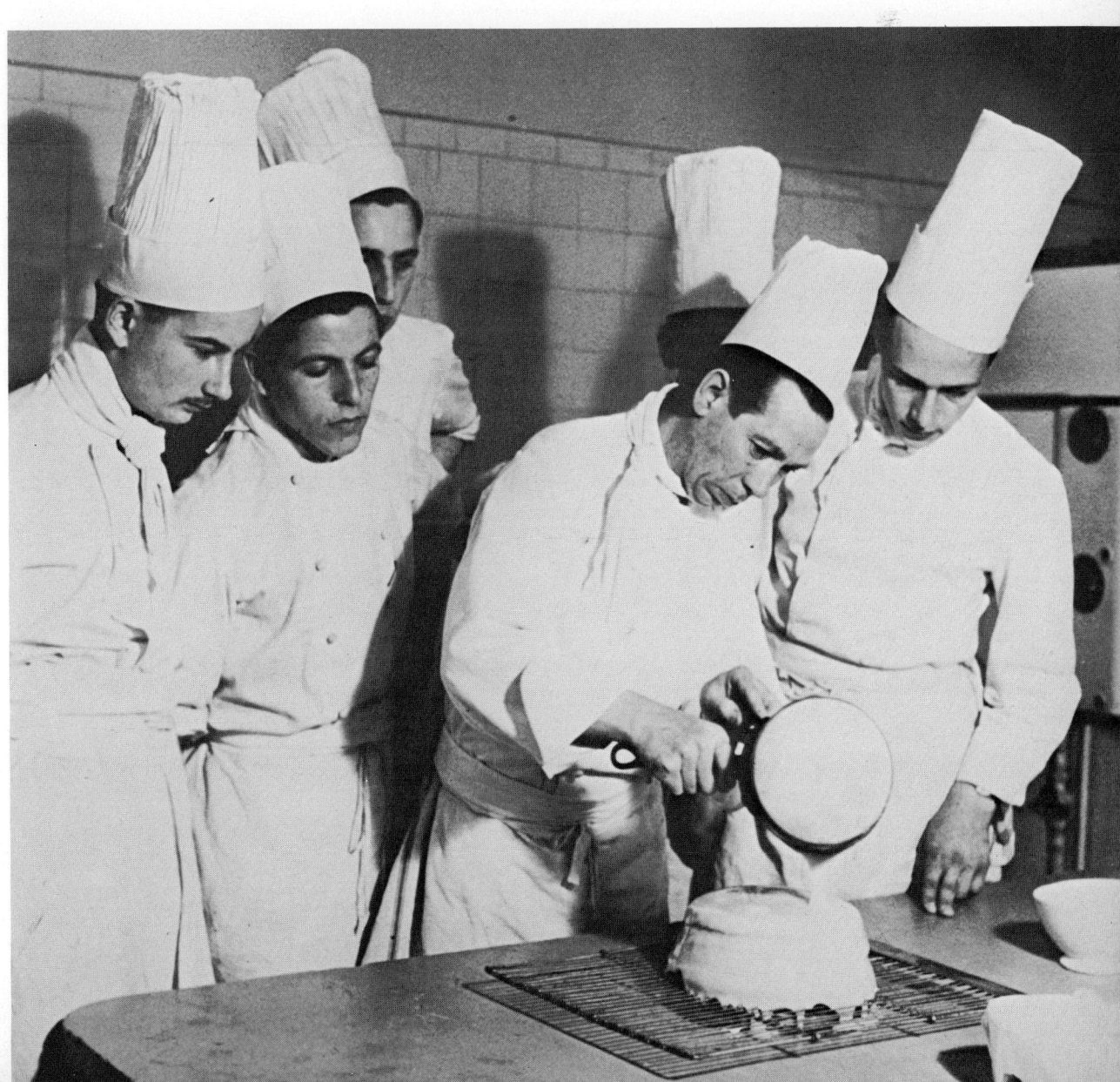

Paris determines French artistic and intellectual tastes to a remarkable degree, but each province has a life of its own. Each town cherishes its own history, customs and traditions.

Even Annecy, nestling in an Alpine valley, French for little more than a century, has been successful in combining its Savoyard heritage with its pride in being part of today's France.

Street scene, Annecy

Biarritz

GEOGRAPHY AS WELL AS HISTORY DETERMINES THE DIFFERences between the provinces and the capital. The intense blue sea, the long, dry summers and the pleasant beaches along France's Mediterranean coastline have made the area an international playground. Generations of aristocrats have bestowed an aura of glamour to the very names of southern French towns—Biarritz, St. Tropez, Cannes, Nice. In the evenings, the resorts strung out along the Côte d'Azur glitter like jewels of a vast tiara set upon the calm, dark sea.

Menton

The fishing fleets of the southern coast have largely given way to pleasure craft and cruise ships; but in the far northwestern corner of France, in Brittany, the primeval rhythms of the tide still govern the lives of those who live at the edge of the sea and look to it for their livelihood.

This isolated province has preserved most of its heritage intact. The Celtic language of the region, Breton, is still commonly spoken, and the women proudly wear the starched lace headdresses that their mothers and their mothers' mothers wore before them.

All over France, in cities, towns and villages, ordinary French citizens still work and play much as did their ancestors. Many farmers still cultivate their fields by hand. The time-tested rituals of distilling brandy and curing cheese have been lovingly preserved. Yet, at the same time, in modern laboratories and plants, researchers and engineers work at the forefront of scientific knowledge. In leisure hours young peasants will don their inherited finery to dance at traditional harvest festivals; in calm retirement the old pursue their hobbies with friends from childhood days.

The endless fascination of France is seen in the faces of her people—in the shy curiosity of a little boy on a country road, in the gaze of a crack Alpine guide, in the rugged calm of an old Breton grandmother.

Its people, its land, its artistic heritage—every aspect of its life—have combined to produce a unique nation: France.

THE LAND

PAGE	
30	THE FRENCH REGION *Geological History...The Coasts...Mountain Systems...Climate...Rivers...Vegetation...Wild Life*
37	POLITICAL ORGANIZATION *Geographical Limits...Administrative Divisions...Constitution...Administration of Justice...Religion...Education...Language...Monetary System and Measures...The French Community*
43	PHYSICAL GEOGRAPHY *The Land, Climate and River Systems of...Northern France...Northeastern France...The Paris Basin...Northwestern France...The Aquitaine Basin...The Massif Central...The Alps and the Jura...Mediterranean France...Corsica*
61	HUMAN GEOGRAPHY *Earliest Settlements...The Celts, Romans and Franks...The French Kingdom...Nineteenth and Twentieth Centuries...Internal Migration...Immigration...Population Density...Forms of Rural Settlement...Villages...City Life*
66	CITIES AND SETTLEMENTS *Paris...The Paris Basin...Northern France...Northeastern France...Northwestern France...The Aquitaine Basin and the Pyrenees...Massif Central...The Alps and the Jura...The Mediterranean Region and the Rhone Valley...Corsica*
93	ECONOMIC GEOGRAPHY *Agriculture...Cereals...Potatoes and Industrial Crops...Vegetables...Orchard and Other Fruits...Grapes and Wine...Forests...Livestock...Fishing...Industry...Mining...Electric Power...Engineering...Textiles...Chemicals...Food and Other Industries...Communications...Tourism*

FRANCE FORMS A BRIDGE BETWEEN the central and the western lands of the great European peninsula, and a natural link between the Mediterranean, the Atlantic and the North Sea.

The fact that France faces the Mediterranean enabled her inhabitants to take part in the life and culture of the classical world. Later, France's position on the Atlantic allowed her to enjoy a privileged position in transoceanic communication with the Americas. Moreover, the absence of natural barriers in Central Europe made migration from east to west easy, and favored the fusion of differing cultures.

Where such foreign influences met and were absorbed over the centuries, French culture arose. It is interesting to observe that the area where these cultures meet contains the general geographic structure and mountain pattern most typical of Europe.

Geological History

The original structural nuclei of the terrain of France were situated in

Paris, the city of light, is seen from a bridge across the Seine River. The river runs right through the heart of the nation's capital and divides it roughly in half.

the northwestern and south-central areas of the country. It was part of the ancient Hercynian mountain system, which in the Paleozoic or Primary geological era stretched as far as Ireland, central England, central Germany and Poland.

These original masses underwent intense erosion and at the beginning of the Mesozoic or Secondary era the land was leveled out into an immense plain. Invasions by the sea followed, which washed the land during almost the entire Mesozoic era. Lime, sand and clay sediments were deposited in layers on the sea bed. The rocks thus formed varied in thickness according to the length of the periods of invasion by the sea.

After the seas finally withdrew in the Tertiary period, faulting, folding and other developments created the land masses and the depressions. The uplifting and renewed erosion resulted in the survival of only the more resistant rocks.

The great Alpine folds to the east were created during the Tertiary period. Their enormous mass is reckoned by geologists to be around twelve miles deep. Folds were formed and were raised up with titanic force to dominate the adjacent plains. This great mountain-building energy also affected neighboring areas, causing huge wavelike formations in such places as the Jura and Burgundy, and raised up the mountainous zone around Lyons.

Volcanic phenomena of the Tertiary and the Quaternary periods complete the picture of France's geological evolution and put the final touches to its landforms. Evidence of this volcanic activity of the Tertiary period can be traced in Auvergne and in Velay, while water and temperature together carved the deep Alpine and Pyrenean valleys and formed the alluvial plains.

The Coasts

France faces bodies of water in three directions: the Strait of Dover and the English Channel, the Bay of Biscay and the Atlantic Ocean, and the Mediterranean Sea. The over-all length of the French coastline is nearly 2000 miles, which exceeds that of the land boundaries.

There are four different coastal sectors. The first is the coast of the Paris Basin in Picardy and Normandy, where the shoreline is of white cliffs much eroded by the waters of the English Channel. The second sector begins with the Cotentin Peninsula, and includes the rocky coastline of Brittany. Here signs of a recent subsidence are seen in the many long estuaries of the rivers and the continually eroding shoreline. Rocks and islets, at one time part of the land, dot the coastline, and some of the deepest inlets occur in the Brest Roads and the Bay of Douarnenez.

Between Brittany and the Spanish border, the French coast is washed by the Bay of Biscay, famous for its 40-foot tidal range, one of the world's greatest variations. The coast is broken only by the river estuaries, where great centers of population are situated. Between the newly-forested Landes region and the sea are several large marshy lagoons. These have been formed by sand dunes blocking the short watercourses.

The Mediterranean coastline of France has a double aspect: that of the Gulf of Lions and the Rhone delta is low and regular, while that of Provence is high and indented, with chalky cliffs and sandy strips. Here the Alpine foothills of Provence face the sea in the wild and splendid Côte des Maures, the Côte Rouge and the Côte d'Azur or Riviera, whose beautiful countryside, mild climate and rich flora have made it one of the most attractive tourist resorts in the world.

Mountain Systems

The mountain and hill systems of France fall into three categories: massifs, mountain chains and the areas having in some degree a mixture of the first two forms. The massifs or uplands, which are in the western and south-central regions, are upraised portions of Paleozoic strata, and are therefore the oldest surfaces of France. The Massif Central covers a vast area (33,000 square miles), having its center at 45° North. The outstanding feature of this massif is a plateau, but there are many small hills, lowlands and true mountains, such as Plomb du Cantal (6096 feet)

The man directing traffic here is not a gendarme. He is called an agent pivot, or traffic officer. Gendarmes are roughly equivalent to state troopers or Mounties. Regular city policemen are called agents de police, or, in slang, Flics.

FRANCE

FRANCE
Principal Cities
Pop.,—Thousands

33	Agen	E 4
68	Aix [-en-Provence]	F 6
39	Albi	F 5
26	Alençon	C 4
41	Alès	E 6
32	Alfortville	g10
105	Amiens	C 5
115	Angers	D 3
48	Angoulême	E 4
43	Annecy	E 7
35	Antibes	F 7
82	Argenteuil	C 5, g10
42	Arras	B 5
82	Asnières [-sur-Seine]	g10
71	Aubervilliers	g10
48	Aulnay-sous-Bois	g11
73	Avignon	F 6
32	Bagnolet	g10
37	Bayonne	F 3
34	Beauvais	C 5
24	Bègles	E 3
48	Belfort	D 7
96	Besançon	D 7
36	Béthune	B 5
34	Blois	D 4
30	Bois-Colombes	g10
38	Bondy	g10
250	Bordeaux	E 3
107	Boulogne-Billancourt	C 5, g 9
49	Boulogne [-sur-Mer]	B 4
33	Bourg [-en-Bresse]	D 6
61	Bourges	D 5
136	Brest	C 1
40	Brive [-la-Gaillarde]	E 4
31	Bruay [-en-Artois]	B 5
91	Caen	C 3
70	Calais	B 4
33	Cambrai	B 5
58	Cannes	F 7
41	Carcassonne	F 5
37	Castres	F 5
29	Caudéran	E 3
42	Châlons-sur-Marne	C 6
44	Chalon-sur-Saône	D 6
44	Chambéry	E 6
58	Champigny-sur-Marne	g11
25	Charleville	C 6
31	Chartres	C 4
45	Châteauroux	D 4
27	Châtellerault	D 4
37	Cherbourg	C 3
41	Choisy-le-Roi	g10
37	Cholet	D 3
48	Clamart	g10
128	Clermont-Ferrand	E 5
56	Clichy [-la-Garenne]	C 5, g10
52	Colmar	C 7
77	Colombes	g10
59	Courbevoie	g10
29	Denain	B 5
30	Dieppe	C 4
136	Dijon	D 6
48	Douai	B 5
66	Drancy	g10
30	Épinal	C 7
37	Évreux	C 4
37	Fontenay [-sous-Bois]	g10
24	Fougères	C 3
43	Gennevilliers	g10
157	Grenoble	E 6
26	Houilles	e 9
52	Issy [-les-Moulineaux]	g10
53	Ivry-sur-Seine	g10
67	La Rochelle	D 3
34	La Seyne [-sur-Mer]	F 6
39	Laval	C 3
34	Le Creusot	D 6
184	Le Havre	C 4

Pop	City	Grid
132	Le Mans	C 4
43	Lens	B 5
25	Le Puy [-en-Velay]	E 5
62	Levallois-Perret	C 5, g10
193	Lille	B 5
118	Limoges	E 4
61	Lorient	D 2
22	Lunéville	C 7
529	Lyon	E 6
51	Maisons-Alfort	g10
34	Malakoff	g10
778	Marseille	F 6
27	Maubeuge	B 5
103	Metz	C 7
41	Montauban	E 4
29	Montceau-les-Mines	D 6
55	Montluçon	D 5
119	Montpellier	F 5
92	Montreuil [-sous-Bois]	g10
45	Montrouge	g10
24	Moulins	D 5
109	Mulhouse	D 7
129	Nancy	C 7
83	Nanterre	g 9
240	Nantes	D 3
34	Narbonne	F 5
73	Neuilly [-sur-Seine]	g11
39	Nevers	D 5
100	Nice	F 7
39	Nîmes	F 6
38	Niort	D 3
25	Nogent [-sur-Marne]	g10
84	Orléans	D 4
46	Pantin	g10
2,800	Paris	C 5, g10
60	Pau	F 3
39	Périgueux	E 4
83	Perpignan	F 5
62	Poitiers	D 4
40	Puteaux	g 9
134	Reims	C 6
152	Rennes	C 3
38	Roanne	D 6
29	Rochefort	E 3
26	Romans [-sur-Isère]	E 6
113	Roubaix	B 5
121	Rouen	C 4
55	Rueil-Malmaison	g 9
43	St. Brieuc	C 2
94	St. Denis	C 5, g10
201	St. Étienne	E 6
35	St. Germain-en Laye	g 9
70	St. Maur-des-Fossés	g10
58	St. Nazaire	D 2
52	St. Ouen	g10
61	St. Quentin	C 5
25	Schiltigheim	C 7
36	Sète	F 5
229	Strasbourg	C 7
39	Suresnes	g 9
47	Tarbes	F 4
162	Toulon	F 6
324	Toulouse	F 4
89	Tourcoing	B 5
93	Tours	D 4
67	Troyes	C 6
53	Valence [-sur-Rhône]	E 6
45	Valenciennes	B 5
30	Vannes	D 2
87	Versailles	C 5, g 9
31	Vichy	D 5
32	Vierzon	D 4
46	Villejuif	g10
105	Villeurbanne	E 6
50	Vincennes	g10
66	Vitry [-sur-Seine]	g10
41	Wattrelos	B 5

MONACO
Principal City
Pop.—Thousands

| 22 | Monaco | F 7 |

The low, sandy coast of Pas de Calais department is made of the same limestone as the white chalk cliffs of Dover, England, twenty-two miles across the water. The Strait of Dover, or Pas de Calais, as it is called in France, which separates England from continental Europe, is a recent geological development. Until some 20,000 years ago, Britain was connected to France by a low, flat area called the Flemish plain. Today, those parts of the plain that are still above water, like the Pas de Calais coast of France, are among the flattest regions of Europe. Dull gray in color, barren and windswept, the Pas de Calais shore line offers little for any form of life to exist on.

and Puy de Sancy in the Mont Dore (6188 feet).

There are smaller massifs in the eastern sector of France, such as the Ardennes, the Vosges and the Morvan, which are smoothly-rounded formations covered with a thick mantle of forest; to the south is the Montagnes des Maures massif, where climate varies between summer dryness and violent autumnal cloudbursts.

The mountain chains in the southeast, east and southwest, namely, the Alps, the Jura and the Pyrenees, are more recently formed masses. For climatic reasons, the Alpine sector is divided in two: the northern and the southern Alps. The former include the highest peaks in the range (Mont Blanc, 15,781 feet; Les Ecrins, 13,461 feet), and are separated from the Alpine foothills by a long trench. Great valleys such as those of the Arve, Isère, Arc and Romanche cut into the relief, and contain the entire range of Alpine vegetation. The southern Alps are lower but broader than the northern Alps, and merge unobtrusively into the Alpine foothills.

THE PYRENEES

The steep Pyrenean slopes are largely of crystalline rock first shaped during the early Tertiary period and modified by the movements which occurred later, when the Alps were formed. The highest peaks are in the High Pyrenees, very nearly the most impassable area in the chain, where Vignemale reaches a height of 10,820 feet.

Between the Alsatian plain, the Rhone valley and the plain of the Saône rise the Jura Mountains, which are mixed formations of the type mentioned above. Rather low in altitude (5652 feet at Crêt de la Neige), and covered with woods and pasturelands, they form a crescent-shaped mountain chain, composed of limestones of the mid-Mesozoic era. From these mountains is derived the name of the Jurassic geological period.

More than half of France consists of scattered plains, which are most widespread in the basins of Paris and of Aquitaine. Plains in the Paris Basin are grouped in Champagne and on either side of the Loire River. But there are also plateaus and hilly parts, and the vegetation is variegated. The plains of Aquitaine are more uniformly flat, and except for some undulation in the center, the basin is a large terraced expanse with many watercourses.

Among the other plains, those of ancient origin in Brive, Berry, Flanders and the Marais Breton are below sea level in places. Those of more recent origin are often surrounded by higher ground, apparent in Alsace, and in the Saône, Rhone and Alpine valleys.

Climate

Most of France falls within the moist temperate region of northwestern Europe. It is one of the few countries in Europe which includes the three main groups of European climatic types: the Mediterranean Sea area, the Atlantic Ocean or maritime area and the central or continental area. The French climate is especially influenced by these two great bodies of water and by extremely variegated terrain.

There is the typically oceanic climate of Brittany, characterized by relatively slight changes in temperature, generally mild winters, early and long springs, short autumns and moderate, well-distributed rainfall in all seasons. There is the "transitional" climate of the Paris Basin, with winters colder than those of Brittany but milder than those of more easterly areas, with relatively fresh summers and regular and not-too-heavy rainfall.

There is the continental climate of Lorraine, Alsace and the Saône valley, characterized by cold winters, relatively hot summers and rainfall mainly in summer. There is the climate of Aquitaine, with moderate winters, humid autumns and springs, and rainfall distributed throughout the year. Finally, there is the Mediterranean climate of mild winters, rainy springs and hot, dry summers.

The influence of relief is noticeable in studying climate that varies from that of the surrounding area, such as the climate of the Massif Central and, above all, that of the Alpine zone: such variations are determined by the position of the valleys in relation to the direction of prevailing winds, by the height of the relief and by differences in the sunlight falling on their slopes.

The greatest Alpine heights are in the north, in the Savoy and Dauphiné Alps, and the climatic contrast between this area and the Maritime Alps in the southern sector is noteworthy. In the latter area a warmer and drier climate predominates, because of the nearby Medi-

FRANCE • *The Land* / 35

Not all French beaches are on the Riviera. These two sun worshippers are at Deauville, on the English Channel. Deauville is about forty miles east of Omaha Beach, one of the beachheads stormed by Allied troops on D-Day in World War II.

View of Mont Cenis across Mont Cenis Lake. Mont Cenis Pass on the French-Italian border extends for about forty-six miles between two peaks of the Mont Cenis Massif. The break in the mountains at Mont Cenis has been known at least since the 4th century A.D. Historians believe that Hannibal may have taken this path across the Alps when he invaded Roman Italy in 218 B.C. The Mont Cenis tunnel, sixteen miles southwest of the pass, was the first tunnel ever built through the Alps. Opened in 1871, it took thirteen years to build and runs for eight and a half miles.

terranean.

France has abundant rainfall; only a few zones corresponding to the most pronounced depressions have annual falls of less than twenty-four inches. The coastal areas are generally rainier than the interior, especially near reliefs, where there is a higher than average rainfall.

The highest annual averages are recorded in the northern Alps, in the Jura, in the Cévennes on the southeastern borders of the Massif Central and in the western Pyrenees. The entire Mediterranean area, including mountainous zones, has a low rainfall. The Alps, the Pyrenees, the eastern Jura and the interior of the Massif Central are covered with snow for five or six months of the year. These enormous deposits swell the rivers in the warmer weather of spring and summer.

The principal winds affecting France are those from the west, which blow in from the ocean throughout the year, from the north and northeast, which are fiercest in winter, and the southeast winds that originate from the Mediterranean. There are also local winds, such as the *mistral,* a cold, dry wind that sweeps the lower Rhone valley and part of the Riviera; the *marin,* a warm and moist southeast wind on the coast of Languedoc; and the *autan,* a warm, dry southeast wind of the area around Toulouse.

Rivers

The French climate and landforms are augmented by a close network of rivers, concentrated in the great basins. The great rivers of the French region—the Rhine, the Seine, the Loire, the Garonne and the Rhone—drain nearly 80 per cent of its surface, and the plentiful rainfall continually replenishes the rivers.

Rivers flowing through hills and plains have high waters in the cold seasons and low waters in the hot seasons; rivers rising in mountains of lesser heights have high waters in spring and low waters in summer and winter, while rivers that descend from the High Alps have high waters in the summer. In the Mediterranean area, rivers are low in summer and full in spring and autumn.

Among the basins of the oldest geological regions, the largest are those of the Seine, the Loire and the Garonne. The Seine, the most navigable waterway, flows for more than 480 tortuous miles from Burgundy, through Champagne and the Île de France or Paris Basin, into its estuary at Le Havre.

The Loire River, 625 miles long, is the longest in France. It rises in the Massif Central, crosses a large alluvial plain, where it is largely canalized, and reaches the Bay of Biscay west of Nantes. It is not an easily navigable river, but is a great source for hydroelectric power.

The Garonne River, over 400 miles long, drains a vast section of the Pyrenees and the Basin of Aquitaine, then flows into the great estuary of the Gironde and the Bay of Biscay.

The rivers of eastern France are mainly torrential in character, and their drainage is shared by neighboring countries. In the northeast, Alsace faces the left bank of the Rhine, into which water from the Vosges Mountains flows. The great waterway of Alpine France is the Rhone, 505 miles long, which flows 350 miles in France through a long valley south to the Mediterranean, where it has formed a swampy delta of accumulated debris that includes the Camargue. Hydroelectric plants have also been constructed on its course.

French rivers are widely utilized for irrigation and for transport, and the valleys are consequently the most prosperous areas in the country.

Vegetation

The hand of man has, of course,

considerably altered the countryside of France, but there still remain areas of the ancient forest mantle, amounting to about 18 per cent of the entire territory. The different areas of natural vegetation are the *temperate forest* of the central, western and northern areas, the *Mediterranean* of the southeast and the *coniferous forest* of the mountain areas.

Characteristic of the temperate forest vegetation are woods of broad-leaved trees, variously distributed according to climate and soil. Among these trees are the oak, the beech, the chestnut and the hornbeam. In the drier areas, man has succeeded in his work of reforestation largely with the aid of pines, which also take root in the sandy parts of the Landes district. Here the vegetation consists of broom, rushes and heather, while farther south, Mediterranean tree species are already noticeable in the Basin of Aquitaine.

Mediterranean vegetation spreads into the interior along the course of the Rhone as far as its junction with the Roubion, just south of Montélimar. It consists largely of the southern and Aleppo pines, the cluster or maritime pine and the ilex or holm oak. There are also cork oaks and thickets of evergreen shrubs. Subtropical plants thrive on the Mediterranean coast (although they are generally not spontaneous growths), together with the characteristic olive tree.

Trees grow in rich profusion in the French mountains. In the Alps, oak and beech cover the lower areas, leaving the high ground to conifers such as pine and spruce. These conifers grow up to the lower limits of the Alpine pastures, at from 6500 to 7200 feet. The upper limit of woods in the Vosges is about 3500 feet, and about 5000 feet in the Jura. Trees of the Massif Central are chestnut, beech, pine and spruce, which grow up to an altitude of over 5000 feet. Among Pyrenean flora the hooked pine predominates, and the woods reach up to 7900 feet in some areas.

Wild Life

It is, of course, no longer possible to study the original wild life of the French plains and lower mountain regions, but it is still quite easy to recognize the various surviving species where they enjoy the protection of high altitude and forest. In such places are found marmots, chamois, wild goats, mountain cocks, birds of prey (including the golden eagle) and extremely varied species of insects.

The Basin of Aquitaine and the Rhone valley have a great variety of reptiles, frogs, toads and vast numbers of insect species. The Alsatian bear became extinct in the 18th century, the lynx in the 19th, but one can still encounter wolves in the Poitou and Limousin areas, and find small colonies of beavers along the lower reaches of the Rhone.

Tuna, anchovies, lobsters and sponges abound in the Mediterranean, sardine and cod in the Bay of Biscay and herring along the northern coasts. Fish are also plentiful in the estuaries, in the rivers and in the coastal salt lakes.

POLITICAL ORGANIZATION

Geographical Limits

FRANCE FACES THREE BODIES OF water: the Atlantic, the English Channel and the Mediterranean. These form natural boundaries to the west, the north and the south, respectively. Other natural boundaries are the Pyrenees in the southwest, the Alps in the southeast, and the Jura Mountains in the east, forming frontiers with Spain, Italy and Switzerland. To the north of the Swiss border the Rhine provides a natural frontier with Germany for a considerable distance, but some way below Strasbourg it ceases to be a frontier and the boundary continues toward the northern coast for another 300 miles.

This portion of France's boundary with Germany, Luxembourg and Belgium is not marked by any natural barriers or outstanding features. In recent centuries, this northeastern frontier of France has changed many times because of various wars.

The northernmost point of France is near Dunkirk on the North Sea

The tributaries of the Loire feed in at two sections of the river. Some, like the Allier, join the Loire in its upper course in the Massif Central. Other rivers, like the Cher (shown here), feed in farther west, in the province of Touraine. There, the river deposits have made the land rich. The soil of Touraine is so fertile that the province has been called "The Garden of France."

38 / FRANCE • *The Land*

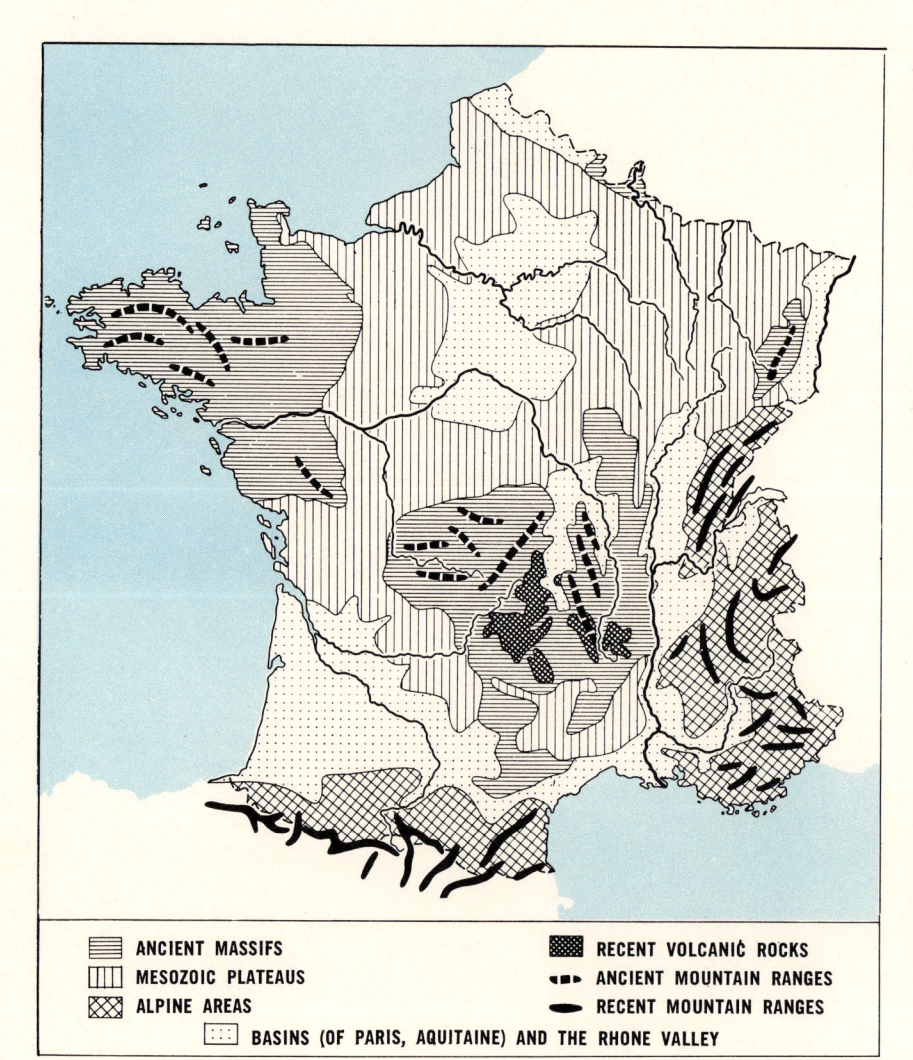

Six thousand, four hundred and thirty-nine feet up in the Pyrenees is Tourmalet, a col, or pass, between two mountains, Pic du Midi and Pic d'Arbizon. Tourmalet is one of the few passes through the high Pyrenees that can accommodate wheeled vehicles. Glaciers in the Pyrenees about 15,000 to 20,000 years ago carved hollows like this pass out of the solid granite mountain rock.

(51°5' North) and the southernmost point is in the Pyrenees (at 42°20'). In Brittany it reaches its farthest continental western point at Pointe de Saint-Mathieu (4°47' West), and its most eastern point is where the frontier leaves the Rhine at 8°11' East.

Administrative Divisions

France was formerly divided into provinces, with traditions and varying privileges, and locally autonomous administrations. The provinces were abolished at the end of the 18th century under the First Republic and divided into many smaller divisions.

These new divisions were called *départements* and took their names from outstanding natural features, such as their positions in regard to the sea (Manche: the French term for the English Channel), important rivers (Seine-et-Oise, Moselle, Dordogne) or mountains (Vosges, Alpes-Maritimes, Cantal). At present there are ninety departments (see table on page 64).

Each department is divided into *arrondissements, cantons* and *communes*. Each of the almost 38,000 communes is administered by a Municipal Council of from ten to thirty-six members elected for six years by universal suffrage. The Mayor, elected by the Council, represents the commune, but also acts for the central government, and is head of the local police. His actions are supervised by the Prefect of the Department.

There are over 3000 cantons, com-

The physical geography of France today was shaped by tremendous forces above and beneath the earth's surface millions of years ago. The glaciers, which covered northern Europe more recently (from 15,000 to 20,000 years ago) never reached the borders of France. The older mountain ranges in the west and center of the country are lower and rounder than the jagged peaks of the Alps and Pyrenees because the action of wind and water through eons of time have worn them away. Eventually erosion will slowly weather even the most rugged faces of the Alps.

ANCIENT MASSIFS
MESOZOIC PLATEAUS
ALPINE AREAS
RECENT VOLCANIC ROCKS
ANCIENT MOUNTAIN RANGES
RECENT MOUNTAIN RANGES
BASINS (OF PARIS, AQUITAINE) AND THE RHONE VALLEY

prising on the average about twelve communes each (some cantons are made up of fewer, but bigger communes). The 311 arrondissements in the whole country are primarily tax districts, and each arrondissement has a Council with as many members as the number of its cantons.

The Municipal Council of Paris is made up of ninety members, and the city is subdivided for administrative purposes into twenty arrondissements, each of which has a mayor.

Although the ancient provinces have no political or administrative significance today, their names, identities, boundaries and traditions are still very real to the French.

The Constitution

France is a republic, and the present republic, the fifth, dates from 1958. It is described in the Constitution as being "indivisible, secular, democratic and social. It shall ensure the equality of all citizens before the law, without distinction of origin, race or religion...."

The national emblem is the tricolor flag of blue, white and red. The national anthem is "The Marseillaise," and the motto of the Republic is "Liberty, Equality, Fraternity."

The Preamble to the Constitution solemnly affirms the Declaration of the Rights of Man of 1789 as reaffirmed and complemented by the Preamble to the Constitution of 1946. "National sovereignty belongs to the people, which shall exercise this sovereignty through its representatives and by means of referendums." There is universal suffrage and voting is secret.

Parliament consists of two bodies, the National Assembly (with 482 Deputies) and the Senate (with 274 Senators). Ordinarily it meets twice a year, from October to December and from April to June, but it may also hold extraordinary sessions if the Premier or a majority of the members of the National Assembly so desire.

Executive power is in the hands of the President of the Republic and the government is headed by the Premier, who is appointed by the President, and need not be a member of Parliament. The President is elected for seven years by the French electorate, much as is the President of the United States. The President of the Republic presides over meetings of the Council of Ministers, and appoints three members of the Constitutional Council. He is President of the French Community, Commander of the armed forces and is empowered to conclude treaties with foreign powers. When public administration is in danger or constitutional government is interrupted, the President may assume all powers to deal with the state of emergency after consultation with other governmental bodies.

There is an Economic and Social Council, which gives the government advice on economic and social questions when requested. The Constitutional Council consists of nine members elected for nine years, and also former Presidents of the Republic. It watches elections to see that they are properly conducted and also determines whether the laws passed by the government are constitutional.

The Administration of Justice

There are 455 Tribunals of Instance, under a judge for each, which administer justice in minor matters. There are 172 Collegiate Tribunals of First Instance (*Tribunaux de Grande Instance*) for more serious cases.

Police Courts deal with minor

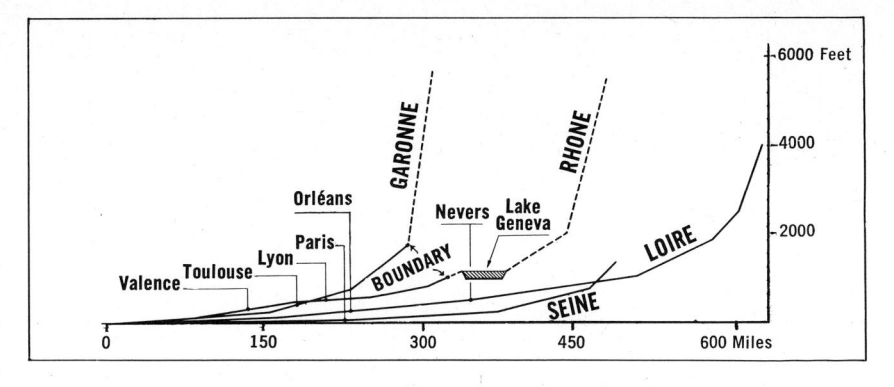

The river profiles in this chart indicate the length of the rivers from mouth to source. The numbers at the right indicate the height of the river at its source. The heights are drawn to scale—the Rhone is about 600 feet above sea level at Lyon but less than 400 feet at Valence. The dotted lines represent portions of the rivers that are outside the boundaries of France.

Rain falls all year round in the western Pyrenees, especially along the Atlantic coast. This Basque countryman, well acquainted with the variable weather of his native region, carries his umbrella papoose-style as he goes about his errands, just in case.

criminal offenses, and are presided over by the judges of the Tribunals of Instance, one for each canton. Correctional Courts, composed of three judges and no jury, are concerned with more serious civil and criminal cases, and can impose sentences of up to five years' imprisonment. Minor industrial and commercial cases are decided by Conciliation Boards and Commercial Tribunals composed of members of the industries and trades concerned, who are elected for two years. There are twenty-seven Courts of Appeal for the whole country, each composed of a president and a varying number of other judges.

Assize Courts judge grave criminal cases, and are composed of a president, two magistrates, who are members of the Courts of Appeal, and a jury of nine. There is one Assize Court for each department. A Court of Cassation has power either to re-examine the validity of a judgment of a lower court, decide whether there has been a fault in procedure, or annul a judgment.

Religion

Since the breaking of the Concordat with the Roman Catholic Church in 1905, the French State has been a lay one and recognizes no official religion, while guaranteeing freedom to all religions. Religious buildings were placed in the hands of religious associations of lay people, who were forbidden to sell or transfer title to them without permission from the State.

The great majority of the population is Roman Catholic, and there are currently 85 dioceses, including the archbishoprics of Paris and Lyon, and also a special Prelature founded in recent years at Pontigny as the center of a "Mission to France." Bishops are nominated by the Pope without consultation with the French Government. There are about one million Protestants and about 500,000 Jews.

Education

Education is divided into primary, secondary and higher categories. Kindergartens may be attended by children from the age of two to six, and compulsory primary education lasts till the age of sixteen. Secondary education is divided into classical and technical courses, which are given in high schools (*lycées*) and *collèges*. Each course lasts six years, and at the end of it the student may gain the first part of his *baccalauréat*, which is at about the standard of a first year in an American university.

Education is free, and primary education has been required by law since 1882. The State supervises education, but it need not be given in State institutions. Many schools and colleges exist which are private, or supported by institutions such as the Catholic Church.

The sixteen universities are under the control of the State, and they are located as follows: Aix-Marseille (founded in 1409); Besançon (1485); Bordeaux (1441); Caen (1432); Clermont-Ferrand (1808); Dijon (1722); Grenoble (1339); Lille (1530); Lyon (1808); Montpellier (1289); Nancy (1572); Paris (1150); Poitiers (1431); Rennes (1735); Strasbourg (1567); Toulouse (1230).

The principal faculties are those of Law, Medicine, Science and Humanities. Although there are special courses for foreign students, for

The meeting of two large waterways is a natural place for a city to develop. Lyon, situated at the junction of the Rhone and the Saône, has been inhabited continually since Roman times and is now the third largest city in France. The Roman military settlement began on the right bank of the Saône, but as it grew, it spilled on to the wedge of land between the two rivers. In modern times, Lyon has spread to the eastern shore of the Rhone.

Connected to the Mediterranean and central Europe by its rivers and canals, Lyon has long been an international market place. The silk-weaving industry introduced by King Louis XII at the end of the 16th century, has flourished at Lyon, and the city is now the most important center of silk manufacture in the world.

The 15th-century castle of Val, which is well preserved, was built on a spit of land jutting out into the Dordogne River to make it impregnable to siege. The castle could only be attacked effectively from the landward side, and it could always get supplies by water.

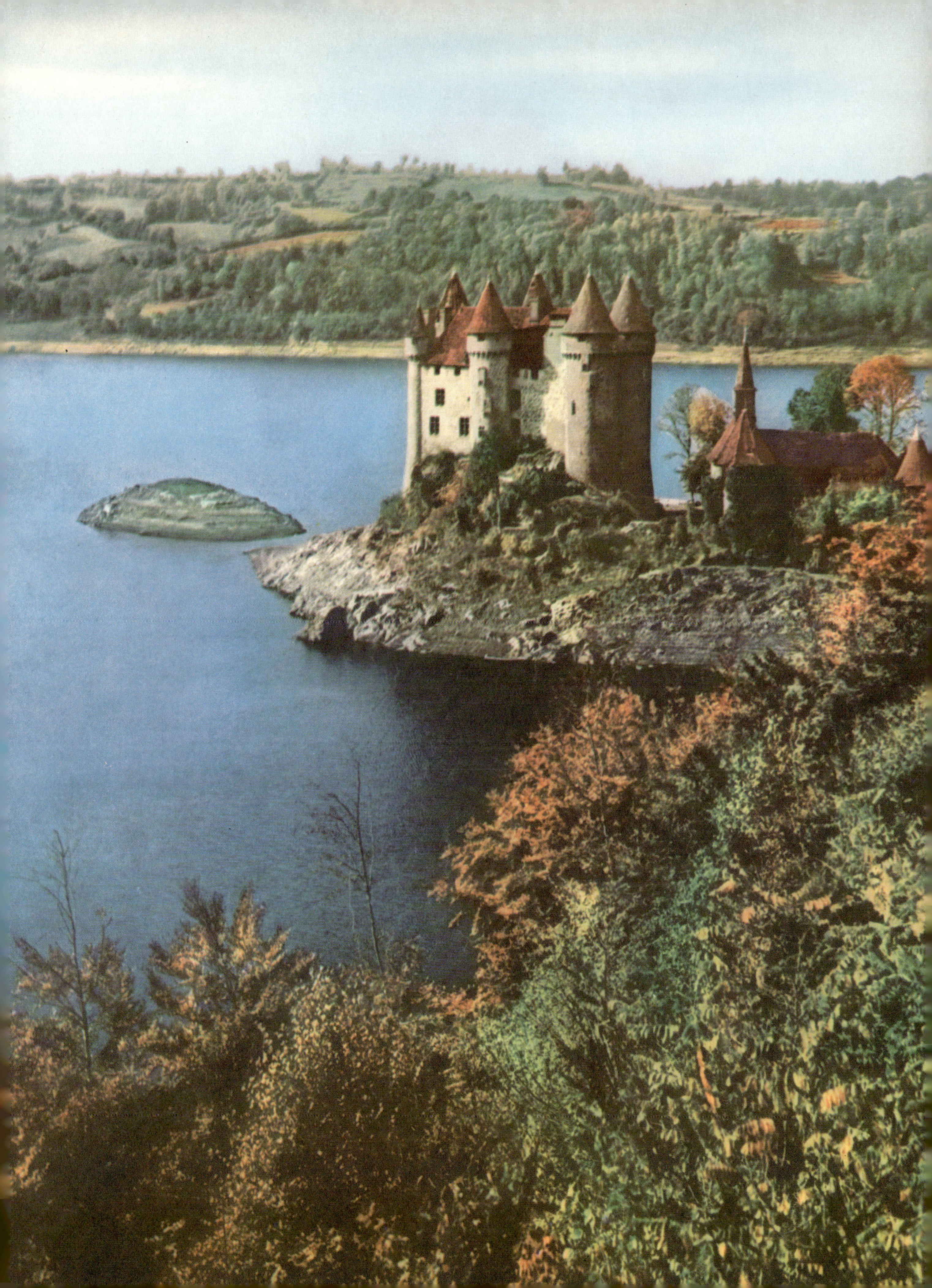

42 / FRANCE • *The Land*

The cattle ranchers of the Camargue, a marshy island in the Rhone River delta, are known throughout France for their skill as cowpunchers.

France for weights and measures. The monetary unit is the franc which is worth about twenty cents in United States currency.

The French Community

The adoption of the new Constitution by a referendum on Sept. 28, and its enactment on Oct. 4, 1958, changed the status of the territories, colonies and dependencies of the former huge French colonial empire that covered about 5,000,000 square miles. They became members, together with metropolitan France, of a French Community of Nations; only Guinea refused to enter this new organization, thereby severing its ties with France and becoming independent on Oct. 8, 1958.

A further step, the May 18, 1960, amendment to the new Constitution, provided that the new states could choose to become independent without losing their membership in the Community. The twelve former colonies in Africa immediately availed themselves of this right, resulting in the following structure of the French Community:

Member States of the Community. There are seven member states: France (the French Republic), the Central African Republic, the Republic of Chad, the Republic of the Congo, Gabon Republic, the Malagasy Republic and the Republic of Senegal. The French Republic, in turn, is divided into ninety metropolitan departments, the four overseas departments of Guadeloupe, French Guiana, Martinique and Réunion, and the seven overseas territories of New Caledonia, Saint-Pierre and Miquelon, the Comoro Islands, French Polynesia, French Somali-

whom degrees are available, foreign students can enroll in the universities on the same basis as French students. There are also numerous other educational institutions controlled by the State, such as the military academy of Saint-Cyr, the mining school at Saint-Etienne, the naval school at Brest and the artillery school at Fontainebleau.

Language

French is the national language, and is spoken or known by all. Originally it was the language of the North only, known as the *langue d'oïl*, to distinguish it from the *langue d'oc* of the South (*oïl* and *oc* are old forms of "yes"). After the Capetian and Valois kings of France brought the whole of the territory under their rule, the language of the North became the official and literary one.

Many different dialects—*patois*—are, however, still widespread. Of other languages spoken within France, only Catalan, used in Roussillon near the Pyrenees, is a Romance language. Flemish, spoken in Flanders, and German, used in Alsace and part of Lorraine, are Germanic languages, while Breton is a Celtic language. In the southwest, around Bayonne, the people speak Basque, a tongue unrelated to any other.

Monetary System and Measures

The metric system is used in

Deep hollows worn out of the ancient rock by the incessant pounding of the sea mark the northwestern shore line of France. This scene, from Pointe du Raz in Brittany, is typical.

land, the Southern and Antarctic Territories, and the Wallis and Futuna Islands.

States with special relations with the Community. There are six such states: the African republics of the Cameroons, Dahomey, Ivory Coast, Mauritania, Niger, and Upper Volta.

State with de facto co-operation in limited matters with the Community: The west african Republic of Mali.

State with co-operation agreed to by exchange of letters with the Community: The west african Republic of Togo.

As the islands of the New Hebrides in the Pacific Ocean form a "Condominium," the rule being shared equally with Britain, it does not form a part of the Community.

Algeria, formerly included in metropolitan France, achieved complete independence in July 1962, and, together with the two former Saharan departments of Oasis and Saoura, is not included in the French Community.

PHYSICAL GEOGRAPHY

Northern France: the Land

NORTHERN FRANCE LACKS PHYSICAL and historical unity, but its mineral resources and its great industrial development make it an important economic region. It has benefited from extremely close contacts with the surrounding regions.

It stretches from the hills of Artois, the upper course of the Somme and Oise Rivers and the wooded heights of the Ardennes as far as the sea at Dunkirk. It is separated from Belgium by an artificial frontier only. Therefore, it occupies the extreme southwest fringe of the Great European Plain, apart from the low hills on its southern border. It is made up of French Flanders, eastern Picardy and Artois.

French Flanders is part of the Brussels basin or Flemish plain which originally was an extension of the London basin, an area similar to that of which Paris is the center. The Flemish plain has been separated from England by the Strait of Dover since the beginning of the Quaternary period. This plain has been subjected to severe erosion and is one of the flattest regions of Europe—the highest points of the French section, Mont Cassel and Mont des Cats, are only 515 feet and 538 feet above sea level.

The Flemish coalfields lie under the hills in parts of Flanders and Artois. The original soil was covered

The Mediterranean Sea continually beats against the limestone outcrops along the shore near Marseille. The action of the wind and water here is less violent than along the Atlantic coast of Brittany (see bottom picture on the opposite page), but the Mediterranean limestone is softer than the ancient granite of the Brittany coast, so these rocks are smoother and more rounded.

by rich mud, from which the countryside derives its fertility, and wheat and sugar beet are cultivated. The development of the steep scarps of the hills of Artois which overlook Flanders is parallel to that of the folds of the coal-bearing layers. These are exploited at Lens and Douai, and coincide for a great distance with a fault which has made more ancient terrains appear on the surface.

The coalfields of northern France spread from the Belgian frontier east of Valenciennes as far as the vicinity of Aire-sur-la-Lys. This area is 75 miles long, and never more than 12 miles wide.

It is a "Black Country," where work goes on continuously above and below ground, and where the landscape is marked by numerous slag heaps, steel pithead towers, thousands of little brick houses, huge electrical works, and coke plants. Covering everything is a dense cloud of smoke, which rises from the chimney stacks. The whole area is crossed and recrossed by a maze of railroads, roads and canals.

MOORS, FORESTS AND LAKES

The landscape changes in the upper valley of the Sambre in Flanders, where there are moors, strips of forest and lakes stretching up to the foothills of the Ardennes. The soil under the forests is sandy, but there is also arable land, and thin pasture is to be found on the slopes of the low hills formed by the extreme western section of the Ardennes Massif.

The Flemish plain has been altered by the hand of man on its coastal side, where there is a close network of canals. These cut through

These stones, called menhirs *(meaning "long stones"), have been standing near Carnac in Brittany for some 4500 years. Ruder than the stone circles at Stonehenge, England, but similar to them, the* menhirs *were erected by the prehistoric inhabitants of Brittany for some unknown purpose. Archaeologists speculate that the stones may have been connected with religious observances, either as monuments to the dead or as indicators of seasonal change. During the course of the year, as the earth rotates about the sun, the position of the sun changes in the sky. This is reflected by the* menhir *shadows, which shift their positions on the ground as the sun moves across the sky.*

the dark, clayey soil of the polders—land reclaimed from under water. The polders are treeless, and lie behind the low, straight and sandy coast on the North Sea. The original clay soil has been covered with sand and peat, and closely resembles the soils of Holland.

The region around Boulogne, however, is undulating and woody, and the coast is a picturesque series of cliffs and little beaches. Inland are great fertile meadowlands and ancient forests near Boulogne, Desvres and Hardelot, and short streams with stony beds such as the Liane, the Slack and the Wimereux. It is a verdant region, and marks the boundaries of the two great natural regions of the Low Countries (Belgium and the Netherlands) and of the Paris Basin.

Northern France: Climate and River Systems

The climate of northern France is largely produced by its latitude and the influence of the sea—which is felt even as far inland as the Ardennes, where the Continental climate really begins. Depending on their direction, the winds favor or restrict the moderating influence of the sea. This makes the climate rather unstable, except close to the coasts where a temperate Atlantic climate usually prevails.

The inland temperatures are subject to great seasonal variations, and over the whole area summer usually comes late. There is much cloudy and rainy weather in the late autumn and early winter, when most rain falls. The rainfall increases from west to east, and that of the Ardennes is one third more than that of Lille. The atmosphere is very humid and the sky often is heavily overcast, especially in autumn and winter.

Except for the Somme and the Oise, all the major rivers of northern France empty eventually into the North Sea. Some flow there directly, while others are tributaries of the Scheldt, which, under its French name of the Escaut, rises south of Cambrai. It has been canalized near Cambrai, and is navigable from that point, where it also begins to supply water to numerous canals on either side of it. It is thus one of the most important rivers of the north. The Lys rises in the hills of Artois, and joins the Scheldt at Ghent in Belgium.

Northeastern France: the Land

The northeastern part of France stretches from Champagne to the Rhine and includes the southern slopes of the Ardennes, the Vosges and the Alsatian alluvial plain.

The southern section of the ancient massif of the Ardennes has been leveled by severe erosion, and is composed of an upland plain about 1300 feet high, covered by forests and peat fields and interrupted only by the deep incisions of the valleys of the Meuse and the Semois. The valley of the Meuse is an important means of communication between north and south.

The Vosges Mountains rise between Alsace and Lorraine and are largely characterized by gentle slopes and a thick forest cover, which tends to hide the harshness of the terrain. There is a chain of peaks—from the Ballon d'Alsace in the south to the German border in the north—and the slopes differ on either side, those toward Alsace being short and steep, while those toward Lorraine are more gradual.

The Vosges are usually divided into the High Vosges and the Northern or Lower Vosges. The High Vosges stretch from the Belfort Gap to the Col du Bonhomme pass. They include the Vosges of Lorraine, which consist of a rather low upland plain (about 1500 feet high) between the valleys of the Moselle and the Meurthe.

This high section of the Vosges is made up for the most part of crystalline rocks. The valleys form a complicated network. The highest peaks of the High Vosges are the Ballon d'Alsace (4100 feet), the Ballon de Guebwiller (4672 feet) and the Hohneck (4465 feet).

The Northern Vosges are made up of upland plains, and their gentle slopes are clothed with thick forest. The highest point of the Lower Vosges is Le Donon (3307 feet).

ALSACE

The plain of Alsace is a typically Rhenish terrain and stretches for 124 miles in a generally north-south direction between the left bank of the Rhine and the eastern side of the Vosges. In spite of its narrow width (on the average about twelve miles separates the Vosges from the Rhine), Alsace has a variegated landscape, depending on the covering soils of the region.

Agriculture flourishes on the very fertile loess (yellowish-brown loam) terraces, and there are thick forests on the sandy terrains. The areas subject to flooding along the banks of the Rhine and the Ill are marshy and damp.

The plain tilts slightly from south to north, and this permits the division of the region into three parts: Upper, Middle, and Lower Alsace. Upper Alsace is partly mountainous and is cut by the valleys of the Thur and the Doller; it is flat at the foot of the Vosges, terraced along the Rhine and consists of a clayey upland plain toward the Jura. Middle Alsace has the typical post-Tertiary cover soils found between the Vosges and the Rhine. Lower Alsace is mainly flat and fertile.

LORRAINE

The region of Lorraine is on the fringe of the Paris Basin, and has special features that separate it noticeably from the rest of the Basin, in comparison with which it has a more rugged landscape and a harsher climate.

The southern part of the region is made up of hills covered with thick forest, and the flatlands of the valley of the upper Meuse.

Northern Lorraine is broader and lower, and on the east it includes the upland plain drained by the Sarre and the Seille. On the west are hills rising above the Meuse and the Moselle which dominate the clayey flatlands in the valleys. The Meuse and the Moselle have formed frequent alluvial flats along their courses, which facilitate communications. There are rich deposits of iron ore in the western area, coal in the eastern area and salt in the central area.

Northeastern France: Climate

The regions of northeastern France have dissimilar climates. Their varying distances from the sea and the different kinds of relief cause distinct types of climate.

In Lorraine, winters are severe, and there are prolonged periods when temperature stays below the freezing point. Spring comes late and suddenly, and vigorously brings the abundant vegetation to life. The

For seaborn passengers, Le Havre is the likeliest port of entry into France. Situated on the English channel, at the mouth of the Seine, Le Havre is the second largest port in the country.

The two spires of the cathedral of Notre Dame have dominated the city of Chartres since the 13th century. The famous Gothic cathedral, dedicated in 1260 by St. Louis (King Louis IX) was built on the site of a still older church that had burned down in 1194. It was in that church that St. Bernard of Clairvaux preached the Second Crusade.

summers are hot, with many storms, and autumn comes so early that there is often a danger that the crops will not have time to ripen. Rain, brought by humid winds from the west, is abundant.

Rainfall is also heavy in the Ardennes, where the climate is also harsh. The Vosges, however, are open to the influence of the sea, and there are clear differences between the climates of the Lorraine and Alsatian sides. The western slopes are exposed to humid winds from the west, which, when they strike the hills, produce heavy rainfall. These winds generally do not penetrate beyond the summits of the Vosges, so the Alsatian slopes have drier weather.

The Alsatian plain has a climate dependent on conditions prevailing in Central Europe. Winters are severe (in January the temperature is usually at the freezing point) and summers are very hot. Alsace has the lowest rainfall of the entire French region, and since the weather is almost always bright and clear it is possible to raise crops usually found in more southerly regions.

The northern edges of the region, however, are without the protection afforded by the Vosges to the rest of the area, and westerly winds make the climate in Strasbourg and Saverne cold and cloudy.

Northeastern France: River Systems

The river systems of northeastern France were formed in various geological periods by very complicated phenomena. Most of the rivers penetrate the massif of the Ardennes and send their waters to the Rhine and the North Sea. The principal rivers are the Meuse and the Moselle.

The Meuse rises in southeastern Lorraine and passes from south to north through the chalk hills bordering the Paris Basin on the east. Near Verdun its bed widens, and it receives the waters of the Chiers near Sedan. It then follows a winding course between the schist and chalk terrains of the Ardennes and enters Belgian territory near Givet.

The Moselle is a tributary of the Rhine, and rises near the Bussange Pass in the southern Vosges. It flows in a generally northwesterly direction and is fed by the Moselotte and the Vologne. It leaves the mountainous area near Epinal, and further north flows between high banks in a narrow and winding valley cut out of the upland plain. The Meurthe and the Seille flow into it, and it leaves French soil northeast of Thionville.

There is also a dense network of navigable canals, the most important of which are the Marne-Rhine and the Canal de l'Est.

The Ill (with its tributaries like the Fecht and Bruche), Moder and Sauer Rivers flow from the Alsatian slopes of the Vosges to the Rhine, and are valuable as sources of power for the important papermaking industry of the region. Because

The Paris Basin comprises the whole north-central portion of France. The region is called a basin for strictly geological reasons—layers of ancient rock dip from all sides toward a center, where the city of Paris has grown up. This cross section map of northern France cut from west to east—the Atlantic is on the left, the Rhine is on the right—shows clearly the vast bowl or basin of sunken rock on which Paris is built. The granite rock of the Brittany peninsula on the extreme west sinks deep below the ground and only rises to the surface again on the extreme eastern border of the country. The oldest rock forms the outermost layers of the basin and has sunk the deepest. The most recent deposit is on the surface at the lowest point of the basin, right at the center, where Paris has developed.

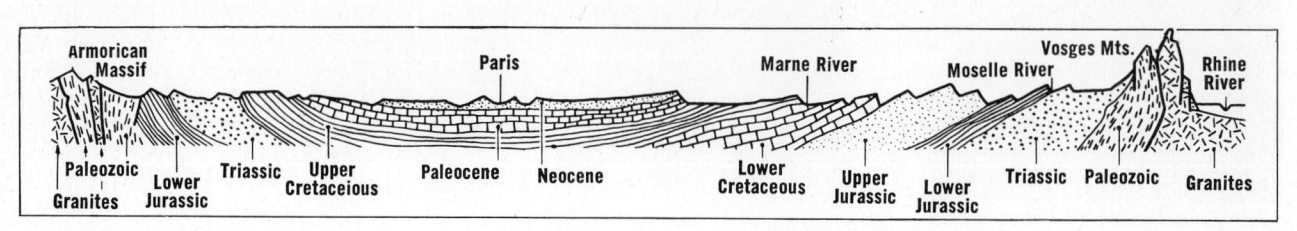

Alsace faces the Rhine, France is able to share in the intense commercial life of the river, and Strasbourg is a very important inland port at the junction of the great Marne-Rhine and Rhone-Rhine canals.

The Paris Basin: the Land

Its position and its history have made the Paris Basin the center of French life. It is bordered by the ancient Armorican, Central, Vosges and Ardennes massifs, and it stretches as far as the English Channel, where it ends in a line of great cliffs. It is one of the most important geographical units in the French region.

The term Basin has been applied to this area on strictly geological grounds; it is not so named because it is the watershed and basin of the Seine River. Indeed, it also supplies water to the Loire, the Meuse and the Moselle.

The countryside is made up of a series of plains and hills having an even, regular appearance. This landscape varies only on the hills around the edges of the region. The hills of the Paris Basin are lower where the ancient rock formations have sunk and are covered with sedimentary strata. These strata have been affected in various ways by erosion, and so the different regions of the Basin have differing characteristics.

The Paris region, or Île-de-France, contains all the various types of land forms to be found throughout the Basin. There are chalk uplands covered with loam deposits, used for the cultivation of wheat, little wooded hills *(buttes)*, steep hills *(coteaux)*, and river valleys with sharp and steep slopes.

To the east in Champagne, there is a series of hilly undulations *(côtes)* composed of soil that is rich in lime, and therefore very suitable for vineyards. These hills dominate the chalk plains, which have thin steppe vegetation, and the clay flats of the wetter part of Champagne, which are covered with thick forest. The series of *côtes* and the fringes of the flats are cut into by the valleys of

This aerial view of the Place de l'Etoile, one of the most important intersections in Paris, shows how the crossing got its name (Star Plaza). Major traffic arteries radiate from the Arch of Triumph at its center to all points of the city. The Place de l'Etoile and many other plazas, boulevards and parks owe their existence to the foresight and skill of Baron G. E. Haussmann, Prefect of the Seine in the middle of the 19th century. On his design old city walls were torn down and boulevards were opened up, bridges were built across the Seine, and broad avenues were laid down, carrying traffic around the city or across it. The work took sixteen years, but in that time Paris was transformed into a modern city, capital of an industrialized nation.

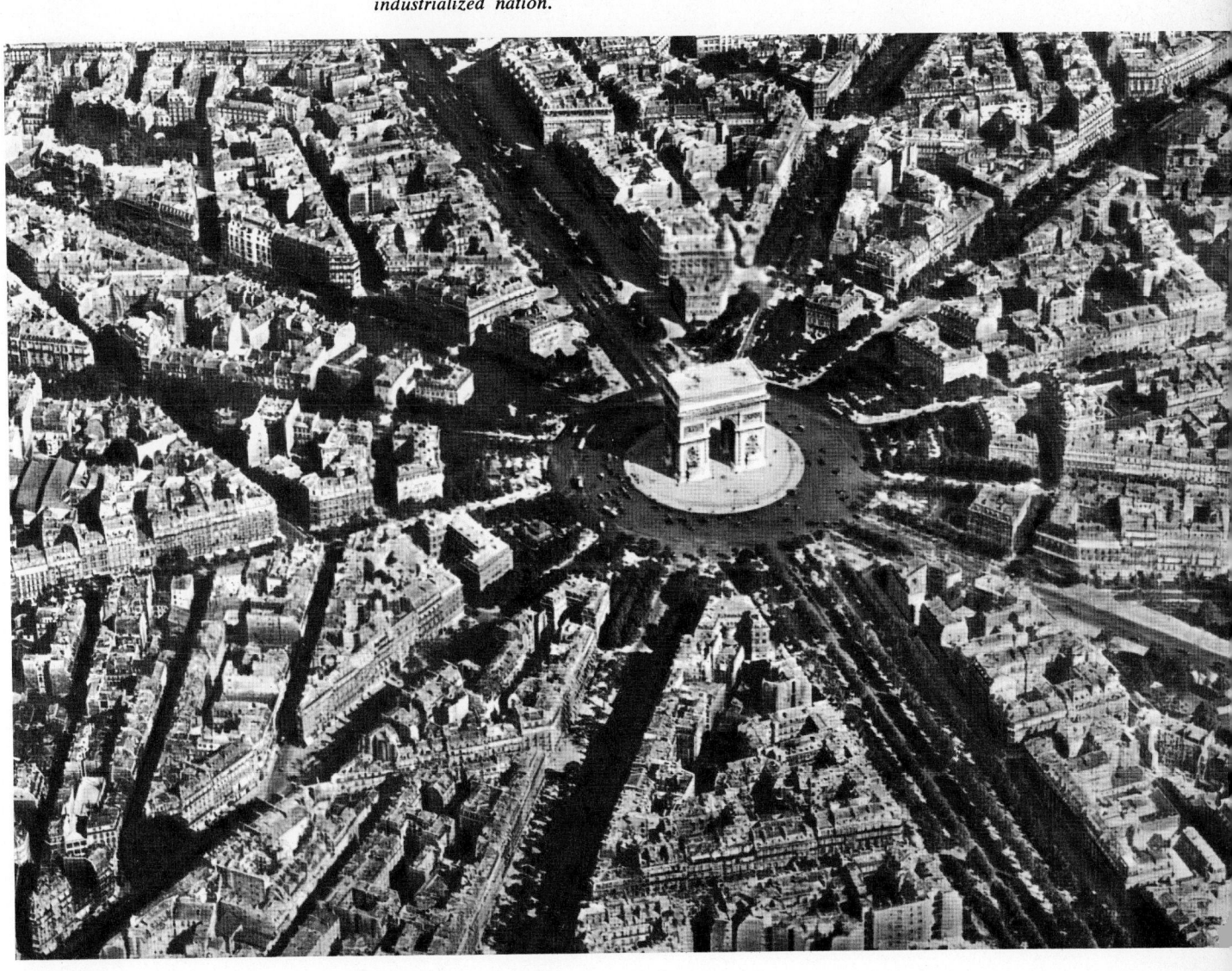

The Col d'Iseran, 9085 feet up in the Alps, is crossed by one of the highest roads in Europe. The pass connects the valleys of the Arc and Isère rivers.

the great rivers, which are bordered by fertile meadowlands.

To the north stretches the plain of western Picardy, where the undulations never rise to more than 650 feet above sea level. The adjoining eastern part of Normandy belongs to this area. A clayey layer on the chalk covering of these plains makes them very fertile, even though they lack trees.

The most characteristic plains of the Paris Basin are those in the valley of the middle Loire, where the landscape is particularly flat and uniform. Only in the southeastern part of the Basin is there variety. There the northwest foothills of the Massif Central give diversity to the Nivernais region.

The Paris Basin: Climate

The Paris Basin is a transitional region between the Maritime and Continental climates. Temperature does not vary greatly, and rain, though sparse, is regular. The influence of the sea loses strength as one passes from west to east, but it tempers the naturally harsh winters and very hot summers of the Continental climate.

The climate of the Basin is thus rather temperate, without excessively high or low thermometer readings, and is usually known as the Parisian climate. In eastern Normandy rainfall is regular and is evenly distributed, though it is inclined to be heavier in autumn than during any other season. Rouen has a higher rainfall than the rest of the region, and the coastal area has a maritime climate.

In Champagne, temperature variations are the same as in Paris, but rainfall is higher. In the middle of the Loire valley, the influence of the Atlantic weakens as one goes from west to east, and in Nivernais the climate is the Continental one of the Massif Central.

The Paris Basin: River Systems

Most of the waters of the Paris Basin flow into the Seine, and only a few outlying areas are not included in the watershed. To the north, the Somme takes the waters of western Picardy to the English Channel, and the Meuse and the Moselle in the east those of Lorraine to the North Sea. The Loire, a large river flowing through several French regions, crosses the southern section of the Basin, and in the north, rivers flowing from the hills of Normandy, such as the Touques, the Dives and the Orne, empty directly into the English Channel.

The Seine is 482 miles long and rises at the height of 1545 feet on the Plateau of Langres. It descends fairly steeply for 50 miles to reach flat country at Bar-sur-Seine. It crosses the flat part of Champagne and enters the Paris region, where the pitch of its descent decreases. From this point to its mouth it flows between high banks that it has cut out of the surrounding tableland.

Its volume of flow is relatively small, for it depends almost exclusively on the rainfall of the zones through which it passes, and these are some of the most arid parts of France. Because of the very gradual pitch of its descent the Seine flows slowly, and this makes it easily navigable; but in places it has been canalized to improve navigation. It has many bends which, like the one at Paris, lengthen river travel: from Paris to Rouen by road is 77 miles, by rail 79 miles, and by river it is almost 150 miles.

The level of the Seine begins to rise in October with the autumn rains, and reaches its highest level in February. Evaporation during the summer causes it to reach its lowest level in August and September. Weirs and locks have been built between Montereau, at the mouth of the Yonne, and Rouen to improve navigation. It is thus the most navigable river in France and the key to the whole inland water transport system.

The chief tributaries of the Seine are all somewhat similar in their lengths, their courses, the terrain through which they pass and the characteristics of the terrain. The most important of them are the Marne, the Aisne-Oise and the Loing.

Northwestern France: the Land

On the west, the Paris Basin is bounded by the ancient Armorican Massif. It is made up mostly of granites and other hard rocks. This region largely coincides with the great peninsula of Brittany.

North of the Armorican Massif, between the Bay of the Seine and the

Gulf of Saint-Malo, extends the Cotentin Peninsula. Further west, the coast of the Massif includes the low and regular sector of the Bay of Mont-Saint-Michel, where at low tide many miles of beach are uncovered.

There are many islands of differing sizes off the coast, the most important being the Channel Islands. All of these, with the exception of the Chauseys, belong to Great Britain. The western face of the Massif is marked by steep and rocky coasts, numerous reefs and islands, and river estuaries reaching far inland.

Most of the Breton inlets from the sea are to be found on the west coast and are connected with river valleys. One of these is the Gulf of Morbihan, which means "little sea" in Breton. It is a sack-like inlet whose shoreline is very broken and whose tides are very strong. Other similar formations are the mouth of the Vilaine and the estuary of the Loire.

The interior of Brittany, called "Arcoat" in Breton, rises in the west to the Montagnes d'Arrée up to 1283 feet, and in the Montagnes Noires, to 1070 feet. These dominate the not very fertile upland plains to the north and south. Farther south, the Landes de Lanvaux parallel the Gulf of Morbihan and are 1115 feet high. The ancient forests that used to cover Arcoat have been almost totally destroyed by man, but reforestation with pines is now being attempted.

The region of the lower Loire, north of the river, is made up of impermeable terrain and of a series of terraced hills on which grow famous vineyards. The valleys below these terraces have fertile fields, meadows and orchards.

Northwestern France: Climate and River Systems

The climate of Brittany is a typically maritime one, having generally mild winters, late springs and mild and fresh summers. Excessive heat or cold is rare and the region is exposed, more than any other part of France, to humid winds from the west. Average annual rainfall is thirty-three inches at Brest, and the periods of greatest rainfall are in spring, autumn and December. The weather in the interior is more severe than on the coast, and rainfall decreases from west to east.

There are two river systems, one in the north and one in the south of the peninsula, which flow into the English Channel and the Atlantic, respectively. The rivers of Brittany, such as the Arguenon, the Trieux, the Rance, the Guer, the Aulne and the Blavet, are generally not very long and their mouths flow into long, narrow inlets. The Vilaine River, which is about 140 miles long, has a larger watershed than the others.

THE LOIRE

The lower Loire passes through the Nantes region, Anjou and Touraine. It is an important watercourse, and rises in the Massif Central to reach the Breton coast after passing across the fringe of the Paris Basin.

About 625 miles long, the Loire is the longest French river and has the largest watershed in the French region, about 45,000 square miles. It rises at a height of about 4400 feet on the slopes of Mont Gerbier de Jonc.

In its upper course the river flows through the volcanic terrain of Velay and the Tertiary basins of Roanne and Forez. Beyond Roanne, where its valley broadens, the river turns to the northwest. It then passes through Bourbonnais and Nivernais to cross the southern part of the Paris Basin. At Orleans it changes direction and turns toward the west. It is now very broad and slow and flows through Touraine, Anjou and the Nantes region to the Atlantic near Saint-Nazaire, where its estuary is about 35 miles long.

The lower Loire flows through a great alluvial plain, and many sandbanks break up its flow into different channels. Dikes along its course protect the rich land around it from flooding. One group of tributaries is formed by rivers such as the Allier that flow down from the Massif Central joining its upper course. The second consists of watercourses such

The city of Blois, on the north bank of the Loire, surrounded by hills, dates back to Roman times. Part of an aqueduct built by Julius Caesar's engineers still stands. Later residents of the city have filled it with beautiful buildings of many periods. This one is the medieval church of St. Nicholas.

The great glacier originating in the ice cap of northern Europe never reached France during the ice ages, but independent glaciers originating in the Alps and the Pyrenees changed the appearance of the southern and southeastern sections of the country. Great rivers of ice, carrying huge rocks, gouged out U-shaped valleys, rounded off mountains and left small lakes as evidence of their passing. This circular hollow cut out of a mountainside in the Pyrenees is called the Cirque de Gavarnie.

as the Cher, the Indre and the Vienne, which also rise in the mountains, but which flow across parts of the plain to the middle Loire.

Because of its fluctuating flow the Loire is not suitable for navigation; instead, its waters are used in parallel canals. Its upper reaches and those of its tributaries are used for hydro-electric works.

The Aquitaine Basin and the Pyrenees: the Land

The Aquitaine Basin resembles that of Paris in the nature of its terrain and its origin, but it has more unified geographical characteristics. To the northeast and south are clearly defined boundaries formed by mountainous country. The greater part of Aquitaine is a single vast watershed feeding the Garonne and Dordogne rivers, which meet in their common estuary, the Gironde.

The structure of the region is simple. In the east, on the fringes of the Massif Central, lies the Causses, a limestone plateau. Here, the valleys have been deeply cut into by watercourses, and contain gorges and caverns. These valleys are often fertile and richly covered with vegetation, in sharp contrast to the surrounding country, which is arid. The higher plateau is to be considered a part of the Massif Central.

In the Pyrenean foothills, in the south, are the regions of Armagnac, Chalosse and the Lannemezan Plateau, which tilt northward toward the heart of Aquitaine and are famous for their vineyards. The area between the two hill zones is a vast sedimentary plain, where watercourses move slowly, and meander among frequent marshes and swamps.

To the west is the great triangular plain of the Landes, composed of sand deposited by the sea, marshes and rivers, now covered with steppe vegetation and pines.

THE PYRENEES

The mountain chain of the Pyrenees stretches for about 270 miles from the Atlantic to the Mediterranean. Only one third of the area belongs to France, the rest, including the highest peak, Pico de Aneto, 11,168 feet high, is on the Spanish side of the border.

The steep French side of the Pyrenees rises suddenly like a great wall from the Aquitaine Basin. Unlike the Alps, the Pyrenees are a serious obstacle to communications, for there are very few usable passes into Spain.

THREE SECTIONS OF THE RANGE

The position of the massifs allows us to divide the whole range into three sections—the Atlantic, Central and Mediterranean.

In the Atlantic section of the French Pyrenees, heights are rarely over 6500 feet although the Pic d'Orby rises to 6614 feet. The heights and valleys are covered with green pastures and beech woods, which flourish because of the wet climate.

The highest French peaks are in the Central section, such as the Vignemale (10,821 feet) and the Pic Balaitous (10,321 feet). These are always covered with snow, and the chain here is never less than 6500 feet high. On less exposed slopes there are short glaciers which today cover a total area of about 15 square miles.

The peaks in the Mediterranean section are lower than the others and the section has a number of upland plains which are not large, and are

Along the Atlantic coast of southern France sand dunes extend for miles parallel to the coastline. On the southern shore of the Gironde estuary, where the Garonne and Dordogne rivers meet the sea, sand dunes reach a height of 350 feet.

due to valleys having been widened out and flattened.

The Aquitaine Basin and the Pyrenees: Climate

The climate of the Aquitaine Basin is conditioned by the fact that it faces the Atlantic Ocean and by the presence of the Massif Central to the northeast. There are therefore two climatic regions: the Maritime area, and the more inland one, which has a transitional Continental climate.

The Atlantic region has even, seasonal temperature, mild winters and fresh summers. Rainfall is heavy in all seasons of the year, and the greatest fall occurs in spring and autumn. In the interior there are wider variations in temperature; the winters are cold and prolonged, and summers are very hot. Rainfall is lighter, and the greatest falls occur in spring and autumn.

The Pyrenees may also be divided into two regions from the point of view of climate. The Atlantic region has abundant and regular rainfall and, above 8200 feet, snow. But the Mediterranean region, eastward from the Ariège River, has little rainfall at any time of the year, and the summers are particularly dry.

Temperatures usually decrease as the altitude increases, and vary according to the exposure of the slopes. Perennial snows begin at about 9200 feet.

The Aquitaine Basin and the Pyrenees: River Systems

The rivers of the Aquitaine Basin all flow to the Bay of Biscay. Most of the region comprises a great collecting area with its point of discharge in the estuary of the Gironde. Only the southeastern sector delivers its waters directly to the sea, both through short, parallel streams flowing through the western Landes and through the Adour River.

The Garonne, over 400 miles long, has the most water of all the rivers of southwestern France. It rises in the Spanish part of the Pyrenees, and descends toward the northeast to Toulouse. There it makes a wide turn and flows northwestward, continuing in this direction until it forms, with the Dordogne, an estuary known as the Gironde.

When the Garonne is high, it is violent and rapid, and it can quickly rise thirty or forty feet. It is therefore not very suitable for navigation, and a canal alongside it has been constructed for this purpose. However, sea-going ships are able to reach Bordeaux.

The rivers of the Garonne basin are suitable for hydroelectric works, and there are numerous stations in the Pyrenean valleys and on the rivers flowing down from the Massif Central. The Garonne's principal tributaries are the Neste, Save, Gimone, Gers, Baïse and Ciron on the left bank, and the Salat, Ariège, Tarn and Lot on the right.

The Dordogne, which is about 300 miles long, rises in the Massif Central and flows in a general westerly direction. For 100 miles above Beaulieu-sur-Dordogne, the river flows through a narrow and uninhabited gorge, but lower down there are picturesque wide banks covered with vineyards. It combines with the Garonne just north of Bordeaux to form the estuary of the Gironde.

Le Puy, capital of the Haute-Loire department is located in the region of the volcanic Velay Mountains. The site of a 10th-century Romanesque cathedral and a 12th-century Gothic church, the city is still famous as a place of pilgrimage. Across from the cathedral, overlooking the city from the top of Mont Anis, is an immense statue of the Virgin Mary.

Most of the rivers that flow down from the French slopes of the western and central Pyrenees send their waters to the Garonne and the Adour. But the Bidassoa goes directly to the Bay of Biscay and the last few miles of its course mark part of the frontier between France and Spain.

The rivers of the eastern or Mediterranean sector, the Aude, Têt, Tech and others, flow into the Mediterranean. All these Pyrenean rivers offer great potentialities for hydroelectric installations.

The Massif Central: the Land

The Massif Central forms a vast and distinctive natural region in the heart of France. It is made up of a number of elevations and depressions which generally rise from the northwest toward the southeast. Geologically, it is dominated by ancient

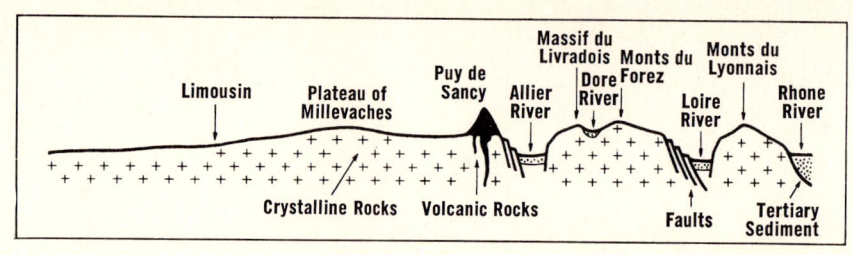

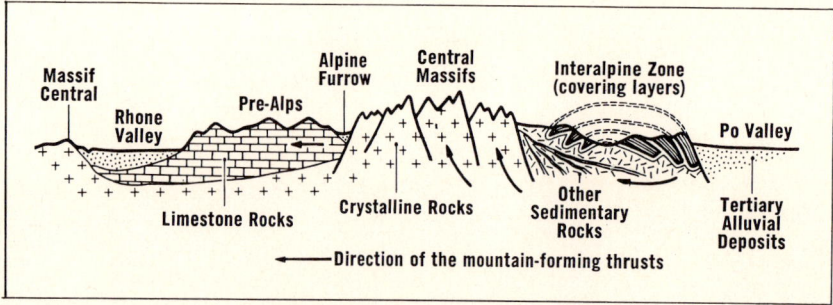

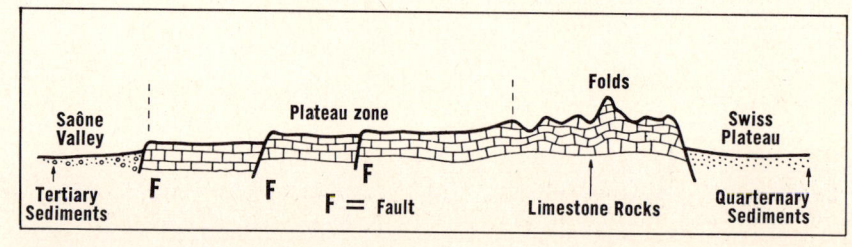

The geological make-up of much of France can be seen in these cross sections of the Massif Central, the western Alps and the Jura Mountains. The most ancient rock in France is exposed over a large area in the Massif Central (top). This crystalline rock was once part of the ancient Hyrcenian mountain system that spread over much of western Europe. It was worn down by intense erosion and then submerged under vast seas during the Mesozoic era.

During the Tertiary period, the age that followed, the waters withdrew, leaving sedimentary deposits on top of the Massif. But at the end of this period, tremendous forces within the earth thrust up whole mountain ranges. To the east of the present Massif Central the ancient crystalline rock was wrenched from its Mesozoic sea bed and impelled upward, forming the Alps and the Jura Mountains. Millions of tons of dense rock were heaved up. Some of it crumpled, slid back down or cracked to form jagged peaks, furrows, faults and folds. Even on the Massif Central, which was relatively stable, mountains rose and fractured. Lava streamed from these fractures, creating the volcanic mountains which still dominate the landscape. Puy de Sancy (6187 feet high) is a mountain formed by the volcanic lava flowing out of the fracture visible in this cutaway on the western shore of the Allier river bed.

The cross section of the western Alps (middle diagram above) shows how the ancient crystalline rock pushed through the limestone and other sedimentary rock deposited by the Mesozoic sea. The forces at work beneath the Jura Mountains (bottom diagram) were not as intense as those beneath the Alps to the south, so the Juras did not rise as high. Instead, there are a series of level limestone plateaus in the west that rise in steps (caused by faulting in the rock when the mountains were formed). The highest peaks in the Jura range lie in the east, where the rock crumpled in narrow folds.

crystalline rocks, and only certain areas are covered with sedimentary strata and volcanic material.

Covering one-sixth of France, it is of very ancient origin and, after being worn down by erosion, was largely submerged during the Mesozoic era. At the time the Alps were formed, its mountains arose as if to provide a counterweight, and intense fracturization occurred. Great masses of lava flowed out through these fractures and formed the present volcanic structure of the Auvergne Mountains. Old volcanoes form the highest points of the Massif. Though they have been greatly reduced by erosion, they still dominate the gently rolling or flat surrounding countryside. Such peaks are the Puy de Sancy (6187 feet) and the Plomb du Cantal (6096 feet). Near these volcanic areas are massifs and upland plains of uniform crystalline or schist rock.

There are two deep valleys running between these peaks from the heart of the Massif; they contain the upper courses of the Allier and the Loire.

The area then slopes toward the west, and the lines of the Massif here become simpler and more uniform in the plateau of Millevaches and the Monts du Limousin. The eastern section of the Massif is composed of mountains aligned toward the south, and separated by deep depressions. The most important of these is the depression of Jarez, centered on Saint-Etienne, which contains vast coal deposits and which connects the upper basin of the Loire with the valleys of the Rhone and the Saône.

The mountains are continued to

FRANCE • *The Land* / 53

Mont Blanc, the highest mountain in the 660-mile sweep of the Alps, straddles the French-Italian border and stands 15,781 feet high. The funicular, or cable railway, in the foreground connects the French town of Chamonix with Aiguille Vert (Green Needle), a peak in nearby Switzerland.

the south by the chain of the Cévennes, which forms the raised southeastern edge of the Massif Central. Seen from the valley of the Rhone and lower Languedoc, the Cévennes appear as a huge, magnificent wall, suddenly rising up. The Montagne Noire range, rising to 3970 feet, marks the extremity of the chain, and its slopes and foothills reach as far as the region of Toulouse.

Northwest of the Cévennes is the limestone plateau of the Causses, the lower part of which has been described under the Aquitaine Basin. It varies in height between 2000 and 4200 feet and is divided into various blocks, clearly separated by deep valleys with steep and almost vertical sides.

The Massif Central: Climate and River Systems

There are often marked climatic variations in the Massif Central zone. On the western slopes of the Massif a temperate oceanic climate prevails, which brings rains to the area. On the chain of the Cévennes the climate is more Mediterranean, and in the interior there is a Continental climate, more marked on the higher portions than elsewhere.

Though it is not possible to speak of a typical Massif Central climate, certain climatic conditions are found over the whole region—such as long and rigorous winters, intensely hot and dry summers, and finally heavy rains in autumn and spring.

Rainfall is distributed very unevenly. The mountains that form the western, eastern and southern borders of the Massif receive a high yearly average, and even higher rainfall occurs on the upper slopes of the Cévennes and the volcanic massifs. Rainfall is less in lower regions.

The Massif Central contains the sources of the greatest and most important river systems in the French region, and constitutes a huge watershed feeding France's great waterways.

To the north, the upper courses of the Loire and the Allier cut deeply into the Massif, and collect most of the rain that falls on the inner slopes of the ranges that border the region. To the west, the Charente and the Dordogne flow down toward the Atlantic, and most of the rivers in the western region are their tributaries. Farther to the south, the Lot and the Tarn (with its chief tributary, the Aveyron) flow into the Garonne. Shorter streams, such as the Orb and the Hérault, flow from the southern slopes of the Cévennes directly to the Mediterranean. On the east, all the rivers descending from the Cévennes flow into the Rhone.

The Alps and the Jura: the Land

The outer western section of the great circular chain of the Alps belongs to France, and stretches along the Italian border for 180 miles, from the Mediterranean to Lake Geneva, varying between 60 and 90 miles in width.

The rocks that form the crystalline core of the Alps are of very ancient origin, and were submerged during the Mesozoic era. Over them were laid down thick strata of diverse sedimentary deposits. The mountain-forming disturbances that took place at the end of the Tertiary period caused the Alpine chain to re-emerge. From that time, it was subject to continual, though sometimes very slow, erosion.

More recently, the great Ice Ages of the Quaternary period had great effect on the entire region. It is still possible to see the results, typified by valleys with the characteristic U-shape produced by glaciers. There are also moraines and glacial deposits which are often arranged in long concentric strips and form amphitheaters at the mouths of the bigger Alpine valleys. In addition, there are cirques, depressions on the high lands, which were once occupied by glaciers; in them little lakes are often formed.

At the height of its development this extensive glaciation covered the whole Alpine area, and left only the highest peaks and the more exposed portions of the surrounding regions free. Today, however, there are only a few, not very extensive glaciers left.

The French Alps fall naturally into two great sections, differing from each other structurally and climatically.

The Alps in the north are higher, and have more glaciers. The outstanding point of difference between them and the Alps in the south are their wetter climate and their more clearly defined relief. The northern Alps are arranged in two very distinct chains, the High Alps in the interior, and the Pre-Alps at the edge. They are separated by a deep trough, the Alpine Furrow, along the whole length of which flow the Arly, the middle course of the Isère, and the Drac.

The southern Alps are generally lower, have a noticeably drier climate, and are less clearly defined and arranged.

FIVE GREAT MASSIFS

In the northern Alps the deep valleys of Faucigny, Annecy, Chambéry and the Grésivaudan are occupied by large tracts of alluvial and moraine deposits. On the north and west of the Alpine Furrow are five great Pre-Alpine limestone massifs. The Chablis, immediately south of Lake Geneva, rises to a height of 10,200 feet in Mont Buet. The

The Durance River, which flows into the Rhone just south of Avignon, has cut a steep valley through the Alps.

High up in the Alps, twenty-two miles south of Geneva, is Lake Annecy, a vacationer's delight. Sailing, swimming and hiking in the beautiful lower slopes of the mountains surrounding the lake make for a perfect summer holiday.

Bornes or Genèvois chain dominates the northern side of the valley of the Arly. The Bauges lies between Lake Annecy and Lac du Bourget. The Grande-Chartreuse, a steep wooded relief, rises to 6847 feet in the Chamechaude. The Vercors, a series of vast upland plains, is bounded by steep slopes.

To the east of the Alpine Furrow are three crystalline massifs. Mont Blanc (15,781 feet) contains huge glaciers, the largest of which, Bossons and Mer de Glace, reach as far down as the wooded zone. The Belledonne range, whose peak is 9781 feet high, dominates the Grésivaudan from the southeast. The Massif du Pelvoux has many glaciers and high peaks, the highest being Les Ecrins (13,461 feet).

Farther to the east, toward the Italian frontier, is the Massif de la Vanoise, where the Grande-Casse reaches 12,668 feet.

Some deep valleys spread out from the Alpine Furrow and penetrate far into the central massifs. Since they run across the general line of the mountain chains, they are important as means of communication and as zones of human settlement. They are the Tarentaise, a wide, fertile valley through which the upper Isère flows; the Maurienne, which corresponds to the basin of the Arc; and further south, the Oisans, a wide alluvial basin.

The Alps in the south have a much more complicated geological structure than have those of the north. Some Pre-Alpine limestone massifs are to be found here too. The Dévoluy, where the Obiou reaches 9163 feet, lies to the west of the Drac. The Pre-Alps of Dauphiné are between the valley of the Buëch and the Rhone trench. The Monts de Vaucluse are parallel to Mont Ventoux, which reaches 6273 feet. The Pre-Alps of Provence extend from the lower course of the Durance almost to the Italian frontier, and form a convex arc toward the southwest.

The relief becomes more complicated toward the interior. The only crystalline massif is one between the Italian frontier and the middle course of the Tinée. Farther to the north, as far as the Massif du Pelvoux, there are mountains originating from eroded cover layers.

THE JURA

The Jura mountain chain stretches to the north of the French Alps between the Swiss Plateau to the east and the Saône valley on the west, and its foothills reach the Gate of Burgundy. It originated during the Tertiary period in a reaction against the mountain-forming phenomena that raised up the Alpine chain. The Jura suffered less intense pressure, and therefore did not rise as high as the Alps, the highest peak being Crêt de la Neige (5652 feet).

The Jura's structure is limited to a uniform series of narrow folds, elongated in the general northeasterly direction of the chain. There are broad plateaus in the west. The presence of limestone has favored differing developments on the folds, where normal erosion prevails, and on the plateau, where a great deal of water flows underground through deep caves and gorges, and comes out at the base of the mountains.

The central Jura possesses all the characteristics typical of the whole chain, and only a long, narrow spur of it lies in Swiss territory. In the east, the higher mountains are arranged in long strips, like Mont Reculet (5643 feet). But on the west are vast limestone plateaus at three different levels. Finally a steep scarp, about 650 feet high, dominates the valley of the Saône. It is deeply cut by valleys which penetrate far into the plateau itself.

The southern Jura begin south of the Nantua-Bellegarde valley. They are entirely French, and their more numerous and thicker folds are without plateaus. South of the Rhone the Jura are noticeably less extensive, and the farthest elevations are low. They reach as far as the Pre-Alpine limestone massifs of the Grande Chartreuse.

In mountain communities in the French Alps, the crafts of another century are still being practiced. This man is a malletmaker. With a young apprentice or two he works every mallet he sells, from tree log to finished product.

THE SAÔNE-RHONE VALLEY

Between the plains of Burgundy and the Massif Central on the west and the Vosges, the Jura and the central section of the Pre-Alps to the east there is a deep depression running south, down which flow the Saône and the Rhone. This valley is a very important means of communication. To the north, the low elevations of Burgundy and the pass known as the Belfort Gap or Burgundy Gate *(Porte de Bourgogne)* give easy access to the Paris Basin and to the central Rhine valley. In the south the Rhone valley spreads out toward southern France. In the west, the Jarez provides easy access to the heart of the Massif Central. Finally, in the east, the valleys of the Durance, the Isère, the upper Rhone and their tributaries, and the short furrows cutting into the Jura provide excellent means of communication with the Po valley in Italy and the Swiss Plateau.

The Alps and the Jura: Climate

The Alps have noteworthy variations in climate from zone to zone, affected by differences in height, the orientation of the valleys and the tilt of the mountains. In the higher regions there are notable changes in temperature during the day, rain is abundant, and there is snow during long periods of the year. In the interior of the range where the influence of the sea is less felt, a high-mountain climate prevails.

It is possible to draw a rather clear distinction between the northern and southern French Alps, for their climates and flora are very dissimilar. In the north the winters are often very cold but in the south winter temperatures are higher.

There are notable differences in rainfall. The Alps are much wetter in the north, where more rain falls on the higher parts than on the lower. Snow is also very abundant and the falls can be many feet deep. In some places the snow does not thaw until late summer.

The southern Alps, on the other hand, share many characteristics of the Mediterranean climate. Rainfall is largely restricted to the autumn and winter months, but on the upper levels it can be heavy. Except in some areas, snowfalls are not heavy, and the summers are usually hot and dry.

The Jura have generally a harsh and very wet climate. Winter is particularly cold and in January the average temperature is below the freezing point. Rain falls constantly and heavily and is distributed rather evenly over the whole region. In winter, snow is abundant on the western scarp and on the plateaus, and more than seven feet of snow may fall upon the highest peaks.

The Saône-Rhone valley has a Continental climate in the north, but in the south there are Mediterranean influences. Temperatures vary greatly during the year; the winters are particularly cold, especially in the interior zone, while the summers are very hot. Rainfall is rather evenly distributed along the whole valley furrow, summer rains prevailing in the north and autumnal ones in the south. Because of the influence of the Mediterranean, summers in the south are dry and sunny.

The Alps and the Jura: River Systems

The rivers of the French Alps and those of the outer sector of the Jura deliver their waters directly or indirectly to the Rhone with only a few, unimportant exceptions. The Rhone, 505 miles long, enters French territory a little below Lake Geneva. It then descends to the southwest through the southern sector of the Jura, where it takes a broken course following the configuration of the land. After receiving the Saône at Lyon, it flows to the Mediterranean through the deep valley between the Massif Central and the French Pre-Alps. Only in the last short length of its lower course, from Arles to its mouth, does it flow across plains.

TRIBUTARIES OF THE RHONE

Its principal tributaries are the Isère, the Drôme and the Durance from the Alps, the Ain from the central Jura, the Saône which rises in the Vosges and collects the waters of several rivers from the Jura, and the rivers that rise in the Massif Central. Except for the Ardèche, the

These children from southwestern France are not carrying around Christmas decorations in the midst of the summer. The garlanded branches they hold are memorial flowers to be put on the grave of a member of their family.

Some parts of the ancient walls around Carcassonne in southern France were erected by the Visigoths in the 8th century A.D. The walls are the most complete still standing anywhere in Europe. Carcassonne had a turbulent history in the Middle Ages, when it was taken during the Albigensian Crusade by Simon de Montfort and later by Edward the Black Prince during the Hundred Years' War. Today, in the more modern sections of the city, wool, cloth, linen and leather are manufactured.

58 / France • The Land

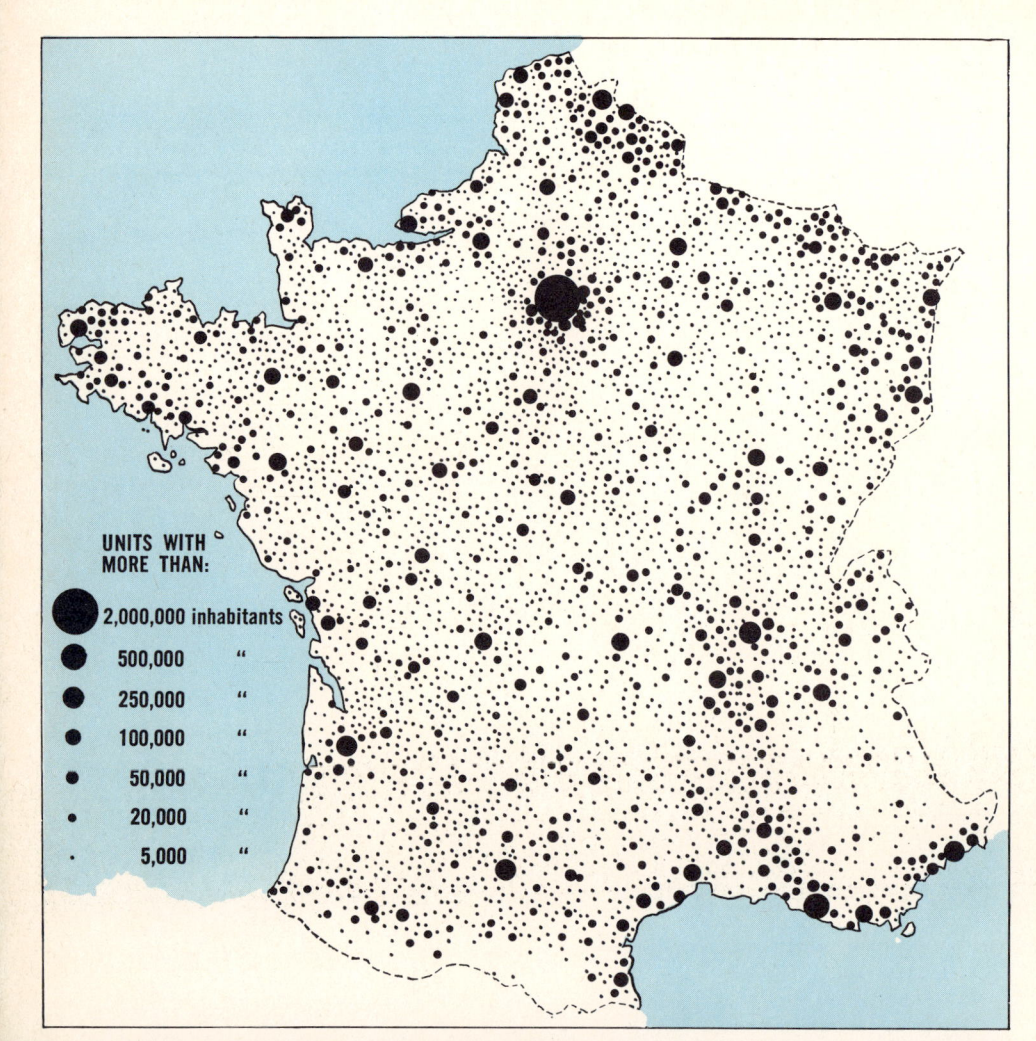

UNITS WITH MORE THAN:
- 2,000,000 inhabitants
- 500,000 "
- 250,000 "
- 100,000 "
- 50,000 "
- 20,000 "
- 5,000 "

Many masterpieces of French art and architecture have served religion. This chapel at Ronchamp was designed by Le Corbusier, the foremost French architect of the 20th century.

The population distribution of France today reflects the continuous migration to the cities that began in the 19th century. The map also indicates the dominance of Paris in French life. It is the only really large city in the entire country. France is remarkably underpopulated for its size, wealth and industrial development. Until the end of World War II it had one of the lowest birth rates in all of Europe. As a result, immigration of workers from other European countries to France has been encouraged.

Cèze and the Gard, the latter are generally short.

When the Rhone's waters are high, the river flows at about eight and one-half miles an hour, causing dangerous floods in the flat areas near its mouth. The Rhone takes enormous quantities of silt down with it, and the finer sand reaches the mouths, where a broad delta has formed. Because of the heavy rains that fall in its vast watershed, the Rhone has the greatest volume of all rivers in France.

The Rhone is navigable from Lyon to the sea, but its unstable course and swift current make it difficult for boats. It is excellent, however, for hydroelectric power, and besides the plants at Pougny, Bellegarde, Donzère and Génissiat, many new generating stations are being built or planned.

TORRENTIAL RIVERS

The other watercourses of the slopes of the French Alps and the Jura are torrential. The rivers of the northern Alps have greater volume, because of the heavier rainfall. The various Alpine lakes and glaciers cause the flow to be more regular throughout the year, though the lightest flow is in winter. The rivers from the southern Alps have less water because less rain and snow fall there.

The rivers of the Jura have an almost constant flow throughout the year because the vast limestone plateau holds the water and distributes it gradually. Their highest levels occur in spring and autumn.

In the Alps and the Jura there are innumerable little lakes. There are also some large lakes, the biggest of which are the Lake of Annecy and Lac du Bourget, lying between the Pre-Alpine massifs of the north.

Mediterranean France: the Land

The region that extends along the Mediterranean coast from the Spanish to the Italian frontier is geologically very diverse, but its climate gives it a geographical unity.

The alluvial plain of lower Roussillon stretches from west to east. It is an ancient gulf of the Mediterranean that has been filled up with silt from Pyrenean rivers. Lower Languedoc is composed of a narrow coastal strip made up of sedimentary terrain. Farther to the north is the limestone tableland of the Monts Garrigues, which are from 650 to 1000 feet high.

Next come the plains of Vaucluse and Crau, composed of alluvial deposits, and the low marshy island plain of Camargue, in the Rhone delta. Finally, there is the coastal part of Provence, which has a rich variety of forms with diverse origins. Oustanding features are the Monts de Maures Massif (2556 feet) and the Esterel Massif (2021 feet), which are separated by the deep depression of the Argens River.

The coast is also highly diversified. From the Spanish frontier up to and including the great delta of the Rhone, the shores are low and unbroken. They are alluvial, and were formed by rivers flowing from the Pyrenees and the Massif Central. The coastal region is sandy and there are many coastal lakes and lagoons, which are continually silting up.

Farther east, the coast of Provence is mainly high and rocky, but is broken at times by little alluvial bays. This coast, especially the celebrated Côte d'Azur, or Riviera, is of rare beauty.

Mediterranean France: Climate and River Systems

The climate of the south of France has clearly defined characteristics. Average temperatures are high in both the summer and winter because of the Mediterranean. The exceptional warmth of its waters, never less than 55°F, has great influence on the winter temperatures.

Rainfall is heaviest in Provence. In the west the rainfall is less. Average yearly rainfall is below twenty-two inches only in some parts of Languedoc, southwest Provence and the Rhone delta.

By far the most important river of the region is the Rhone, whose vast and marshy delta extends far into the Mediterranean. There are shorter and less important rivers to the west of it, such as the Tech, the Têt, the Agly and the Aude, flowing from the eastern Pyrenees. These are often torrential, and in its lower reaches the Aude flows through the open corridor between the Pyrenees and the Massif Central.

The Orb and the Hérault rise in the Massif Central, as do several minor streams. The rivers to the east of the Rhone delta are of little importance, the most notable being the Argens and the Var. They are torrential streams, which cause damaging floods in winter; in the summer they have little volume.

Corsica: the Land

Corsica is an island about 110 miles from the southern coast of France, in the Mediterranean. Geographically, ethnically and historically it is Italian, but since 1768 it has been politically a part of France.

Its geological structure is fairly simple. Granite prevails throughout the southwestern and central sectors, and limestone schist in the northeast. A mountain range runs from northwest to southeast, containing the highest peaks on the island. These include Monte Cinto (8891 feet), Monte Rotondo (8612 feet) and Monte d'Oro (7552 feet). Several high spurs stand out from this central chain and stretch toward the southwest, where they go down to the sea in great rocky promontories. In the northeast, another chain extends southward, and then, from the middle course of the Tavignano, turns toward the north.

Between these two mountainous regions is a series of internal basins of varying size, which help communication between the western and eastern sides of the island.

The character of the coast varies greatly. On the west the coast is generally high and rocky. It is marked by deep inlets from the sea, like those in Brittany, and these are separated by the mountain spurs already mentioned. On the east, however, the coast is unbroken and ringed with coastal lakes and lagoons, which make the alluvial plain of Aleria unhealthy.

Corsica: Climate and River Systems

Corsica has a generally Mediterranean climate. The summers are very hot and dry in the coastal areas, up to a height of 650 feet. The winters are mild and wet. Farther inland, as the height of the land rises, temperatures fall and rain is more abundant. Olive trees and chestnuts grow up to and above the 2600-foot line. Higher up, vast areas are covered with beeches and pines.

The rivers of Corsica are few and of little importance because of their

About 110 miles off the southern coast of France is the rocky, mountainous island of Corsica. Historically, Corsica is much more Italian than it is French. Even today, the folk costumes, traditions and dialects on the island are closest to those of nearby Sardinia, which is still Italian. For many years Corsica was under the jurisdiction of the Genoese Republic. But in 1730 the Corsicans revolted, seeking to win their independence. Unable to suppress the revolt, Genoa called in the French, who only subdued the armed bands of mountain revolutionaries with great difficulty. Not until 1768, thirty-eight years later, was the revolution finally crushed. In that year France took control of the island.

shortness and torrential character. They are very low in summer and in winter cause dangerous floods. The Golo and the Tavignano are the most noteworthy, and have contributed to the formation of the alluvial coastal plain at the foot of the eastern slopes of the mountain chain. On the western side of the island, the more important rivers are the Taravo and Gravone, which empty into the gulfs of Valinco and Ajaccio respectively.

The foreign quarter of Marseille in the northwestern part of the city is marked by a triumphal arch. As an international port on the Mediterranean, Marseille has a large foreign population, which comes mostly from North Africa and from the southern European countries.

HUMAN GEOGRAPHY

FRANCE HAS A STRONG TRADITION OF national unity, which has grown up over the centuries and has been helped by geographical, historical and economic conditions. These have given the whole population of the region a distinct character.

The importance of the country's geographical position arises from the fact that it lies between five natural frontiers: the North Sea, the Atlantic, the Mediterranean, the Pyrenees and the ranges of the Alps and Jura. These frontiers have tended to limit migrations of peoples from Eastern Europe and Central Asia. Since the 13th century, France has been an independent state, and, though it had alternating periods of expansion and contraction, it has played a leading part in the history of Europe.

Its national unity also rests on economic interdependence among its regions. This was created over the centuries by the activity of millions of peasants and artisans. Moreover, a really remarkable fusion of the Celtic, Latin and Germanic components in the population took place. Finally, the Catholic Church exercised a powerful unifying influence, even during the long periods of crisis it underwent in France.

Earliest Settlements

There is little concrete evidence regarding the Paleolithic Period. It is known that in the period before the last Ice Age, northern France was inhabited by people who knew the use of flints; probably these people migrated to the south when the last Ice Age began.

Later, new peoples from the south and east entered the French region. They were more advanced, and perhaps also more numerous, than the original inhabitants. They easily dominated, and then fused with them.

In the Neolithic Period the territory was inhabited by two different peoples. In the west lived Iberians, who came from the Iberian Peninsula; in the east lived Ligurians, who were soon joined at various points along the Mediterranean coast by Phoenicians.

The Celts, Romans and Franks

At this period in history, scattered tribes belonging to a new stock from Central Europe appeared in the valleys of the Seine and the Saône. These were the first Celts, and they were soon followed by other, more numerous, related groups, who fell in successive waves upon the territory. Because of their advanced culture the Celts overcame the Iberians and Ligurians, who were partly driven to the edges of the regions and partly absorbed by the conquerors.

Having settled down, the Celts, whom the Romans called Gauls, took up agriculture and trade. They established trading stations at important crossroads, and several of the great cities of modern France owe their origin to these settlements.

At the time of the Roman Conquest, ancient Gaul roughly corresponded to the area of modern France. But the Gauls proper lived only in the vast central area; Aquitanians inhabited the basin of the Garonne (modern Aquitaine), while the Belgae, or Gauls who had adopted a somewhat Germanic culture, lived in the northeast.

Other Gallic groups lived along the Mediterranean coast, and had already adopted the highly developed Roman civilization. The Romans were unable to take a census over such a vast area, so sparsely populated by moving tribes. Nevertheless, one can assume that a great rise in population resulted from the long period of peace and tranquillity that followed the Roman Conquest. In these years there was a constant increase of cleared and cultivated land, and trade and industry developed.

Gaul was deeply and entirely Romanized, as is evident by the spread of Latin and the disappearance of the Celtic languages, except in a few outlying regions.

In the 5th century A.D. new invasions began. Germanic and other tribes from the east entered the territory and remained there for years at a time, until they were driven further west by new invasions from across the Rhine. The Vandals were followed in this manner by the Visigoths, Saxons, Huns and others. But only the Franks, who later gave their name to the country, and the Burgundians, who were later absorbed by the Franks, remained. Between the 8th and 9th centuries the

Marseille is by far the most important port in France. It exports the products of all southern France and the cities of the Rhone valley. To it come luxury goods and raw materials from everywhere on the Mediterranean Sea and points east (via the Suez Canal).

Franks restored to the territory the political and administrative unity that it had lost after the barbarian invasions of the 5th century.

The French Kingdom

Unfortunately, we have little information about the size of the population at this time, nor is very much known about it for centuries. There were plagues and economic crises, often due to disastrous wars, and periods of prosperity. Thus, the population of France must have varied a great deal during the course of the Middle Ages, even within periods of a few years.

The kings of France promoted internal colonization. It proceeded slowly but produced results. The population fell again as a result of the foreign and civil wars of the second half of the 16th century. Afterward it rose steadily until it reached 20,000,000 around 1700 and 26,000,000 in the last decades of the 18th century.

At this time France had the largest population of any European country. The increase continued at a faster rate during the following decades. In 1800 the population was 27,500,000, more than 30,000,000 in 1821, 34,000,000 in 1841 and 37,000,000 in 1861.

The Nineteenth and Twentieth Centuries

The population continued to increase up to the end of the 19th century and after, but at an increasingly slower rate. However, births exceeded deaths in only a few regions; in some parts births and deaths balanced each other, while in many other areas the population actually began to decline.

From 1861 until 1945 the over-all increase was only 3,000,000. This figure is very low in comparison with the population increases in other countries, such as Italy, Germany and England. It was not due solely to natural factors, but also to immigration, which became very great, as will be seen.

The depopulation of the countryside assumed disturbing proportions toward the middle of the 19th century, when the development of communications made internal migration easier. The cities attracted great numbers of men and women, who were absorbed into new industries and trades.

The introduction of machines destroyed many crafts, crafts which had been carried on largely in the provinces in association with agriculture. Therefore, millions of persons had to go to the cities to look for new work.

The situation was gravest in the poor mountainous regions. But, paradoxically enough, the richer agricultural regions showed a greater and quicker fall in population than the less favored areas.

This seems to have been due to the increase of middle-class ideas and the desire of the peasant proprietor to pass his entire property to a sole heir, rather than have to divide it up among several, as the law required.

The gravity of the population crisis was increased by the fact that France was surrounded by countries with higher birthrates. Thus, the country was simultaneously faced with great political, military and economic problems. The population crisis helped to weaken France's position in the already unstable balance of power in Europe.

In the last century, censuses revealed that the birth rate was falling continuously. In the first decade of the 19th century it was thirty-two live births a year per one thousand population. By the middle of the century the figure had fallen to twenty-eight per one thousand, and fell even further, to twenty-three, in the last decade.

The situation grew worse in the 20th century, and in the decade immediately after World War I the rate fell to eighteen. Just before World War II it was down to sixteen.

Since the end of World War II there has been a notable recovery. Births have increased, and deaths, partly because of progress in medicine and hygiene, have declined. But it is impossible to make firm forecasts. Time will tell whether there has been a permanent recovery, or whether the recent improvement is only a temporary result of the special conditions produced by the war.

Internal Migration

The improvements in methods of communication and travel, especially the building of railroads during the 19th century, made it easy for large population movements to take place.

The capital and other large cities, such as Marseille, Lyon and Bordeaux, attracted most people, and movement also was heavy to the industrial areas of Alsace, the Rhone valley, Flanders and Lorraine.

Naturally those regions that were too undeveloped to support a relatively dense population lost great numbers. Notable among these regions were Brittany, some parts of the Alpine region, the Pyrenees and the Massif Central.

IMMIGRATION

Internal migration was not sufficient to right the economic imbalance caused by industrialization. Therefore, about the middle of the last century, France began to allow increased immigration into her territory. This brought her new life, and helped to make some changes in the character of the population.

About the middle of the 19th century there were approximately 380,000 foreigners in the country, and they made up one per cent of the population. This proportion rose noticeably in the following decades, and was three per cent at the end of the century. In 1930 it was seven per cent, a very high figure for a European country. Since then the number of foreigners has been falling, and in recent years has

For centuries artists have attempted to capture on canvas the beauty of Paris.

become stabilized at about four per cent.

The presence of numerous foreigners created social problems in some areas, especially after World War I, when many Poles, Czechs, Greeks and Africans arrived. They found it particularly difficult to absorb French culture and learn the language, tended to form separate groups, and occasionally came into conflict with their French neighbors.

Italians and Belgians, on the other hand, assimilated quickly and well. There has also been considerable immigration from Spain.

These foreign workers have been of primary importance to French agriculture and various industries, especially mining, construction, steel and glass making.

Immigrants are most numerous in the Paris area, in the industrial departments of the east and north, along the Mediterranean and the Pyrenees, especially in Lyon and around Bordeaux. About half of the 1,500,000 foreigners at present working in France are Italians.

Population Density

On Jan. 1, 1963, the population of France was estimated at 47,600,000, and it was distributed over an area of 212,680 square miles, a density of 223.8 per square mile. This density is far below that of its neighbors (except Spain), and also below that which its natural wealth could make possible.

The French population is distributed very unevenly. Zones of very high density alternate with zones that have been all but depopulated. The most heavily populated areas are those of the industrial northeast (Alsace and Lorraine), the north (Flanders, Artois and Picardy), and the northern part of the Paris Basin, especially in and around Paris, Rouen and Le Havre.

The population is relatively dense along the coasts of Normandy and Brittany, but it decreases noticeably in the interior. The wide valleys of the Loire and the Garonne are heavily populated, as are the valleys of their main tributaries.

The winegrowing Mediterranean areas (Languedoc and Provence), which many tourists visit throughout the year, also have large populations. Other densely populated areas are the valleys of the Rhone, the Saône and the Isère, where industry is concentrated.

The most sparsely populated re-

The café-lined Champs Élysées is the perfect place for a stroll on a sunny Sunday in Paris. As you go by you can look at the people sipping iced chocolate in the cafés. Should you get tired, you can stop for some yourself and see how the avenue looks from the sidelines. The Champs Élysées, which has often been called the most beautiful street in Paris, is named after the Elysian Fields, the paradise of Greek mythology.

gions are the interior chain of the Pyrenees, the Alps of Provence, the Landes, the higher interior parts of the Massif Central and great areas of Champagne, Burgundy and the Orléans region.

Forms of Rural Settlement

In the French countryside the peasants live either in villages separated by great stretches of cultivated fields, in single, scattered homesteads or in hamlets. In the north and northeast, villages are most common (Lorraine, Picardy and the Paris Basin), and in the south and west, hamlets and isolated farms prevail.

In the flat or undulating countryside of the north and east the population is concentrated in large centers. These are places which have been centers of commerce and communications for thousands of years. Almost all the invaders who have entered France have passed through these places. The peasants therefore came together in large villages and towns in order to facilitate defense as well as economic development.

In these same regions a particular kind of rural farm economy, which is still quite common, led the inhabitants to live together in large towns. This kind of economy is the old practice of *assolement,* by which all the owners have their land divided into three sections. A strict rotation system is practiced and the work is done in common.

In western France, in the south and in the central regions, it is more common for farms to be isolated, and for villages to be social and economic centers. These are signs of greater security in previous centuries. They also reflect a less intense exploitation of the soil, and a greater personal liberty for each owner.

Hamlets prevail in Brittany, in Maine and in the Vendée, and are more common than isolated farms throughout the whole of central France and in northern Alpine regions.

Villages

Villages are most common, as previously noted, in the north and

POPULATION: DEPARTMENTS OF FRANCE

DEPARTMENT	AREA (Sq. miles)	POPULATION (1962)	DEPARTMENT	AREA (Sq. miles)	POPULATION (1962)
Ain	2,248	327,107	Ille-et-Vilaine	2,697	614,268
Aisne	2,866	512,920	Indre	2,664	251,432
Allier	2,848	380,221	Indre-et-Loire	2,377	395,210
Alpes-Maritimes	1,443	618,265	Isère	3,178	729,789
Ardèche	2,144	248,516	Jura	1,951	225,685
Ardennes	2,027	300,247	Landes	3,604	260,495
Ariège	1,892	137,192	Loire	1,852	696,348
Aube	2,326	255,099	Loire-Atlantique	2,693	803,372
Aude	2,448	269,782	Loiret	2,629	389,854
Aveyron	3,385	290,442	Loir-et-Cher	2,478	250,741
Bas-Rhin	1,848	770,150	Lot	2,017	149,929
Basses-Alpes	2,697	91,843	Lot-et-Garonne	2,078	275,028
Basses-Pyrénées	2,977	466,038	Lozère	1,996	81,868
Belfort, Territoire de	235	109,341	Maine-et-Loire	2,811	556,272
Bouches-du-Rhône	2,025	1,248,355	Manche	2,475	446,878
Calvados	2,197	480,686	Marne	3,167	442,195
Cantal	2,229	172,977	Mayenne	1,986	250,030
Charente	2,305	327,634	Meurthe-et-Moselle	2,036	678,078
Charente-Maritime	2,791	470,897	Meuse	2,408	215,985
Cher	2,819	293,514	Morbihan	2,738	530,833
Corrèze	2,272	237,926	Moselle	2,403	919,412
Corse	3,367	279,111	Nièvre	2,658	245,921
Côte-d'Or	3,391	387,853	Nord	2,228	2,293,112
Côtes-du-Nord	2,786	501,923	Oise	2,272	481,289
Creuse	2,163	163,515	Orne	2,371	280,549
Deux-Sèvres	2,337	321,118	Pas-de-Calais	2,606	1,366,282
Dordogne	3,550	375,455	Puy-de-Dôme	3,090	508,928
Doubs	2,052	384,873	Pyrénées-Orientales	1,598	251,231
Drôme	2,532	304,227	Rhône	1,104	1,116,664
Eure	2,330	361,904	Saône-et-Loire	3,330	535,772
Eure-et-Loir	2,291	277,546	Sarthe	2,410	442,899
Finistére	2,729	749,558	Savoie	2,388	266,678
Gard	2,270	435,482	Seine	185	5,646,446
Gers	2,428	182,264	Seine-et-Marne	2,275	524,486
Gironde	4,140	935,448	Seine-et-Oise	2,184	2,298,931
Haute-Garonne	2,457	594,633	Seine-Maritime	2,448	1,035,744
Haute-Loire	1,930	211,036	Somme	2,443	486,225
Haute-Marne	2,420	208,446	Tarn	2,231	319,560
Hautes-Alpes	2,178	87,436	Tarn-et-Garonne	1,440	175,847
Haute-Saône	2,074	208,467	Var	2,333	469,557
Haute-Savoie	1,774	329,230	Vaucluse	1,381	303,536
Hautes-Pyrénées	1,750	211,433	Vendée	2,690	408,928
Haute-Vienne	2,119	332,514	Vienne	2,711	331,619
Haut-Rhin	1,354	547,920	Vosges	2,303	380,668
Hérault	2,402	516,658	Yonne	2,892	269,820
			TOTAL		**46,521,597**

Economic and geographical reasons can usually explain the position and even the existence of a village, but there are exceptions to the rule. In the south of France, for example, it is not uncommon to find villages placed at the top of high hills; they are far from fertile land, do not have abundant water and are reached by a difficult winding road. Their position can only be explained by the necessities of defense during the long periods of insecurity and warfare.

Such villages tend to spread downward; there are many examples of a second town being founded on the plain below (sometimes near a railroad station), or of the upper town spreading down the hillside into more modern streets and buildings. The two parts then have very different characteristics, the twisted medieval streets of the upper town often contrasting strongly with broad modern ones.

City Life

France has an ancient civilization, and a highly developed urban life is to be found in every province. Cities differ from villages not only in size but also in their more complex economic, social and cultural life. The characteristic form of economy in most cities is trade, while that of villages is agriculture, crafts, mining or fishing. To a great extent, it was trade that turned the original small villages on great highways and crossroads into huge modern cities.

Some French cities that arose at crossroads are Angers, Lille, Reims, Saint-Quentin, Metz, Nancy, Dijon, Le Mans, Rennes, Montpellier, Nîmes, Aix-en-Provence and Poitiers. Others have grown up beside fords on great rivers, such as Tours, Perpignan and Paris. Still others are situated at the confluence of two rivers, such as Lyon, Grenoble, Montereau and Avignon.

CITIES WHERE REGIONS MEET

There are cities that became important centers of trade because of their position at the junction of two regions. Pau, Tarbes, Foix and Perpignan are all situated at the foot

northeast, but they are also numerous in other regions. The variety of their appearance and their location make them one of the most picturesque features of the French landscape. They are often separated by vast stretches of cultivated or pasture land, and almost always have a modest appearance, being made up generally of small houses grouped around a church, a market or some other natural center.

Seen from the surrounding fields the villages reveal notable regional differences. Some have the backs of the stone houses turned to the fields, and have neither gardens, orchards nor trees to relieve the monotony, as in Champagne and the Côte d'Or. Others are surrounded by gardens, hedges and woods, as in Lorraine. In Normandy villages are hidden in thick woods to protect the people from the cold winds from the Atlantic.

Villages are usually situated near the richest and most fertile land in the district, or at the point of contact between one region or economy and another. They are frequently along highways or at junctions of two valleys.

There are two islands in the Seine River at Paris. The larger one, the Île de la Cité, was the site of the original Gallic settlement of Paris and now houses the cathedral of Notre Dame and the Palace of Justice. Just east of the Île de la Cité is Saint Louis, the smaller island, which offers an excellent view of the back of the cathedral.

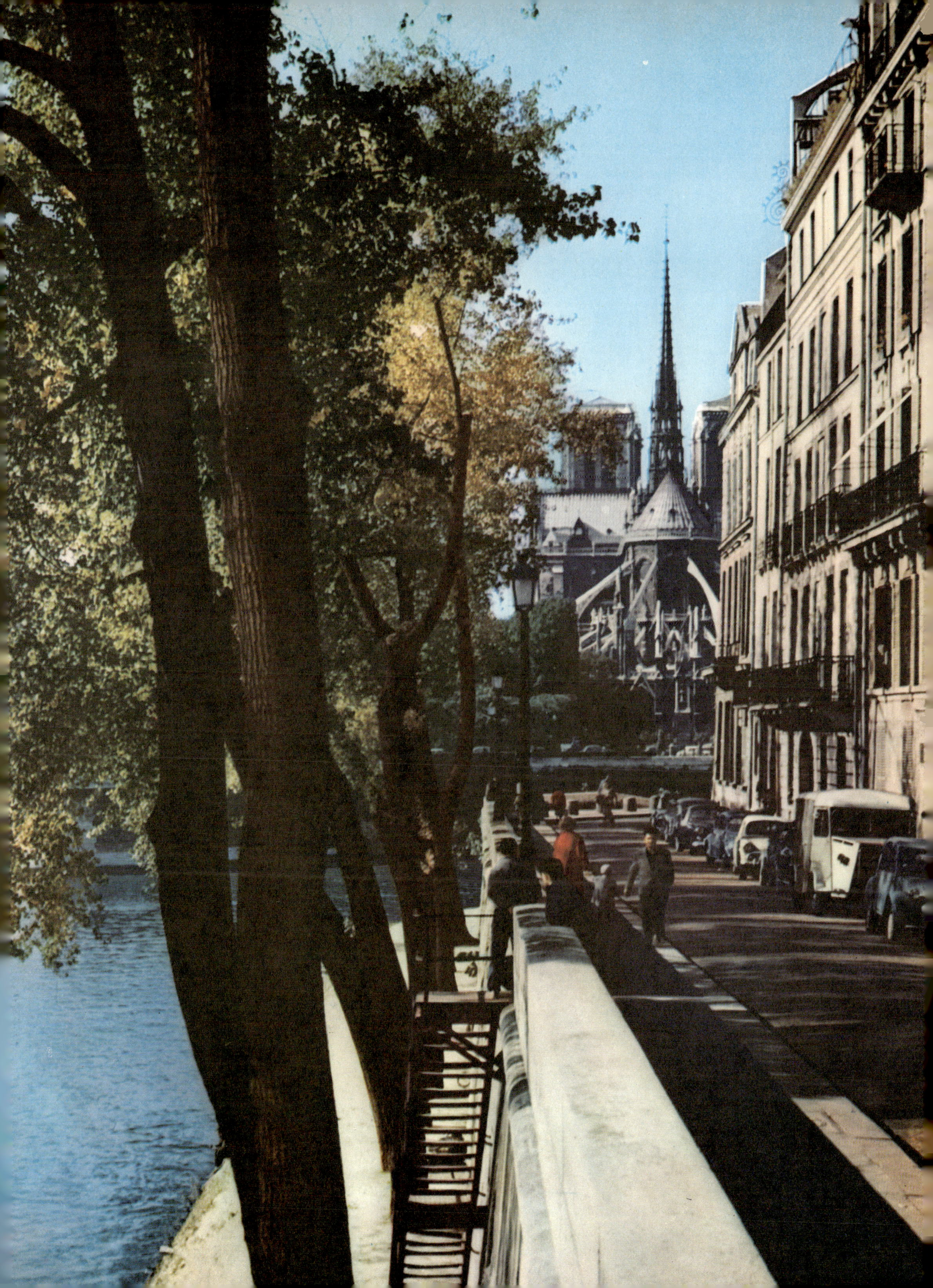

of the Pyrenees, in valleys that run far back into the mountains and provide contact with Spain.

Clermont-Ferrand, Montluçon and Aurillac are similarly situated at the foot of the Massif Central, Besançon and Lons-le-Saunier are at the foot of the Jura, and Grenoble is in the center of an important Alpine valley. Other cities such as Vierzon have developed in recent times at great rail junctions. The growth of modern industry has also caused many cities to expand (some of previously little importance), such as Saint-Etienne, Roubaix, Douai and Hénin-Liétard.

PRINCIPAL PORTS

Cities have always risen at favorable points on seacoasts. In France there are twenty-six maritime cities with more than 20,000 inhabitants. The most important are the great commercial ports (Marseille, Le Havre, Dunkirk, Rouen, Nantes and Bordeaux), which are usually on the estuaries of great rivers, and thus in a good position to trade with the hinterland.

Some ports are largely for passenger ships (Dunkirk, Calais, Cherbourg, Le Havre, Brest, Saint-Nazaire).

They are mostly situated along the Channel, and are more easily accessible than the great commercial ports on the same coast. Still others are mainly for pleasure boats and yachts (Nice, Cannes), or for great fishing fleets (Boulogne, Lorient, La Rochelle), and are connected by fast means of transport with the big cities. Toulon, with its magnificent natural harbor, and Brest are the main naval bases.

Many French cities show clear signs of their origins and preserve characteristics of the ancient villages from which they arose. The central parts still have narrow twisted streets, little plazas and squares, and complicated blocks of houses intersected by alleys. In the center there is often a cathedral or a castle.

EXPANDING CITIES

In the late Middle Ages and the early Renaissance wider streets, laid out on a more rectangular plan, were built, and new circles of walls and bastions erected to protect these new areas. When these walls were rendered useless by improvements of artillery they were usually demolished and replaced, as in Paris, by wide avenues; these are known, from their origin, as *boulevards* (which means "ramparts" or "bulwarks").

Since the Industrial Revolution the cities have spread out beyond the limits of the walls. Paris, for example, has had several circles of such walls. Most other cities have developed similarly but some, especially in the south (such as Carcassonne), have kept their medieval character.

In mining and heavily industrialized areas where development has been enormous over the last century, the residential and industrial districts have often spread out like tentacles, reaching neighboring towns and cities. In this way great combinations of cities have arisen, and have received the name of "conurbation."

In France there are seventy-six cities with a population between 30,000 and 50,000. Greater Paris comes first in size and importance (8,569,238). (All population figures for cities are taken from the 1962 census.)

CITIES AND SETTLEMENTS

FOR MANY CENTURIES PARIS HAS been the political, economic, financial, intellectual and artistic capital of the country. With its suburbs and

The Sorbonne, the central college of the University of Paris, has been stimulating the intellectual life of Europe for centuries. The University of Paris was founded in the middle of the 12th century, but the Sorbonne, its first endowed college, was not established until 1257, when Robert de Sorbon, the chaplain of St. Louis (King Louis IX) opened a seminary for poor theology students. The name was soon extended to the entire faculty of theology. Wealthy patrons like Cardinal Richelieu donated buildings and books to enrich the college, but the entire theology school was suppressed by the revolutionary government in 1792. In the extensive administrative reforms that were introduced in the 19th century, the name Sorbonne itself was dropped, and all the schools were incorporated in the University of Paris. Today, the Sorbonne is the unofficial name of any part of the University, and the old buildings house the public courses of the faculties of science and letters.

contiguous communes it contains more than one seventh of the whole population of France.

It has an excellent geographical position, its great development and its place in French history being largely due to the convergence of many complex geographical, historical, economic and political factors.

The topographical features that led the first inhabitants to choose the site were the low hill of Sainte-Geneviève, which was developed for settlement in the 5th century B.C., that dominated the left bank of the Seine and the Île-de-la-Cité, site of the Gallic village. This island, surrounded by marshes, made crossing and defense easy. On the right bank there was a semicircular plain, enclosed by a chain of low hills (*buttes*) with easy slopes (Passy, Montmartre, Ménilmontant). The slopes of the hills provided good land for cultivation and abundant building material.

The Roman city, *Lutetia Parisiorum*, spread from the island to Sainte-Geneviève hill. The remains of its theater and baths are still to be seen on the Boulevard Saint-Michel.

During the barbarian invasions the island in the Seine became the center of the settlement, for it was easier to defend. The city remained there for several centuries. In the meantime, monks undertook intense reclamation on both sides of the river and several great abbeys arose: Saint-Germain-l'Auxerrois, Sainte-Chapelle, Saint-Germain-des-Prés, Sainte-Geneviève and Saint-Denis. These became centers for urban development outside the walls of the *Cité*.

THE EXPANSION OF PARIS

The first great expansion took place in the beginning of the 10th century. The principal reason for this was the succession of the Capetian dynasty to the throne of France in 987. In two centuries of struggle they succeeded in unifying the country. Paris now became almost the first city of France. Its advance was favored by the fact that it stands in the vicinity of the main river communications (the Seine, the Yonne, the Oise and the Marne). The roads that meet there also link the city with every part of France.

During the 16th and 17th centuries Paris continued to expand over the narrow plain on the right bank, where the new districts became the commercial center. Other areas grew up around the great monuments of the recent past, such as Notre-Dame Cathedral, the Louvre and the Hôtel de Ville. During the absolute rule of the Bourbons all political and administrative power was centered in Paris, and the cultural life of the country was attracted to the Court. The city went on spreading over the flat areas on the right bank, and reached the foot of the hills of Montmartre and Belleville.

DEVELOPMENT OF THE LEFT BANK

Until the end of the last century the districts that had grown up on the left bank had not spread as much as those on the right bank. The Left Bank was occupied by the University buildings and a number of monasteries and nunneries. Between these there were large open spaces and parks, such as that of the Luxembourg Palace gardens. Only when the bridge tolls were eliminated in 1848 did the Left Bank begin to develop on a large scale.

Like many other French cities with fine buildings, Amiens has had to find some way of integrating modern structures with the old. Located on the Somme River, seventy-five miles north of Paris, Amiens was severely damaged in World War II. Since 1945 architects and city planners have worked to rebuild the city in harmony with the architectural monuments of the past.

From the 13th to the 16th centuries the population of the city remained almost stationary at about 200,000, but by the beginning of the 18th century it was about 500,000, and it reached 1,500,000 in the middle of the 19th century. In spite of the planning measures previously taken by Louis XIV and Napoleon I, Paris was still a maze of narrow, tortuous streets, unable to bear the ever-increasing volume of traffic. In 1859, Baron Georges Eugène Haussmann was commissioned to transform it radically. He was Prefect of the Seine for sixteen consecutive years, and conceived a great plan for municipal improvements that gave the city the modern and monumental appearance that it has today.

The more important boulevards and avenues were opened up. These either circled or ran through the city, making it easy for traffic to pass from one side to the other. New bridges were built over the Seine, and entire districts were hollowed out to provide room for great new

68 / FRANCE • *The Land*

The Vosges Mountains in eastern France are older than the Alps and the Pyrenees. Erosion and weathering have rounded off their peaks, and thick forests cover their slopes. The northern Vosges are lower and more gentle. The highest peak in the range is Ballon de Guebwiller, which rises to 4672 feet. This picture, taken from Ballon d'Alsace, the third highest peak, reveals how harsh the terrain is under the covering.

squares and parks. These developments spurred many to leave the center and seek new homes on the outskirts, and the old city was filled with offices and shops.

Paris was now the leading commercial and industrial city of the country, and new strength flowed into it. The population increased, and residential suburbs stretched out in all directions. The *buttes* of Montmartre and Belleville as well as their opposite slopes were built upon. New tentacles were thrown out toward the neighboring villages, which were soon devoured by this expansion.

Today the city is not only the center of French politics, administration, culture and art, but also the greatest commercial and industrial city in the country. This is due to the availability of vast numbers of workers and the fact that all communications, by land, sea and air, are centered there.

An important Parisian industry is the tourist trade. Its beauty and its reputation as a commercial and social center attract foreigners in great numbers to the "City of Light" from all over the world.

The Paris Basin

The capital exerts an influence over a large part of the great agricultural region surrounding it. This area, known as the Paris Basin, extends throughout the Île-de-France, and includes the lesser areas of Beauce, Gâtinais and Brie. Parts of Champagne, Picardy and the middle Loire valley (Orléanais) also form part of the Paris Basin.

In the Île-de-France the people live mostly in farming villages. The cities beyond the large Parisian suburbs are generally market towns with some industries, and include Chartres, Melun, Château-Thierry, Beauvais, Compiègne and Etampes in the Île de France.

Like a large part of the Île-de-France, Champagne is sparsely populated. The people live mostly in large farming villages in the fertile valleys of the rivers. Large towns and cities such as Reims, Châlons-sur-Marne and Troyes have grown up at important crossroads.

In Picardy also the towns arose at the crossroads and developed as market centers. The more important are Amiens, Saint-Quentin, Abbeville and Péronne.

AMIENS *(pop. 105,433).*

After serious destruction in both world wars, Amiens is being rebuilt in the medieval style typified by the great cathedral, the largest in France. Standing on the swampy banks of the lower Somme River, it was the historical capital of Picardy. Capital of the Somme department, it is about 70 miles north of Paris, and is an important rail and textile center. Formerly famous for its velvet making, it now also produces chemicals and machinery.

BEAUVAIS *(pop. 33,995).*

This beautiful town is the capital

This fountain in Lyon was designed in the 19th century by Frédéric Bartholdi, who also sculpted the Statue of Liberty in New York harbor. Beyond is the city's 17th-century hôtel de ville.

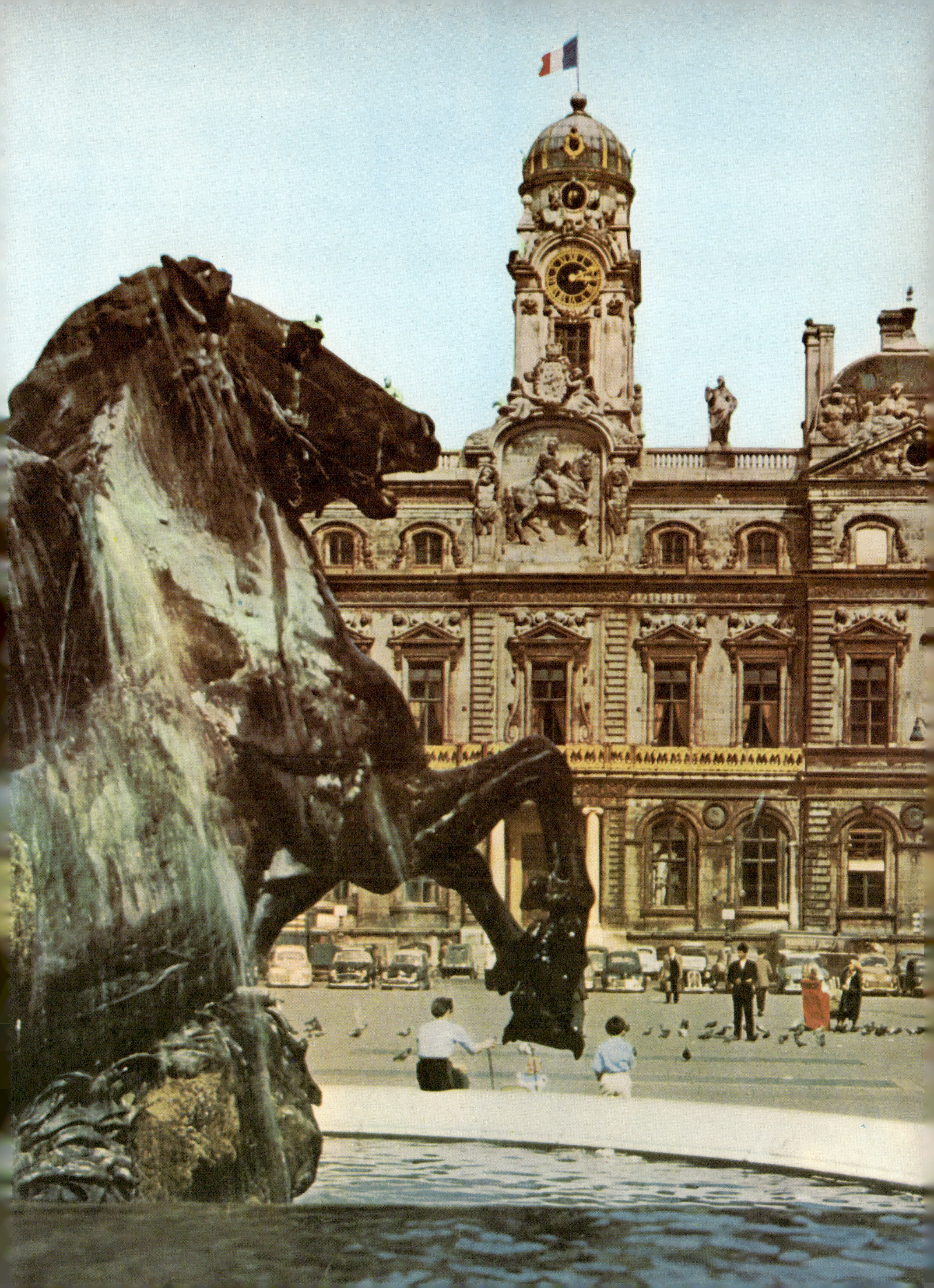

of the Oise department, and is situated on a hill beside the Thérain River, about 40 miles north-northwest of Paris. Its historic central sector was partially demolished during World War II, but it has since been rebuilt.

CHÂLONS-SUR-MARNE (pop. 41,705).

Capital of the Marne department, it is situated on the right bank of the Marne in a champagne-producing district. It stands at the junction of important commercial and historical routes and has played a great part in history. The great battle of the Catalaunian Fields (451 A.D.), in which Attila and his Huns were defeated, took place nearby. Châlons is about 100 miles east of Paris.

CHARTRES (pop. 31,495).

Capital of the Eure-et-Loir department, the city stands on the left bank of the Eure River. It has picturesque streets along the river. The most outstanding of its medieval buildings is the Gothic cathedral, which can be seen from a great distance across the fields of Beauce. Chartres existed in Roman times, and became first a county and then a duchy in the 16th century. It is a road junction on the route to Brittany, about 50 miles southwest of Paris.

LAON (pop. 25,078).

The city stands on a rocky hilltop about 325 feet above the surrounding plain. It is the capital of the Aisne department, and is a manufacturing and rail center 83 miles northeast of the capital. It has notable historical and artistic monuments, the most outstanding being the church and the medieval walls.

REIMS (pop. 133,914).

The city lies in a broad basin surrounded by vineyards in the Marne department, about 85 miles northeast of the capital. In spite of almost total destruction during World War I, the city has again developed toward the Vesle River and the Aisne-Marne canal. The southeastern suburbs have reached the slopes *(buttes)* containing the famous champagne cellars. Reims is one of the principal centers of champagne production and its allied industries (glass, packing cases, etc.). The most important artistic monument is the Gothic cathedral.

SAINT-QUENTIN (pop. 61,071).

A picturesque town in the Aisne department about 80 miles northeast of Paris. It stands in an amphitheater on the right bank of the Somme River and on the Saint-Quentin canal. Besides its museums, this capital of medieval Vermandois county is notable for numerous battles that have taken place around it, the most celebrated being the hard-won victory of the Spanish over the French in 1557. The main industries are the traditional textile industry and metal working.

TROYES (pop. 67,406).

Capital of the Aube department, it is situated on the left bank of the Seine in a broad alluvial valley. Capital of Champagne in the Middle Ages, Troyes was a famous market town and art center, but suffered at the end of the 17th century from the revocation of the Edict of Nantes, which drove away its most energetic commercial citizens. Its present development is largely connected with the textile industry. It is the center of the French knitting mill industry, especially hosiery. It also shares in the flourishing champagne industry.

Lille, in the northeast, has become the nearest thing to a French Pittsburgh. In the center of the mining and steel-refining districts, the city is a major rail center, produces chemicals, refines metal ores and manufactures textiles. The expansion of Lille and the neighboring cities of Tourcoing and Roubaix has made a large urban complex that transcends old town boundaries.

In the rich iron fields of eastern Lorraine is the manufacturing city of Nancy. The city has many historic buildings, some of which face out onto this statue of Stanislas Leszczynski on the Place Stanislas. Stanislas, who was the deposed king of Poland, had been supported by France in the complicated politics of eastern Europe in the early 18th century. He became the father-in-law of the French king when his daughter, Marie Leszczynski, married Louis XV of France in 1725. Leszczynski's forces were decisively defeated at the siege of Danzig in 1733, and he fled west to his son-in-law, who named him Duke of Lorraine and Bar. The ex-king then took up residence in Nancy in 1737 and stayed in France until his death.

It is a road and rail junction about 100 miles southeast of the capital.

VERSAILLES (pop. 86,759).

Eleven miles to the west of Paris, this city is the capital of the Seine-et-Oise department. The royal court lived there from 1682 to 1789, and the government had its seat there from 1871 to 1879. It stands on an undulating plateau in a wooded region and is divided by three broad avenues converging at the Palace, which was begun in the 17th century. The city has begun to grow in recent times, and because of the ease of communication with Paris it is a favorite residential district and is often visited by tourists.

Northern France

The northern region of France has been densely populated for many centuries. The soil and the advantages accruing from trade with neighboring regions have made constant economic and social advance possible. During the last ten years the development of mining and industry has caused a rise in population in the industrial areas, and consequently in rural regions that supply their needs.

The density of population is very high in the Pas-de-Calais, which corresponds broadly to the old province of Artois. In the Nord department, coinciding with Flanders, the density is the highest in all of France.

The population is generally concentrated in small cities and towns. Most of the smaller towns have an agricultural appearance, for example, Orchies, Hazebrouck, Montreuil, Saint-Omer and Saint-Pol. The mining towns are larger and more important, such as Hénin-Liétard, Denain, Anzin and Liévin. These, and industrial towns such as Aulnoye, Jeumont and Aniche, have long monotonous streets lined with interminable rows of low, gray workers' houses.

There is more life in the bigger cities, such as Arras, Cambrai, Douai, Valenciennes, Lille, Roubaix and Tourcoing, and in the ports of Dunkirk, Calais and Boulogne. In the summer the numerous resorts along the sandy coast, which have come

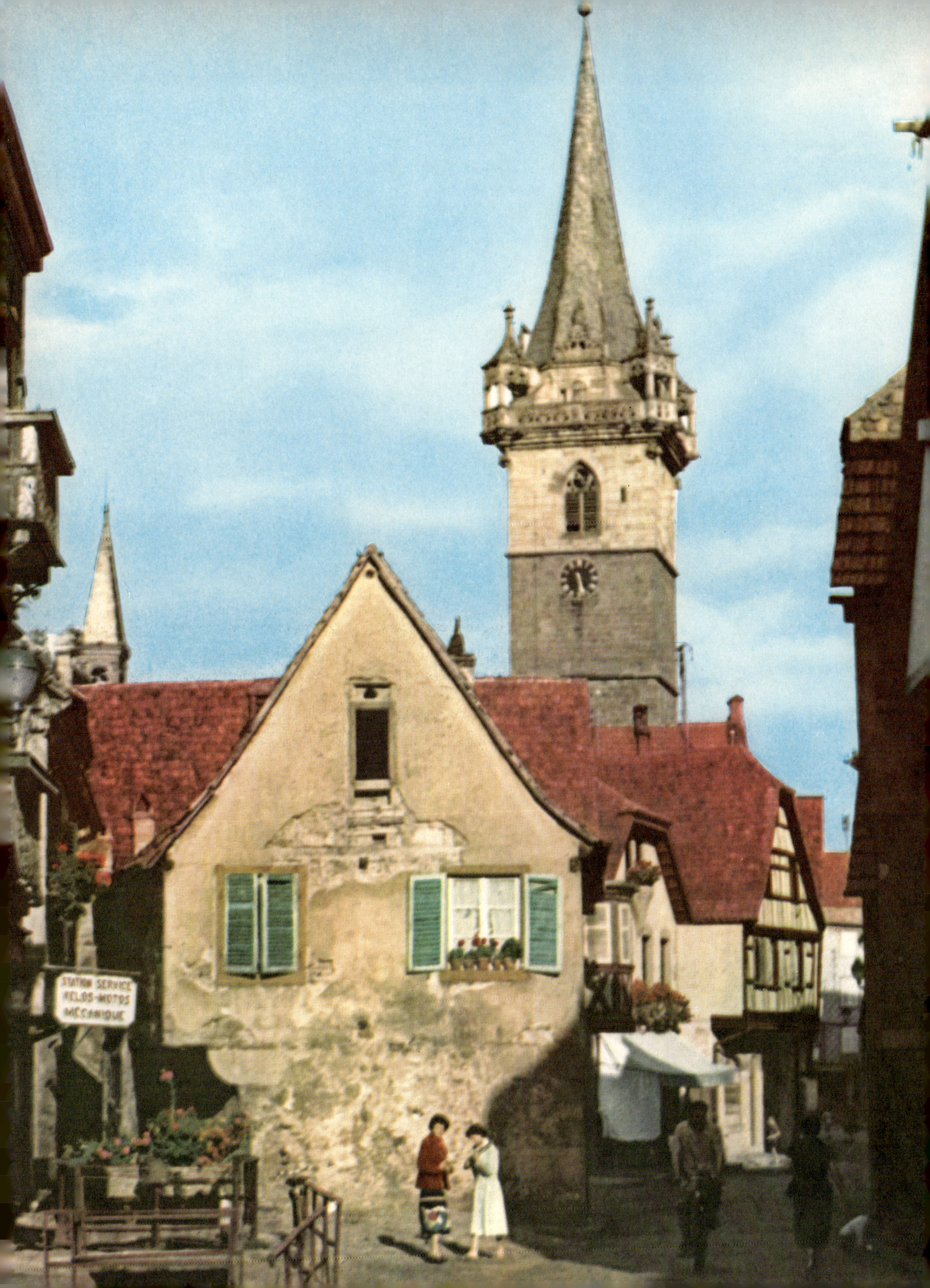
STATION SERVICE
VELOS-MOTOS
MÉCANIQUE

into being because of the nearness of Paris and the great industrial centers, are very lively.

THE 'CROSSROADS OF EUROPE'

There were very few towns or cities in this area in Roman times and Arras and Cambrai were but frontier posts, but in Carolingian times its position at the "crossroads of Europe" favored the growth of towns and cities. After the Norman invasions the region resumed its commercial life, and market towns such as Douai, Béthume and Saint-Omer flourished. More recently the opening of vast coal deposits has caused many new towns to arise and ancient ones to develop in new directions as the economy of the region was transformed.

ARRAS (pop. 41,761).

Capital of Pas-de-Calais department, it is a road and rail junction on the canalized Scarpe River. In Roman times it was an important crossroads. Because of its strategic location and economic importance it was the scene of battles from the time of the Norman occupation to World War I, after which it had to be entirely rebuilt. Famous for its wool trade and former tapestry works, the city's name became synonymous with tapestry. Historical capital of Artois, it is about 110 miles north-northeast of Paris.

BOULOGNE-SUR-MER (pop. 49,281).

Situated on the shores of the English Channel in the Pas-de-Calais department, it is the most important fishing port in France, and also an important port for communications with England. It is connected by rail with the capital, about 150 miles away. It formerly had great strategic importance, and was long fought over by France and England. Its industrial area was badly damaged during World War II. Its economy depends on fishing and allied industries, and more recently it has become a tourist center because of its beaches and its nearness to both the hinterland and to England.

CALAIS (pop. 70,372).

This city stands at the mouth of a series of canals which connect it with the rich industrial hinterland. Because of its strategic position it was fought over by France, England and Spain from the 14th to the 16th centuries. The port area was virtually leveled during World War II. It is the most convenient port for trade and travel to Dover (27 miles away) and Folkestone in England. It is also a notable fishing port and has engineering and lace industries. It is connected by rail to Paris, 170 miles to the south.

CAMBRAI (pop. 32,897).

A historic town in the Nord department, standing on a hill on the right bank of the Scheldt (Escaut) River. Its beautiful 17th- and 18th-century houses give it an aristocratic air, but there is also a modern part, built after the destruction caused by World War I. The city owes its importance to the rich farming region surrounding it and to its position at a crossroads between Artois and the Ardennes. The powerful and often famous bishops of Cambrai also ruled the surrounding county of Cambrésis. The town's name is also linked with the famous League of Cambrai, which was formed in 1508 against Venice.

DOUAI (pop. 47,639).

An industrial city and a rail and road junction, it is about 125 miles northeast of Paris in the Nord department. The dwellings in 17th-century style on the right bank of the canalized Scarpe River give it a tranquil and dignified appearance. It lies in a coal region, and is surrounded by a belt of industrial suburbs. Douai has historical, cultural, literary and religious links with England, and the Douai Bible was prepared at the Roman Catholic college here around 1600.

DUNKIRK (pop. 27,616).

A North Sea port standing on the dunes of the sandy coast of Flanders, in the Nord department, at the convergence of numerous canals. Boat-building and fishing are carried on, and much raw material is imported through Dunkirk for the engineering, chemical and textile industries of the area. As it was an important means of communication with England, it was fought over between France, Holland, England and Spain from the 16th to the 17th centuries. It became famous in modern times for the troop evacuation carried out there in 1940 by the retreating British. Near the Belgian frontier, it is connected by rail with Paris, about 175 miles to the south.

HÉNIN-LIÉTARD (pop. 25,527).

A typical mining city of the Pas-de-Calais department, it has a uniform and monotonous appearance, and owes its recent development to the coal mines in the area and the new industry founded because of the mines. It is about 125 miles northeast of Paris.

LENS-LIÉVIN (pop. 77,717).

These twin cities are in the Pas-de-Calais department, situated on the southern edge of the great Anglo-Flemish coal field. The main industries are coking and metal-working. Lens is a rail hub, and is located about 125 miles from the capital.

LILLE (pop. 193,096).

Capital of the Nord department and former capital of Flanders, it is an industrial city with beautiful 17th- and 18th-century buildings in the old town. Founded on an island in the Deûle River, its position on the highway between Flanders and Paris favored its development as a commercial center. It is a historic linen market. The discovery of vast coal deposits in the region led to the development of a great modern industrial complex of 700,000 people, the Lille complex. The city is a major road and rail center and is engaged in such industries as chemicals, textiles and metallurgy. It is also an educational city, having one of France's largest universities.

ROUBAIX (pop. 112,856).

A great textile center in the Lille complex, it is in the Nord department, near the Belgian border, and is a rival of Lille. Royal charters in the 15th and 18th centuries granted Roubaix the privilege of making cloth of the kinds "made by the English."

TOURCOING (pop. 89,258).

The third of the three chief cities of the Lille complex, in the Nord department. It specializes in woolens, which have been manufactured there for many centuries. In the 19th century the introduction of power machinery resulted in expansion of the industry and the city.

VALENCIENNES (pop. 45,379).

An industrial and commercial city and a rail junction in the Nord department near a vast coal basin.

A few miles south of Strasbourg on the eastern hills of the Vosges Mountains is the small town of Obernai. German influence is strong in the Alsatian towns near the Rhine, as the construction of the houses shows.

It is on the Scheldt River, which is canalized from the city's port to the North Sea. It is engaged in light engineering and a revived lace industry. There are also food industries, centered on the surrounding fertile plain of French Flanders. The city is only a few miles west of the Belgian border.

Northeastern France

Northeastern France stretches from Champagne, which belongs to the Paris Basin, to the Rhine. It is made up of the undulating regions of Lorraine and northern Burgundy, the mountainous massif of the Vosges, and the low plain between the Vosges and the Rhine, Alsace.

Southern Lorraine is essentially rural and has preserved the ancient rotation system of farming, the people living in modest villages. The cities are generally small and quiet, such as Mirecourt and Neufchâteau, but there are two watering places, Vittel and Contrexéville, and a few industrial towns along the valleys of the Moselle, such as Thaon-les-Vosges and Charmes, and along the Meurthe, such as Lunéville and Baccarat.

NORTHERN LORRAINE

Northern Lorraine is a densely populated mining and industrial region. The population tends to group in villages, and is thickest in the Moselle valley, where the more important cities, Metz and Nancy, also lie. The population is relatively dense also in the Meuse Valley. In this area the more important cities are Verdun, Revin, Vireux-Molhain and Mézières.

The demographic structure of Lorraine was profoundly altered by the industrial developments that began in the last decades of the 19th century. At that time the population was predominantly rural. The opening of

If these streets look like part of a little German town, they should. They are in Colmar, not twenty miles from the French-German border. Because it is so close to the boundary, Colmar has been the scene of fighting whenever France and Germany have been at war. Today the city is noted for its textile manufactures.

the iron mines brought about a great increase in population and in immigration, especially from Germany, to which country the area originally belonged. German, the predominant language of Alsace and eastern Lorraine, then began to be spoken in western Lorraine also.

ALSACE

From ancient times Alsace was always important as a route between central and western Europe. This was because of the easy communications along the low plain between the Vosges and the Black Forest, and the low passes through the mountainous massifs on either side. The intense trade and the industrial and agricultural activity of the Rhine valley have always resulted in a dense population. Large agricultural towns and industrial cities that have developed recently contain most of the population.

The cities of Alsace have grown up at important junctions and crossroads. Strasbourg is at the junction with the Rhine and the road that crosses the Vosges and the Black Forest in Germany.

Mulhouse stands at the point where the road from central France passes through the Belfort Gap, or *Porte de Bourgogne,* on its way to the Alpine regions of the Swiss Plateau. Belfort, at the Gap, and Colmar, Haguenau and Sélestat, near the left bank of the Rhine, also grew in the same way. The more important industrial centers in northern Alsace are Saverne, Bischwiller, Reichshoffen, Niederbronn-les-Bains and Woerth.

The appearance of the province, its language and customs are profoundly German. It was first annexed by France during the Thirty Years' War.

THE VOSGES AND BURGUNDY

In spite of harsh conditions there, the Vosges Mountains also have a high population density. The people live in separate settlements, but there are large towns in the foothills, such as Thann, Guebwiller and Molsheim, and in the valleys (Ribeauvillé, Munster and Sainte-Marie-aux-Mines).

Beyond the Vosges, to the southwest, is a vast hilly, mainly wine-growing region, Burgundy. The population is generally sparse, and the density is lower than the average for France.

The principal town is Beaune, a busy wine market. The more important towns are all in valleys tributary to the Saône, the Loire and the Seine.

Chaumont, Langres, Montbard and Auxerre are notable towns, and Le Creusot and Montceau-les-Mines are industrial centers. Dijon is the ancient capital and the economic center of the province.

AUXERRE *(pop. 31,178).*

Capital of the Yonne department, the city stands on two hills overlooking the left bank of the Yonne River. The original town is separated from its suburbs by an uninterrupted circle of boulevards built on the site of the former ramparts. It is an important market for Burgundian wines, and is about 95 miles southeast of Paris.

BELFORT *(pop. 48,190).*

This industrial city is capital of the Territory of Belfort, a department created after the war of 1870. It stands between the southern Vosges and the Jura, in a position dominating the Belfort Gap or *Porte de Bourgogne* (the Gate of Burgundy). Once a strategic point, it is today a road and rail center between the Paris Basin and the Rhine valley, about 230 miles southeast of Paris.

COLMAR *(pop. 52,355).*

Situated near the foot of the Vosges on the alluvial plain of the Rhine, the city is the capital of the Haut-Rhin department. It is a typical

The grapes grown in Alsace, along the gentle eastern slopes of the Vosges mountains, produce white wines similar to those made in Germany just across the Rhine.

Alsatian town, with historical buildings and celebrated museums. Linked to the Rhone-Rhine Canal, it is a road and rail junction and textile center about 245 miles east-southeast of Paris.

DIJON *(pop. 135,694).*

A center of Burgundian art and culture, with historic buildings and a famous museum. Here is the palace of the dukes of Burgundy, and the city is now capital of the Côte d'Or department. It stands on the Ouche River near the Burgundy Canal, on the northeastern slopes of the Côte d'Or and on the edge of the Bresse plain, stretching toward the Saône River. It is an important market town and a road and rail center. It has chemical, metalworking and food industries. Dijon is about 160 miles southeast of Paris.

METZ *(pop. 102,771).*

Capital of the Moselle department, it is a rail and road junction standing on an isolated hill at the confluence of the Seille and the Moselle, about 175 miles from Paris. Because of its strategic position, Metz has often been besieged. Its importance as a military stronghold with a strategic position retarded its economic development in the last century. But it is now an industrial center, and its

Boulogne-sur-Mer on the English Channel is the largest fishing port in France. Because of its strategic location, Boulogne has had a troubled history. The city was demolished by invading Norsemen in 882, by Emperor Charles V in 1553, and more recently by Allied forces in World War II. Taken by the Germans in May 1940, Boulogne was won by Canadian troops in September 1944, after four days of bitter fighting.

metalworking and tanning industries benefit from the nearness of the Lorraine mining areas.

MULHOUSE *(pop. 108,995).*

The industrial center of Alsace in the Haut-Rhin department, it stands on the river Ill and the Rhone-Rhine Canal between the Vosges and the northern slopes of the Jura. Formerly a Free City, it was a member of the Swiss Confederation from 1515 to 1798, then voted for union with France. In 1800 it had only about 6000 inhabitants, but the exploitation of neighboring potash deposits and the opening of the Rhone-Rhine Canal caused the city to develop quickly. It is a commercial center near the Belfort Gap. It specializes in the textile and chemical industries, and is about 245 miles east-southeast of Paris.

NANCY *(pop. 128,677).*

Formerly the capital and cultural center of Lorraine, it is now the capital of the Meurthe-et-Moselle department. It stands between the left bank of the Meurthe on the east and the forest of Haye on the west, in a hilly area rich in iron. After the return of the province to Germany in 1871, capital and skill poured into the city and it rapidly developed industrially and commercially. It is a road and rail junction about 175 miles east of Paris.

STRASBOURG *(pop. 228,971).*

Standing on the left bank of the Rhine at the mouth of the Ill, the ancient center of the Alsatian capital lies on an island formed by the two rivers. An important and prosperous city because of the waterways linking it with the North Sea and the Mediterranean, and its road and rail connections with central Europe, it is situated 250 miles east of Paris. Its main industries are food processing, engineering and chemicals.

A German city until its annexation by France, it became German again from 1871 until 1918, and was reoccupied by Germany during the last war. It is the capital of the Bas-Rhin department, has fine museums and educational institutions, and its Gothic cathedral is one of the finest in Europe.

Northwestern France

Northwestern France comprises Brittany, Normandy and the valley of the lower Loire, which includes the historic regions of Maine, Touraine, Orléanais, Berry, Anjou and Poitou.

In Normandy human settlement is generally sparse. The peasants' houses seem lost in the green of the trees and gardens surrounding the farms, which are sometimes grouped into hamlets. The population density is low, almost everywhere lower than the average for France. A higher density is found along parts of the coast where there are fishing ports such as Honfleur, Carteret, Saint-Vaast-la-Hougue, and especially Granville and Cherbourg, and also along the Orne River, on the estuary of which stands the port of Caen, Ouistreham. The population of the inland area is decreasing. The more important towns here are Alençon and Saint-Lô, which are the capitals of the Orne and Manche departments.

The population density is greater in eastern Normandy, which is not exclusively agricultural. Rich industrial towns such as Fécamp, Elbeuf, Louviers, Lisieux, Dieppe and Evreux alternate with sparsely inhabited areas. The estuary of the Seine, where Le Havre and Rouen are situated, is thickly populated. These two ports, formerly distinct, are tending to amalgamate. Le Havre, on the open sea, is a more recent port than Rouen, which is some distance inland, and a center for transferring goods from ships to river barges.

BRITTANY

Brittany has markedly varied densities of population. The inhabitants tend to prefer to live along the tortuous coastline, where they raise early vegetables and fruit and engage in fishing. The most common form of settlement in the countryside and the mountainous interior is the isolated hamlet. Here even the towns and villages have a very rural character. The fishing centers along the coasts, such as Saint-Malo and Paimpol, have great economic importance, and send out fishing fleets to the Newfoundland Banks and the coasts of Iceland.

Lorient is an important commercial center, as are Saint-Brieuc, Quimper and Vannes, the capitals of the departments of Côtes-du-Nord, Finistère and Morbihan, respectively. The largest city in Brittany is Rennes, which stands at the junction of several important routes. Finally, Brest is a great naval base and passenger port standing at the extremity of the peninsula and having a well-protected harbor.

The Breton language, which the people call *Brezoneg* (or *Brezonek*), is spoken in Brittany in four different dialects. It is quite unlike French, and is related to Welsh, Gaelic and Irish, being, like them, a Celtic language.

MAINE AND THE LOIRE VALLEY

Maine is also sparsely settled. There are only a few market towns, such as Mamers, Château-Gontier, Mayenne, Conlie, La Suze-sur-Sarthe and Laval, which is capital of the Mayenne department. The only city is Le Mans, which stands at the junction of several highways.

The valley of the Loire is one of the most thickly populated parts of western France. It is like a fertile oasis dotted with towns and villages all along its length, from Orléans to the sea. The proximity of Paris and the presence of great market towns such as Orléans have led to the development of a rather complex agricultural economy.

There are great cattle-raising estates producing milk and beef for the big cities, and also many smaller farms growing fruit, vegetables, grapes and wheat. Anjou has the largest population, the population being sparser lower down the river and around Orléans and in Touraine.

Towns, villages and hamlets line the roads running through the valley, and there are also many on the low undulating hills above. Throughout the countryside there is great activity and wealth and a sense of well-being. For centuries this region was a favorite one of the kings and nobility, who built many residences there, and today thousands of tourists visit it every year. The several large cities along the Loire include Orléans, Blois, Tours, Angers, Nantes and Saint-Nazaire.

The folk costumes of the Brittany peninsula are among the most distinctive of all France. The white lace caps the women wear are heirlooms handed down from generation to generation.

The appearance of the valley changes in the lower course of the river. Industry and navigation prevail over agriculture in this area, and although life is as busy, it is less picturesque. Nantes stands not far from the mouth of the river, and its satellite towns stretch along the banks toward the sea. These are La Basse-Indre, Pont-Rousseau, Couëron and Paimbœuf. Saint-Nazaire stands on the estuary, and is well known for its naval dockyards.

BERRY, POITOU AND VENDÉE

The region of Berry, between the Massif Central and the wide loop made by the Loire between Nevers and Blois, is sparsely inhabited. Urban life is found in a few centers in the main river valleys, such as Châteauroux and Bourges, which are the capitals of the Indre and Cher departments. They are industrial towns, and nearby Vierzon is a road and rail junction.

West of Berry is the broad plain of Poitou, which is almost treeless and has few villages. There are some agricultural villages and towns such as Mirebeau, Loudun, Châtellerault, La Roche-sur-Yon and Niort. The two last named are the capitals of the Vendée and Deux-Sèvres departments. The principal town is Poitiers, a commercial and industrial center of historical importance on the great route linking Paris with Bordeaux.

In Vendée, farther to the west, the population is more scattered and the countryside is less uniform. There are few towns, and these have little importance. The coast is almost entirely bordered by sand dunes, and since this has forced the population to live inland, it is lonely and deserted. The most important fishing port is Les Sables-d'Olonne.

ANGERS (pop. 115,252).

Former capital of Anjou, and now chief town of the Maine-et-Loire department, it stands on the Maine River a little above where the Loire, Sarthe and Mayenne join it. The older part of the city stands on the left bank, and the medieval castle there is surrounded on three sides by boulevards separating the old from the modern districts. In spite of the great changes that have taken place in recent years, Angers is still one of the most interesting cities in France. Its many monuments bear witness to its great past. Because of its strategic road and rail position between northwest France and the Aquitaine Basin, it has recently taken on new life as a commercial and industrial center.

BLOIS (pop. 33,838).

Capital of the Loir-et-Cher department, it is one of the most beautiful and picturesque towns in the Loire valley. It stands in an amphitheater of hills on the right bank of the river, and has, with its famous royal château, a typically medieval appearance. It is the leading commercial center of the area because it stands at the junction of several important roads and railways.

BOURGES (pop. 60,632).

Capital of the Cher department, it stands on a low terrace at the confluence of the Yèvre and the Auron, which meet here and surround the city on three sides. It is an industrial center, but is most interesting as an artistic center because of its Gothic cathedral, civil and ecclesiastical buildings and its old wood and stone houses. It was the seat of the dukes of Berry, and is about 125 miles south of Paris.

BREST (pop. 136,104).

The largest city in the Finistère department, it has an important naval base at the mouth of the Penfeld River, where the roadstead is comprised of the estuaries of several submerged rivers. During World War II it was a heavily fortified German base, and suffered severe damage. Much of the present city is new. Because of its remote position its trade is purely local, and its economy rests largely on manufacturing. It is about 315 miles west of Paris.

CAEN (pop. 91,336).

Capital of the Calvados department, it is located on a pretty plain about 9 miles from the English Channel, at the confluence of the Orne and the Odon rivers. Because of its position in the metallurgical basin of Normandy, it is an industrial city as well as a commercial center. Its development has been helped by the Orne canal, which leads to the English Channel. The city has many churches and museums, and as a cultural seat is known as the "Athens of Normandy." Its buildings suffered 90 per cent destruction during World War II. It lies about 125 miles westnorthwest of Paris.

CHERBOURG (pop. 37,486).

Located on the north shore of the Cotentin Peninsula, it is an important port for transatlantic shipping and is also a naval base on the English Channel. It was heavily damaged during World War II, during which it was one of the main Allied bridgeheads, entry ports and supply bases. There is some industry, but commercial activity is limited by the distance of the city from the main routes. However, the wild beauty of the peninsula attracts many tourists to the Cherbourg area. The city is about 190 miles northwest of Paris.

LE HAVRE (pop. 183,776).

After Marseille, Le Havre handles the greatest ship tonnage in all of France. It lies on the English Channel at the mouth of the Seine River, about 110 miles west-northwest of Paris. It is an outport for Rouen and Paris, has a prosperous hinterland, and extensive sea, river and land transportation facilities. It has large new suburbs and stands on an alluvial plain at the foot of the coastal tableland. Its beach resorts stretch along the coast to the suburb of Sainte-Adresse. Largely destroyed during World War II, it has since been restored and has resumed its place as a world port for coffee, petroleum and cotton, and as a landing place for transatlantic passengers. Its shipbuilding yards have also been rebuilt.

LE MANS (pop. 132,181).

Capital of the old province of Maine, it is now capital of the Sarthe department. It was founded by the Gauls on a low hill on the left bank of the Sarthe River, and became a Roman colony (Cenomanum). Because of its position at the junction of several main transportation routes of northwestern France, it was the scene of many battles. Today it has a certain commercial and industrial importance, and its Romanesque-Gothic cathedral, begun in the 11th century, is famous.

LORIENT (pop. 60,566).

Situated on the estuary of the Scorff and Blavet rivers near the Atlantic, Lorient was founded by the French East India Company in the middle of the 17th century, and hence its name (L'Orient). It recovered quickly from the almost complete destruction incurred as a German submarine base during World War II, and its fishing port of Kéroman is now one of the best-equipped in France. There is an important shipbuilding industry, and this and its canneries make Lorient one of the most important economic centers of the Morbihan department.

NANTES (pop. 240,028).

Capital of the Loire-Atlantique department and the second most important commercial city on the Atlantic coast after Bordeaux. Most of the city stands on the right bank of the Loire at the confluence of the Erdre. It is now being reconstructed after the grave damage it suffered in World War II. Because of the high tides ocean-going ships are able to ascend the Loire as far as the city. In the 18th century it enjoyed a prosperous trade in fish with England and Spain, and this industry was revived at the end of the 19th century by the establishment of canneries. The port is very busy and a good road and rail system link it with its hinterland.

ORLÉANS (pop. 84,233).

Capital of the Loiret department and a great commercial and transportation center, Orléans stands on the right bank of the Loire, 70 miles south-southwest of Paris. The oldest part of the city is almost a pentagon, and is separated from the newer districts by broad boulevards which

The port of Rouen is the terminal for barges hauled down the Seine from Paris. The road distance between Paris and Rouen is only seventy-seven miles, but the many bends and loops the river makes between the two cities increases the distance by water to 150 miles.

took the place of the ancient walls.

Orléans was originally a city of Gaul, and has played a very important part in the history of France. It is most famous for its great defense against the English siege of 1428-29, relieved by Joan of Arc. It stands at the junction of several very important highways leading to the heart of France, and has several flourishing industries.

POITIERS (*pop. 62,178*).

The old capital of Poitou and the present capital of the Vienne department. Founded by Gauls, it stands on a plateau above the confluence of the Boivre and Clain Rivers. Now an important road and rail junction, it has played an important part in the history of France. In 732, Charles Martel halted the advance of the Moslems near Poitiers and turned them away from Paris. It is rich in Roman, Romanesque,

Gothic and later buildings and is one of the most interesting artistic centers in France.

RENNES (pop. 151,948).

Capital of the Ille-et-Vilaine department, the cultural and intellectual center of Brittany, it stands at the confluence of the two rivers after which the department was named. After suffering heavy damage during World War II, part of the city has been reconstructed in the modern style. Its economy rests on trade, for it is an important road and rail junction on the route to Brest from Paris. It is about 190 miles west-southwest of Paris, at the beginning of the Ille-Rance canal, which reaches, via the Rance River, the English Channel at Saint-Malo. The important international airport of Rennes-Saint-Jacques is about 37 miles from the city.

ROUEN (pop. 120,857).

Capital of the Seine-Maritime department, it stands at the extremity of one of the loops the Seine makes before reaching the sea. About 70 miles northwest of Paris, of which it is the outport for river barges, it has extensive port installations, and in the 14th century already had trade with Africa and the Hanseatic ports. Rouen has a rich hinterland and an excellent system of communications to all parts of northern France. It handles one of the greatest ship tonnages of all French harbors. It also has a very fine Gothic cathedral.

SAINT-BRIEUC (pop. 43,142).

Capital of the Côtes-du-Nord department of Brittany, it is a commercial center on the important railway linking Paris with Brest, and is about 240 miles west of the capital. It grew up around a monastery founded by a Welsh monk in the 6th century, a few miles from the sea. On the estuary of the nearby Gouët River is the mercantile and fishing port of Le Légué. Brest's old quarters, grouped about the cathedral, still maintain the appearance of a medieval Breton town.

SAINT-NAZAIRE (pop. 58,286).

In the Loire-Atlantique department, it is an important commercial and industrial center. The modern reconstruction plan undertaken after World War II separates the residential quarters from the industrial ones along the banks of the Loire by means of green belts of pasture land.

Until the middle of the 19th century Saint-Nazaire had a population of only 3000. It expanded because of its position on the Loire estuary, and became the outport for Nantes.

TOURS (pop. 92,944).

Capital of the old province of Touraine and now of the Indre-et-Loire department, it stands between the Loire and the Cher, near their confluence. A long broad street divides the city into two distinct parts. To the east is the older quarter with its administrative buildings and aristocratic houses, and to the west is the business section, which is typically medieval in appearance. Farther south there are wide boulevards in place of the old walls, and the modern districts reach as far as the River Cher. Tours is largely a residential town, and is an important commercial center on the route linking Aquitaine to Paris.

In the Middle Ages the southern counties and dukedoms of France formed what was really a separate country from the lands to the north. The southerners spoke a different language from the north, called langue d'oc or Provençal, and developed an independent culture in the 11th century. The poetry of the Provençal troubadours had a strong influence on the forms and subject matter of other, later poets, including Petrarch and Dante.

The city of Toulouse was the center of this southern culture. The counts of Toulouse not only patronized the poetry of others but wrote poetry themselves.

In the 13th century the Albigensian Crusade and the institution of the Inquisition brought devastation to the region, and the independence of Provence was crushed. Yet even today Toulouse remains an important cultural center, housing a university, academies of art, science and literature, an observatory, a botanical garden, a museum and the largest Romanesque church in France.

The Aquitaine Basin and the Pyrenees

The Aquitaine Basin stretches from the Massif Central to the Pyrenees and the Bay of Biscay, and is a vast region, mainly agricultural and lightly populated. The land throughout Aquitaine is in the hands of small holders, and there are many hamlets, known locally as *mas*.

There is little city life. The larger cities are spread out along the line of the Garonne valley, and Bordeaux and Toulouse are the most important of these. Bordeaux is near the sea and stands on the main route from Paris to the Spanish frontier, and Toulouse is in the corridor joining the Massif Central to the Pyrenees.

Castres, Albi, Cahors, Souillac, Terrasson and Périgueux are at the foot of the Massif Central, and farther to the northwest stands Angoulême, on the route connecting

FRANCE · *The Land* / 81

Bordeaux to Paris. At the foot of the Pyrenees are Foix, the capital of Ariège department, Tarbes, Pau and Bayonne, the latter near the mouth of the Adour on the Bay of Biscay. To the north of the Garonne are Montauban, Villeneuve-sur-Lot, Bergerac and Libourne. To the south of it are Auch and Mont-de-Marsan, capitals of the Gers and Landes departments, respectively, and Saint-Sever and Dax.

These cities stand on important lines of communication and are generally market towns for their regions. Other market towns are Angoulême, Jarnac, Cognac, Saintes and Rochefort, along the course of the Charente. La Rochelle is a celebrated Atlantic port.

THE LANDES

The lower courses of the Garonne and the Adour form a huge triangle with the sandy ocean coasts. In this triangle is the region of the Landes, which was once almost uninhabited. The population is still very sparse, but it has risen as a result of the replanting of the forests and the subsequent growth of the sawmilling industry. In less than a century it has increased by one third.

The narrow French strip of the Pyrenees is also sparsely inhabited. The main occupations are farming and cattle raising. The population is relatively thick in the valleys of the larger rivers, which contain modest villlages and watering places such as Bagnères-de-Luchon, Eaux-Chaudes and Bagnères-de-Bigorre. Lourdes, the famous place of pilgrimage, which a century ago was an unknown village, is also in this area. Permanent dwellings become rarer in the upper mountain valleys, and where agriculture is absent only shepherds' huts for use in summer months are found.

In the western section of the Pyrenees live the Basques in the Basses-Pyrénées department. There are about 200,000 Basques in France, and 1,500,000 live on the Spanish side of the frontier. The Basques are quite a different people from either the French or the Spanish. Their language is entirely different from any other in Europe.

AGEN *(pop. 32,800).*

This city stands on the right bank of the Garonne, at the foot of a range of steep hills. It is the capital of the Lot-et-Garonne department, and a road and rail junction on the route crossing through the Gates of Aquitaine to connect with the other cities of Languedoc. It is the market town for its region.

ALBI *(pop 38,709).*

Capital of the Tarn department and one of the most picturesque and interesting cities in France. It was once a Roman city *(Albiga)*, and is situated on the left bank of the Tarn River. The old city is grouped about the church of Saint-Salvi and the famous Gothic cathedral of Sainte-Cécile, and is separated by wide boulevards from the modern residential and industrial quarters around it. Albi is famous as the center of the Albigensian movement in the 12th and 13th centuries, which was suppressed with great force by the Catholic Church in a celebrated Crusade. It is also the birthplace of Toulouse-Lautrec, the artist. The local museum is named after him.

Bordeaux is most famous for the red and white wines that come from the vineyards of the district, but Bordeaux is also a major Atlantic port for southern France. Situated near the mouth of the Garonne River, Bordeaux has a history going back to the Romans. The cathedral in the foreground of the picture was built in the 11th century. The stone bridge across the river was built in 1821 and has seventeen arches.

The small village at the foot of this castle in the Auvergne, is typical of many hamlets in the mountainous regions of the Massif Central and the Alps. They often date back to medieval times, when they were laid out to give maximum protection to the villagers. The castle of the lord was built on a prominence, where it commanded a view of the valley below. The peasants who farmed the surrounding countryside lived near their fields at the bottom of the hill. In times of civil disturbance, the peasants stored their grain and livestock within the castle walls, and took refuge there themselves if the settlement were under attack.

ANGOULÊME *(pop. 48,190).*

A road and rail junction on the ancient highway linking Paris and Bordeaux about 235 miles southwest of Paris, it is the capital of the Charente department. It is the most important commercial and industrial town in the Angoumois region. The old city, which is still surrounded by its walls, stands in a good defensive position on a limestone spur dominating the left bank of the Charente River. Modern residential and industrial quarters have developed at the foot of the promontory.

BORDEAUX *(pop. 249,688).*

Capital of Aquitaine and of the Gironde department, and the largest city in southwestern France. It is one of the five most important ports in the country, and stands on a broad plain on the left bank of the Garonne, about 60 miles from the Bay of Biscay. It was inhabited in prehistoric times because of its position where the routes from Spain and southeastern and northern France meet.

In recent centuries it has derived much of its prosperity from overseas trade, especially with the French colonies. The main export is wine, a great deal of which goes to England. It has flourishing industries, most of which have developed in relation to the products of the hinterland. Bottles, packing cases, copper oxide for vines, and liqueurs are all made in Bordeaux. The overseas trade has developed local sugar refining, petroleum refining and the processing of rubber and fine woods. Bordeaux is an important cultural center, and has a university.

CAHORS *(pop. 17,046).*

Capital of the Lot department, it is a commercial center and a road and rail junction. It is about 60 miles north of Toulouse, and stands on a peninsula formed by a narrow bend of the Lot River, which surrounds it on three sides. On the fourth side the remains of the city wall are still visible. The older part of the city has a typically medieval appearance, and centers around the cathedral, which is dedicated to St. Stephen.

LA ROCHELLE *(pop. 66,590).*

Former capital of Aunis and at present capital of the Charente-Maritime department, it stands on a well-protected bay opposite the Île-de-Ré. In the Middle Ages it was the chief French Atlantic port, but lost its pre-eminence to Nantes and Bordeaux after the 17th century. Today it is mainly a fishing and transatlantic passenger terminus, served by its outport, La Pallice. It has some industry, but its development has been retarded by the lack of communications with the hinterland. It still has part of its old walls and many historic and artistic buildings. It was also a famous Huguenot stronghold.

LOURDES *(pop. 16,023).*

Located in the Hautes-Pyrénées department, it has been famous as a place of pilgrimage from all over the world since the vision of Bernadette Soubirous in 1858. It stands on the northern slopes of the Pyrenees and is divided into two very distinct sections, separated by the Gave de Pau and the old castle above the town.

MONTAUBAN *(pop. 41,022).*

Capital of the Tarn-et-Garonne department, it is an important road and rail junction. The older part of the city contains buildings of one of France's oldest fortresses, and stands on an alluvial terrace on the right bank of the Tarn. Modern residential quarters surround the old town. Founded in the Middle Ages, it became famous in the 16th and 17th centuries as a Protestant stronghold as a result of the Treaty of Saint-Germain (1570), which accorded it to the Huguenots. In 1629 it fell to Richelieu, who demolished its fortifications.

PAU *(pop. 59,937).*

Formerly the capital of Béarn, and now capital of the Basses-Pyrénées department, it is about 100 miles west-southwest of Toulouse. Frequented by tourists in summer and winter, it is a road and rail junction. Pau was once the residence of the French kings of Navarre. The oldest part of the city stands around the castle and spreads along the right bank of the Gave de Pau.

PÉRIGUEUX *(pop. 38,529).*

A road and rail junction about 75

miles east-northeast of Bordeaux, it is the capital of the Dordogne department. It is an important commercial center. Of Roman origin (*Vesunna*), it stands in an undulating countryside on the right bank of the Isle River, which touches the old city. The cathedral in the center of the old town is dedicated to Saint-Front.

TARBES *(pop. 46,600).*

Capital of the Hautes-Pyrénées department, it stands on the left bank of the Adour River at the foot of the mountains. Its favorable position for communications and the abundance of water-generated electricity have made it a notable industrial and commercial center. In spite of its ancient origins it has a very modern appearance. It is one of the most popular of the Pyrenean watering places.

TOULOUSE *(pop. 323,724).*

Formerly the capital of Languedoc and now capital of the Haute-Garonne department, it stands on the right bank of the Garonne where the river forms a wide semicircle. Its historical and economic importance derives from its excellent geographical position in the center of a fertile plain on the shortest route between the Atlantic and the Mediterranean, now traversed by roads, railways and the *Canal du Midi*. The valleys of the southwestern Massif Central and those of the central Pyrenees also converge at Toulouse.

Recently it has acquired large chemical and engineering works. It is an important artistic and historical center, has museums and cultural institutions including a university, and is often visited by tourists. Its population has expanded enormously since the last century. In 1821 it had a little more than 50,000 people. In 1866 the figure was 127,000 and today it is the sixth largest city in France. The old city is surrounded by tree-lined boulevards along the Garonne, and beyond them there are large residential districts built in modern times, which reach as far as the *Canal du Midi*. There are large suburbs on the other side of the canal.

The Massif Central

The population of much of the Massif Central is very sparse, especially in the southern peripheral departments of Lozère, Aveyron, Cantal, Corrèze, Haute-Loire and Creuse. The departments of Haute-Vienne, Puy-de-Dôme and Loire have higher densities because of the industrial development that has followed the exploitation of coal and manganese deposits. Steelmaking and engineering are the main industries in the principal cities of the region, which are Limoges, Clermont-Ferrand, Roanne and Saint-Étienne.

In Marche and Limousin most of the people live in scattered hamlets and isolated farmhouses. The large centers are usually agricultural markets, such as Guéret, capital of the Creuse department, Nontron, Bellac, Brive and Uzurche, but Limoges is not. Aubusson, Saint-Junien, Tulle and Aurillac are small industrial centers; the two last named are the capitals of the Corrèze and Cantal departments.

THE ALLIER VALLEY

In the higher parts of Auvergne the population also lives in hamlets or isolated farmhouses, but in the Allier valley settlement is concentrated in large agricultural towns and villages. The countryside is also very different there, for in contrast to the neighboring region, its willows and poplars grow abundantly on the gently undulating landscape, and its little fields of potatoes and beets give it a markedly prosperous air.

Farther along the valley of the Allier and beyond the great industrial and commercial city of Clermont-Ferrand is the famous watering place of Vichy, and still lower down is the agricultural market town of Moulins. To the southwest the industrial city of Montluçon stands on the banks of the Cher.

The upper valley of the Loire cuts deeply into the Massif Central, and forms a natural line for communications. Important industrial and commercial cities along the banks of this part of the river are Nevers, Roanne (in the heart of an important cotton-milling district), Montbrison and Le Puy.

The most thickly populated area in the Massif Central is a short corridor connecting the upper Loire

Many of the small towns and villages in the province of Auvergne in south-central France have hardly changed at all through the centuries. This building with its pointed medieval towers is in the Auvergne market town of Salers.

with the middle course of the Rhone. It is important as a road and rail route and also because of its vast coalfields, which have been mined for a very long time. Its population has increased greatly in a few decades.

Saint-Étienne is the most important industrial and commercial city of the Massif Central, and it is surrounded by a number of lesser cities such as Firminy, Saint-Chamond, Unieux, Rive-de-Gier, Le Chambon, Terre-noire and Lorette.

The difficulty of communications and the lack of resources have inhibited the growth of urban life in the southern departments of this region. The villages are usually situated in the desolate valleys near some spring, and usually appear poor and lifeless. The few larger towns such as Decazeville, Le Vigan, Ganges, Rodez, Mende and Privas are almost all on the edge of the Massif, and the last three named are capitals of the departments of Aveyron, Lozère and Ardèche.

CLERMONT-FERRAND *(pop. 127,684).*

Capital of the Puy-de-Dôme department, it stands at about 1300 feet above sea level in a circle of hills, with the volcanic Monts Dôme on the west and the fertile plain of Limagne to the east. The old city of Clermont (*Clarus Mons*—bright hill) stands on a height dominated by the Gothic cathedral. The appearance of the town has hardly changed since the 18th century. Montferrand is about one and a quarter miles away on the other side of the city from Clermont, and two miles west is the spa of Royat.

Founded by the Romans, the city began as an important communications center and later became capital and tourist center for the Auvergne. But later the great tire-making and rubber industry made it the "Akron of France" and produced a great rise in population.

LE PUY *(pop. 25,125).*

The old capital of Velay and present capital of the Haute-Loire department. It is a picturesque city and was already a place of pilgrimage in the 5th century A.D. It lies on the Borne River near its confluence with the Loire, on Mt. Anis (about 2500 feet). On the top of this mountain stands a colossal statue of the Virgin Mary. Le Puy is surrounded by volcanic peaks characteristic of the Velay.

The oldest part of the city is on the southern slopes of the hill, and is overlooked by the great mass of the cathedral. The modern streets are farther to the south, and are centered on the broad Place du Breuil. Le Puy is about 317 miles south-southeast of Paris, on the direct route from the capital to the south of France.

LIMOGES *(pop. 117,827).*

The city is shaped like an amphitheater looking out over the green fields of Limousin, and was originally in two sections, both on the right bank of the Vienne River. In spite of frequent reconstruction the city has not lost its historic appearance. Capital of the Haute-Vienne department and known today for its

The delightful Lake Oô on the French side of the high Pyrenees is one of the pleasanter examples of glacial action.

The settlement at Col de Vars is almost 7000 feet above sea level, but in its Alpine setting, it is the local lowpoint. It is at the bottom of a saddle between the mountain peaks that separate the valleys of the Durance and Ubaye rivers in the Alps.

porcelain and footwear, it is also a market in a smaller way for grain and wine. A rail junction, it is about 225 miles south-southwest of Paris.

MONTLUÇON *(pop. 55,184)*.

A highly industrialized city, with steelworks, and rubber, tire and synthetic textile mills, which owes its development in the last century to the opening of the Commentry mines close by. It is situated in the Allier department, and the Cher River flows through it. Montluçon stands at the beginning of the Berry canal, and is a railroad junction on the line connecting the south with Paris, about 193 miles south of the capital.

NEVERS *(pop. 39,085)*.

Capital of the Nièvre department, it stands on the slopes of a hill at the confluence of the Nièvre and the Loire, near which stands the medieval quarter (capital of the former Nivernais province). After the crisis caused by the end of river navigation, Nevers regained importance as a rail junction and a center for china and pottery production. It is about 145 miles south-southeast of Paris.

ROANNE *(pop. 51,723)*.

The city stands on the left bank of the Loire where the river flows out onto the plain, and at the beginning of the Loire Lateral canal. In spite of its ancient origin (the Romans knew it as *Rodumna*), the city has a very modern appearance. It developed as an industrial and textile-milling town because of its favorable position where railroads and roads cross the Loire River. It is about 200 miles south-southeast of Paris, and is in the Loire department.

SAINT-ÉTIENNE *(pop. 201,242)*.

Capital of the Loire department, it is essentially an industrial city built on a uniform plan, and lacks interesting buildings. Its most obvious characteristic is a great cloud of smoke rising from the famous steel mills standing in a gently undulating landscape on the banks of the Furens. The coal mines in the area and its favorable position for communications with the valley of the Rhone and the Paris Basin turned it into a great industrial center during the last century. Its population consequently rose from about 17,000 in 1800 to 130,000 in 1880.

The Alps and the Jura

In the valleys of the Jura the people generally live in large villages that are often more like small towns. On the shaded slopes there is far less settlement, and on the higher levels none at all. The Doubs valley has the densest population, and the next most densely populated area is the undulating country along the foothills facing the Rhone.

In this area are the cities of Montbéliard, Besançon, Vesoul, Lons-le-Saunier and Bourg, the last three being the capitals of the Haute-Saône, Jura and Ain departments. They stand along important lines of communication linking the Rhine and the south of France.

The population of the Alpine areas is very irregularly distributed. The central departments, Hautes-Alpes and Basses-Alpes, have typically Alpine economies. The population is much denser in the two southern departments of Savoie and Haute-Savoie, mainly because of tourists' centers and great hydroelectric works there.

The departments of Isère, Drôme, Var and Alpes-Maritimes cannot be compared with the other departments for population density because they contain large tracts of non-Alpine country.

LARGE VILLAGES ARE COMMON

In the Alps the people live mostly at the bottom of the valleys or on the slopes exposed to the sun. Large villages are most common, but there are also hamlets and scattered temporary dwellings. The Grésivaudan has several small cities and industrial centers such as Froges, Lancey, Sassenage, Brignoud, Domène, Le Cheylas, Pontcharra and Allevard.

The chief town is Grenoble, which is the most important city in the whole of the French Alps. The Grésivaudan valley has a high density of population. In Savoy there are also several towns of note, such as Aix-les-Bains, Thonon-les-Bains, Chamonix, and especially Chambéry and Annecy.

The south-central part of the French Alps has a few large towns and a low population density. Besides Briançon, a tourist center on the upper course of the Durance, there are also Gap, Barcelonnette, Sisteron and Digne, capital of Basses-Alpes department, all market towns in the valley of the Durance or in its vicinity. Much farther to the south is Draguignan, capital of the Var department.

ANNECY *(pop. 43,255).*

Capital of the Haute-Savoie department, it lies at the northern end of Lac d'Annecy. There is an old castle and modern suburbs along the lakeside. Although it is an industrial center, it is visited by many tourists because of the beauty of its surroundings.

BESANÇON *(pop. 95,642).*

Capital of the Doubs department and a commercial center on the route linking the valley of the Rhine with those of the Rhone, Saône and Loire, it is about 242 miles southeast of Paris.

The old city is situated on a wide bend of the Doubs with the new districts facing it on the other bank, on a circle of hills. It has Roman remains, historical and artistic monuments, museums and mineral springs. Since the 19th century its industries have made striking progress, especially clock- and watchmaking, for which Besançon takes first place in France. After 1676, it was capital of the Franche-Comté.

CHAMBÉRY *(pop. 44,246).*

Capital of the Savoie department, it is a pleasant town in an Alpine basin that also contains Lac du Bourget and is a means of communication with the Isère valley and the upper Rhone. It is a rail junction and has some light industries, but it is best known for the beauty of its surroundings. It was the capital of the dukes of Savoy, until their headquarters was moved to Turin in Italy in 1562.

GAP *(pop. 20,478).*

Capital of the Hautes-Alpes department, it stands on the Luye, a tributary of the Durance. It is 2424 feet above sea level, and is surrounded by a circle of barren mountains. It was a Gallo-Roman city and capital of medieval Gapençais, and recently has become an important commercial center and road junction. It is a popular summer resort.

GRENOBLE *(pop. 156,707).*

Capital of Dauphiné and of the Isère department, it is a commercial, cultural and tourist center. It stands in the Grésivaudan, at the convergence of the Alpine valleys of the Isère and the Drac. There are many large hydroelectric plants in the vicinity. Grenoble is also a road and rail junction.

The Mediterranean Region and the Rhone Valley

In the south of France the population is distributed in a very irregular way. Physical, climatic and historical factors have caused the population to be thickest in certain restricted areas. Because of the great expanses of arid land and for reasons of defense the earlier inhabitants of the region were obliged to gather in large villages. These often flourished and took on the characteristics of small cities.

The region was always full of cities, and two axes may be discerned along which they grew up over the centuries. One axis runs along the ancient coast route connecting Italy and Spain. It passes through harsh rocky zones in the interior and marshy ones on the coast, but it always connects points where fresh water and places for defense could be found. The other route penetrates Provence and thrusts farther between the Alps and the Cévennes toward the valleys of the Rhone and the Saône.

Important cities grew up along both of these axes at crossroads, fords and good defensive positions. Toulon, Marseille, Aix-en-Provence, Saint-Rémy and Arles are typical cities of the Mediterranean route. So are Avignon, on the lower Rhone, Nîmes, at the junction with the highway from the Cévennes, and Montpellier, within easy reach of the sea. Sète, an important mercantile port where the two navigable canals of the Rhone-Sète and the Midi meet at the sea, Béziers, on the Orb, from which access is easy to the Massif Central, and Narbonne, a junction for the two highways from Spain and from Aquitaine, are other important cities.

All of these cities have known periods of great prosperity and splendor, and today they are busy commercial centers for the olive and wine growing regions around them.

CITIES OF THE RHONE VALLEY

The cities of the Rhone valley,

Les Sables-d'Olonne has been an important fishing port for centuries. Today it is a shipbuilding community and processes canned sardines and anchovies. But in the years following the discovery of the New World, the port was the home base for many privateers. One of the most vicious pirates in the West Indies, Pierre L'Olonnois came from Les Sables-d'Olonne.

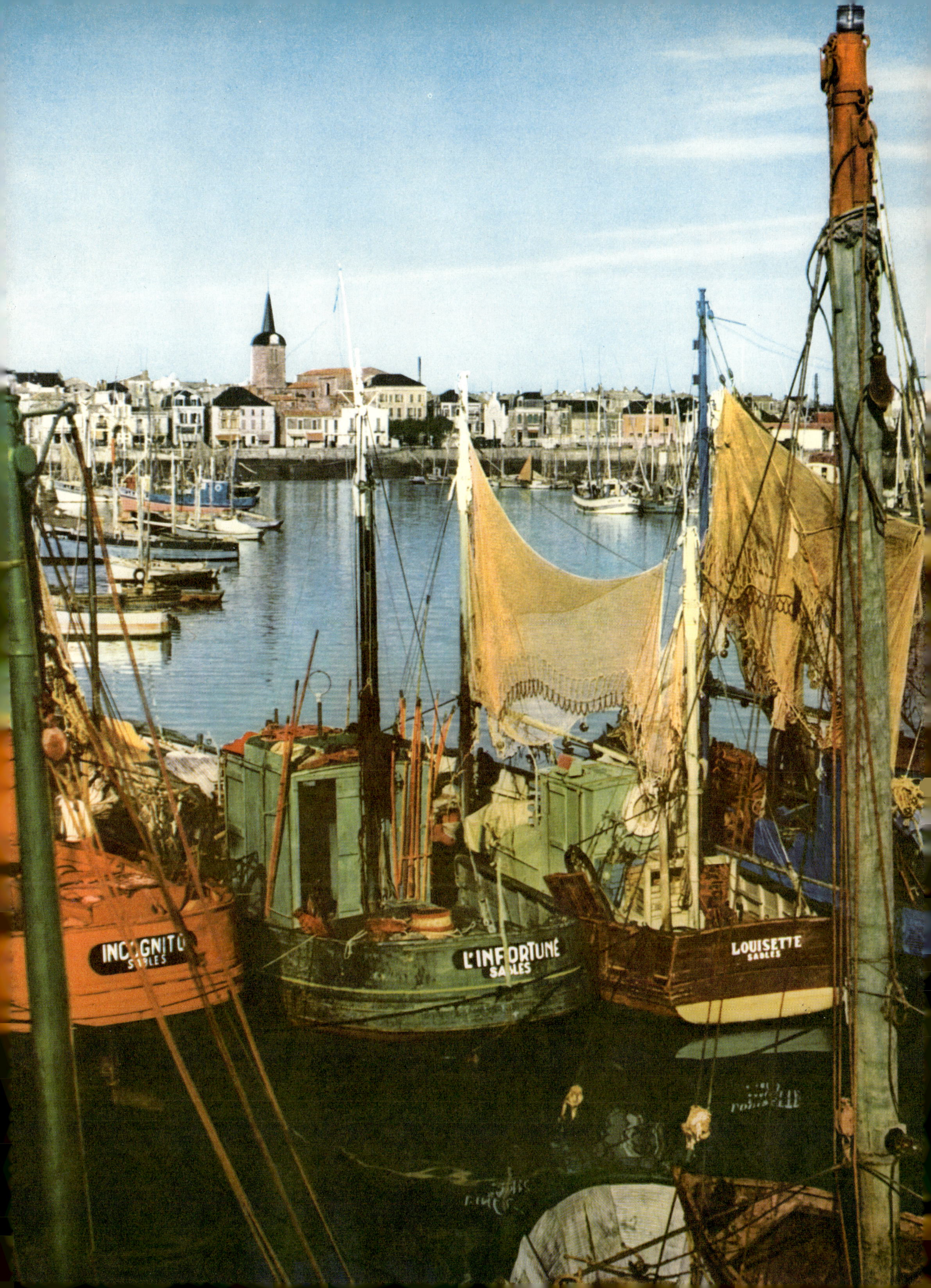
INCOGNITO
L'INFORTUNÉ
SABLES
LOUISETTE
SABLES

Seventy miles south of Paris, where the Loire bends west toward the sea is Orléans, an important river port with a history going back to Roman times. Orléans is most famous for its resistance during a year-long siege by the English in 1428-29, in the course of the Hundred Years' War. A peasant girl from the northeast, Joan of Arc, obeying her visions of angels and saints, led an army to the relief of the beleaguered city and won immortal fame for herself. Under her leadership the city repelled the English. French people everywhere, inspired by the example of Orléans, began to take pride in being French. They started thinking of France as a nation rather than as a collection of communities belonging to the king. The relief of Orléans was a turning point of the war. Today a statue of Joan of Arc in the Place du Martroi *in Orléans commemorates the critical victory in the siege.*

except for Lyon and Valence, did not know prosperity in ancient and medieval times like that of the cities along the coast. However, they had great historical importance because of their position on the great highway of the Rhone valley. These cities and towns often stood at points where this highway was crossed by roads leading to the Alps or the Massif Central.

The cities on the lower course of the Saône, such as Chalon-sur-Saône and Mâcon, capital of the Saône-et-Loire department, have historical and economic characteristics similar to those of the Rhone valley.

In recent times the eastern stretch of the coast of Provence has developed greatly. This is the Riviera or Côte d'Azur. The climate is exceptionally pleasant and mild, and from Saint-Tropez to the Italian frontier there is an almost uninterrupted line of holiday resorts, such as Fréjus, Saint-Raphaël, Cannes, Juan-les-Pins, Antibes, Nice, Menton, and Monte Carlo and Monaco (both outside French territory). Vast numbers of French and foreign tourists visit this coast every year.

AIX-EN-PROVENCE *(pop. 67,943).*

This historic city stands on a beautiful and typically Provençal plain near the Arc River, in the eastern part of the Bouches-du-Rhône department. It is of Roman origin (*Aquae Sextiae*) and enjoyed great prosperity as a spa until the 4th century A.D., when it declined with the rise of Arles. From the 15th to the 18th century it once more enjoyed importance as the capital of Provence.

In the 16th and 17th centuries new areas, which are still models of urban building, were developed around the old center of the city. Aix has an ancient cultural tradition, is the seat of a university and an art center, and is often visited by tourists. It is an important rail junction, and it is about 17 miles from Marseille. It stands at the crossing of several ancient and important highways.

ARLES *(pop. 41,932).*

A former medieval capital of Provence, it is now in the Bouches-du-Rhône department. It stands mostly on the left bank of the lower course of the Rhone, on the branch known as the Petit-Rhone, near the delta. Its many monuments and churches bear witness to its historical importance from Roman times through the Middle Ages and down to the 18th century.

It is one of the most interesting and artistically rich cities in France. The former cathedral and monastery of Saint-Trophîme, the Roman amphitheater and the collections in the museums are of outstanding interest. It is about 56 miles northwest of Marseille, and is an important road junction. The main products of the district are olives and grapes.

AVIGNON *(pop. 72,717).*

Located on the left bank of the lower course of the Rhone, a little above its confluence with the Durance, Avignon is capital of the Vaucluse department. It still has its city walls, and extends over a spur dominating the river and over the slopes to the south and east.

The older part, some of it transformed into a magnificent park, is on a higher level, and the Palace of the Popes and the cathedral are both there. The Palace is one of the best examples of 14th-century Gothic architecture, and was the residence of the Popes from 1305 to 1378. Some antipopes lived there also during the Great Schism (1378-1408).

The city is of Gallo-Ligurian origin, was capital of the Comtat Venaissin (1229-71), and is famous for its buildings and works of art from the Papal period. It is about 58 miles northwest of Marseille, and is a commercial center for wine and fruit. It also produces textiles, chemicals and food products. In recent years new suburbs have been built.

BÉZIERS *(pop. 73,538).*

A picturesque town in the Hérault department, founded by the Celtiberians before the Roman occupation. It stands on a hill overlooking the left bank of the Orb. Its older upper town is separated from the modern districts by boulevards, and it has several fine churches, an old bridge and an art museum. It is a market for the rich, wine-producing countryside, and a road and rail junction. At Béziers the *Canal du Midi* flows into the Orb.

CANNES *(pop. 58,079).*

A very fashionable resort on the Riviera, visited by tourists from all over the world. It stands on a bay of the Gulf of La Napoule between the hills of the Maritime Pre-Alps and the sea. Off the coast are the beautiful Îles de Lérins.

Behind the modern tourist town stands old Cannes, on a hill to the west. It is an elegant and beautiful relic of old Provence. There are many hotels of all kinds, and each year an International Film Festival is held there. It is about 18 miles west of Nice, and is a port of call for passenger ships sailing between America and Italy.

CARCASSONNE *(pop. 40,897).*

Capital of the Aude department, it is a wine market and road and rail junction about 50 miles southeast of Toulouse. It is situated between the Montagne Noire and the northeastern spurs of the Pyrenees. It owes its historical and economic importance to its position on the shortest route between the Atlantic and the Mediterranean.

The *Cité,* with the finest town walls in Europe, stands on a steep hill to the right of the Aude. The more modern district, the *Ville-Basse,* lies between the Aude and the Canal du Midi, and was laid out in the 18th century in a chessboard design.

LYON *(pop. 528,535).*

Situated at the confluence of the Saône and the Rhone, it is the third largest city in France, and is capital of the Rhône department. The original part of the city was on the right bank of the Saône, and spread toward the east to occupy the alluvial wedge between the two rivers. The fashionable quarter and the commercial and financial districts are here.

The city of Poitiers has a history dating back to Roman times. In 732, just north of Poitiers, Charles Martel checked the advance of the Moslem invaders who had already conquered Spain. England claimed the whole region for several hundred years, and it was not until 1416 that Poitiers became part of the French crown lands.

The Loire River valley is dotted with magnificent castles. This one, the Castle of Blois was a residence of three kings—Charles VIII, Louis XII and Francis I.

The city's industrial suburbs and its residential and university districts extend to the left bank of the Rhone. The whole city is attractive to tourists because of its historical interest and its fine museums.

Its prodigious commercial development is due to its position at the crossing of the great routes connecting the Mediterranean with the Paris Basin and those linking the Rhone valley with Central Europe. In Roman times it was therefore an important military station, and in the Middle Ages it held fairs to which traders came from all over the continent.

In more modern times it has had close relations with the Orient, and its silk industry has flourished. It also has chemical, metallurgic and engineering industries (cars and aircraft). Railroads leave Lyon in all directions, and it has an important airport at surburban Bron. It is a road junction, and is about 250 miles southeast of Paris and 175 miles north of Marseille.

MARSEILLE *(pop. 778,071).*

Capital of the Bouches-du-Rhône department, the largest French port on the Mediterranean and second city in France. It extends along the shores of the Gulf of Lions and over the low white limestone hills behind it. It owes its development to its convenient position near the mouths of the Rhone and to its resultant maritime trade.

It was founded by Phocaeans from Greece about 600 B.C. In modern times it has been particularly concerned in trade with the Near East and with America, North Africa and India after the 16th century. The city developed at a greater rate after the French conquest of Algeria and the opening of the Suez Canal. It became a great Mediterranean commercial center dealing in fruits and vegetables, cotton, coffee, petroleum and other raw materials.

The oldest part of the city is surrounded by quarters built in the 17th century, and farther out are others, developed since the 19th century. It is a great cosmopolitan city, and some of the faculties of the University of Aix-en-Provence are situated there. It is a road junction and a very important railhead. It is also an important port of call for passenger ships, and is visited by many tourists. It is about 425 miles south of Paris, and it has a large international airport at Marignane. The historic Château d'If lies just offshore.

MONTPELLIER (pop. 118,864).

Capital of the Hérault department, a commercial center and a road and rail junction, 80 miles west northwest of Marseille. The city extends along the right bank of the Verdanson River near its confluence with the Lez, and its old central part is separated from the modern residential and industrial areas by wide boulevards. Its university, founded in 1289, is one of the oldest in Europe.

NICE (pop. 292,958).

One of the largest tourist centers in the world, it stands in the Paillon River valley along the Baie des Anges (Bay of Angels) on the Riviera. The Phocaeans founded a colony here in the 5th century B.C. After the Roman conquest it shared in the fortunes of Provence, and in the 14th century passed to the House of Savoy, which ceded it to France in 1860, when it had only 66,000 inhabitants.

Tourists began to visit it in the middle of the 19th century because of the beauty of the Côte d'Azur and the mild winter climate. There is an old section as well as typically French modern sections along the seafront and on the hills behind. It is the capital of the Alpes-Maritimes department, and a market for oil and flowers.

Since 1932, Nice has been the site of a Mediterranean campus of Aix-en-Provence University, and it is the principal passenger port for Corsica. There is a modern international airport (Nice-Californie) near the mouth of the Var, about four miles to the southwest.

The fortunes of Marseille have depended on the sea since its founding thousands of years ago. The first known settlement on the site of the city was made in 600 B.C. by the Phocaeans, Greeks from the Ionian islands. Massilia, as they called it, developed an active trade with tribes up the Rhone and along the Mediterranean, and established several new colonies on the Spanish coast. The colonies were lost when Julius Caesar conquered Massilia in 49 B.C., but the city continued to prosper. In the centuries that followed, Marseille declined when trade throughout the Mediterranean was curtailed by the collapse of the Roman Empire and the Moslem conquest of North Africa. The city became independent in the 13th century, but passed to the French crown in 1481. A band of men from Marseille, who came to Paris in the summer of 1792 to aid the Revolution, first sang the song, composed by Rouget de L'Isle, that has since become the national anthem of France, the Marseillaise.

NÎMES (pop. 99,802).

Capital of the Gard department in Languedoc, it is an important commercial and industrial center. It stands at the junction of highways and railroads from the valley of the Rhone, the Massif Central and the coastal cities.

It is situated at the foot of the Cévennes, and is made up of a medieval center around the cathedral and newer residential districts beyond the wide circle of boulevards. It is of prehistoric origin, and enjoyed great splendor under the Roman Empire. Many monuments of that period still exist, the most notable being the amphitheater, which was built in the 1st century A.D.

PERPIGNAN *(pop. 83,025).*

Capital of Roussillon and the modern Pyrénées-Orientales department, it is an old fortified town 9 miles from the sea, at the confluence of the Basse and Têt rivers. The older part of the city lies between the Basse and the great citadel that dominates the southern section.

New residential districts grew between the two rivers to the northwest after the fortifications were dismantled. It is an important wine market and a rail and road junction on the route linking Spain with the southern coast of France.

TOULON *(pop. 161,786).*

A city in the Var department of Provence, it has important engineering works and dockyards, and stands at the foot of Mont Faron, which has been fortified. The city is at the innermost point of Toulon Roads, which are well protected from the winds.

The older part of Toulon dates mainly from the 18th century and is bordered on the north by the Boulevard de Strasbourg, on the other side of which are modern residential districts. The city was known to the Romans as *Telo Martius*. Toulon was of little importance throughout the Middle Ages and until the reign of Louis XIV. That monarch extended the fortifications and made the port the strongest naval base in the Mediterranean.

VALENCE *(pop. 52,532).*

Capital of the Drôme department, it stands on the left bank of the Rhone, a little downstream from the confluence of the Isère, in the heart of a fertile alluvial plain. It is a center of communications and trade. It was settled in prehistoric times, and was known to the Romans as *Julia Valentia*. Later, it was the capital of the duchy of Valentinois, and it possesses an 11th century Romanesque cathedral.

Corsica

The whole of this large Mediterranean island makes up a single department, with a very low population density. In the past, the people preferred to live in villages in the inland valleys, avoiding the coast because of the inhospitable high cliffs and the danger of malaria in the marshy and low-lying areas. But the few cities, Ajaccio, Bastia, Calvi and Bonifacio, are all on the coast, for purposes of trade with the mainland.

The poverty of the island obliges thousands to leave it each year for the south of France, especially Marseilles and Nice, and for Paris. In recent years, because of the improved

Situated on the east bank of the Rhone, Arles began to flourish after 103 B.C., when the Roman consul Marius built a canal connecting the settlement with the Mediterranean Sea. Arles became the most important trading port for the entire province of Gaul. After Rome, Arles was the richest city in the early days of the Roman Empire. The wealth of its citizens is reflected in this Roman amphitheater called Les Arènes, *which has been preserved largely intact.*

At the south end of Corsica, overlooking the narrow strait that separates the island from Sardinia is the walled city of Bonifaccio. According to local tradition, the fortress on the strait was established in 828. During much of Corsica's turbulent political history this armed stronghold maintained relative independence.

standard of living, people have tended more and more to settle on the coast. At present one fourth of the population lives along the coastal strip.

AJACCIO *(pop. 41,006).*

Capital of the Corsica department, and the second most important market town after Bastia. It is also the major road junction, for it is connected by road with the interior and every part of the coast. The city stands on the gulf of the same name on the west coast, and stretches for about two and a half miles along the shore on a series of wooded hills. The older part of the city stands on a promontory having a citadel at its tip, and is quite separate from the new districts to the north and west.

BASTIA *(pop. 50,117).*

This city is the most important commercial center in Corsica. It is directly linked with Marseille, Nice, Leghorn in Italy and Porto Torres in Sardinia by regular ship services, and with Ajaccio, Calvi and Porto-Vecchio by rail.

It is situated on the northeastern shore of the island and stretches for some distance on low hills along the sea. There is a citadel to the south of the city on a fortified rocky promontory. This is surrounded by the two old districts of Terra-Vecchia and Terra-Nuova. The modern district of Capanelle is to the north. Bastia was the Corsican capital until 1791.

ECONOMIC GEOGRAPHY

THE ECONOMIC STRUCTURE OF FRANCE is a well-balanced one. Industrial activity is highly diversified, and this characteristic is traditional for France. The country's natural resources and its differing soils and climates have been exploited in many different ways.

The primitive landscape of France has been profoundly altered by the labor of millions of men through the centuries. The last century saw the rise of heavy industry, which was closely connected with the exploitation of coal resources. In France heavy industry has to some extent followed the national tradition of diversity and individuality, in the spirit of the ancient crafts.

Agriculture

Agriculture plays a notably important part in the French economy, and agricultural products make up about 15 per cent of the value of the gross national product. France is generally able to consume her agricultural products herself, but is one of the biggest wine-exporting countries in the world. More than one fourth of the working population and one twelfth of the whole population lives directly off the soil.

These are relatively high figures, even though they are low in comparison with the proportion of agricultural population at the beginning of the century, which was 42 per cent of the whole. Secondary industry has absorbed many of the workers displaced from the land; it has also brought about an extensive mechanization of agricultural methods, with the result that in the last hundred years agricultural production has improved. Agriculture has lost first place in absolute terms to secondary industry, but this is only because secondary industry has expanded at a prodigious rate.

French agriculture always traditionally aimed at supplying all food necessary for the country. But in recent years there has been a tendency to reduce the area of cereals grown and to increase the cultivation of fruit, fodder and sugar beets, which are more profitable, and to breed more beef. More cereals have therefore been imported.

Agriculture is favored because there are great areas of fertile land and a relative abundance of water. Besides highlands and mountains, there is ample pasture, as well as the rich lands to be found in the many river valleys.

The climate is generally mild, with

Menton, on the Mediterranean, first became French territory in 1860. Until 1848 it had been part of nearby Monaco, and in the twelve intervening years it was an independent republic. It is famous as a year-round resort.

The two islands of Lerins in the Mediterranean make the view from the beach at Cannes magnificent. Just a few miles off shore, on Saint-Honorat, the smaller island, stand the ruins of a fortified monastery, one of the oldest in western Europe.

enough rain even during the summer (though the south lacks summer rains). Finally, the variety in the nature and composition of the various soils, and the different positions of the various regions (ranging from the wet northeast coasts to the relatively arid south), make it possible for good crops of many kinds to be grown.

AGRICULTURAL REGIONS

The great Paris Basin is very suitable for cultivating cereals and industrial crops, because its soil is made up of fertile alluvial terrains. The flat, treeless countryside is suitable for the use of modern agricultural machinery on large estates. In the west and southwest the countryside is less uniform, because the land is generally undulating, and is divided into a greater variety of fields and crops.

In the north the countryside is divided into clearly defined holdings. The same system is found in parts of the Massif Central, where timber is also grown. Other regions, such as Languedoc and Champagne, have extensive vineyards. In Burgundy and Limousin there is large-scale cattle-breeding, and the eastern departments have vast forests.

Less than one third of all farms have more than 125 acres, and the great majority have between 12 and 25 acres. These figures show that small farms are the most common. Indeed, such farms cover about 70 per cent of all agricultural land in France. These smaller holdings often have better modern agricultural techniques than those that are used on large estates.

There are also a variety of social conditions to be found in the agricultural world. A great majority of peasant families own their land and work it themselves (67 per cent), but large estates, especially those in the Paris region and in the north, employ many wage laborers. It is less common for land to be rented or share-cropped.

In the northeast, where there is less employment of wage labor, the contrast between the profits from working the small holdings and the wages to be obtained in heavy industry in the region has led to a depopulation of the countryside. Immigrants, mainly Poles and Italians, have been brought in to work the land. The problem of lack of agricultural labor has also been met by the increased use of machines (on Jan. 1, 1962 there were 830,000 tractors in France).

Farms cover over 60 per cent of the total area of France. Forest areas account for about 20 per cent of the territory. Only about eight per cent of the total area is unproductive. The remainder is devoted to cities and towns.

Cereals

Almost one half of all the cultivated land is planted to cereals, and wheat represents about one half of the cereals. Wheat began to be extensively grown in France about the middle of the 19th century.

Cereal production was more than 22,000,000 metric tons (1 metric ton = 2204.6 lbs.) in 1960, but the actual yields vary widely from season to season. The north produces the greatest yields.

France takes fifth place in world production of wheat, and she is able to provide almost all of her own needs. Only hard or special grain is imported, and in very good years France exports part of her production. The production of wheat in 1960 totaled 11,000,000 metric tons.

Corn is a far less important crop than wheat. It needs humidity and a rather high temperature and is limited to the south, especially the Atlantic departments. Aquitaine produces 80 per cent of the crop.

BARLEY, RICE AND OATS

Barley production has also increased in recent years, reaching 3,043,000 metric tons in 1961, and is cultivated on the poorer soils in the center and especially in the north, where it is used for making beer.

Rice is a relatively recent crop in France, for it was introduced only during World War II. Its cultivation expanded greatly at first, but now there are only about 60,000 acres planted with rice, almost all in the Camargue.

Oats are grown on about one third of the whole area devoted to cereals. The crop takes fourth place in French cereal production, and one of the leading places in world production. It is grown wherever wheat is grown, and sometimes alternates with it or is grown together with it. Oats are to be found mostly in the north.

The rye-growing areas are growing less every year, and the crop is now only found on poorer soils in the Alpine valleys, in the Pyrenees and in the Massif Central, in addition to a few other small areas.

Potatoes and Industrial Crops

French potato production is among the highest in the world. The annual yield in 1960 was 14,892,200 metric tons. The soils of Alsace, Auvergne, Limousin and Brittany are best adapted to it, and excellent spring potatoes are raised on the Mediterranean.

The sugar beet is widespread, and is often cultivated together with wheat, especially in the Paris Basin and in the north. Several hundred thousand acres are planted to it, and the yearly crop is one of the largest in the world, the production in 1959 being almost 7,800,000 metric tons. As a root crop it helps enrich the soil for cereals, with which it is often alternated. It is also an important fodder crop.

FIBER PLANTS

Fiber plants have far less importance. The area devoted to hemp has been continually reduced, from more than 120,000 acres in the last decade of the 19th century to about 5000 today.

Flax is cultivated mainly in the wet regions of the north, the Seine estuary and Morbihan in Brittany, and it covers about 150,000 acres in all. Part of the yield is used to make linen, the rest being used to produce oil.

Hops are grown especially in the northeast, in Alsace and Lorraine, where most of the beer is consumed, and chicory is grown in many places in the north as a complement to imported coffee.

Tobacco is cultivated in fifty departments, especially in the region of Aquitaine, the southeast and Alsace. Production amounts to only about 46,500 metric tons a year, and does not satisfy the national demand.

Vegetables and Miscellaneous Crops

Vegetable growing has great importance in France because of the huge domestic demand and because of the foreign market for early vegetables. Formerly the supply for each city was grown nearby, but modern transportation and communications have led to vegetables being raised at great distances from their markets, under more favorable conditions.

Brittany has a mild climate because of the sea, and its soil can be cheaply manured by means of seaweed. It produces many vegetables, as do Roussillon, Provence (especially the plain of Avignon) and irrigable areas such as in the Somme valley near Amiens. Lettuce, tomatoes, cabbages, spinach and many other kinds of vegetables are all cultivated in one or the other of the regions.

The Côte d'Azur is particularly suitable for flower-growing, both in the open and in greenhouses. The area under cultivation is not very large, but flowers are an important source of income, and they supply the raw materials for the perfume industry that flourishes at Grasse.

The Promenade des Anglais runs along the coast of the Baie des Anges (Bay of Angels) in Nice, one of the greatest tourist cities in all France. Over five and a half million foreign visitors converge on the country each year, and increasing numbers of them visit the Riviera, traditionally the resort of only the very rich.

Orchard and Other Fruits

There are many different kinds of cultivated fruit in France, but they have only secondary economic importance. The olive, which is a typically Mediterranean tree, is widespread in the Corsica, Alpes-Maritimes, Vaucluse and Gard departments. The average yearly crop of olives is between 20,000 and 40,000 metric tons.

Apricots grow best in Roussillon and in the region of Avignon. Peaches are cultivated on the Mediterranean coast, in the valley of the Rhone and throughout Aquitaine. The Dordogne and Garonne areas in the southwest, and Alsace and Lorraine in the east, produce plums. Cherries abound particularly in the Vosges.

The apple and pear harvests combined make up more than all the other fruit production put together. Apple production totaled 684,100 metric tons in 1960, and pears another 278,200 metric tons. Large quantities of apples are used to make cider, especially in the northwest, and apple brandy (calvados) in Normandy.

The science of wine-making (oenology) as practiced in France today is basically the same as it has been for centuries. The techniques and machinery, such as wine presses, fermentation vats, bottling and corking machines, have been developed to a high degree; but the skill of the cellar master is still the telling ingredient and is only acquired after an extremely long apprenticeship.

Grapes and Wine

The vine has a place to itself in any consideration of French agriculture, for France has the largest grape and wine production in the world, and the largest export trade in wines. Despite this, because of the large domestic consumption, France imports more than it exports. Choice wines and grape brandies in particular are exported from the southwest (Bordeaux, Médoc, Graves, Charente, Sauterne, Cognac and Armagnac), from Burgundy, from Alsace, from the *côtes* of Lorraine and from Champagne. The ordinary table wines of France come mostly from Languedoc, Roussillon, Provence and Algeria.

The cultivation of the vine has a clearly localized character. It has been abandoned in the northwest because of the climate, and in some other places it has ceased because of poor returns. French vineyards once covered a much greater area than they do now; at present they comprise over 3,600,000 acres.

Toward the end of the last century phylloxera (plant lice) gravely damaged the French vines during a series of bad seasons, and the vineyards were restored only after much patient research and work, and with the introduction of American roots.

The yield per acre was raised, the area under vines reduced, and a number of experiments in cultivation were made. Vines were associated with seed crops, others intermingled with orchard trees, and still others grown alone—as is now most common. In 1962 wine production was almost two billion gallons. Part of the grape harvest is eaten at the table as fruit.

Forests

As previously noted, one fifth of the territory of France is forest. Only one third of these forest areas are in mountain regions. Reforestation of denuded areas is going on steadily. These forests are not able to produce enough timber to supply the country's needs, and France must therefore import considerable quantities of lumber.

Some cork is produced in the south and on Corsica. Resin production has fallen because of the damage done to pines by forest fires. The plantations of oak and maritime pines in the Landes are famous, and other plantation areas are to be found in Sologne and Champagne. The slopes of the Alps and the Pyrenees are

Modern agricultural methods have helped France to be the world's biggest producer of wine.

generally covered with conifers of various kinds.

Chestnut trees are common in Corsica and the Massif Central, oak and beech groves are most common in Normandy and the Loire region, and oaks and hornbeams grow in the Paris Basin. Vast forest areas exist in Alsace and Lorraine, in the Ardennes, the Vosges and the Jura. Timber production amounted to 42,000,000 cubic meters (1 cubic meter = 1.308 cubic yards) in 1960, making France the second largest producer in Western Europe.

Livestock

The vast pasture areas of the country and the land occupied by grass and fodder crops favor cattle and sheep raising. There are over 20,000,000 head of cattle, and their number has increased greatly since the last century, partly because of the greater demand that has been created in a more prosperous society. The best cattle pastures are in the damp northwest. Brittany, Anjou and Poitou have almost 65 per cent of the total number of cattle. There the animals are reared in the open, not in stalls, as in the northeast. In mountainous regions these two systems are alternated according to the season.

Milk cows predominate in Brittany, Flanders and Normandy, and make up about half of all the cattle in the country. They produce an average of 22,156,000 metric tons of milk a year. One third of this production is consumed directly, one third is turned into butter, a sixth goes to make cheese and the rest is used to feed animals.

Draft animals prevail in some places, such as the Charolais (north of Lyon) and Gascony. All beef cattle in the country produced

Wine is produced in many regions of France but only a few have become legendary. Some of the vineyards in the more famous wine districts are worth as much per acre as real estate in the heart of New York City. Although France is the world's leading wine producer, her internal demand is so great that she imports more wine than she exports. Fine vintage wines come from many regions, the most famous of which is Bordeaux. The Midi in southern France produces vin ordinaire, *the cheap wine that Frenchmen drink every day.*

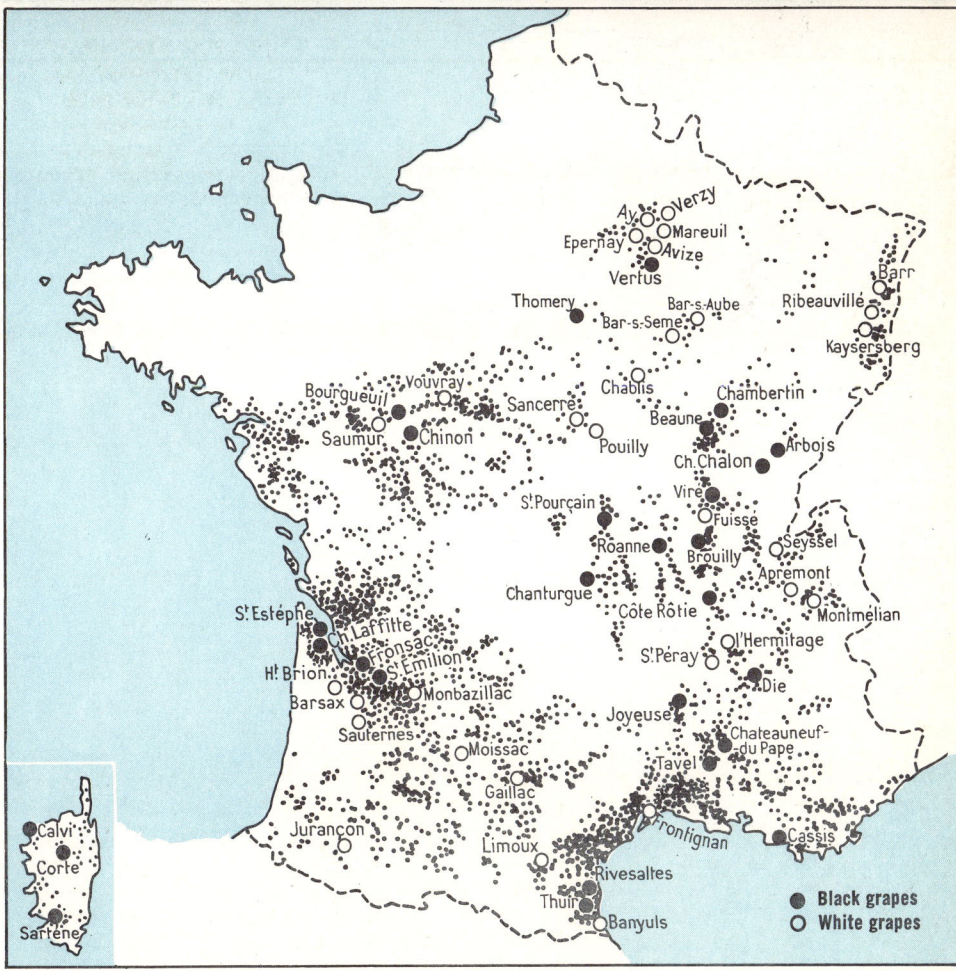

1,873,000 metric tons of meat in 1960. The hides of these beasts have great economic importance.

In the Mediterranean area, in the southwest and in the Massif Central, where pastures are rather thin, sheep and goats take the place of cattle, goats being particularly numerous in the southeast. There are over 9,000,000 sheep and about 1,200,000 goats, but their numbers are decreasing.

HORSES AND PIGS

There are about 1,742,000 horses, and horse breeding is particularly important in the north and northwest. Some breeds, such as the Breton and the Percheron, are much sought after. Mules and donkeys are more numerous than horses in the south.

Pigs are raised everywhere, and they totaled about 9,100,000 in 1960, the greatest number for any European country, and a notable increase in comparison with the past.

Poultry and rabbits are raised, the former especially in Bresse, in the valley of the Loire and in the southwest.

Beekeeping is also in decline, but because of improved methods the production of honey has remained almost constant.

Fishing

Fishing is important in France because of the opportunities offered by the extensive coastline, but it is carried on in very different ways in the Atlantic and the Mediterranean. The large amounts of plankton present in the Atlantic waters and the regular currents and tides assure a large number of fish.

Consequently, fishing is organized as an industry, especially in the Bay of Biscay and around the Breton coastline, which has so many bays and inlets and a broad, sloping seafloor. Most of the French fish supply comes from Atlantic ports such as Boulogne, Dieppe, Fécamp, Lorient, Douarnenez, La Rochelle and Arcachon.

Atlantic trawlers catch migrating fish, such as anchovies and sardines, and from some ports, Fécamp especially, ocean-going trawlers go as far as the Newfoundland Banks in search of cod. In the Mediterranean, more primitive and less productive methods of fishing are still practiced.

In 1960, some 960,000 metric tons were caught, consisting largely of herring, cod and sardine. Crayfish are trapped along all the coasts (especially the Atlantic), and more than 100,000 metric tons of oysters are produced. There are about 12,000 French motor fishing vessels, and fewer than 3000 sailing ones; the total displacement of all these vessels is a little more than 265,000 metric tons. About 45,000 work afloat in the fishing industry.

Industry

Secondary industry now has the predominant place in the French economy. It furnishes the greater part of the national income and employs about 35 per cent of the working population (which makes up 16 per cent of the whole population). Its development has depended strictly on raw materials and available power. Steelworking in particular has depended directly on the development of iron and coal mines and on steam and electric power, as have all the engineering industries.

The location of the various industries has been determined to some extent by the location of available sources of raw materials, and by other factors such as local aptitudes and traditions, commercial relations and nearness to markets. Industrial development has reached a very high level of technical achievement.

Mining

Coal mining is now carried on in France mainly to provide fuel for electric power stations. France is the world's fifth largest producer, mining over 38,000,000 metric tons of coal in 1960, one of the highest figures in Europe. But France produces only 70 per cent of its needs; the rest is imported. Coal is mined by the nationalized company, *Charbonnages de France,* and the most important coalfields are in the north and the Pas-de-Calais, Lorraine and the Massif Central.

More than 2,200,000 metric tons of lignite were produced in the departments of Vaucluse and Bouches-du-Rhône in 1960, and peat is cut on the Somme and the lower Loire. There are about 219,000 coal miners, only about 179,000 of them French. (Only half the miners actually working at the coalface are French; the rest are foreigners, chiefly Poles.)

Very little petroleum has been discovered in France, but oilfields have been found in Alsace, in the south and in the southwest, at Lacq. By 1960 almost 2,000,000 metric tons were produced annually, and 4,500,000,000 cubic meters of natural gas.

As the country needs more than 20,000,000 metric tons of oil a year, most of its petroleum is imported, chiefly from the Sahara. In 1958 almost 30,000,000 tons were imported, but some of this was re-exported after processing. There are many big oil refineries near the great ports, such as at Le Havre on the English Channel, Bordeaux on the Bay of Biscay, and Lavéra, Martigues and Berre near Marseille.

IRON ORE AND BAUXITE

Iron ore and bauxite are also found in France. It has more iron ore than any other country in Europe, excluding the Soviet Union. Its production exceeds 66,000,000 metric tons, and takes third place in the world. Ninety-two per cent is mined in Lorraine, where the average yield is between 30 and 35 per cent from the ore. Production exceeds the national demand, and some iron ore is exported to Belgium, Germany, Britain and the Netherlands.

In 1960 more than 2,000,000 metric tons of bauxite were mined, mainly in the southern departments of Var, Hérault and Ariège, especially around Brignoles and Les Baux (which gave its name to the mineral). Bauxite is used to make aluminum, cement and in other industries. The main countries to which it is exported are Germany, Switzerland and Britain.

There are smaller deposits of several other important minerals, such as lead and zinc, which are mined on the northern and southern foothills of the Massif Central and in Provence. Tungsten and manganese are found in the upper valley of the Vienne, magnesium in Savoy and Dauphiné, nickel in Savoy, pyrites (giving a 42 per cent yield of sulfur) around Lyon and in the Aude. Alsace has great deposits of potash, producing over 1,700,000 metric tons of potassium salts a year.

Throughout the country there are many quarries of building-stone and marl, which are used for cement. Uranium mining has increased greatly in recent years, and France is the largest producer in Western Europe. In 1962 about 1500 tons were mined.

Underneath the forested hills of Alsace are important mineral deposits. Potash mined near Mulhouse is one of France's few mineral exports.

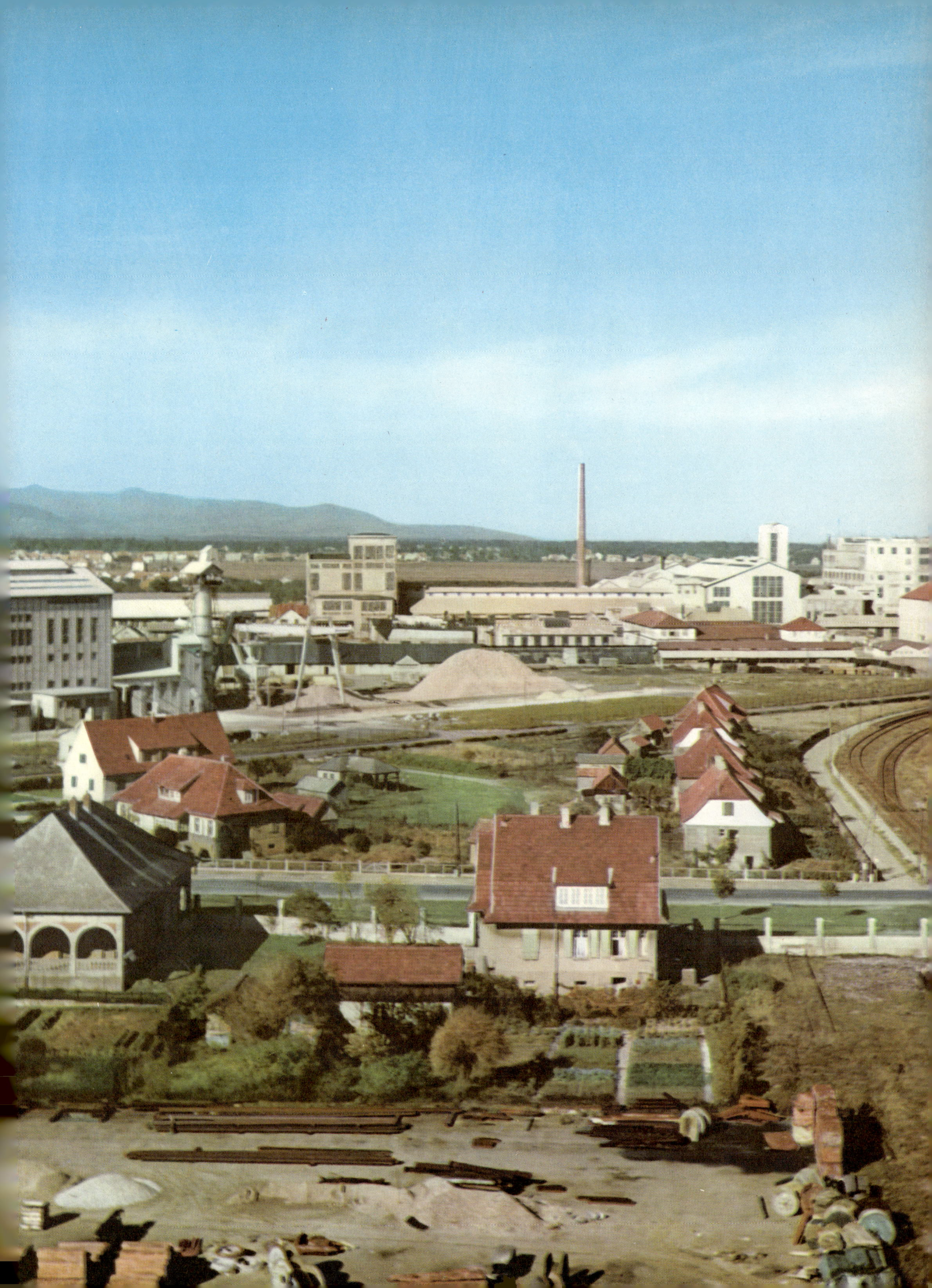

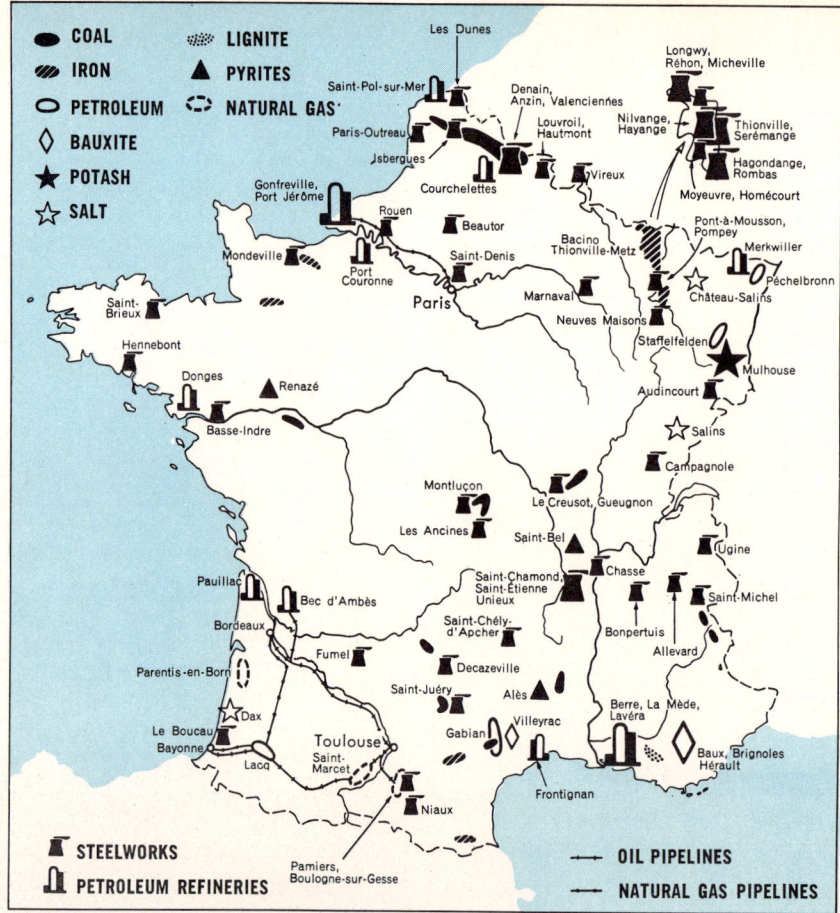

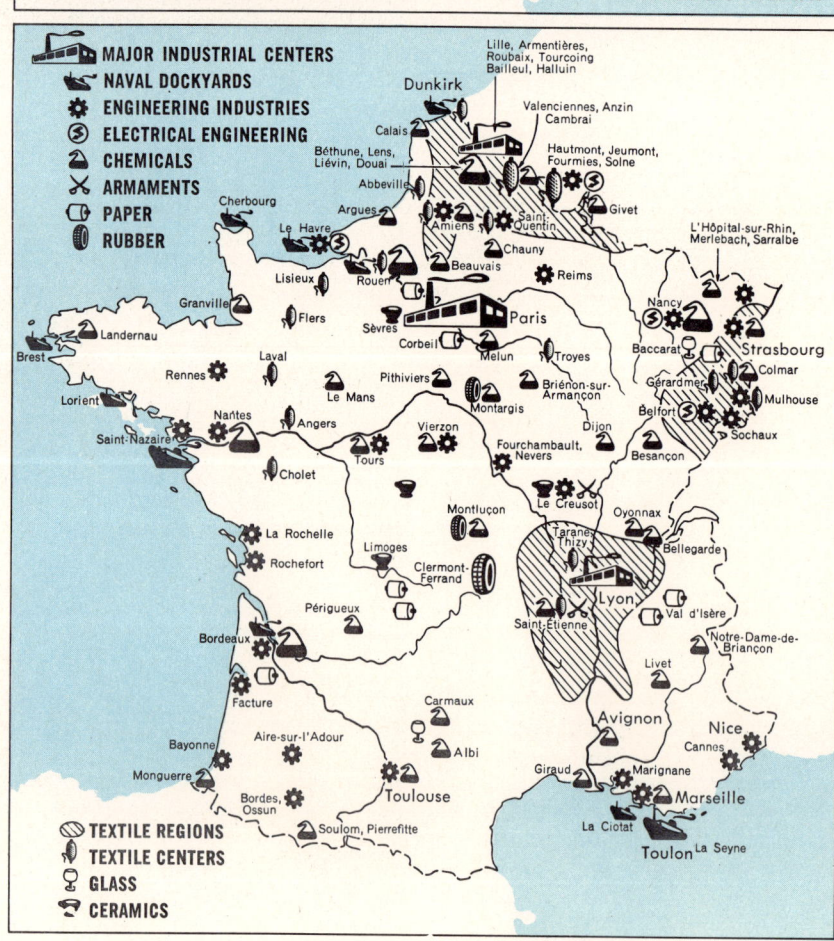

The Electric Power Industry

In view of the country's lack of sufficient coal and petroleum for industry, it is natural that great attention should have been given to electrical energy. Electricity is produced partly through using coal to power turbines and partly by exploiting the many mountain rivers and the favorable geographical conditions of the French terrain to establish hydroelectric works. (Petroleum and gas are also used to some extent to drive turbines.)

Today enough power is produced to supply the country's need for electricity: 83,100,000,000 kilowatt-hours, almost half of which is from hydroelectric plants. About 56 per cent of the almost 22,000,000 kilowatts of installed power is derived from waterpower.

In the north, electric energy is produced in central powerhouses and almost entirely consumed in the locality. Great hydroelectric plants in the east and the Alps supply local needs and also furnish Lyon, Paris and the Rhone valley with their power. Paris, however, has the largest powerhouses in the country.

In the Alpine and Pyrenean regions almost all electricity is produced from waterpower, as is most of that used in the Massif Central. The Pyrenees supply almost all of the southwest.

Nuclear energy installations have been built in recent years. The first three plants were at Marcoule and two others are being built at Chinon.

Metal-Producing Industries

The French steel industry is naturally located near iron and coal deposits. In 1960 more than 14,000,000 metric tons of pig iron and 17,280,000 metric tons of steel were produced. Three quarters of all French steel mills and furnaces are in the northeast: in the Moselle valley, along its tributaries such as the Orne, and along the Meuse. These plants account for 70 per cent of the national production.

The northern mills and furnaces,

The mineral-resource map, at top, shows how poor France is in coal deposits. Except for the coal in the northeast and some minor deposits in the south, France must depend for her power on oil, hydroelectricity and imported coal. The heavy industries, shown at bottom, are located near mineral deposits, but finishing and manufacturing plants are widely distributed throughout the country.

in the valleys of the Sambre and the Scheldt, provide 15-20 per cent. The steel industry of central France has declined in recent years, and is mainly concerned with producing special steels, as at Le Creusot. It supplies 6 per cent of the total. In the west the furnaces use coal from the mines of Normandy as well as imported coal. These plants are generally near great ports, Caen, Rouen, Nantes and Saint-Nazaire.

The determining factor in the south is the availability of electric power. Electrometallurgical plants exist in some of the Alpine valleys, in the Pyrenees and in the Massif Central.

About 280,000 metric tons of aluminum are produced by these plants each year, and they also produce a number of different kinds of ferrous alloys for various sorts of stainless, fine, and special steels: ferromanganese, ferrochromium, ferrosilicates and ferrotungsten.

Lead is refined in Le Havre, in Brittany and in the south. Zinc is refined in Flanders, and copper in Flanders and the Seine valley. Half of the copper produced is used in electrical installations.

Engineering Industries

The economic events of the last few decades have led the French engineering industries to concentrate on specialized production. These industries have expanded considerably because of the rise in production of steel, iron and alloys.

In 1962, 1,535,000 vehicles were produced, including 1,305,000 passenger cars. All together more than twenty firms, with more than 200,000 workers, produced 1,352,000 vehicles in 1960, including 1,118,000 passenger cars (200,000 of these went for general export, and 75,000 were sent to former French overseas possessions).

Bicycle production was about 800,000 in 1962, and motorcycle production was more than 1,000,000 in the same year. The railroad engineering industry manufactured more than 115,000 metric tons of products in 1958. This industry is located mainly in the east and north. (Lille supplies one third of all locomotives made in France.) The tractor industry is in a similarly prosperous state.

SHIPBUILDING AND AIRCRAFT PRODUCTION

Shipbuilding production has risen since the war, and at present ships totaling almost 600,000 tons are built annually by a work force of 40,000 men.

Most aircraft factories are owned by the State. The most important centers of the industry are in the Paris region, and in Toulouse, Marseille, Nantes and Bordeaux. The industry has not recovered the important place it held before the last war, but nevertheless it produced 2,900 airplanes in 1961 (excluding light sports craft). The French aircraft industry is fourth in the world and employs about 83,000 workers.

Arms manufacture is concentrated especially near Lyon, as at Le Creusot, at Sèvres, and at Saint-Étienne and nearby Saint-Chamond. Most electrical equipment comes from the Paris region, but other important centers are in the Marne department and around Lyon, and in most other great industrial cities. About 276,000 persons are employed.

Textile Industries

Weaving and clothmaking is a very old industry in France, and in recent years it has been extended to include synthetic fibers. The industry is dependent on imports for its raw materials. It is highly mechanized and employs a high proportion of women workers (55 per cent), and has a very diversified production.

Apart from the synthetic fiber mills, there are about 10,000,000 spindles and 350,000 looms in operation. Though 80 per cent of the industry's raw material is imported, the production of synthetic fibers from locally produced materials is going up. Textiles make up one seventh of the value of all French exports.

Textile factories are found in all parts of the country, but the main centers are Lyon, (silk), Alsace and Lorraine (cotton), Normandy (cotton) and the north—Flanders, Artois, Picardy (wool, silk, cotton and flax). Eighty per cent of woolcombing mills are in the north, and 50 per cent of the spinning and weaving mills. The north also produces 90 per cent of all linen.

The cotton industry has 6,834,000 spindles and 127,000 looms in action. Less than half of these machines are automatic, and about 131,000 persons are employed. In 1960, 303,800 metric tons of spun cotton and 249,000 metric tons of woven cotton were produced. In the same year the woolen industry produced about

Oil tankers can unload their cargoes right at the refineries on the English Channel near Le Havre.

The suburbs of Paris are not all residential. Just west of the capital, at Boulogne-Billancourt is the Renault automobile plant.

The hydroelectric installation at the Genissiat dam on the Rhone River generates billions of kilowatt-hours each year. Waterpower drives the turbines that produce more than half the electricity of France.

87,000 metric tons of combed wool, 147,000 tons of spun wool, and 69,000 tons of woven wool. This industry also employs about 100,000 people. Only a small part of the raw wool comes from France or the French Community.

The silk industry has 120,000-160,000 spindles and 60,000 looms, employs about 50,000 persons, and produced about 32,000 metric tons in 1962. About 10,000 persons are employed in the flax spinning and weaving industry, where there are more than 200,000 spindles and 40,000 looms. In 1957, 25,000 metric tons of spun flax were produced. This is the only textile industry that gets its raw material from the soil of France. The production of jute products (121,000 metric tons in 1961) has been falling in recent years.

Half of the synthetic fiber industry is located in the vicinity of Lyon, but many factories are also to be found in Paris and in the north. In 1961, 56,000 metric tons of spun rayon and 63,600 metric tons of flock were produced.

Chemical Industries

The chemical industries are continually expanding. There were 7897 factories in 1960, employing 215,000 persons, and the export trade in chemicals is one of the most important elements in the national economy.

A large part of the production of chemicals is based on the processing of coal and its derivatives. The main plants are near the northern coal basin. There are also factories for making ammonia and artificial fertilizers and numerous other derived substances. Additional important factories are situated at the foot of the Massif Central and of the Pyrenees.

The fertilizer industry uses phosphates from North Africa and imported pyrites. Therefore some superphosphate factories stand near the great ports and others near the consumption areas. More than 3,362,000 metric tons are produced each year.

The potash industry is localized in the northeast near the Alsatian potash and rock-salt deposits. Almost 2,000,000 metric tons of sulfuric acid and 350,000 metric tons of dyes are produced annually.

The plastics industry, which is concentrated in the Paris region, is developing steadily and produced 380,000 metric tons in 1961.

The photographic materials industry is also on the increase. The rubber products industry (including synthetic rubber) employs about 70,000, and produces about 483,000 metric tons a year. More than half of this goes to the automobile industry for tires and fittings. The main centers are Clermont-Ferrand, Montluçon and Paris.

There are more than 200 factories making drugs and medicines, the main ones being at Paris, Lyon and Rouen. Scent is made mainly in the south (essences are extracted on the Côte d'Azur at Grasse), and factories are also situated at Paris, Lyon and Bordeaux. This industry has an international reputation.

The soap industry (39,790 metric tons in 1962) and the vegetable oil industry (365,000 metric tons in 1960) have their most important works near the great ports (especially Marseille), in Paris and in other large market areas.

Food Industries

Sugar refineries use both domestic sugar beets and imported sugar, and are usually found in the great ports and near the main consuming areas. In all, more than 2,500,000 metric tons of sugar were refined in 1960.

A great deal of cheese is also produced, since there are abundant pastures and milk supplies. Many of the cheeses are of choice quality that find ready markets abroad. Many regional varieties are made. In 1960, 430,000 metric tons were produced.

There are also numerous regional wines, brandies and liqueurs. More than 450,000,000 gallons of beer were produced in 1960.

The milling industry is located largely in great ports such as Marseille, through which grain is imported, in Paris, and in all the greater grain-growing districts. Cereal foods of all kinds are made mainly at Lyon and Paris.

Other Industries

The tanning industry produced about 218,000 metric tons of leather in 1961. Much hide is imported, and most of the tanneries are in Paris, Lille, Bordeaux, in the middle and lower Loire areas and in Grenoble.

Shoe factories are connected with them.

The glassmaking industry employs about 39,000 persons. Production is about 400,000 metric tons of plate glass and about 780,000 metric tons of mechanically curved glass.

Majolica and ceramic factories are found in many places, but are particularly centered in the north, the center (Saône-et-Loire), the east and the Paris region (industrial and kitchen ware). Porcelain is made especially in Limousin and in the Lyons district. It has a long and brilliant tradition, represented particularly by the fine products of Sèvres, a suburb of Paris.

Abundant clay in many parts of the country makes possible the production of great numbers of bricks. There are more than 1500 kilns, mostly in the north, around Paris, in Provence and near Bordeaux. The annual production, which was about 5,950,000 metric tons in 1960, meets the national demand. Cement is also produced in many places. The largest factories are in the big industrial areas and the annual production was 14,175,000 metric tons in 1960.

Optical goods are made mostly in the Paris region and in the valley of the Meuse. Paris is the center of the goldsmith, jewelry and costume jewelry trades, but specialized factories and workshops exist in the provinces. Clockmaking is concentrated in Franche-Comté and Haute-Savoie, and also in the Paris region.

Twenty State tobacco factories treat 70,400 metric tons of native or imported leaf every year. Most factories are in Bordeaux, Paris, Lyon, Alsace and Lorraine and in the north, and they employ 8,000 workers. More than 44 billion cigarettes are made every year (half of them *Gauloises*).

Communications

France's geographical position and many other complex human and environmental factors have led to a highly developed communications system.

Many French ports are well situated at the mouths of great rivers near estuaries and in fine natural harbors, and in 1960 they handled

The airport at Orly, about eight miles south of Paris, is the point of debarkation for most transatlantic air travelers to France. Orly is one of the largest international airports in the world.

55,000,000 metric tons of unloaded cargo and 19,000,000 of loaded cargo.

Marseille on the Mediterranean receives the trade of the whole of the south and of the Rhone valley, and it also serves as a port for parts of Switzerland. It is not only the most important French port, but also the most important Mediterranean one, since it has considerable trade with the Near East, the Far East and the former French possessions in Africa. The naval base of Toulon, and Nice and Sète, also play an important, though lesser, part in the national economy.

There are numerous ports on the Atlantic seaboard. Some, such as Dunkirk, serve particular industries in their hinterlands. Others, such as Calais and Boulogne, are important

Scenic Alpine highways, though full of curves and frequently hazardous, offer the traveler who can trust his car a trip through some of the most spectacular country in Europe.

means of communication with Great Britain. Le Havre (as well as Rouen to a lesser degree) serves the industries of the Seine basin, and Le Havre also handles many transatlantic passengers.

Cherbourg specializes in the transatlantic passenger run. Brest and Lorient are naval bases. Nantes is an important industrial and commercial port and Bordeaux exports wine, handles passengers, and has a large trade with Africa and Central America. In 1961 the French merchant fleet was composed of about 800 ships, totaling over 5,000,000 gross registered tons.

The road system is about 500,000 miles long, and carries more than 70 per cent of French merchandise. The roads are also continually increasing in importance for passenger transport, as more people purchase cars. Fruit, vegetables and corn are largely transported by road, and the roads are also used in transporting industrial products to other European countries. There are more than 7,000,000 vehicles in France, almost one for every seven persons.

The rail system is built parallel to the highways. It is about 25,000 miles long, and is particularly well developed in the flat industrial regions of the north, the east and the Paris Basin. The railways are run by a State-controlled company (*Société Nationale des Chemins-de-Fer Français*, or *S.N.C.F.*).

About 20 per cent of the national production of goods is transported by rail, most of this being made up of coal, minerals and metal manufactures (more than 225 million metric tons). The railways are still important carriers of passengers between the big cities and from the outlying suburbs of these cities to their centers. This is also true of international travel, especially to Germany, Belgium and Italy. More than 570,000,000 passengers are carried each year.

INTERNAL WATER TRANSPORTATION

About 5000 miles of navigable rivers and canals play an important role in the transportation system. Almost all of the important rivers are interconnected, and where these rivers are not navigable canals run parallel to them. The canal system is particularly heavily developed in the north, but the *Canal du Midi* in the south, the eastern canals and the Rhine-Rhone canal are also very important. The traffic along the greater canals and through river ports such as Strasbourg is very heavy. Most of the cargoes consist of raw materials such as fuel, oils and building materials.

French overseas air communications are especially heavy with the Atlantic countries, particularly North America, and also with the former French possessions. The principal international airports are at Orly and Le Bourget near Paris, at Marseille and at Nice. There are about a dozen other large airports for internal and international use, such as Toulouse. French planes flew about 3,300,000 miles in 1960.

Foreign Trade and Tourism

France is able to supply itself with most agricultural products and export some. But its industries must import great quantities of raw materials, such as coal, petroleum, nonferrous minerals, rubber, wool and cotton.

In 1962, imports were valued at $7,364,000,000, and exports at $7,362,000,000. Imports come mainly from France's former colonies, the United States, Belgium, the Netherlands, Italy, Britain and the Middle East. Exports go mostly to France's former colonies, Belgium, the United States, Italy, Britain and Switzerland.

Trade with the countries of the French Community is well balanced, and an increase in this trade is highly probable. France now derives very important raw materials from these areas, and can profit from the expanding markets of these emergent countries.

Every year more and more foreigners from all over the world converge on France, and many Frenchmen spend part of their summers discovering their own country. The wealthier classes have traditionally sought relaxation at Paris, Deauville, Biarritz and on the Riviera. In recent years, however, members of all classes have been traveling and vacationing in increasing numbers.

In addition, about 5,600,000 foreigners visit France as tourists every year. Most of these come from Belgium, Britain, Germany, Switzerland, Spain, the Netherlands, Italy and the United States. The country has much to offer the traveler. There are great artistic and historical treasures as well as the various coasts and mountain chains. The Alps have fine winter sports centers, and there are celebrated spas and mineral springs, such as Vichy, Aix-les-Bains and Évian-les-Bains. The greatest attraction, however, is still Paris, "City of Light."

THE PEOPLE

106   CUSTOMS AND BELIEFS
Customs Concerning Birth...Christenings...Infancy...Betrothal and Marriage...Love and Superstitions...Rejected Suitors...Marriage by Capture...Wedding Guests and Gifts...The Bridal Gown...The Church Ceremony...The Wedding Feast...The Honeymoon...Good and Bad Luck at Weddings...The End of Life...The Lament for the Dead...Lighted Candles...Care of the Grave...The Funeral Feast...Mourning

129   RELIGION AND FOLKLORE
Lourdes...Rural Religious Customs...Patron Saints of Winegrowers...Harvest Rites...The November Feasts...Christmas and Twelfth Night...Witches and Fairies...Christmas Social Customs...Carnival...Easter...Whitsun Games...Branding Day

151   SHEPHERDS AND THEIR FLOCKS
The Shepherds...Leaving for the High Slopes...Tending the Flocks...Their Enemy—the Wolf...Shepherds' Saints

157   THE FRENCH AT PLAY
Children's Games...Draftees' Festivities...University Customs...Paris, City of Light...Montparnasse...Montmartre...Place Pigalle...First Nights at the Theater

173   THE CRAFTS
Ceramics...Tapestry...Furniture Makers...Metalwork

181   FOOD AND DRINK
Regional Specialties...Norman Recipes...Fish of Brittany...Burgundian Wines and Recipes...Dishes of the Loire Valley...Fish of La Vendee...Wines of Bordeaux...Basque Eels and Oysters...Fish from the Rhone...Savoy and Provence

FOR GENERATIONS THE NAME OF France has been charged with the highest and most precious meaning. It has signified the country of Liberty, of joy in life, and of the supremacy of the intellect—and the home of everything *chic* in dress, food and drink.

Paris has for the modern the fascination that Athens had for the ancient world—it is seen as the capital of refinement, a center where ideas are generated, the meeting-place of every mental and spiritual current worthy of notice, and the inventor of every kind of worldly pleasure. When Paris approves, the world listens, and its decision holds not only in the matter of the length of women's skirts, but also for the theater, for a dance step and for a painting.

All these things have earned France and the French widespread and well merited affection. But enthusiastic lovers of France and superficial observers may well be led into errors of valuation when they consider the nature and character of the people. The fact is that the French have constructed a picture of France for foreigners that often has no foundation in reality.

The real France is not to be found in Paris, which is an island of a special kind, an artificial thing, in spite of its great age and the leading role it has played in the history of the French. Rather, the true face of France is found in the provinces, in regional capitals and in the little villages that have preserved their centuries-old traditions intact.

Therefore, to deal accurately and objectively with French life *we must give most of our attention to the villages and the countryside* where we will find the authentic personality of this great European nation. There, also, we will sometimes discover surprising things, such as the presence of pagan and primitive elements embedded in ancient customs and traditions.

Some of the habits and customs that will be mentioned in the following pages have already disappeared, or are disappearing. The movement of peasants to the cities, other migrations within the country, the development of industrial centers, improved communications and television's tendency to produce a common level of thought and feeling are all helping to destroy the characteristics and the defenses of provincial life. But we will describe that life as it is or has lately been, in all its simplicity and occasional crudity, in order to make possible a deeper understanding of the French people.

CUSTOMS AND BELIEFS

CUSTOMS CONCERNING BIRTH

IN CONSIDERING THE CUSTOMS AND traditions which precede the birth of a child in France one needs to take into account outworn as well as surviving traditions, their variety and their nature. It may be said that rather than being mere folklore, these customs and ceremonies have the character of magical practices that, it is believed, invoke supernatural powers. Though some of them, especially those observed during pregnancy, are partially concerned with hygiene, there are many that can be classified only as superstitions.

For instance, pregnant women are forbidden to look at red cloth, lest they have a miscarriage; they are warned not to spill wine on themselves, and not to scratch themselves. These and other injunctions are evidently founded on magical ideas, and are still quite common.

Practices concerning childbirth are more complex. In Toulouse it is believed that a woman who wants to have a successful delivery should wear a cincture (a small belt-like garment) blessed at the shrine of Notre Dame de la Daurade. Other protective cinctures are those of Our Lady of Lourdes and of Saint Margaret, who is the patron of pregnant women.

Very often, to discover what the sex of her unborn child is, a woman will stand in her nightdress and let a coin slip down the front of her body. If it falls to the right the child will be a boy, if to the left, a girl.

CHRISTENING

The first ceremony in a child's life as a separate individual is his

In the spring, on the island of Corsica, young people take picnics on the lower mountain meadows and bring home armloads of flowering hawthorn branches. The folk costumes of Corsica are similar in color and design to those on the nearby island of Sardinia, which belongs to Italy.

christening. Above all, on this occasion, the baby must be dressed in rich cloths and wear a cap shaped like a priest's biretta, over which is put a hood decorated with ribbons and lace. The cap is always white, and is called an *aubette*. In some parts of the North it may be edged with red. It is preserved with great care in the family and used in future christenings.

The greatest attention, however, is given to the baptismal robes, which are often wonderful examples of lace and embroidery, and which, when the child is held in the godmother's arms, reach right down to the ground.

In the country the old custom is still largely preserved of announcing the arrival of a new fellow townsman —the baby—to the parish, and to the neighboring ones also, by means of the church bells. Indeed, the church bells are rung extremely frequently in the French countryside. They are heard before all religious services, for births, birthdays and marriages, for deaths and funerals, for practice and exercise.

When a boy is born the big bell is rung, but only the little bell is rung for a girl. For a boy the bells ring longer, and the peals are preceded by three separate strokes— but only two in the case of a girl. However, the length of the peal often depends on the generosity of the godfather. If he is very generous and rich he may well keep the bells ringing for a whole week, almost without pause.

The christening ceremony in the church has kept all its traditional features and omens are still widely drawn from the way it is carried out and the incidents that occur during it. Conclusions will be drawn from whether the child cried or not when the water touched it, whether the godparents made the responses correctly, and whether the priest spoke in a loud or a soft voice.

CUSTOMS DURING INFANCY

As the child grows many differing practices and customs are observed. In Savoy, in Bessans and in the valley of the Arves the various stages of infancy are marked by changes of headgear. When still very young the child wears a so-called "nursing cap" and when it begins to walk it adopts a kind of hood decorated with ribbons. After receiving his first Communion a boy may wear a man's hat, and a girl puts on an embroidered headdress called a coif.

This 18th-century fountain supplied water for both horses and people in Saint-Paul-de-Vence, a small village on the Mediterranean coast. The stone basin in front of the fountain is a public washing trough.

It is very common to find lucky charms decorating children's clothes. Care is taken not to let them walk under tables, lest they should not grow; but they are made to walk between certain trees and rocks which are thought to cause them to grow quickly.

In some places a child's nails must not be cut at all until he is one year old. And in other places they may not be cut until he reaches the age of seven years, and then not with scissors, but the mother must bite them off. If they are cut before, the child will become a thief or a bad character. For similar reasons the hair is allowed to grow long even up to the age of five or six.

ADVICE TO THE HUNGRY CHILD

The French have a great store of ironic remarks reserved specially for children. Irony is so common among adults in France that the French have difficulty in understanding how other peoples may find it humiliating and offensive. For instance, English people consider it cruel of the French to tell a child complaining of hunger to "eat one of your hands, and keep the other for tomorrow."

108 / FRANCE • *The People*

July Fourteenth, Bastille Day, is celebrated in France with dancing in the streets and picnics in the country, much as July Fourth is celebrated in the United States with parades and speeches. The holiday commemorates a high point of the French Revolution of 1789, the storming of the Bastille, the fortress housing political prisoners.

In France such remarks are meant to teach the child not to whine, not to lie and not to be vain or greedy. The idea behind them is to avoid spoiling the child by taking pity too easily on him for his little misfortunes. There is also a desire to accustom him to adults taking a strong line with him, and to teach him to be ready to look after himself.

In Brittany adults actually encourage children to fight among themselves, and in many of the region's towns and villages little groups of children are always being formed to go looking for chances to fight. Conflicts between towns are also encouraged, and after the processions on Rogation Days (the three days before Ascension Day) the boys of Saint-Malo and of Saint-Servan engage in furious stone fights. At that time a violent struggle also takes place in the public square between the youths of Great and Little Paramé in the presence of an excited crowd.

BETROTHAL AND MARRIAGE

Marriage and funeral customs survive longer than any others. One reason is that they, more than any other traditions, best express the attitude of a people toward life. In France, as elsewhere, marriage customs begin with the betrothal, if not before. There are customs associated with the asking of the girl's hand, with the preparations for the marriage, with the ceremony, and still more follow the marriage itself.

It is considered very much better for marriages to take place between inhabitants of the same village or of the same parish. There is a strong tendency for matches to be restricted to couples from families following the same trade or profession, and there is considerable diffidence toward strangers, though this is decreasing.

In the past every attempt was made to discourage girls from becoming interested in young men from neighboring villages, to whom they were often attracted. And there were frequent pitched battles between youths from different villages, because of rivalries stemming from this custom.

This unwritten law and its breaking has led to the existence of thousands of village Romeos and Juliets, very few of whom ever succeeded in conquering the taboos and coming together at last. It consequently often happens, and not only in remote places, that all the inhabitants of a village are related to each other. In the past, their mutual relationships were so close that all old women were once called "aunt" for very good reasons. The spread of modern ways of living and communications, however, and the movement of the peasants into the cities have done much to weaken the force of the old saying: "Choose wives and oxen from your own village." The custom, though weakened, has not died out. In the big cities a person from the provinces will prefer to marry into a family of the same background as himself rather than choose a girl from some other part of France.

LOVE AND SUPERSTITIONS

There are many practices associated with courting and betrothal that seem to be directed partly toward harnessing supernatural powers. In La Vendée girls offer a kind of dry bread to the youth of their choice. In the Var they offer a little water in the hollow of the hand from the spring of Bonne Fontaine. In Auvergne the girl who wants a youth to propose plucks a mandrake root at midnight and puts it on the altar where the first mass will be said in the morning.

People employ other strange methods to win love. They leap through fires on the first Sunday of Lent or on St. John's night (June 23); there are also certain other nights that are believed to be particularly suitable for finding a husband. That between April 30 and May 1 is very important, for then many young men declare their love by hanging a flowering branch or a bunch of flowers over the girl's bed or at her doorway.

The custom of "planting the may" is a very ancient one. In the countryside around Retz if a girl wishes to know to which of her admirers she should give her hand she gets up before dawn on May Day (May 1), and goes with a pail and a sprig of hawthorn to a brook or a spring. She then kneels down, recites a special prayer, plants the hawthorn, fills the pail with water, stirs it with her left hand and pronounces three mysterious words: *Ami, Rabi, Voni.*

When the sun appears over the horizon she must have repeated the magic formula nine times. Then, if she has pronounced it accurately and was seen by no one either at the spring or on her way there, she will see the face of her future husband at the bottom of the pail.

Such preliminaries are followed by customs called "frequentations." These "frequentations" are various means for letting persons know whether their feelings are shared or not and fairs, wakes, balls and religious festivals provide opportunities for them.

Everywhere in France a declaration of love may be made by rubbing the other's thigh with one's own; in Morvan one slaps the other's shoulders or back; in Gers the young man squeezes the girl's arms until she yields and sits on his lap; in Quimper arms are twisted and slaps on the shoulders exchanged; in the Côte d'Or a flower is placed on the forehead; in the Vosges the lovers shake hands; in Brittany they spit into each other's mouths.

APPLES OF LOVE

In Ille-et-Vilaine an apple is bitten and offered to the beloved; in Provence the girl throws stones at the wooer she prefers; in Gascony she throws burning brands; in Normandy the man offers to carry the girl's basket, and at Vallespir he offers to carry her umbrella.

Finally the young man asks for the girl's hand. There are many

Open-air concerts are always part of the July Fourteenth festivities. The hot sunshine may induce some members of the band to don sunglasses, open their jackets or undo their heavy belts, but they keep on playing. The music continues until dark.

different ways of doing this. In the Basses-Pyrénées, in Savoy, Flanders, Limousin, Marche and Lorraine he asks her father directly. In Picardy, Gascony, Brittany and the Meuse and Ardennes departments, his own father makes the request.

An unusual method is used in Morbihan, where the young man makes his request in tears, lamenting the death of his parents if they really are dead, and the bad state of the crops and the livestock, until the girl's family bursts out weeping too. At Ouessant the girl goes with all her relations to ask the young man's hand, while on the island of Is the girls may choose their husbands during leap years. In most cases there are two stages in the procedure, for the young man first sends someone to discover whether his suit is acceptable, and he waits to hear the result before appearing on the scene himself.

SIGNS OF REFUSAL

Some of the methods used to show that a suit is refused can be amusing. In the countryside care is taken to avoid an open refusal, for fear of arousing long-lived enmities. So a language of signs is used, which tells the rejected lover all.

In Auvergne an offer of marriage is refused by turning a broom upside down. The gift of an empty sack is a sign of refusal almost everywhere, and so is a handful of oats or other grain placed in the pocket. An invitation to be seated is a sign of acceptance throughout France, however, as is the action of sweeping all around the seated aspirant.

Another sign of acceptance is to burn some twigs and put them well in evidence in the middle of the fireplace. But if the fire is put out, or the key of the house turned three times in the hand, the lover has been rejected. In Berry he is refused if he is offered a plate of eggs, but accepted if an apple or a pear is put to roast in the ashes of the hearth.

In Bourbonnais the gift of a capon means acceptance, and an omelette means rejection, and in Burgundy the girl roasts a fine rooster to show that she yields. In Brittany she offers her lover broth and meat, but porridge and milk tell him that she refuses.

An omelette means acceptance in Nivernais, and refusal is shown by a cross traced in the ashes and the offer of coarse cheese and water. In Roussillon the lover knows how he stands with the girl from whether she will dance the ceremonial dance with him immediately after Sunday Mass.

Negotiations between the families of the lovers last for several days, and are marked by continual exchanges of visits, during which the talks over financial arrangements may break down and be resumed. In Ille-et-Vilaine the betrothal ceremony resembles the marriage ceremony, and takes place in church in the presence of the priest. Then all go to the girl's house, where a great banquet is held, often with a roast calf or an entire cow, and much wine and brandy.

Toward the end of the feast the groom's father presents the so-called promises—a book, rings and coins —to the girl's parents, who place them before their daughter. It is her duty now to burst into tears.

GIRLS IN THE PULPIT

In some villages in the Auvergne a girl who wants a husband goes up into the pulpit with the priest on Sunday. He describes her virtues and states what her dowry would be. Then he announces to the faithful: *"Ti la ti, la donzella à paroudà!"* (Here is the girl who desires to be married.)

Another custom still to be found here and there throughout the country is that of "planting the peg." A great bough of a tree, or even a whole tree, is planted in the courtyard of the newlyweds' house, or in the house of either his or her parents if they are going to live there.

When the groom brings home his bride he first must uproot this bough or trunk, and if he cannot do it with his bare hands, he may use an axe. Sometimes his whole family will help. In certain villages the first blow with the axe is given by the bride, the second by the groom, and the succeeding blows by the rest of the family and friends in order of rank until the tree has been felled.

In Corsica, in the regions of Ajaccio and Sartena, there is a curious method of forcing parents to accept the claim of an unwanted suitor. The young man joins the promenade—the ceremonial walk through the village square—with a handkerchief in his hand. If, when he meets the girl, she takes out her handkerchief, he knows that she returns his love. From then on the lover, accompanied by all his friends, goes to serenade her every evening under her window until her parents give their consent, partly, no doubt, to be rid of the noise he is making and the talk that his wooing is causing among the neighbors.

REJECTED SUITORS

In the country an engagement always arouses great curiosity, especially when there is a betrothal procession, ceremony, blessing and banquet. Every person in the neighborhood takes part, even if only by standing to watch and applaud the engaged couple as they pass. Sometimes white arrows are painted along the way from the groom's to the bride's house so that everyone will know who have become betrothed; sawdust, oats or ashes are also laid down over the way.

Ceremonies at the Arch of Triumph on Bastille Day honor those Frenchmen who died defending their country. France's Unknown Soldier of World War I lies buried under the Arch. Here, a member of the crack Republican Guard salutes the colors as they pass in review.

The Seine, which runs through the heart of Paris, is not just a beautiful waterway. It is a heavily traveled commercial supply route for the capital. Canals connect it to the surrounding suburbs.

The rejected suitor is presented with a bunch of onions to help him to weep, or a bunch of rosemary or thistles. Sometimes straw is placed in front of his house, or he is given a cabbage. He may also be offered a band of black crepe to wear on his arm in mourning, or a necklace of onions. In some places the rejected suitor has the right to invite the girl to a ball, and she may not refuse to dance with him.

There have been examples of real persecution of poor youths who have failed to win the girl they loved. Long processions may be formed and make a devilish uproar outside their windows, and on other occasions an enormous wig is fixed to a pole in front of the disappointed lover's house. An ironic and scurrilous

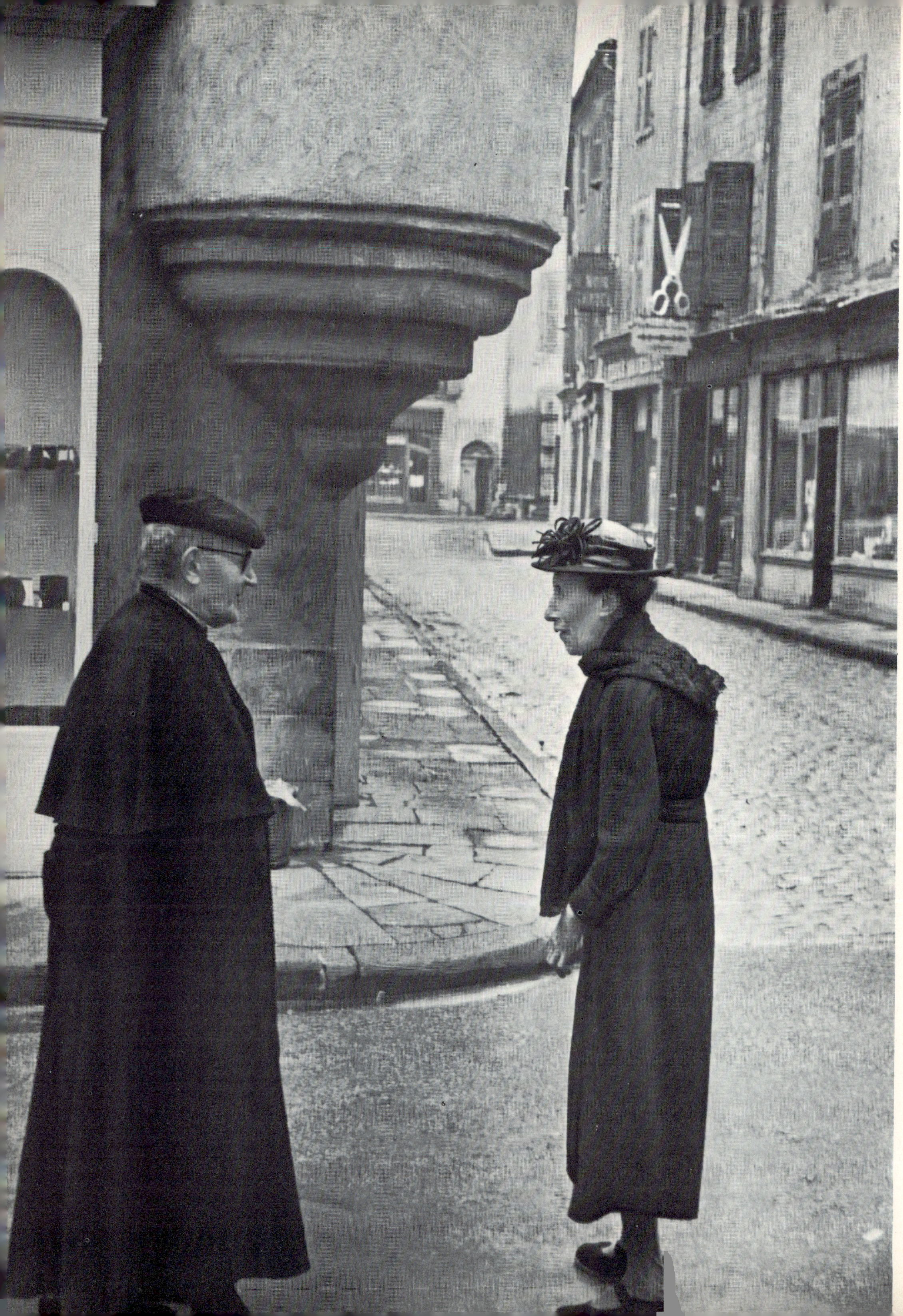

Two old friends stop to chat early in the morning on the street of a provincial town.

speech is made to him, and then during the night the crowd sings bawdy songs and dances about the bewigged pole, which is finally thrown into a fire. Girls who have been abandoned by their lovers get similar treatment, but in their case the wig is replaced by an enormous man's hat.

An even more unpleasant fate awaits rejected lovers in a few places of the Southeast. They are obliged to dance the so-called "dance of the rejected lover," all alone on a little mat. All this derision must be taken by the victim in good part, and he is expected to offer drinks to his tormentors.

These customs seem at first glance to be very cruel, but there is a sound though primitive wisdom in them. The rejected suitor is not allowed to keep his sorrow and pain to himself and brood upon his unhappiness. Rather, he throws these feelings off by means of the ceremony, and more often than not finishes in a state of well-being and joy, joining happily in with the others. In this way, all's well that ends well.

MARRIAGE BY CAPTURE

A very unusual betrothal custom is found in some places in Corsica, Provence, Montpellier, Gard and other regions. If the girl's parents are against the suitor, he may carry her off, and after having spent a certain number of nights with her earns the right to keep her. This custom was quite common until the end of the last century, but is now found only in rather backward districts.

In Corsica the lover seizes the girl and they ride off into the woods. They stay there one night and one day before returning to claim the parents' consent. Often such highly romantic escapades have finished tragically, because of the violent reaction of the girl's family. Suitors have been ambushed and shot dead. Certain episodes in the history of brigandage in Corsica started with such situations; the suitor, knowing what kind of reception awaited him if he returned to his village, preferred to become a brigand, sometimes keeping his sweetheart with him.

In Provence, even though the girl's parents may agree to the marriage, the custom of carrying her off persists, and has become somewhat institutionalized. She may make a legal deposition before two witnesses that she desired to be carried off, and the lover is thus saved from being prosecuted at law.

Other very ancient betrothal customs still found in France are those of the Hidden Bride and the Fleeing Bride. The first custom occurs on the wedding eve, when the bride is entertained by a group of her friends, and hidden in one of their houses, or even in the house intended for her after marriage. When the groom learns that she has hidden herself he goes with his friends to demand that "the lamb be handed over." He receives the answer that in that house "there are no lambs belonging to him."

He and his friends then go in and search the house from top to bottom until they find the bride. Often she hides in a bedroom with her friends, and the demand for the lamb to be delivered up is then repeated at the bedroom door. Generally this is all done by means of traditional demands and replies sung by each group, and the girl is then handed over to her lover.

Sometimes, however, as in parts of Savoy, the women do not soften so easily because prolonged resistance is regarded as proof of the girl's virtue. They shut the doors and windows, and the men have to take the house by assault. The struggle may be carried on in a spirit of

Farms are still a family business in France. Although large-scale, mechanized farming has been introduced in some parts of the country, more than half of all agricultural products come from small, family-operated farms.

In at least one respect, French cities and towns are no different from their American counterparts—neighborhood streets belong to the children. Who will win the next round of marbles is far more important at the moment than the beauty of Nôtre Dame cathedral in the background.

gaiety, but it can become heated.

THE FLEEING BRIDE

Because of the custom of the Fleeing Bride, one of the hardest tasks that a man in the north of France has to carry out is that of conducting his bride to the church. From the door of her own house to the steps of the church she thinks of nothing but escape—naturally, in order to be recaptured. If she notices a path leading off from the street she will take to her heels, and all her relatives and the guests run to catch her.

To prevent such attempts a bodyguard is needed, and he (the *garçon d'honneur*) watches every move she makes. Should she flee, he must bring her back to her parents, and if she does get away, he will not easily find her again, because she may hide in the woods, in the vineyards or elsewhere.

Even when she is found she will put up strong resistance, and it is not uncommon for a comic battle to break out between the bride and her *garçon d'honneur*. Her gown may be torn to shreds in the struggle, but this is a sign of good luck, and any girl who reaches the church in this condition is proud indeed.

Here again, her resistance is a proof of her virtue and devotion, for the longer she resists the greater will be her fidelity and love. In Puy-de-Dôme the bride hides on the wedding night, and the groom must find her if he wants to spend the night with her. This custom, however, applies only to marriages that have been celebrated in church.

GUESTS AND WEDDING GIFTS

In Paris a fashionable wedding requires that the bride and groom have at least six bridesmaids and groomsmen. Such retinues are also found at marriages in Alsace, Burgundy, Brittany, Gascony, Languedoc, Lorraine, Maine, Normandy and Savoy, though of course everything is simpler in these places.

Rules about guests and invitations are much as they are in other parts of the Western world, but in some places curious old customs still regulate these matters. In Alsace the groom and his men go on horseback to invite the guests and are greeted with cheers and pistol and cannon shots. In Auvergne a special messenger with a long staff decorated with ribbons comes to the door and fires pistol shots to announce his mission.

In the Bourbonnais the invitation ceremonies last for weeks. One invitation is sent each day and every recipient must entertain the messengers to dinner. In Burgundy the invitation is given by means of the cry, "Clean your boots!" and in Bresse the bride and groom themselves carry the invitations. Every recipient offers them tobacco and sweets.

In Brittany an invitation to one person includes all members of his family, including any children and the servants. In the Argonne an invitation to young people goes with a white ribbon, and that to adults with a colored ribbon.

In Gascony the messengers are known as "Chasse-chien" (dog chasers) because they must beware of the dogs at the houses to which they go. The invitations are brought in the evening, and the messengers are given supper. Since they have other invitations to give they may eat as many as twenty suppers in one evening.

In the Landes the bride and groom issue invitations to each other by means of special messengers, and in La Vendée each guest attaches a colored ribbon to the messenger's garments, so that at the end of a day he looks like a harlequin.

THE BRIDAL GOWN

At last the wedding day comes,

Along the quiet, narrow streets of Châteaudun everyone knows everyone else. The people in this small, tranquil community, which was founded by the Gauls, have been tending to their own business for more than two thousand years.

But seventy-five miles away, Paris sparkles with life. This is the Avenue de Wagram, which runs east from the Arch of Triumph.

and with it the ceremony of preparing the bride. The dressmaker presides over this, and is assisted by the bride's mother and her attendants. It almost always lasts several hours, because bridal gowns are still very complicated and have many folds.

White is not the usual color. Red is preferred, and other colors are used in this ceremony in different regions. In La Vineuse the bride wears violet silk, which is rather unusual, because violet is also the color of mourning. In Gascony the normal color is red, but blue and brown gowns are also seen, as well as a white sash, as in Picardy.

In the Argonne the bride wears rose, and in the Isère she wears shot silk called *gorge de pigeon* (pigeon's breast) because of its varying tints. In Limousin the colors also vary, but they are bright, as they also are in the Nivernais. In Normandy dark shades are preferred, and in the Île-de-France white is most usual, though several other colors are used. The most elaborate and beautiful bridal gowns are certainly those found in Brittany, where at Bourg-de-Bats the bride wears four petticoats one on top of the other, the

Holy-day processions offer a good opportunity for villagers to get dressed up in their inherited finery. The embroidered shirt bands and sashes and the double-breasted coats of these young men mark them as Bretons, people of Brittany. They are observing the Feast of the Great Pardon at the shrine of St. Anne of the Marsh.

outermost being red or violet with black embroidery; the sleeves are scarlet, the bodice yellow, a broad embroidered sash is worn about the waist, the stockings are red, and the shoes white.

The dominating feature of the bride's costume all over France, however, is the bridal crown, which is often of orange leaves. But it can also be complicated and heavy and made up of flowers, imitation pearls, ribbons and feathers, as in Alsace. Gilded paper crowns are used in the Lower Loire region, and headgears covered in roses in Picardy.

In Languedoc the bridal crown is made up of very beautiful arrangements of wild flowers, masterpieces of folk art. In Normandy rosemary and roses are used, and myrtle in Franche-Comté. In France, except in Paris, the bridal veil is less important than it is in other countries.

The veil is being adopted in the provinces, but only slowly, while the custom of putting a cincture about the bride's waist is as vigorous as ever. It may be done by the groom, or by one of the bride's family (as we have seen, in Limousin it is done by the bride's father), or a young man may be specially chosen for the task.

WHEN BRIDES MUST WEEP

When the bride has at last been dressed, and the groom has arrived, the procession to the church is formed. This journey is a very solemn part of the whole ceremony and is usually accompanied by minor rites, such as the traditional weeping by the bride as she leaves her father's house, and his blessing given on the threshold.

The order of the procession is also important, and varies from place to place and also according to the social standing of the bridal couple. In Paris and other big cities the bride goes first on the arm of her father, the groom follows with her mother, and the bridesmaids, groomsmen, relatives and guests come after them. After the ceremony the newly-married couple take the head of the procession, and are followed by all the others in the same order as they set out for the church.

In the big cities this procession is now almost always confined to the interior of the church, for the rest of the journey is made in cars or carriages, but in the country the whole way from house to church and back is covered on foot.

The procession will often not be a peaceful one, because it may be stopped by the traditional barrier. In Alsace a heavy iron chain is stretched across the road, but in other places only a red ribbon is used (in Biederthal the priest's sash). In Auvergne the route is blocked with tree trunks, boards, carts and other farm implements.

In Bresse the barrier is made of boards, but bottles of wine are placed on it, and the relatives of the bridal couple may take them in return for money. In general, the main purpose of the barrier today seems to be to make the families and the guests pay a kind of toll, which the young people of the village afterward use for a feast of their own.

THE CHURCH CEREMONY

When all obstacles have been overcome, and the bride recaptured after her flight, the procession reaches the church and the ceremony begins. During the Middle Ages it was customary to use the *pallium,* a canopy held over the heads of the bride and bridegroom through the ceremony or during the blessing, and this is still done in the regions most attached to tradition. The Catholic Church terms the pallium the *velatio nuptialis* (marriage veil); it is a survival from the time of the Roman occupation of Gaul.

When the groom reaches the altar he places the wedding ring on a dish, the priest blesses it, and the bridegroom puts it on the finger of the bride. But not always on the ring finger. In certain districts he puts it first on the little finger, then on the forefinger, finally on the ring finger. In some places the ring is made not of gold, but of silver, and bears two crowned hearts.

Often the bridal couple bring, together with the ring, silver and gold coins to be blessed. There are usually thirteen of them, six for the husband, six for the wife, and one for the priest. The bride may remain veiled until the blessing begins, and in some places an ox yoke is placed across the shoulders of the couple, or they are linked together by a chain.

Symbolic gifts are offered to the bride when she returns from the church to her own home, or at the door of her husband's house. These are usually a broom, a distaff, a cradle and a saucepan. When, as happens in most cases, she has to go to live with her husband's family, she is said to go as a daughter-in-law *(elle va bru).* If the husband for any reason decides to go live with her family he is said to go as a son-in-law *(aller gendre).* If he does this he is not well thought of.

THE WEDDING FEAST

If you were present in the house of a large peasant family in France at the solemn moment of the beginning of the wedding feast, you would see at least seventy guests seated about the banquet tables, all dressed in gorgeous colors, all tired from walking in the procession and from the emotions they had experienced. Some would be rather "high" from the numerous glasses of fine wines and liqueurs that they had been offered along the way.

The room is splendidly decorated, and the table is covered with ribbons, flowers and good-luck charms. A great rustic garland hangs from the ceiling or is suspended from the wall above the bridal seat.

It is important to eat something from all the many courses and dishes, because if you do not you will deeply offend the relatives of the happy

Also part of the feast-day celebrations are folk dances, performed to the skirling accompaniment of the bagpipe, a traditional Breton instrument.

Brittany was called Armorica when it was conquered by Julius Caesar in 56 B.C. After 500 A.D., Britons, the Celtic inhabitants of the British Isles, came across the Channel to Armorica, fleeing from the Angles and Saxons, who had begun their invasion of England. The Britons found a welcome haven in Armorica and gave the region its present name. Breton, the language of Brittany, which is still spoken in many villages, is related much more closely to Welsh than it is to French.

couple. To start, each guest will be served a whole chicken—even though there are seventy guests. It does not matter if you send yours back to the kitchen almost untouched as long as you do at least taste it, and praise it.

Your praises should then be given to the mutton, veal, beef and pork that will follow. You must also praise the tarts, the accompanying pastries and the pies.

The final obligatory dish is the wedding cake, which can take many forms. Some, such as the *gateaux-monstre* (monster cakes) in Anjou, are so big that they have to be brought in three or four sections and set up in the dining-room. There may be a little figure on the cake that represents the bride, as in the Bourbonnais. Sometimes the wedding cake is broad and flat and is carried in on the bride's head, from which the bridegroom takes it to cut and distribute the pieces to the guests.

In Languedoc the cake is heart-shaped, and in Normandy it has a sugar cupid on it. In the vicinity of Orleans it has the shape of a castle, and in Burgundy, La Vendée and Savoy special dances are performed as it is brought in.

Sometimes the bride's parents do not take part in the banquet, but stay in charge of the kitchen. Usually the bridal couple sit side by side, but sometimes they are kept apart, and *garçons d'honneur* watch to see that they do not embrace each other.

SMASHING PLATES AND GLASSES

An exciting moment occurs when the plates and glassware are broken. Since this can be a rather costly custom it is usual to restrict the breakage to three or four pieces as a symbolic gesture of propitiation. But in Languedoc as soon as the feast is over the table is overturned with shouts of *"que le mariage tienne!"* (may the marriage last!) and care is taken that nothing is left unbroken.

It may be asked how peasant families can bear the enormous expense of ceremonies, gowns, decorations, food and breakage. Indeed, a family could ruin itself in this way. They have, however, learned how to put on marvelous feasts and at the same time recover what they spend, at least in part.

At the end of a wedding banquet the bride herself may go around the guests and all—especially her close relatives—are expected to give her money. The same custom is observed on the wedding eve, when the bride goes the rounds of the village, but on this occasion she is expected to give at least a glass of wine in exchange.

The custom is observed in many places, but even when it is not, no guest can expect to be relieved of the duty of bringing a gift to the wedding banquet. Contributions are also asked for to pay the bellringers at the church, who, in order to ensure a good fee, are likely to deafen the village with the bells for three days on end without stopping.

PAYING THE COOKS

The musicians, servants and above all the cooks must also be paid from the guests' subscriptions. In Alsace the cooks send two masked clowns around to collect at the tables, and in the Ile-de-France the *garçons d'honneur* dress up as cooks for this purpose. In Gascony, the cooks cover anyone who refuses to pay with flour, while in Lorraine the cook pretends to have burned herself and when she asks for money it is said to be in order "to heal the burn."

The guests may be tired out after the procession, marriage ceremony and banquet, but they still have at least one more duty to perform. They must go to the ball, which may begin several hours after the wedding feast is over or may start at once.

The whole village takes part without having to be invited, and the guests will sometimes change from their holiday costumes to dance more easily. By this time, everyone has eaten well and drunk deep, and it is easy to imagine how many a marriage ball quickly degenerates into a wild, noisy rout. Everyone leaps about according to his fancy, liberties are boldly taken, dangerous practical jokes played and the young men seize and embrace the girls. In most of France the only rule observed is that one requiring the bride to open the ball with her husband and to dance with each of the guests.

On the other hand, in places where, as in Gascony, behavior at the balls is too outrageous, the bride is prohibited from taking part in the ball at all. In Gascony all kinds of bold remarks and insults are exchanged during the dancing, as if to show that every once in a while people need to shed their inhibitions so as to have the satisfaction of revealing their repressed selves.

In Brittany games are preferred to dances. Each young man takes a tart or pie and tries to break everyone else's. Whoever manages to keep his own tart intact wins and is allowed to kiss his favorite girl. In Champagne the pavane is danced, in Lorraine the quadrille, and in the Nice region, the farandole.

THE HONEYMOON

Relatives and guests do everything possible to stop the bridal couple leaving the feast, and often even try to prevent them being together during it. Naturally, the bride seeks every opportunity to get away, and she and the groom try every means to evade their guards. This is not easy, and even after the ball is over they are still watched. They are given no peace all night even though they succeed in locking themselves in their room.

An old custom, widespread until a few decades ago and still observed in some places, required the bridal couple to pass the first night, or even from three to ten nights, without consummating the marriage. This custom is known as "the night of Tobias." (In the Old Testament it is related that he did not consummate his marriage for several nights as a cure against an evil spirit.)

Other forms of the custom still exist. In Bresse the bride returns to her parents' house after the wedding and the groom goes away until the following Saturday. In Bresse, it is said, all marriages take place on Fridays!

In Brittany the bridal couple are kept awake all night long by the joking and singing of a little crowd of relatives and friends. This goes on until dawn, and the next night another group takes over.

In Franche-Comté "the nights of Tobias" take place only if the bride so desires, and it appears that advantage is taken of this privilege if the groom has drunk too much at the wedding or the bride is shy. In Picardy, if the bride consummates her marriage on the wedding night the old people of the village will condemn her to draw a cart through the main streets.

UNPOPULAR MARRIAGES

The kind of wedding that we have been considering so far is that in which the couples are thought to be well matched. But the customs and traditions already described do not apply at all to unusual marriages that do not meet with popular approval.

The classic case for popular scorn occurs when an old man marries a young girl or a young man a much older woman. It is considered even worse when an old widower or widow does the same thing. The least they can expect is to suffer the *charivari*—that is, uproar, shouts, whistles and loud music, which may end in scuffles and fights if the ill-mated couple are defended.

An old bridegroom in these circumstances is acting wisely if he enables the young men of the village to eat and drink well at his expense. In this way he can reduce public demonstrations against himself, or even avoid them. Anyone who reacts with violence or threats, refuses to pay for a feast, or goes to law gets opposite results from what he intended.

Once in Toulon an old widower refused to pay for or to give dinners for this purpose. Instead, he went directly to the police and demanded their protection against the *charivari*. On his wedding night the police guarded the street where his house was, but the windows and doorways along its whole length were black

The women of Brittany are justly proud of the beautiful heirloom lace on their folk costumes. The white lace caps, called coifs, and collars receive the most attention, but good needlewomen also like to show their skills on the dark dress materials as well. The blue satin of this girl's costume has been quilted and embroidered.

The Bretons have always regarded Brittany as distinct from the rest of France. Long after the province passed by marriage to the French royal house, the Bretons retained their own provincial government and laws. In the 19th century a movement to make Brittany an independent country won wide support in the province. Even today, Bretons are very slow to adopt the ways of their neighbors. They keep to themselves and follow the traditions of their fathers. Here a musical procession winds its way through the streets of Saint-Flour.

with people, who gave him and his young bride a night of uproar such as was never heard in Toulon before or since.

A FORBIDDEN CUSTOM

The usual way of carrying out a *charivari* is to assemble an orchestra of empty barrels, pots and pans, bells, cowbells and horns. But the shouts and yells of the people provide most of the noise. *Charivari* has always been forbidden by the Catholic Church, by the kings and by the Republic, but it has survived all the changing French governments and the centuries. Indeed, it is certainly the most widespread and vigorous of all forbidden customs in France.

It is only some twenty years since one of the most scandalous *charivaris* ever recorded occurred at Saint-Pierre-d'Entremont in Savoy. An old widower married a young widow of twenty. They were a gift from the gods for the youth of the town. But the old man was very rich and arranged with his friends in the ministries at Paris for special police protection.

Someone revealed his plan, and the organizers of the *charivari* determined to put on an unforgettable performance. They brought hundreds of persons by car from the surrounding villages and by the evening more than 1500 people filled the streets of the town. Money poured into the inns and bars. The moment when the police arrived was chosen to begin the uproar. Pots and pans were struck and bells rung while a farm cart bearing two enormous figures representing the bridal couple was hauled through the streets.

The gendarmes tried to block it, and took the names of the more troublesome demonstrators. Tempers got so heated that one of the ringleaders leaped onto the wagon and incited the people against the police, who were driven back and roughly handled. A government inquiry followed and the demonstrators were accused of seditious behavior and attacks on the safety of France. The affair ended months later with about one hundred people being sentenced to short periods of imprisonment.

Similar treatment is given to husbands who beat their wives and to those whose wives are known to be unfaithful, especially if the husband condones her infidelity. Girls who take too long to marry also have to undergo public criticism. But in their case the taunts and jokes, which occur especially when a younger sister marries before the older ones do, are more benevolent. It is said that the younger has left the elder among the ashes, or that she has cut the ground from under her feet. Sometimes the elder sister has to bear unkinder jokes, as when a plate of oats is served to her at table to let her know she is a donkey for not having found a husband earlier. In the Meuse region an unmarried elder sister has to dance at the younger sister's wedding feast with a bag of straw hanging from her neck. In Isère such unfortunate girls are obliged to eat a plate of garlic and raw onions. There are hundreds of variations on these practices.

GOOD AND BAD LUCK AT WEDDINGS

The ways of knowing whether a marriage will be happy or not are quite another matter, and can be very amusing. In general, a rainy wedding day is a good sign, and fine or snowy days are not particularly favorable. There is a popular saying: "A wet bride is a fortunate bride."

It is obviously bad luck for a wedding procession to meet or be held on the same day as a funeral, just as it is if the groom finds his bride fully dressed when he goes to her house to fetch her. If the bride looks back during the walk to the church or looks in a glass before setting out, bad luck will result. Bad luck also follows if the ring fits only halfway up the bride's finger, or if she kneels on her gown when taking her place in the church. To avoid this danger her attendants raise her skirt as she kneels.

Other unfavorable signs are a setting moon, not having made confession before the marriage, and a cat in the church. Also, bad luck is likely if the bride has any broken pots or pans she has forgotten about, if her procession meets another bridal procession (always possible in a city), if a vehicle crosses the route of the procession, if it is a very windy day, if it is the feast day of a martyred saint, or if the flames on the candles in the church waver during the ceremony.

Some may conclude from all these customs that it is not easy to get married in France. But this is not true. No one is obliged to fulfill any of the traditional requirements, and marriages in the modern style, exactly as in Paris, may be seen even in such strongholds of tradition as Picardy and Burgundy.

Local usages, traditional costumes, processions and even banquets can all be left out. However, they have the effect of impressing the young from their earliest childhood with the importance of their destiny. Indeed, both they and their parents look upon marriage as much more than a normal event. Rather, it has an element of the supernatural about it.

A student of folklore once asked some girls in Burgundy whether they would not prefer to be married without so many complicated ceremonies. "Certainly," they replied, "but how would we get on without the *rôtie*?" Evidently, they believed that without the *rôtie* (a special drink brought to the bridal couple during

FRANCE • *The People* / 121

their first night together) they would not be able to bear children—and this was, for all of them, their chief desire.

THE END OF LIFE

It is a very human desire to play an important part in life at one time or another. From this originated the habit of dramatizing many aspects of existence that is so noteworthy in the traditional customs of France. This tendency is not confined to the joyful events alone, but is also shown during occurrences that some people might prefer to forget as soon as possible.

The death of a member of the family is an occasion in France not only for sincere and often profound grief, but also for a public exhibition of one's wealth. Even if a family is not as rich as it would like to be, the opportunity is seized to show that it is better off than the neighbors thought.

If this is impossible it is an additional disaster. As a Paris wit has said, the relatives of a man who has died in poverty in France are struck simultaneously by three causes for grief: his loss, the lack of any inheritance, and the necessity of telling the mortician that the funeral must be a third class one.

What are the usual, or at least the indispensable elements of the death ceremonies? Almost everyone follows the custom of announcing a death by solemnly composed letters and large announcements in the newspapers. The corpse has to be washed and made ready, the room for the lying in state prepared, the corpse arranged for the visitors, and preparations made for the solemn procession through the streets to the cemetery and for the burial service.

The ceremonies of displaying grief before an audience have not yet finished, however, for the gravestone has to be chosen and decorated. Then a competition begins with other families to keep it supplied with

In the old market of Pont Aven, a small fishing village on the southern coast of Brittany, the women shop the way their grandmothers did fifty years ago. The timeless serenity of Pont Aven has attracted many painters, including Paul Gauguin, and there is now a permanent art colony on the outskirts of the village.

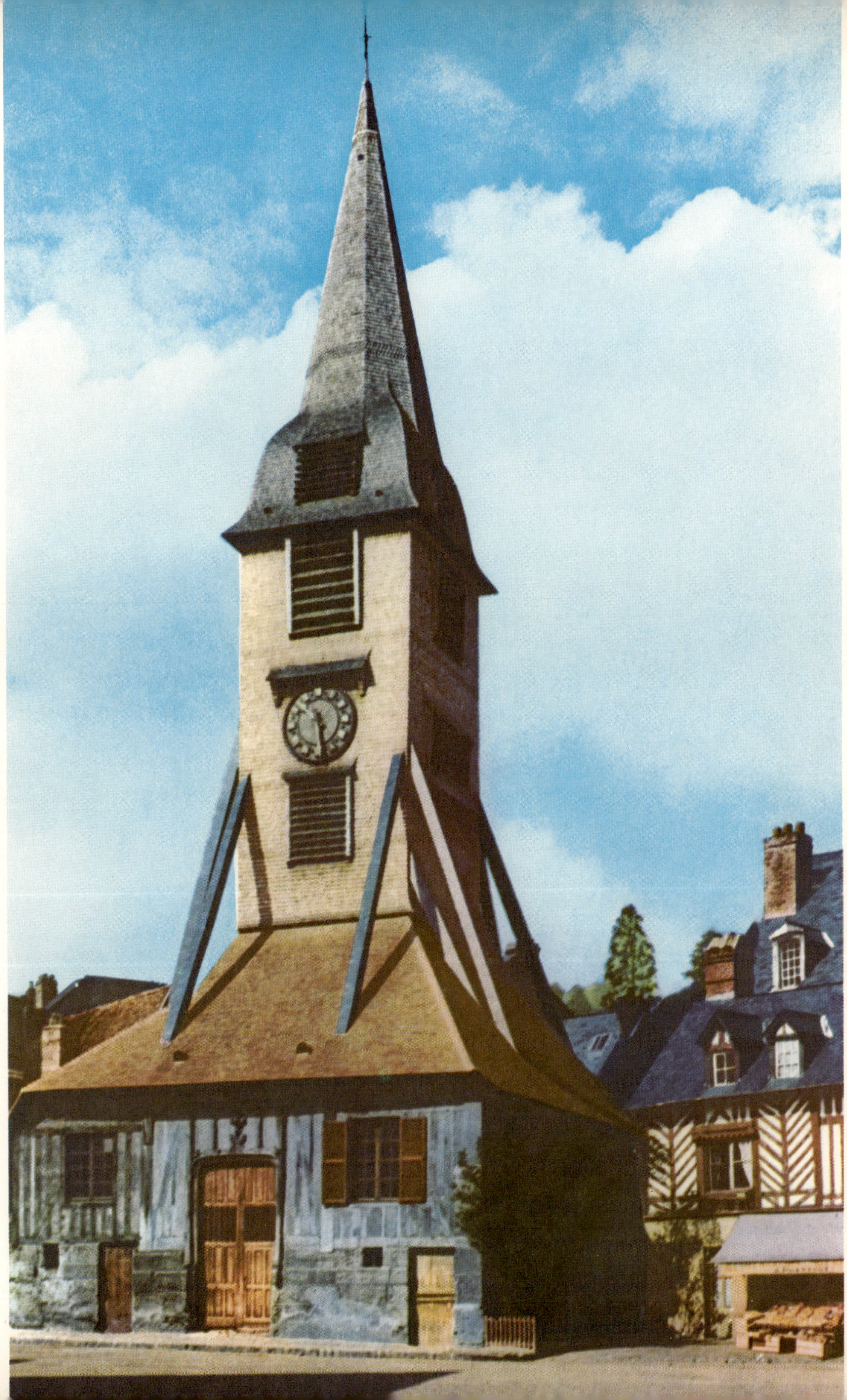

flowers and lighted candles, in order to draw attention to one's devotion. Sometimes the funeral ceremonies are followed by a dinner for relatives and friends. Moreover, the period of mourning continues according to the current custom of most Western countries.

AT THE TIME OF DEATH

These are common forms of behavior in the case of death. In France, however, there are many other customs. In some regions when the dying man is in his agony his bed is arranged parallel to the beams of the ceiling; this is supposed to relieve his sufferings. Sometimes a tile is taken from the roof and brought into the room, or the dying man is made to get out of bed and stand for a minute or so barefoot on the floor. A rooster may be killed in his presence; he may be sprinkled with holy water or touched with candles blessed by a priest or by a five-franc piece. He may be given water from special springs to drink.

An unusual practice is found in Corsica, where, when a person is dying, the whole village hurries in, and the house is filled with silent people. Everyone sits up through the night, and the women surround the bed. When the person breathes his last one of the women screams, and immediately all seats and tables are overturned. The women act like maniacs, shriek savagely, let down their hair and scratch their faces. Peace is gradually restored, and then one of the women stretches over the corpse and sings a kind of lament relating his virtues and describing his character.

A death is not always announced in plain language. A Frenchman may say: "His bread's cooked," or "He's emptied his cellar" or "He's broken his pipe." In Bourbonnais the phrase, "He will plough with his spine," is used, and in Aude and the Côte d'Or "He has gone to see the truth." In Paris one says, "He's gone to Père Lachaise," the name of the well-known cemetery there.

From the moment of the death everybody stops what he is doing, even on a farm or in a workshop. The horses and cows are taken back to the stable or the stall, the women stop cooking and neighbors come in to prepare the frugal meals that will be eaten for the next few days. Neighbors will finish any urgent work on the farm, inform relatives, help to prepare the corpse, arrange for the funeral and undertake any other necessary duties.

It is particularly important not to sweep the dead man's room or move the furniture, and all bells of whatever size have their clappers tied or are stuffed with straw. Almost everywhere it is the custom to stop the clocks at the hour of the death, to cover mirrors, turn pictures to the wall, turn all crockery and other kitchen ware upside down and throw away all the milk and water in the house.

In the country a black cloth is placed over the beehives and special poetical formulas are used to inform the bees of their master's death. These verses are pretty, though mournful.

One runs, *Abeilles, petites abeilles, votre maître est mort.* (Bees, little bees, your master is dead.) The following is recited by the heir: *Petites mouches à miel, c'est moi qui remplace le maître défunt, et qui vous soignerai à l'avenir.* (Little honey bees, I replace your dead

This crucifix overlooks a vineyard in Normandy. Family vineyards often have such crosses set up as a perpetual prayer for the protection of the harvest.

The old church of St. Catherine in the Normandy town of Honfleur is built like a peasant barn of the region. The bell tower has to be held up with struts because the roof cannot support it alone. The wood paneling on this building and the one behind it is a heritage from the Norsemen who conquered the region and settled it over a thousand years ago. Since then Honfleur has seen many battles because of its strategic location on the shore of the English Channel. The town changed hands many times during the Hundred Years' War between France and England, and it became a battleground again after the D-Day invasion of World War II.

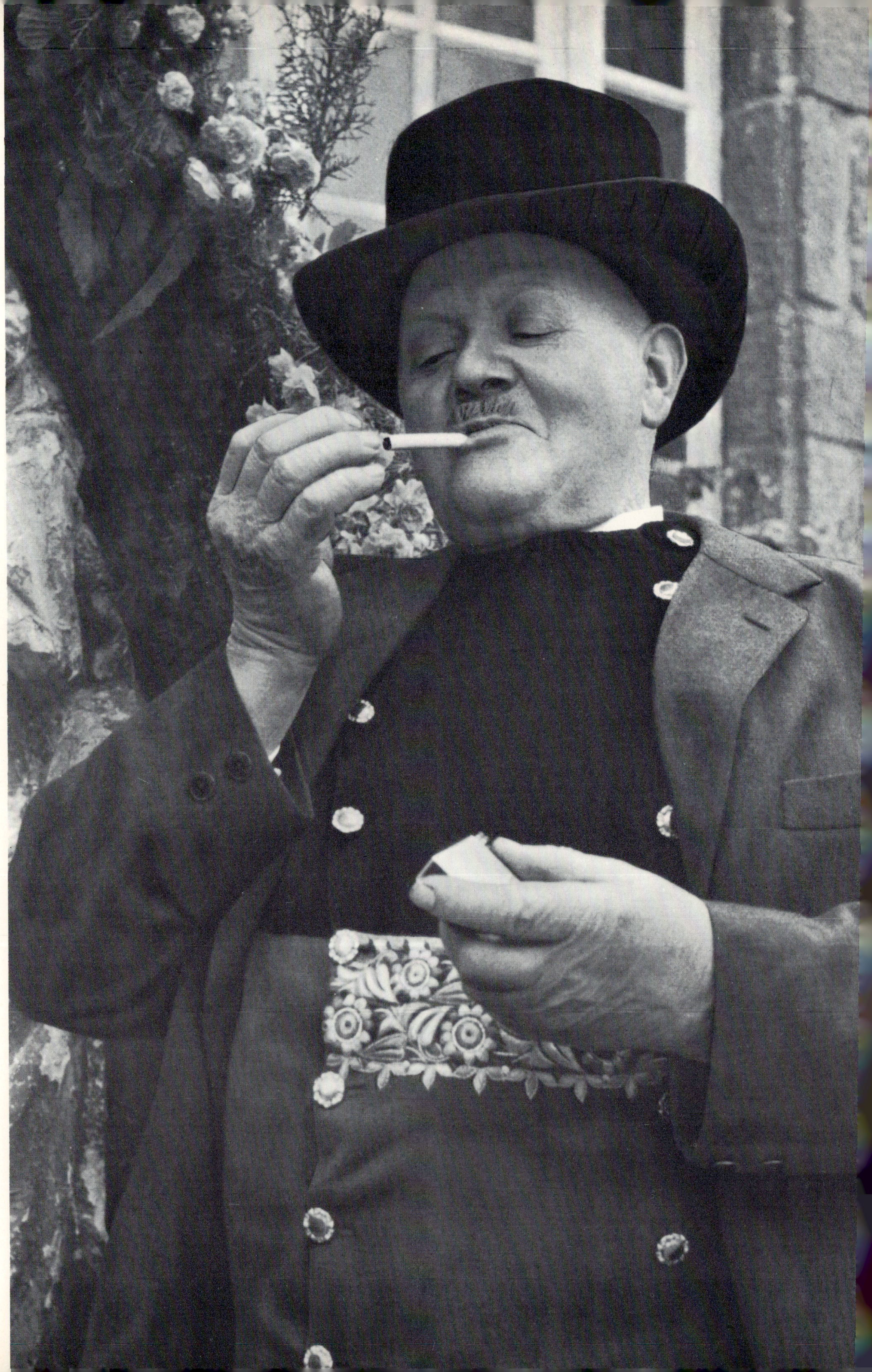

This prosperous looking citizen is from Finistère, the westernmost part of France. The name Finistère means "land's end." On the tip of the Brittany peninsula, the region is noted for its fishing fleets.

master, and I will look after you from now on.) A more rhetorical statement is: *Petites, bêtes du Bon Dieu, réveillez-vous, un grand malheur vient d'arriver; votre maître vient de mourir.* (Little beasts of God, awake! A great sorrow has come upon you, for your master has just died.)

Black mourning is put on cows and goats in Savoy, Isère, Haut-Var, Ardèche and Lozère. In Savoy they are deprived of their bells, and in Pas-de-Calais cats, dogs and bird cages all receive black ribbons.

THE LAMENT FOR THE DEAD

We have already mentioned the laments made by the women in Corsica at the moment of death. These laments are almost never completely spontaneous, but are really funeral hymns; they vary from region to region, and are often derived from very ancient rites. The most remarkable aspects of the lamentations are the wails (or keenings) which are as impressive and interesting in France as in other countries.

One can trace the deep roots of these laments and find connections with age-old popular traditions and customs. In Corsica they seem to go back to the time of the ancient Greeks.

An ordinary lament in Corsica is only a mournful hymn of praise of the dead person, but some, especially the one called the *vocero*, have immense dramatic power. A *vocero* is a terrible cry of rebellion against death and a challenge to the person responsible—it is only used when there has been a murder; it is begun by the victim's mother or wife, and then taken up by all the women. It is not a prayer for eternal rest, but a call to revenge, and is probably also intended to rouse the men to execute vengeance pitilessly and remorselessly. The *vocero*, which is rarely heard today, resembles the laments of the choruses in the plays of the ancient Greeks.

Somewhat similar lamentations, known as elegies, also exist among the Basques and Bearnese, but in all other regions the laments follow the normal pattern. The praises are almost always the same, and the cries and shrieks are often uttered by women whose job it is to do this and to be paid for it.

BELLRINGERS FOR THE DEAD

The custom of using special signs to announce a death is still widespread in France. Sometimes a large wooden cross is put on the door of the house, or one made of straw or black cloth. Black or white hangings are found everywhere, sometimes reaching down each side of the doorway to the threshold. In Brittany, every village has its "bellringer for the dead," who goes about the streets ringing a bell and announcing the death in a loud voice.

As in all Catholic countries, the church bell is rung, and even though the number of strokes and the manner of ringing have been laid down by the Church, in many places variations exist by force of custom. Abel Hugo reports that in the arrondissement of Pont-Audemer when a person is just about to die "the bellringer sounds sixteen peals for a man and twelve for a woman, and immediately all in the village recite the prayers for the dead.

"The bellringer has different kinds of strokes according to the dead man's social standing. A rich man receives the *gros son*, a loud peal; a middling peal, or *son moyen*, if he belongs to the middle class, and the *dindin*, or tinkle, is thrown to the poor as alms."

In Guerande, a village on the southern coast of Brittany, costumed folk-dancers dance around the "Devil's Mill," a local landmark.

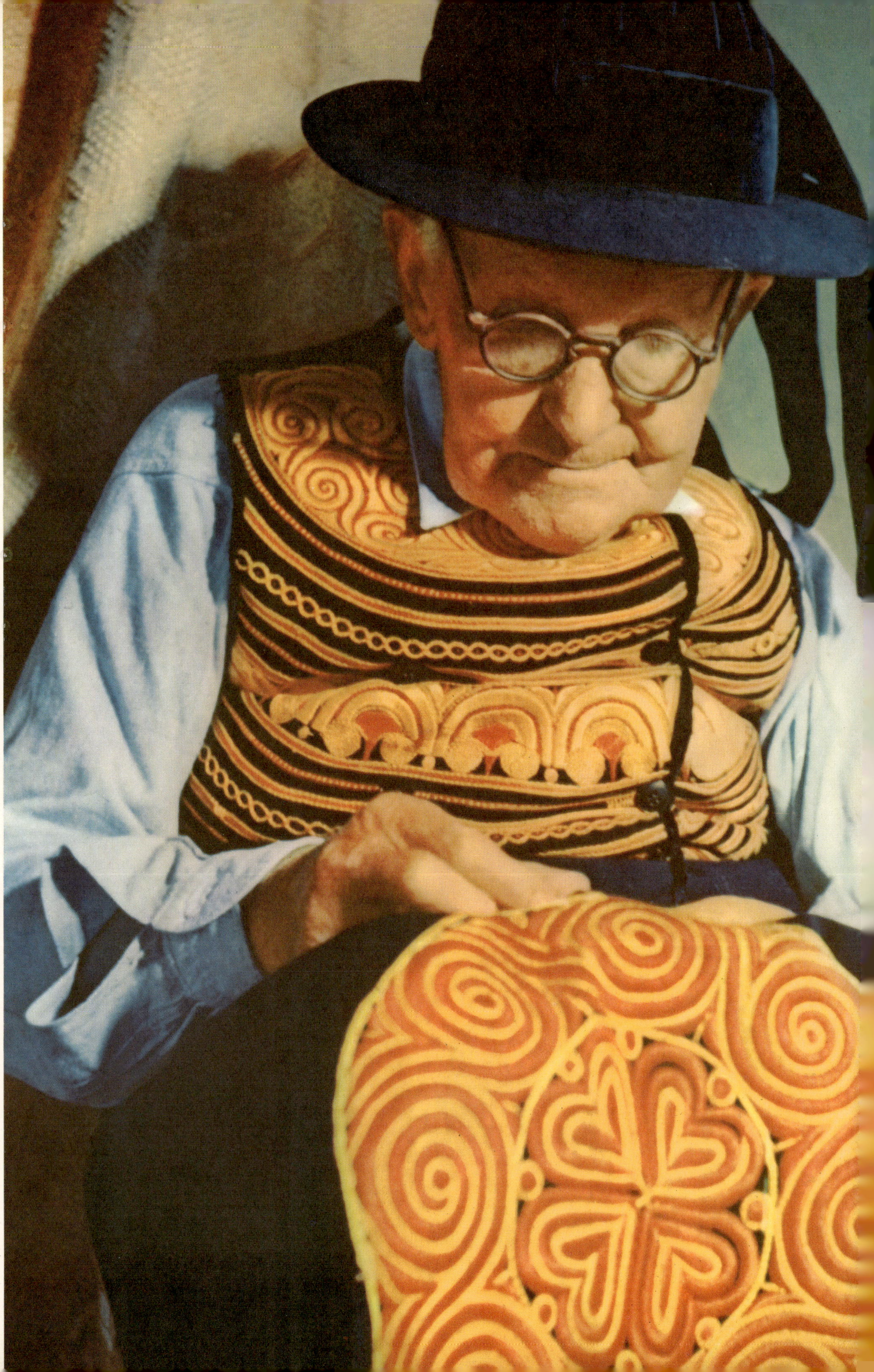

The technique of bellringing is complicated and traditional. In some regions certain bellringers have even become famous for their ability to draw different sounds from the bells.

The *chambre ardente* (candlelit room), or lying in state in the home, hardly known in English-speaking countries, is a custom that exists in France but it is not as widespread as in other European countries. The hangings used in the room are generally white, not black and the *chambre ardente* is, in fact, often called the *chambre blanche* (that is, "white" not "candlelit" room). The richly worked hangings are handed down from generation to generation.

The *chambre ardente* serves not only to give visitors a last sight of the dead person, but also to provide room for the wake, the custom of mourners sitting up at night around the coffin. These wakes are sometimes transformed into merry parties. In the valley of the Moselle, for example, a party is held about the corpse in the coffin, and the guests eat bread roasted and dipped in hot wine, while the members of the family go about pouring out liqueurs. Everyone speaks in a loud voice and it is not uncommon to spend the night telling funny stories.

THE ROLE OF OXEN

Like wedding processions, funeral processions take on various forms in different regions. In Finistère the funeral cart is drawn by at least two oxen, but sometimes four or even more are used, according to the wealth of the family. In the Loire-Inférieure department it is strictly forbidden for anyone to touch the oxen "because Death shows them the way."

Two oxen and a horse draw the funeral wagon at Quimper, and here too it is forbidden to touch them, even with a whip. If they halt, all have to wait patiently for them to go on, and conclusions are drawn from these occurrences concerning the dead person's chances in the other world. Perhaps Death does not want to receive the dead man yet, because he was too good or too useful to his family and to society; perhaps the custodians of heaven stopped the funeral wagon because they were unwilling to let an undeserving soul come in.

In other regions two horses draw the funeral cart, which is usually covered with a white pall and a wreath of laurel. Stops are frequent, especially if the bier is borne on the mourners' shoulders. They rest at the crossroads and wherever there is a wayside crucifix.

Certain people such as pregnant women, the surviving spouse, or the parents of a son are forbidden to join a funeral procession in some areas. Formerly, all the relatives were excluded in some villages, and also some women.

LIGHTED CANDLES

In Normandy everybody carries a lighted candle, and in a wide region comprising the Pas-de-Calais, Flanders, Artois, Ternois, Issart, Ergny, Ponthieu and Boulonnais, the procession is headed by a man carrying a white "funeral cushion," with embroidered borders, on which a crucifix and a wreath of green leaves have been laid. In Normandy and Brittany a small cloth is carried instead, and is then placed in the grave. Sometimes boys ringing bells go ahead to warn of the approach of the funeral procession.

Certain similarities exist between the garments worn at funerals and at weddings, and tradition used to forbid villagers and country people to take part in funerals wearing ordinary clothes. The relatives of the deceased wear full mourning, and keep it on for certain lengths of time. The rest wear special clothes—the women long black capes and the men long cloaks.

There are exceptions to every rule, however, and in Puy-de-Dôme it is correct to wear your oldest clothes. In Dordogne the men wear no ties, and in Lozère they tear the buttons from their coats; in Bouches-du-Rhône they wear working clothes and unpolished shoes, and in Pyrénées-Orientales, Eure, Seine-Inférieure and Var, it is customary to go to funerals unshaven. Black ribbon on the jacket or a black armband are used everywhere as signs of mourning.

In some places, as was mentioned in connection with wakes, the funeral procession also takes on a joyful appearance, and in some villages in Auvergne a comic song is sung which begins: "Turlututu, my wife is dead!"

When they reach the church the men go to the right and the women

This old woman has been embroidering for most of her long life. The patterns she works on are traditional to her village in Finistère.

128 / FRANCE • *The People*

In the northeastern part of France, near the Belgian border, the women wear their starched lace coifs in the shape of a halo. In the 16th and 17th centuries, the fine lace and embroideries of this region were famous throughout Europe.

to the left, but in Ille-et-Vilaine relatives and other mourners remain kneeling on the church steps. Families of good social position take great care to make the proper offering to the church for Masses and prayers to be said for the repose of the departed soul.

Some families even supply cash to everybody present in order to draw attention to the amount they can spend in this way. The money for the Masses is placed on the bier or in a vessel, or is given directly to the priest. The coffin is brought out of the church in the manner usual elsewhere in Europe, but the custom of lining up to embrace or greet the chief mourners *(faire les honneurs)* is a Parisian custom that is followed more and more in other places too.

THE FUNERAL FEAST

After the funeral ceremony, relatives, acquaintances, friends and admirers of the deceased hurry off to a richly-laden and decorated dinner table. It is very likely that the funeral feast stems from a Roman custom. In any case, it still flourishes, and its purpose is to thank all who wished the dead man well and who helped during his sickness and after his death, and to relieve the fatigue and worry of the family.

Such a custom may not seem right to everybody, and some may suspect that it shows hardness of heart or cynicism. But it is wrong to think so. A banquet need not always be an occasion for merrymaking. Centuries ago, the Romans held dinners whenever they felt a need for greater affection, greater family unity and stronger spiritual communion with their fellows. This is the deeper and religious significance of a meal taken in common. Apart from the Roman custom, the Last Supper eaten by Christ with his Apostles on the eve of His death is the supreme example of the profound significance that such occasions can have.

Where the custom is kept up in modern France, the meal is usually a simple one, and the only subject of conversation is the deceased. Meat is usually not served, and neither are pastries, liqueurs nor coffee. In Auvergne and Franche-Comté milk and rice are obligatory, while salads are often forbidden.

In Limousin there is still a tendency to make the dinner an occasion of merriment, and it is said that "the peasants count the empty bottles instead of the number of candles to decide whether the funeral has been a good one." Nevertheless, pastries, coffee and liqueurs are all excluded from the meal. Milk soup is a "must" here, and wine is allowed as a concession. The soup seems to have the practical purpose of stopping the people from drinking too much wine, because it is well known that wine and milk do not agree when they meet in the stomach.

As a general rule, it can be said that funeral feasts are distinguished by sobriety and seriousness. Indeed, the presence of the clergy, at a separate table but eating the same food, assures this.

The diaichottes *dance is performed in Montbéliard on spring and summer holidays. The folk costumes of this area show the influence of nearby Switzerland.*

POSSESSIONS OF THE DECEASED

However great may have been the affection felt for the departed soul, few would welcome his return from the dead. Similarly, no one looks forward to having to come in contact with his possessions, his clothes, or even the furniture of the room where he died. His linen is sent away or given to the poor. This, it is said, will make it easier for his soul to enter eternal life. In reality, however, the motive is a horror at the idea of putting on a shirt of his or sleeping on his mattress or sheets.

It is widely believed that death is contagious, like a disease. As a result, it is usual almost everywhere —not only among the peasants—to destroy the mattress of the deceased, and not to give it away (because no one would take it). Little fires lit for this purpose are always to be seen in the street or the fields on the day after the funeral.

MOURNING

Mourning is the last stage of the funeral cycle. As all know, the bereaved family imposes certain restrictions on itself in regard to social life and amusement, and shows this in its dress. Close relatives are particularly affected. Today the period of mourning and the cut and appearance of mourning clothes has become standardized, but until a hundred years ago very many different forms existed.

Until the middle of the last century the mourning color was not necessarily black. Up to 1840 red was worn in Isère, dark blue was worn in Savoy, blue in Brittany, and in Berry any color except red.

A few interesting and unusual practices remain to be mentioned. In Franche-Comté it was once the custom to bury people face downward, so that they would not see "the hated Spanish invader." In some parts of the industrial Northeast a workman's mates will want to see his face again just before burial, because they fear his body may have been changed for another at the hospital. And the sailors of Brittany hold that a death and the life hereafter will be good or bad according to whether the tide is high or low during the last agony.

Finally, as elsewhere, the dead person is commemorated at certain fixed intervals by prayers and religious services, and such commemorations may go on for years.

Distinctive coifs are not restricted to Brittany. They appear frequently in the folk costumes of all of northern France. Varying widely in shape and size from village to village, the caps often date back to medieval times. Some are enormous creations, like the coif of this woman from Normandy. It is held up by starch and wire supports.

RELIGION AND FOLKLORE

AN ANSWER TO THE QUESTION OF what kind of faith the French have in God might be that faith is an interior experience, felt rather than thought, and that it is a simple thing which cannot be analyzed. Such a reply does nothing to explain the rules by which the people live and what they believe—it is beside the point. One must refer to the outward practices of an interior faith, which itself is affected by these outward practices.

As is well known, there are definite differences among the responses of the various Catholic peoples to their faith. In general, the French may be said to have less obvious religious warmth than some other peoples; but their understanding of their faith is firmer. They are less fanatical, but more rigorous, not as impulsive as others, but more given to the practice of religion when they do believe.

It is enough to go to Mass in a French church to see this. There is little exhibition of fervor and interior struggle, but a greater sense of solidity and maturity than is found in some Latin countries. During Mass the people behave in a disciplined fashion, never chatter, and kneel and rise at the proper times.

These characteristics are to be found everywhere, not only in Paris, but one must not conclude that this necessarily reflects a more submissive attitude than is found elsewhere toward the clergy. Indeed, the spiritual and intellectual liberty that many French Catholics insist on is well known.

As it happens, France offers an outstanding opportunity to anyone wishing to make comparisons among the various Catholic nations. This can be done by observing the pilgrims who flock to Lourdes from many countries.

THE STORY OF LOURDES

Lourdes has a fairly recent history as a famous shrine. On Feb. 11, 1858, a little shepherdess, Bernadette Soubirous, fell into an ecstasy at the feet of the Virgin Mary, who had appeared to her in a grotto. On March 25, she heard the Virgin say to her: "I am the Immaculate Conception." A spring gushed out of the grotto floor; and from that day on sick persons have gone there to pray, and have been cured.

Crowds of cripples, lepers and the paralyzed flocked to Lourdes. The bishop doubted the miracle, and the Prefect of the Department denied it. In the end, Napoleon III gave orders that the people be allowed to go there freely and express their faith. A church was hurriedly built near the grotto, and in a very few years Lourdes became famous all over the world.

There have been many cases of persons pronounced incurable by doctors regaining their full health after bathing in the spring. The Catholic Church set up a special organization to tend the sick pilgrims, to supervise medical attention, and to examine reputed cures.

Today, Lourdes is a great center of pilgrimage, and has four churches, three of them one above the other. The lowest is a vast circular edifice built underground in very recent years. One important use of the underground church is to give shelter from the rain, which often falls, since Lourdes is in the foothills of the Pyrenees. It was opened in 1958, the centenary year of Bernadette's first vision, and is about 660 feet long and 260 feet wide, but only about 33 feet high. The ceiling of reinforced concrete is supported by a great many columns that give a fantastic and mystical effect.

The shrine is always crowded with sick and pilgrims from all over the world, and in the evening splendid and impressive processions are held. Priests from many countries are found there who can speak a large number of languages. One of the most moving sights is that of the volunteer attendants wheeling the sick from the hospitals and hostels to bathe in the spring, or to take part

Floats, elaborate costumes and tons of confetti help to make the Carnival at Nice, on the Riviera, a major tourist attraction. Nice has been attracting foreigners for thousands of years. The Romans took it over from the natives, the Phocaeans, in the 2nd century B.C. For centuries the city was under Italian rule, but it was ceded to France in 1860, when Italy was reunited. Giuseppe Garibaldi, the hero of the Italian reunification, was born in Nice in 1807.

in some of the religious functions, such as the torchlight processions.

Lourdes has an international character, it is true. Nevertheless, it is also an authentic and highly revealing manifestation of the French religious spirit.

RELIGION IN THE PROVINCES

Religion and folklore are closely related. Naturally, prayers for good crops take a leading place in the peasants' minds and formerly such prayers, with appropriate ceremonies, were recited in most dioceses every Sunday from May to September. This period was called "Between the two Crosses" (the reference is to the two Feasts of the Holy Cross—one in May and one in September).

Solemn processions are often held, especially on the Feast of St. Mark, April 25, and on the Rogation Days —the three days before Ascension Day. Most of the peasants keep the feast of Our Lady in May, and in January special devotion is paid to St. Anthony of Egypt and St. Bernard of Vienne. In April, St. George and St. Peter are honored; in February, St. Brigid in Alsace and St. Blaise in Isère; in August, St. Helen and St. Urban.

St. Isidore, whose feast falls in May, is the patron of agriculture and of farm laborers. St. Vincent is the special protector of vineyards. St. Cornelius watches over cattle, St. Anthony over pigs, St. Fiacre over gardeners, and St. Christopher over orchards.

Various popular rites, officially ignored by the Church, exist for averting thunderbolts, storms and hail. For example, in La Bâtie-Divisin so-called St. Adonis' Bread is eaten, and in La Buisse a statue of St. Victor is carried through the streets. In Voissant a pilgrimage is made to La Croix du Mont and in St. Pierre-de-Chartreuse one is made to La Croix du Grand-Som.

In Rives beds are sprinkled with holy water and in other villages the thresholds of houses are blessed in the same way. In Vif the women put on black silk clothes and pray before a candle that has been blessed. In Salagnon and Saint-Siméon-de-Bressieux shots are fired at the clouds to bring rain. And in Livet-et-Gravet as a protection against hail, a handful of hailstones is thrown into the fire.

WHEN WORK IS FORBIDDEN

Work in the fields is generally forbidden on Sundays and holy days, especially on the greater feasts, such as Easter, Ascension, St. John's Day, the Assumption, All Saints and Christmas. There are various interesting legends about punishments suffered by those who disregarded this obligation. Some peasants in Aude, who considered St. John to have been a false prophet, once began reaping on his feast day. St. Dominic happened to pass by,

A holiday cart decorated with flowers passes along the seafront in Nice. The French call their stretch of Mediterranean coastline the Côte d'Azur, the Azure Coast, because of the deep blue color of the sea.

rebuked them, and immediately all the sheaves turned the color of blood.

The ancient practice of offering the first fruits of the harvest to the Church still persists, but is less common than formerly. Until the last century it was rare indeed for the parish priest not to receive the finest sheaf as soon as the harvest was over, the first barrel of wine, the first ripe fruit, the first dish of butter, one tenth of the eggs laid during Lent, a ham from each pig killed in the same period, and so on.

This custom of tithing and the donating of first fruits is, of course, a very old one. It was a legal institution in the Middle Ages, and can be traced back to the ancient custom whereby the priests received portions of the offerings made to pagan gods. Today, the administrator or steward of the agricultural cooperative is more likely than the priest to receive this kind of benefit.

In some regions, the custom survives in a limited or symbolic way, as when an ear of corn is carried into the church to be blessed, bunches of grapes placed on the altar, and strings of apples and pears offered to statues of the saints. In Picardy, during the Thanksgiving Mass after the harvest a handful of wheat and one of oats, and an apple and a pear, are taken into the church to be blessed.

The following prayer is in use among peasants of the North: "St. Christopher, give us apples, pears and plums. Give us little ones and big ones. The big ones will be for us, and the little ones for our children...." The peasants of Pas-de-Calais and the Somme are rather disinclined to make any offerings, even symbolic ones. As self-interest and opportunism spread farther afield these rural rites degenerate to the point where the gifts are made to more visible powers than the deity, such as the mayor, the Prefect and, in a purely symbolic way, the President of the Republic.

THE MIRACULOUS REAPER

Many legends stress the religious character of work in the fields, and they may often be traced back to pagan legends which have been transformed by Christian influence: Christian saints replace heathen heroes. The legend of the "miraculous reaper" is often told about various saints in different regions.

In one part of Burgundy the story concerns St. Claude. This saint was sent by his master to cut grass early in the morning. When the master went to inspect the work and found him still busy sharpening his scythe he fell into a fury and threatened to dismiss him. Without a word St. Claude set to, and the crop fell before his strokes as if it had no weight or thickness.

The farmer was dumbfounded. Soon the whole meadow had been reaped, but the saint was only now warming to his work, and went on. A plantation of poplars fell before him while his anguished master tore out his hair in desperation. This legend may stem from the fact that the banks of the Saône in that area, it is said, used to be covered with poplars, but are now bare.

As we have seen, each kind of agricultural work has its patron saint. And the festivals celebrated in their honor are often of great interest to travelers and to students of folklore, since they are living clues to local history.

French winegrowers are perhaps the world's most celebrated producers of wine, and they also seem to have the greatest number of patron saints. Starting from the New Year, the first festival is St. Vincent's Day, Jan. 22. Although the saint was a native of Saragossa, he is the protector of the most illustrious vineyards in France—those of Champagne. There are several conjectures why this 4th-century martyr should have been chosen, but one of the most common is that, as a deacon, he had the duty of pouring wine for the priest during Mass.

Another reason advanced is that the first three letters of his name spell the French word for wine—*vin*. At any rate, St. Vincent is honored with bunches of grapes and vine leaves placed on his statues and altars. In Anjou, on St. Vincent's Day, the village youths go from house to house early in the morning and decorate all the winegrowers' doors with laurel branches, and the winemakers are expected to give them wine.

SAINT VINCENT'S PROCESSIONS

In Auvergne a procession takes place early on the same day. The statue of St. Vincent is followed by a barrel, a basket, a pruning hook and a spade. As the procession advances, St. Vincent is gradually turned about on his litter, so that he seems to gaze at every vineyard in the district.

The Feast of St. Vincent at Charmes in Ardèche is a time of great excitement. A very long procession of decorated wagons and carts carries peasants in folk costume. Afterward, the peasants meet at a banquet and choose the president of their association for the following year.

Occasionally costume balls for charities are held at the Palace of Versailles. The entertainments and costumes at this ball were modeled on those of the court of Marie Antoinette, who frequently had elaborate masques and parties here.

Even though Carnival is for merry-making it is carefully organized. The various groups in Nice who parade in the front of the processions spend months designing and building their floats and making their costumes. The marchers in the front see where they are going by looking through the holes in the necks of their masks.

The deacon could keep his hat on in church, even during the prayers, like a king. And the women could hold meetings without the men. The bellringers sounded the peals during the festivities. No member was allowed to drink alone, and transgressors were punished by being made to abstain even when their fellows were drinking.

In certain circumstances, the bellringers had the duty of inspecting the houses of the six men, and if any of them was surprised drinking in private and alone he was punished. The host would offer drink to the inspectors and these visits often lasted till three in the morning. At the last house, the inspectors would be given bottles of wine and a dish of herrings—no doubt to stimulate their thirst.

Such customs give rise to rumors of orgies among the French peasants, and of these orgies being more or less tolerated by the Church. Such stories are not true. Naturally, there is a great deal of drinking done at the wine festivals, but the people know how to hold their drink. The Church, being aware of this, uses its influence to limit the merrymaking to exuberant fun and noise.

OTHER PATRON SAINTS

St. Brigid of Ireland, whose feast is on Feb. 1, is the patron of all peasants in many parts of Isère. She is also the particular patron of the winegrowers in the canton of Sassenage, as well as in Alsace. But the St. Brigid whom the peasants near Nice thank on Oct. 8 for a good harvest is the Swedish one.

St. Agatha, whose feast falls on Feb. 5, has been chosen as their patron by many winegrowers in mountain areas. In Savoy phrases such as "by St. Agatha, the hand to the pruning hook," may be heard. The following rhyme is from Vaulnaveys-le-Haut: *Sint-Aguèta, prin ta gouèta, é vai tailla ta vignolèta; se t'a fré u dé, retourna-te pour un mè.* (On St. Agatha's day, take your pruning hook and go to cut your vines; if your fingers get cold, go

In Burgundy the winegrowers carry bread in solemn procession to the church on their festival day. In Champagne the festivities on St. Vincent's day are very solemn, and on the eve of the feast the winegrowers attach the best bunches of grapes from the previous autumn to the saint's statue with ribbons of many colors. Two cannon shots are fired from little mounted cannon made by local workmen. (They are called the artillery of Hautvillers, from the name of the village on the Marne where the custom began in the 17th century.)

The next day a rod believed to have belonged to the saint is carried in procession and is followed by carts bearing pyramids of garlands and candy which are afterward distributed to the crowds. In the evening every winegrower holds a big dinner for his family, staff and workmen.

In other parts of Champagne races are held in which the runners wear masks. Barrels are carried around into which the villagers pour as much wine as they can. From them, everybody drinks together at the end of the day in the public square. It is easy to get drunk, for wines of different colors and qualities are mixed in the barrels and the brew has a very high alcoholic content.

In some cases it is not difficult to see how former sacred feasts have degenerated into profane ones. In Provins in the Seine-et-Marne Department in the 18th century the Confraternity of St. Vincent organized a "procession of Bacchus." The part of the pagan god was taken by a member of the Confraternity, seated on a barrel, crowned with vine leaves and bearing a cup of wine in one hand and a bottle in the other.

A wagon carried him through the streets and the people shouted: "Bacchus is not dead! He still lives! He still lives!" and "St. Vincent, drench us, drench us, drench us! St. Vincent, fill our mouths with wine!"

A COMPLICATED RITUAL

On Jan. 25 the conversion of St. Paul the Apostle is commemorated by the Church. This is a special day in some winegrowing regions. There used to be a Confraternity of St. Paul with a deacon, six men and six women, three musicians and an apprentice, who all carried out a closely regulated ritual.

Storks are considered to be lucky birds in eastern France, and farmers encourage them to nest on the rooftops. The stone post on the roof of this Alsatian farmhouse has no other purpose than to support a stork's nest.

back home for a month.)

St. Valentine (Feb. 14) helps the winegrowers only in the valley of Chambéry in Savoy, and in Maconnais. Though St. Vincent Ferrer has been declared a patron of vineyards his cult is not very widespread. St. George (April 23) has to divide the honor with several other saints: Pancras, Boniface, Mark, Philip, Maximin, Ferdinand and Petronilla.

However, St. George has sometimes been less than honored. Once when the vines in Thurissey in the Saône-et-Loire Department were struck by frost the peasants dragged his statue through the vineyards crying: "George, George, look what you've done to us!"

The story is told that the St. George of Mancey once invited the St. George of the neighboring village of Messey to come and taste wine with him, and got the latter so drunk that it took him seven hours to get back to his own church. In revenge, the St. George of Messey asked God to strike the vines at Mancey with frost.

When frost does injure the vines at Mancey the peasants drag the saint's statue around calling out to him to look at what he has brought upon them. When the vines escape frost they shout with joy: "Long live St. George! Our vines have not been frozen!" In other places, the peasants bathe the statue's feet with the best wine if the vines are not frozen, but use water when damage has been done.

The procession in honor of St. George held at Désertines near Montluçon deserves a visit for its outstanding picturesqueness. It is headed by viola and bagpipe players, who are followed by standard-bearers and peasants carrying vine leaves and tools, and then gardeners with bunches of flowers and bundles of vegetables. Next come statues of the Virgin and of St. George, each on the shoulders of four men. Then follows a paper dragon, made to move and writhe by a man inside it, and finally men disguised as horses.

MORE SAINTS OF WINEGROWERS

The Feast of St. John at the Latin Gate falls on May 6, and he has become a patron of winegrowers because of a play on his name. In French it is *Saint-Jean-Porte-Latine*, which is read as *Saint Jean Porte La Tine* (St. John Carry-Cask). A window in the cathedral in Auxerre does, in fact, depict him bearing a great white cask (or barrel) of wine on his shoulders. Saint-Vernier (May 20) is buried in the diocese of Trèves on the Rhine. He lost his position as a protector of the vines during the last century when so many vineyards were destroyed by the phylloxera disease. The same fate overtook St. Didier of Langres (May 23).

Whitsunday, which falls seven weeks after Easter, is the feast of prime importance in the countryside, and it used to be celebrated with processions in costume and various games. One of these was the Drunken Barrel game, the purpose of which was to sprinkle the bystanders with wine.

Certain other feasts, such as those of St. John the Baptist and St. Michael, are held in a purely religious spirit. St. John is called upon to protect the crops, while St. Michael protects the whole human race from the dangers of nature, especially from floods.

When the ancient world adopted Christianity, St. Michael displaced the gods of many pagan shrines and temples. In France he took over from Apollo and Mercury, and his cult remains strong there. In Aude, ox races are held on his feast day.

St. Michael's Day, Sept. 29, is the day for the flocks to come down from the high pastures of the Vosges, and at Valenciennes, on this date, a famous nut market is held, called *la Saint-Miche a gauques* (St. Michael of the nuts).

The time of grape gathering in France is marked by an atmosphere of great rejoicing. The laborers in the vineyards need to eat and drink well and to enjoy themselves, and therefore the four meals a day are very abundant and wine flows freely. Soup, meat, ham, cheese, sausages, omelettes and fried pastries are eaten in great quantities.

Everywhere, many young women take part in the work, and in the evening dancing lasts till midnight. The girls are subjected to practical jokes as are freshmen at universities. Such initiation ceremonies are very common in Alsace, where a glass of red grape juice is thrown over each girl; in other regions a bunch of black grapes is rubbed against her cheeks. Sometimes a young man will volunteer to repair the damage with a kiss.

Naturally in the excitement the game can become rather rough. Bunches of grapes are dropped inside the girls' dresses. Often they defend themselves and give as good as they get, and real battles between the sexes break out. Married women do not take part in these encounters.

In Yonne men and women dance the *farandole* in the streets and sing many songs. It can even happen that the verses of the *Magnificat* hymn are alternated with those of a popular song.

On the evening of the last day of the vintage great banquets are held. The wine is kept in a big tub in the middle of the table and continually filled. In Champagne the owners of the vineyards bring out their best white wines for the banquet.

HARVEST RITES

Eighteenth-century chroniclers tell curious stories of the rites connected with treading the grapes. In certain provinces there were special buildings equipped with presses for this purpose, called "houses of Bacchus," with a little statue of Bacchus in the center, to which the workmen bowed on entering. Anyone who refused to honor the god in this way was beaten or kicked. The punishment was decided upon by a court of Seven Sages, and read out by the eldest of them.

Everything in the house had a name in a special "bacchic jargon," and to this day in the Île-de-France a jargon is used at the wine harvest which some scholars believe to be descended from words used in Roman times. There is no certain proof of this, nor is there proof that modern vintage rites and festivals are directly derived from ancient sources. Hard work all day long in the vineyard under a hot sun and fresh new wine at night make people behave in the same way in any age and place.

When we see a modern wine festival our minds naturally go back to what we have heard of ancient

The immense cellars of the Pommery Greno in Reims hold vats of delicious, ripening champagne. France is the biggest wine-producing country in the world. Over one **billion** *gallons are made there each year.*

Bacchic orgies. According to the old chronicles "no kind of amusement is forbidden" and "young men and women tell each other bawdy stories and make spicy jokes that provoke roars of laughter."

Alsace is a rather strait-laced province, but even there many liberties are allowed. Youths and girls roughhouse, and the girls laugh heartily without blushing at stories which at other times they would leave the room rather than hear. But such customs have no real connection with Bacchic rites, in which there was far more license.

THE NOVEMBER FEASTS

The Feasts of All Saints and All Souls, which fall on Nov. 1 and 2, are very important to the French. Both feasts are given over to commemorating the dead, and, since the two recent wars, they have become very popular. Cemeteries that formerly were neglected are now often visited and decorated, and even people who are not Catholics observe the feasts in their own way. Flowers are also put on war memorials and the tombs of famous men, after the family grave has been visited.

In the country many prescriptions exist about what must or must not be done on All Souls' Day. There should be no washing; the earth must not be dug, no bread cooked, no journeys made and the house must not be left after dark. Amusements and noise are forbidden, and in some places it is also forbidden to sweep the house out, yoke oxen, take flocks to pasture, or leave the horses in the fields.

In these matters sailors are more superstitious than peasants. No seaman from Dieppe would dream of embarking on All Souls' Day, for his shadow, a real double, would follow him wherever he sailed. It is also important not to fish, for the nets will only bring up broken bones of drowned sailors, which rise from the ocean floor on this day of memories.

It is said in Roussillon that dead men's heads have been taken from the sea on that day, and a fisherman at Toulon is reported to have brought a head with flaming eyes and gnashing teeth aboard. At Menton such a dead man's head, it is said, harshly rebuked the fisherman for working.

St. Martin's Day, Nov. 11, is another important feast. In the past, fireworks were set off in his honor, with a special purpose. This was to

The judges of the harvest in the eastern town of Riquewihr prepare to render a decision on the best grapes of the harvest. Ceremonies honoring the wine harvest are as old as the cultivation of the grape itself, but the rites in Riquewihr only go back four or five hundred years.

"warm St. Martin's feet," for, according to the legend, he stripped himself in order to clothe the poor, and gave half his cloak to a beggar in the snow. He was not yet a Christian when he did this, but his good deed provided the grace that made him one.

Precisely because of his exceptional merits and his humble heroism, the French are particularly devoted to St. Martin, and over the centuries have dedicated thousands of churches to him. His feast is the date for the beginning or ending of labor contracts, as well as the occasion of interesting customs.

On the coast of Flanders, boys under the age of seven carry around lanterns made of coconuts and pumpkins on the night of Nov. 11 and blow horns, trumpets and seashells. In Dunkirk they drag heavy chains through the streets, while wearing their parents' shoes. The parents take part in the conclusion of the festival at eight o'clock at night, when they suddenly turn off all lights.

St. Martin's festival is the day for new wine, and the first chills of the coming winter are driven away by the bubbling wines of the recent harvest. The peasants derived excessive comfort from this custom, even in remote times—as the Synod of Auxerre noticed in 578, when it severely forbade such drinking. But not all parish priests followed its directions, and many of them participated in the St. Martin's wine festival when it did not go to outrageous lengths.

CHRISTMAS AND TWELFTH NIGHT

In France Christmas is not celebrated in the same intimate fashion as in other countries, and some aspects of the French way of keeping the feast seem to be in contrast with its religious character. But the French really have deep feeling for Christmas, and this feeling is shared by believers and nonbelievers alike. All love the happy atmosphere with its snow scenes, roaring fires, crèches in the churches, long Christmas parties and Christmas trees.

The feast is extended to Twelfth Night (Jan. 6, the Feast of the

Epiphany) in most parts of the country, and in some places for an even longer time. In the region of Périgueux it actually lasts from the feast of St. Catherine (Nov. 25) until Epiphany. In Alsace the festive period begins on St. Andrew's Day (Nov. 30) and also lasts until Jan. 6.

In French Catalonia, at the eastern end of the Pyrenees, it falls between the same dates as on the Spanish side of the frontier: Dec. 13 to Epiphany. In the regions of Nevers and Metz the time runs from Dec. 25 till the end of the year, and is called the period between the two Christmases: the birth of Christ and the birth of the New Year.

Advent, the preparatory period of four weeks before Christmas, is observed in much the same way as in the rest of the Catholic world. However, numerous strange popular beliefs are associated with it. For instance, it is considered inadvisable to get married during Advent.

In Menton the following rhyme is sung: *Se marier en Avent aura grand mécontent* (He who marries in Advent will be very discontented). In Limousin pregnant women are warned not to enter empty streets for fear of misfortunes. Also, werewolves are believed to be particularly active at this time.

CHRISTMAS FIGURES

The period between Christmas and Twelfth Night is marked by the appearance of certain traditional figures of special interest to children, for, as La Monnoye remarks, "children need everything to be personified for them." Some outstanding figures are St. Martin, St. Nicholas, Father Christmas, *Père Chalande*, the Child Jesus, the New Year, Father January, the Virgin, *Tante Arie*, the *Chauchevieille*, the *Guillaneau*, and the Old Year.

In French Catalonia the children are told that St. Martin, the doer of good deeds, passes by in the night riding a donkey. He leaves dried chestnuts and fruit on the windowsills and thresholds for good boys and girls, while the lazy and disobedient get ashes and charcoal.

Though the French regard St. Martin highly, St. Nicholas is actually more popular. The reason seems to be that, while it is still possible to work in the fields on St. Martin's Day (Nov. 11), by St. Nicholas' Day (Dec. 6), snow has already fallen over a great part of France, and the people have more time to devote to festivities and to home life.

Consequently, St. Nicholas' Day is a simple home festival, which generally starts with the making and eating of candy. In Picardy dainties are given to the children by hiding them in their shoes, clogs or stockings. The children say a little prayer: "St. Nicholas, my patron, bring me something good; fill the shoes and stockings; St. Nicholas, I will be grateful to you." They also get hay and carrots ready for the Saint's donkey and leave them in the chimney.

St. Nicholas is the chief patron of Lorraine, where he is represented together with an assistant, *Père Fouettard* (Father Whip), who punishes bad children. In Metz men dressed as St. Nicholas go from door to door asking the children how they have behaved during the year and giving them little rewards or penalties.

Recently, St. Nicholas has been known to arrive in some towns of the region by airplane. In Alsace he passes through the streets followed by a man disguised as a donkey. The children are expected to pray as he goes by. If they do not, the donkey carries them off, but after a time they are returned to their parents.

FATHER CHRISTMAS

In some regions St. Nicholas has been replaced by the secular figure of Father Christmas. In France he is regarded as a Protestant invention, but he has now been accepted in Catholic circles. *Père Chalande* is a provincial version of Father Christmas, especially in parts of Savoy.

The figure of the Child Jesus is venerated in all Catholic countries, but he has somewhat different characteristics in the different nations. In Alsace he appears in the guise of a boy or youth who goes from village to village distributing gifts to the children and dancing to amuse them. Elsewhere he is a baby dressed in white who comes to visit good children.

The child who takes the part of the Child Jesus is usually attended by others of his own age. These attendants carry bags of straw to represent the donkey who distributes rewards and punishments. In Lorraine the part is taken by a girl, whose little brothers may sometimes recognize her in spite of her wig and flowing white cloak.

The New Year has also been personified, and is represented on postcards, calendars and posters as a small, smiling, naked—or partly clad—child. In some parts of the countryside he is believed to throw candy down the chimney for the children.

Father January is not celebrated in many places, but on the left bank of the Saône he is honored under the name of *Parrain Zeugni*. Almost everywhere else he has been replaced by Father Christmas, or *Père Noël*, no doubt through a desire to increase the importance of Christmas in children's eyes.

CHRISTMAS SONGS

On the isle of Oleron the children go from door to door at Christmas

In addition to the wine-judging contest, the villagers of Riquewihr celebrate the grape harvest by drawing a decorated wagon through town, offering passersby as much wine as they care to drink. Traminer, a white wine, is one of the wines offered.

time and ask: "Do you want us to wish you a happy New Year?" If the reply is favorable they recite in chorus: "We wish you a happy New Year, perfect health, and at the end of your life Paradise for you and your family."

Then they ask: "Do you want music?" If another positive answer is given they reply with an uproarious outburst of trumpets, trombones and drums. They perform a wild dance and sing comic verses. The money collected is used for festivities, which end with balls, practical jokes—and betrothals.

The really admirable thing about these Christmas customs is the patience with which the children wait outside the doors for the householders to give them money or food. The groups are capable of waiting for a whole morning, monotonously repeating the same verses: "Search your pockets, search them to the bottom; give us money and we shall go away and leave you in peace." They will go on until the victims surrender.

In spite of the long waits, smiles never leave the lips of the youths, and the miserly householders listening also smile, but without taking the smallest coin from their pockets.

The song used by the children in Brittany is a solemn one, almost a hymn: "A cry of joy in honor of the mother, father and children in the house; may the children breathe in health, and may your daughters have the odor of lavender. We wish you a year of abundant fresh dews, oats

Above: The people of Obernai in Alsace re-enact the marriage of Fritz Kobus, the hero of a 19th-century novel, Friend Fritz, *written by two Alsatian writers, Emile Erckmann and Alexandre Chatrian. Fritz, a great lover of good food and drink, a quick wit and a generous, good-hearted friend, has become a kind of folk hero in Alsace.*

Right: In the novel, which was later made into an opera by Pietro Mascagni, Fritz bets that he will never give up his carefree bachelor existence and marry. Such bets are always made to be lost, and this one is no exception. One day soon after, Fritz goes to his farm, where he is served a delicious morsel prepared by Susanna, the lovely young daughter of his tenant. When Fritz learns that Susanna, who secretly loves him, is to be married to someone she dislikes, he goodnaturedly offers himself as a replacement and marries the girl. The wedding is celebrated with a splendid procession and ends in an enormous feast, well suited to please a gourmet like Fritz.

FRANCE · *The People* / 139

and wheat. When the month of May comes may good hemp grow in your courtyard. We wish you flowers in May, grain in June, and white grapes in July." Everywhere these excursions are carried out with great discretion and tact, in keeping with the peaceful spirit of Christmas.

"May we sing a Christmas song?" they ask in Morbihan. If the answer is in the affirmative, they begin: "Let us sing of Christmas, my good lady, let us sing of Christmas; you and I, for an apple, for a pear, for a glass of wine, let us sing of Christmas...."

BATTLES IN GASCONY

In Gascony, where everything is carried to extremes, these quests for money are marked by joyous merrymaking. There are many groups, each led by one of the boldest of the village youths. When the bands meet, furious battles are fought with sticks and stones. Then there is a general reconciliation and all drink together.

These Gascons have their own carol, which, naturally, is less refined than the others we have mentioned: "As Christmas approaches/ here we are outside your house./ Listen to our good wishes/ that your donkeys work harder/ and that God gives you as many daughters as you have pleats in your skirts, woman!"

In Pernes-en-Artois beggars go through the town in a procession, carrying a great star made of gilded paper and repeating the following verses to attract the charity of the bystanders: "We have covered three hundred leagues./ We have found Jesus./ Angels were singing Alleluia./ But the Star,/ No the Star did not come to rest above us!"

In the Pyrenees men wearing bearskins lead the bands of children on their quests. In the Alps pipers and bagpipers go from village to village to beg. In general it may be said that all over the country the customs and traditions help to get the people into a spiritual state of waiting and hope. This is the only way in which the mystical meaning of Christmas may be understood.

Tante Arie or *Tantairie* (Aunt Air) is thought to have been the last of the Druid priestesses, who fled to the mountains of Lomont. There she became a beneficent fairy or sorceress who aids young shepherds. However, we find her as a distributor of Christmas gifts only in the late 19th century in the Jura and the valley of the Ajoie.

Her name seems to refer to her ability to travel through the sky. She is described as having a sweet breath, very strong teeth, and a goose's feet. Tante Arie is represented either as a good housewife who spins, bakes bread and washes clothes, or as a fairy who comes riding on a donkey to help good children. It is said that she wears a crown of diamonds and that she has a chest full of gold at the back of her cave.

She does not confine her gifts to children, for she rewards good maidens by finding excellent husbands for them and giving them a purse full of gold at their wedding. However, she is also very much feared. She is used to frighten bad children, and sometimes she curses a house and sets it on fire. She is thus a very interesting and significant mythological figure.

WITCHES AND FAIRIES

Even more fearful figures are the *Trotte-vieilles*. These are old witches who pierce with their horns children who cry too much. The *Chauchevieilles* or *Chauchepailles* of the Jura region are similar figures. Their name derives from *cauchemar* (nightmare).

Another mysterious figure is *Le Guillaneu*. The word is often heard at the beginning of questers' carols, and is a little like the Alleluia of Christmas hymns. Some are of the opinion that it is the term for a little donkey or gray or white horse. Van Gennep, however, the author of a monumental work on French folklore, believes that it refers to the table on which the gifts are placed.

There are many stories concerning fairies, who are known as the White Ladies, the Good Ladies, or Christ-

The folk costumes of the region have a distinctly German flavor. The hats are black, and the white lace is restricted to the aprons. These women marching in a religious procession are from a small town near Strasbourg.

On feast days in towns along the Rhine, on the extreme eastern border of France, the houses are strung with lights, flowers, flags and boughs of green leaves.

often blessed before being put on the fire, and there are even some families who kneel down around it to pray, as if before a sacred image.

THE ORIGIN OF THE YULE LOG

This misplaced devotion is very revealing, and explains the Church's concern about the spread of figures such as Father Christmas in modern times. The true Christian significance of the feast cannot mean very much to people who prostrate themselves before the log and worship it. In some parts the feast is not called Christmas, but "Log-tide."

There can hardly be any doubt about the pagan origin of this rite, especially since we know that oaks were sacred to the ancient Gauls. Today, a Christian meaning is given to it, and the oak or fruit-tree log is christened by the head of the household. He pours a cup of wine over it, saying: "In the name of the Father, of the Son and of the Holy Ghost," and adds a pinch of salt and sometimes holy water.

In Charente, when the log has been baptized in this way, a chair covered with fine linen is placed before it for the Virgin to sit on, so that while the whole family is away at Midnight Mass the log will not be left alone. Often a member of the family is left to guard it but it is not clear whether the imagined danger is thieves, or witches and their spells.

MIDNIGHT MASS

The final moment in all the ceremonies of Christmas Eve comes when all solemnly recite the *Gloria* together in church. The coming of the Redeemer is proclaimed by tolling the bells, ringing handbells, lighting all the candles on the altars, burning incense and unveiling pictures and statues of the Child Jesus. Then everyone leaves the church and exchanges Christmas greetings in the churchyard and the square. Lanterns are lit, vehicles move off, and the people return to their houses, to find them well warmed by the Yule Log. They go to bed in peace in order to be ready to rise early in the morning and prepare the dinner, which is the main business of Christmas Day itself.

mas Fairies in various localities. A lesser figure is called the Daughter of the Lord of the Christmas Gifts, Berthe the Spinner, and is of German origin.

Most French people like to spend Christmas Eve and Christmas Day in their own homes. But in some regions, especially mountainous ones, ancient customs probably deriving from the pagan rites of the first inhabitants of Gaul are still observed. Bonfires are lit, and fireworks are set off.

The youths of the villages carry torches and firebrands and spend the eve of Christmas around the fires on the hilltops, dancing ritually and singing and celebrating noisily. This kind of collective celebration is more often to be found during the Feast of the Three Kings (Epiphany, Jan. 6), which will be discussed later.

As for the Yule Log, in Alsace the log is usually placed on the fire before the family goes to Midnight Mass, so that the room will be properly warm when they return. Many Alsatians believe that the purpose of this custom is to warm the Child Jesus when He comes into the world. In Charente the log is sometimes a huge oak one, about thirteen feet long. It is cut down for this purpose, dragged into the house, and made to last for many days.

Usually, it burns from Christmas Eve until Jan. 6, and so that it may last that long, it is extinguished at night and dragged outside to avoid filling the house with smoke. It is

The people of the Camargue, a marshy island in the mouth of the Rhone River, celebrate the Festival of St. Sarah with a ceremony blessing the sea. Since many of the island's inhabitants raise cattle, the saint's day is also the occasion for the "tournament of lances," in which French cowboys show off their skills against bulls in an arena. The event is something of a cross between a bullfight and a Wild West rodeo. The mounted man in the center is carrying a lance used in this tournament. The head of the lance has three prongs and is used to fend off the bull if the cowboy falls off his horse.

CHRISTMAS SOCIAL CUSTOMS

The peasants are usually very punctual and regular at their meals, but on this day they sit down later than usual and prolong the meal until the late afternoon or evening. There is much conversation, and many songs, toasts, recitations and performances. Christmas legends are told to the children. At Easter many prefer to eat their dinner away from home, or to go on a picnic. But Christmas is a time of family reunions, and many members of the family may travel long distances to be there.

Christmas is a time for visiting one's parents and relatives, and for discussing family business and deciding on future work. It also gives the people an opportunity to offer condolences and consolations and enjoy the company of favorite rela-

To be a cowboy is the dream of every small boy on the Camargue. The cowboy, who is called the gardien, *or guardian of the herd, must be a crack rider. The bulls raised on the Camargue are featured in the bloodless bullfights of Portugal and France.*

tives. St. Stephen's Day, the day after Christmas, is the best time for this, however, and it is the occasion for another banquet. At Christmas time there are no special dishes, except for turkey and chicken, which are common Sunday foods in any case. Not only is the sign of the Cross made before the meal starts, but the head of the family may also give his blessing, or sometimes make a speech. The children usually receive delicacies and candy, but if they do not, they know these will come at Epiphany, the feast of the Three Kings.

THE FEAST OF THE THREE KINGS

At Epiphany the children sing hymns about the star which appeared to the Three Wise Men and led them to Bethlehem. The feast, which falls on Jan. 6, commemorates the arrival of the Three Kings there. The children sing the hymns for the same reason that they went from house to house singing carols at Christmas—to obtain gifts and money to spend on their feast. The Church takes a direct part in the customs of Epiphany, especially the children's songs and caroling. Once the songs of the Star of Bethlehem were organized by the bishop himself in a village in Saverne, in order to aid three poor students, who were sent around impersonating the Three Kings. Throughout the country, mothers are anxious to obtain this honor for their sons. Each of the kings is clothed in a tunic of red velvet with an ermine border, and wears a gift crown.

In Burgundy, when the kings go on their rounds collecting, they subject the people to what is almost a complete examination of conscience. They ask: "Have you warmed the poor?/ Have you clothed the naked?/ Have you given alms?" The second stanza of the song gives a negative response: "I have not warmed the poor/ nor clothed the naked/ nor given alms./ Therefore I am like a tree that bears no fruit." The people who hear these appeals to their conscience naturally get the meaning, and in the end make a contribution to the questioners, if only to silence them. The first gift offered to the kings is a slice of the Epiphany cake, which is called "God's share." The head of the household cuts this slice with his own hands before seating himself at the table. The following verses explain this ceremony better than any other description: "I come from a strange country/ and have come to this place/ to ask God's share/ from him who has enough to eat./ Get your knife and fork ready/ to give us a slice/ of your cake...."

CARNIVAL

The importance of Carnival derived from the fact that it was the last period of enjoyment before Lent, but today Carnival celebrations have become almost completely secularized and rather vulgar. However, there are celebrations which are still associated with religion and which are interesting from the point of view of folklore.

Years ago, Carnival was a time of widespread masquerading, but the taste for it has declined. People used to dress up as kings, queens or pages. Men wore women's dress, and women men's—and begged alms, in the form of money, cakes, sweets, food and wine.

Hymns were often sung during these excursions. In Champagne the children sang the hymn *Inviolata* on the Tuesday and Thursday of Holy Week in honor of the Virgin. In Bresse, Ille-et-Vilaine and Nice famous collective masquerades took place, and these have become the modern processions of floats. Masquerade horses, made by covering with a sheet and a false head several youths holding a ladder on their shoulders, ran among the crowd and caused a great deal of excitement.

The masquerade animal is a feature of Carnival processions all over the

The Feast of St. Sarah is observed not only by the gardiens, but also by gypsies who come to the Camargue every year to honor St. Sarah, whom they revere as their patron saint. Gypsies always form part of the procession that brings the saint's statue down to the shore for the blessing of the sea.

world, under various names. In Normandy it is known as the "mad horse," and in Provence it is the "horse with a skirt." In Vallespir a bear is represented instead of a horse.

In Arles-sur-Tech an orchestra plays in the main square for the people to dance. Then appears the *Rosetta*—a man dressed as a woman, with a painted face, long hair and a very tight dress. In the afternoon of the same day the *Rosetta* is carried away by the bear, but the beast is soon captured and brought back to the town. As the procession returns, the bear makes an occasional rush into the crowd or throws himself upon Rosetta. The bear is then imprisoned in a cage. In the end he dies, during a final attempt to seize Rosetta. He revives, however, in time to attend the concluding banquet as the guest of honor.

At Prats-de-Mollo, in the Pyrenees, there are five or six bears. The men who play the part of the animals put on bear hides and then approach the town. As soon as they are seen coming the women flee and the men bring out their guns. The bears advance, brandishing big clubs, and the men fire—with blanks, of course.

If a gun goes off the bear at whom it is aimed must fall dead. If it fails to fire the hunter must take to his heels: for the bear is entitled to give him a tremendous blow on the legs with his club, which would fell him and cause him a great deal of pain. If unarmed men do not keep their distance they are attacked by the bears, and women are brutally manhandled if they remain in the street.

THE BURNING OF CARNIVAL

Carnival time in French Catalonia is also very exciting. Elsewhere, people are content to conduct battles with confetti, grain and mustard seed; but the celebrated battles held at Nice pale before those which used to be fought at Perpignan, Moulins, Nantes, Pau and Bayonne.

Races, masquerades, dances and parties all ended with the death, by burning, of the Carnival, which was represented by a giant figure or costumed man. Everywhere in France the role of Carnival used to be taken by a man dressed in straw with a painted face.

Carnival is set on fire at the end of the celebrations, but, since it is not now customary to burn men alive, a papier-mâché figure is used. It makes a fine blaze, and the crowd

According to legend, St. Sarah the Black landed in the Camargue in the company of St. Mary Jacob and St. Mary Salomé after being shipwrecked in a storm on the Mediterranean. During the festival of St. Sarah, the two other saints are also honored. Their statues, standing in a small boat, are carried to the sea.

cries out: "Carnival is dead! Carnival is dead!" In Lorraine, until 1914, a real man was set aflame. The fire was immediately put out with blankets and sand, but the man often received bad burns, and the police finally abolished the custom. It is a common custom in France to leap over the burning remains of the figure of Carnival. This is said to be a quick means for girls to find husbands.

In the countryside of the North, burning wooden disks are hurled into the air. This custom appears to be a survival of ancient sun-worshipping rites. The wheels are stuffed with straw, set alight, and sent careening down hillsides by the peasants during Lent. By the length of time the wheels continue to run downhill the peasants foretell what the next harvest will be like.

Almost all Lenten observances are associated with fire. Often, fanciful ones were invented to satisfy the peasants' passion for fire, and their desire to see it burning, moving and turning. From the Middle Ages down to the 19th century, children made torches from branches of trees by dipping them in oil and pitch, and set fire to sheaves of straw. They carried these about while singing songs of good omen for the vines, the crops, sweethearts and wives. They danced about madly, holding flaming poles in order to exterminate harmful insects and weeds.

At a certain stage it became necessary to impose restrictions on these celebrations, because houses, barns and crops often caught fire. The prohibitions, together with the peasants' own good sense, led the custom to die out in the last century.

THE CARNIVAL IN NICE

The Carnival festivities transport us for a short while into an unreal world of fantasies and folk memories. Carnival is celebrated all over France. But that at Nice has acquired great fame, because characteristics derived

Children who are too young to go out on the marshy beach for the blessing of the sea are brought to the crypt of the church to kiss the saint's statue.

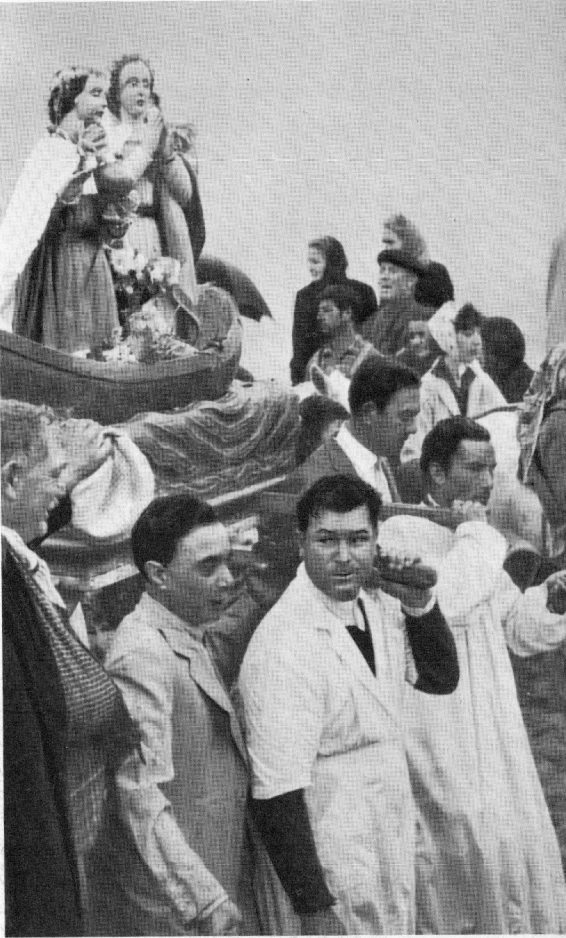

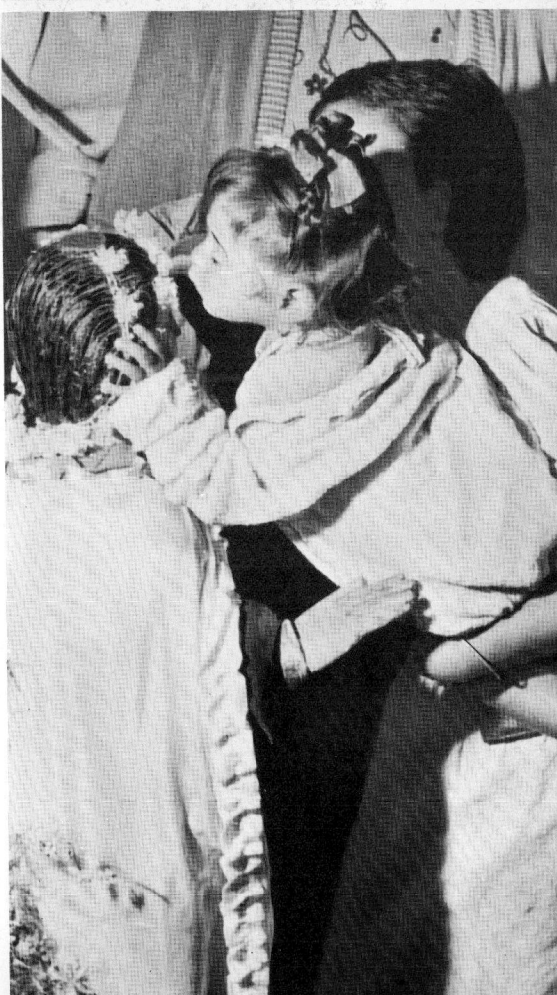

from international society have been added to its spirit of gay and careless abandon.

When Nice became a favorite resort for rich English people, the inhabitants of the city did not hesitate to commercialize their festival. They saw that it could serve to lengthen the winter season into the spring and summer, and in this way be of great benefit to hotel owners and shopkeepers. English people took to the idea, and thirty and forty years ago, during Carnival, they thronged the streets and the sea front in their cars, moving about among the floats, hurling confetti, candy and even small coins at the crowd.

In the evening big hotels, such as the Negresco, gave balls, and rivers of champagne flowed. Foreigners took part, wearing the most grotesque costumes, and naturally a very unusual atmosphere was created. The spirit was one of extraordinary freedom.

The floats are made by local craftsmen with exceptional skill and invention. The long lines of humorous, satirical, allegorical and gigantic figures are extremely interesting and diverting. And the public enthusiastically joins in the fun as the figures pass by.

Nevertheless, the Carnival at Nice has now lost its most attractive quality—international luxury and elegance. Russian princes no longer ride in *landaus* along the promenades; few English lords pass grandly and silently by in their Rolls Royces. Candy and money are no longer the weapons of the street battles—only confetti is used—and orange drinks have been added to the champagne served during the revels.

Races and parties are held everywhere in France at this period, but they generally have no particularly distinctive characteristics from the point of view of folklore. The Carnival itself, however, is a genuine expression of the popular spirit, and the various ways in which it is celebrated reflect more than anything else a desire for complete liberty of spirit.

CARNIVAL DANCES

An essential element in all Carnival festivities is dancing. French country dances have the complicated structure of a ballet. They are performed by large groups of both sexes in full folk costume. Students of folklore take particular interest in the *farandole*, comic dances, shepherds' dances, garter dances, cord dances, sword dances, spinners' dances and the very widely spread Moorish dance. Many of these still flourish, especially along the German frontier, and they are also to be found in the Paris region.

In the Pyrenees the girls of the village invite the men to dance on Ash Wednesday. But the invitation is refused because the time of penance has already begun.

There are numerous prohibitions in connection with Carnival and Lent. Weddings may not take place on Shrove Tuesday, nor may work be done during the Carnival time. Spinning, sewing, and baking are forbidden on Shrove Tuesday. Clothes may not be washed during the whole of Lent.

The significance of these three important periods of the year—Carnival, Lent and Easter—will not have escaped the reader. They represent the force of instinctive joy,

At the feast of St. Sarah, in the Camargue, gypsy women wait their turn to receive holy water blessed in the ceremony at the seashore.

During their wanderings, gypsies rarely have the time to fuss about laundry. But when the caravan stops to rest near fresh water, the women can catch up on the family wash. Bands of gypsies came to Paris in the 15th century and have been roving about the French countryside ever since.

Choir boys of the monastery of En Calcat wait in line to enter the stall of the chapel. The early Romanesque cloister has been in use for centuries.

its mortification or subjection, and its rebirth in a nobler form. The religious meaning of the cycle is clear, and that this is well understood by the Church is shown by the fact that she has never made any attempt to abolish or reduce the Carnival festivities. It is noticeable that the instinctive joy of Carnival is almost boundless, but the mortification of Lent is strictly limited.

EASTER CUSTOMS

Lent, the beginning of the process of Redemption, is the period of preparation for Easter. Although the prevailing spirit is of sorrow and repentance, the signs of the approaching burst of glory can be seen already.

Holy Week is called Great Week in Franche-Comté, Black Week in Limousin, and Sorrowful Week in Boulonnais. For the Church it is a period of great mourning and penance for sin. The sadness is heightened by the knowledge of the joy of the coming Resurrection and also by the brief day of light and glory preceding it, on Palm Sunday. On this day Christ gave one final indication of His mastery and His kingship.

The usual custom in the Church is to bless palm fronds or olive branches on Palm Sunday, but in France twigs of boxwood are frequently used. In Brittany, Gironde, Landes, and the Basque country, laurel is used. In some parts of Creuse juniper is blessed and in Roussillon olive branches are intertwined with those of the palm. In Lorraine holly is used, but the Church officially prefers palm where it is obtainable.

In the past candy and other objects were tied to these branches on Palm Sunday. This custom has almost disappeared, except as a means of rewarding children. In this case, boxwood and laurel are preferred to palms.

Palm Sunday is still dramatized in remoter country districts. In Chalosse the peasants bring whole laurel trees into church to be blessed, and then lock them up in their houses. The twigs are distributed on Holy Saturday, and are hung in every conceivable place—the cowstall, the poultry run, the stables—anywhere in fact where there are living things.

In the Meuse region and in Picardy blessed palm or laurel branches are placed on the family tomb, and fishermen throw branches into the sea for their drowned relatives or friends. In all regions blessed twigs are planted in the fields, and are often stuck onto hats, harness and yokes—a custom that seems to be for protection against lightning.

Church bells are silent from Holy Thursday until Holy Saturday at midnight because the churches are in mourning. The statues and pictures are veiled in purple, so there is little scope for popular customs based on church ceremonies. However, it is interesting to note that until recently some peasants and the children believed that all the church bells left France and paid a visit to Rome during this period of silence.

During the Office of Tenebrae and the other services of these three days clappers are used instead of bells, or a board is beaten with a stick. In some dioceses a mallet or a rattle is used. At one point in the Office of Tenebrae the congregation beats on the benches with their hands and stamps on the floor. This is done to represent the earthquake accompanying the death of Christ.

EASTER BLESSINGS

There is a custom of blessing children during Holy Week. This is done by the priest, who goes about from house to house, where the children await him on their knees. In the country, however, the children go to church, and offer eggs to the priest and the sacristan before being blessed.

On Holy Saturday, water, bread, eggs and sometimes the fire are blessed. In many peasant houses the holy water is kept in special vessels for use during various rites throughout the year. The vessels are emptied on Holy Saturday to receive fresh holy water. Usually, it is carried home from the church; but sometimes it is brought around, and the carrier then gets a small gift, such as an egg, for his services from each housewife.

In Franche-Comté the priests adopt the practical course of blessing all springs and fountains in the village during Holy Week, and so all the water used in the place for the rest of the year will be blessed. But in the Bouches-du-Rhône Department, in Toulon and in the county of Nice, this procedure would be superfluous, because it is believed that the first peals of the bells on Holy Saturday automatically bless all springs and fountains. In these regions women and children may be seen flocking to get water from the springs in all kinds of vessels, and washing in it as soon as possible after the bells ring.

THE PASSION OF BURZET

During Easter Week, passion plays depicting the crucifixion of Christ are performed in parts of France. The most notable one is that in Burzet in Ardèche. It is a very realistic play. Christ carries an extremely heavy cross. He is escorted by Roman soldiers and He is accompanied on His walk by Simon and His mother. The Way of the Cross is very difficult and steep, leading from the church in Burzet to a Calvary more than two thousand feet above it. All the actors are inhabitants of the town. Although the play is realistic, it is not always historically accurate. The Roman soldiers wear firemen's helmets, and their banner is the French tricolor.

Some Holy Week processions have gone out of existence in recent times because they became too realistic, while others have been transformed

The cathedral of Chartres, at the far end of the road, is the destination of these students, who have traveled the road from Paris on foot. The cathedral, which was built between 1145 and 1260 on the remains of a ruined Romanesque church, is famous for its stained glass windows, which have survived the centuries almost without replacement, and for the more than 8000 pieces of sculpture that adorn it.

into theatrical spectacles. In the Pyrenees an unusual kind exists, which are known as "mysteries." The parts are taken by carved wooden figures, which often have a terrifying appearance. The Church ignores this kind of performance, and intervenes only to stop excesses.

EASTER EGGS

Formerly, the Church strictly forbade the eating of eggs during Lent. Consequently, when Easter came there were eggs in abundance. The housewives used as many as they could for the Easter dinner, but they also gave many to children, and painted them to make them more acceptable. The custom of giving Easter eggs as gifts was begun at Court. Until the Revolution the king had the right to the biggest egg laid in France during Holy Week. This Easter egg was offered to the king in a grand ceremony in which many dignitaries took part. Many speeches and grandiloquent greetings were made.

It is notable that there was great disproportion between the importance of the feast and that of the gift, and it became necessary to invent something more spectacular. Since at the Court of France all things were possible, decorated eggs were first introduced, then porcelain or silver ones, and even golden ones, with the real egg inside. Finally, the real egg was replaced by a sugar or chocolate one. The aristocracy imitated the king, and the middle class imitated the aristocracy. The Revolution put an end to this and to many other similar extravagances, but when the Restoration came the middle class still had their chocolate and sugar eggs.

A very picturesque ceremony is the Festival of the Lances at Champagne in the Sarthe area. It was interrupted after three centuries during the German occupation in the last war, but was resumed in 1946. It commemorates the treachery of Judas. A great crucifix is carried in procession by peasant riders all armed with lances. Judas walks behind them, with a purse in his hand and a long black staff. He must bow down before the crucifix and accept the famous thirty pieces of silver. When he has done this he mounts a horse and follows the guards to the church.

EASTER DIVERSIONS

Other Easter diversions are walks, picnics and excursions. These are enjoyed everywhere without any particular religious object in view. In some places the pleasure of taking a trip is combined with fulfilling a religious duty, such as a visit to some shrine, cross, spring or grotto.

The people of the Nièvre region all go together to the miraculous springs of Faubouloin. Those from some villages of Île-de-France and Brie go to Sainte-Aubierge, where they sing and dance. Very often a meal is eaten in the open air. It may consist mainly of boiled eggs, but can also include roast lamb, goose and turkey. Because the weather is usually so fine and beautiful, the Easter dinner has many different forms, unlike Christmas dinner.

There are innumerable kinds of Easter cakes, and every French town has its own specialty. In Savoy a "golden soup" is eaten. It is made with slices of white bread soaked in milk and beaten eggs and browned in oil. In Alsace and Lorraine a soup containing nine different herbs is made, and many kinds of omelettes are eaten.

Excursions and picnics occur mostly on Easter Monday, called "The Angels' Day." On Tuesday work and ordinary social life begin again, to go on till the end of the Paschal season on Low Sunday, the one after Easter Sunday. This is also known as Quasimodo Sunday, because of the first words of the Mass on that day. And the diversions of Easter Monday are repeated.

WHITSUN GAMES

The games played on Pentecost, or Whitsunday—the seventh Sunday after Easter—were entirely different entertainments. The first one, the Rope Game, was surprisingly infantile. It consisted of taking ropes into the ranks of a procession and striking at the participants' legs.

The Pumpkin Game was a little more spirited. A pumpkin filled with wine was offered to passers-by. When a person accepted, and came up to the pumpkin to drink, he found it empty, and the wine ran down his shirt, through a hole in the bottom, from which a cork had been pulled. In the game of the Drunken Barrel, the barrel was raised to the top of two poles by two peasants, who pretended to be drunk, and sprinkled as many people as possible by shaking the barrel. The game resulted in a great deal of merriment.

The Sturgeon Game took place in the Rhone area. Boatmen took a little boat filled with water through the town on a wagon and splashed everybody they could reach as they went along. It is said the spectators were often subjected to absolute floods of water, but seemed to enjoy it. The women watching from the balconies were also drenched by jets of water. In the Gardeners' Game young men threw spinach and carrot seeds over the girls, and at a later period flowers were thrown and water squirted from hoses.

In the St. Christopher's Game a man with a long beard and a long pointed staff went about carrying a child. He tried to prick with the point of the staff anyone in the crowd whose legs were bare. In the Shepherds' Game three very beautiful children were carried about on a donkey, and escorted by a group of shepherds, each of whom had a jar of juniper oil. When anyone came closer to admire the children the shepherds drew moustaches or some other humorous marks on his face with the oil.

BRANDING DAY

A barbaric but very colorful festival is the so-called *ferrade* or Branding Day. In France branding the cattle has kept its old traditions and customs. These festivals, somewhat similar to rodeos in the United States, take place in enclosures like arenas, which may be permanent or temporary. The functions attract crowds of sightseers. Wagons, carts, cars and trucks arrive early in the morning, and horsemen armed with tridents—three-pronged spears—gather about the yard. The vehicles are all decorated with streamers and banners, and everything is full of color and movement. These trucks and wagons provide the seats for the spectators when the ring is only a temporary one.

On one side of the arena a big fire is lit and the branding irons are placed in it. Then the beasts are driven into the arena with the tridents and with shouts. They rush in, overturning anything in their way, leaping, butting and kicking, for they are untamed animals that up to this time have lived in the wild state. Instinctively they know that something unpleasant awaits them. The rest of the day is occupied with the business of branding. The cowmen have the chance to show their skill by tackling the wildest animals and bringing them down, or even riding them, to the delight of the crowd.

SHEPHERDS AND THEIR FLOCKS

THE WORLD OF SHEPHERDS IS A silent, mysterious and closed one—almost incomprehensible to outsiders—for the people belonging to it are accustomed to living in complete accord with the slow rhythm of nature. They live in a world of vast silences. They have deep faith and religious spirit, existing, as they do, close to the very sources of nature where it is easy for religion to be experienced. The life of the nomads is filled with the sense of the presence of the divine, even though this sense may be largely unconscious or directed to more than one god.

Arnold van Gennep, the folklorist, remarks that this religious sense began to decline from the moment that the first shepherd used a bicycle to drive his flock to a barbed-wire enclosure and leave them alone there all day, until the evening, when he returned to get them on his bicycle—or perhaps even on a motorcycle. This may be true to a certain extent. The pastoral life is gradually dying out in France, and in some regions the shepherds have changed their characters. Nevertheless, the great majority of them have not really altered their habits,

When two caravans of gypsies happen to meet on the road, a party always follows. During the singing and dancing, gossip and news of other gypsies are exchanged, new babies are admired, and marriages are arranged. But after the party is over, the gypsies pile back into their wagons and go their separate ways.

their mentality, their beliefs or their religious spirit.

Persons who have met shepherds on the slopes of the French Alps have found that every conversation brought its surprise. The shepherds' ways of thinking and feeling are so different from those of the rest of us, and their knowledge of modern life in the big world is so fragmentary and superficial.

Their earnings are ridiculously low, but if you ask shepherds why they do not earn more, they will answer that their master fixes the wage, and that if he doesn't raise it, nothing can be done. The shepherds rarely pay attention to pasture boundaries, because laws and limitations have no place in their minds. They respect only lightning, hail, cold and wind. All these things are their god, and the wolf is their devil.

The signs of the zodiac serve as guides to their decisions as to when to set out and return. It is dangerous to take the flocks to high pastures under the sign of the Fish (Pisces) because it will still be cold. They can be taken up under the sign of the Ram (Aries), in March, but it is still a risk. April is a kind month, but if cows are taken to pasture under the sign of the Bull (Taurus), they will want bulls to be with them for the rest of the year. May is a favorable month, and the Twins (Gemini) put the cows in a good humor. June is worthless, and the sign of the Crab (Cancer) makes the cows walk backward.

The worst sign is that of the Lion (Leo) in July, because the cows that go out to pasture in that month become nervous and impossible to calm. Bad luck may be avoided, however, if the beasts are given blessed salt to eat on St. Mark's Day or if the priest is asked to read over the beginning of the Gospel of St. John in their presence: *In Principio erat Verbum* (In the beginning was the Word).

LEAVING FOR THE HIGH SLOPES

The most impressive and dramatic occurrence in the life of the shepherds is the departure for the high slopes, which close the shepherds

Not everyone is able to wear poverty as lightly as the gypsies do. The slum section of Marseille is a dismal collection of old tenements. The beams crossing the narrow street keep the front wall of the building on the right from collapsing.

into a life of almost complete isolation. The French word for this movement, *inalpage* (going into the Alps), is a rather expressive one. If we interpret this parting according to our own ideas, we are inclined to sympathize with the shepherds for having to leave their families, houses and their native villages to spend months in solitude.

But the shepherds do not have such feelings at all. The parting has only one meaning for them. They begin a march toward their god, that is, toward those forces that are most real to them: lightning, thunder, hail, wind and frost. The *inalpage* is a kind of yearly testing, during which the shepherd on the mountain finds himself once more alone with the divine power. If he is meant to be saved, nothing but that power can help him, because he is alone, and at the mercy of the elements.

These ideas are present in the shepherd's mind as he kneels for the priest's blessing on himself and his flocks or herds. The blessings are usually quite simple ones. There is little outward ceremony, for there is strong faith and inner awareness.

If shepherds make up most of the population of the village, the priest will go in the morning along the streets past the open stalls to give his blessing to the animals; or he will stand at a crossroads and the flocks and herds will be led past him to be sprinkled with holy water. Sometimes a special Mass is said at the beginning of the *inalpage*, and then all the animals are gathered about the church to share in the ceremony. In some parts of Berry the shepherd's staffs are blessed. In La Châtre the statue of St. Lazarus is beaten with white staffs because in French his name (Lazare) resembles *hasard*, the word for risk.

WHAT SHEPHERDS MUST KNOW

Shepherds are chosen from men whose attitude and ability have shown that they are suitable for the work, since flocks and herds of considerable value are entrusted to them. Generally they are trained by their fathers from childhood, and the calling is very much a hereditary one.

There is no short course to becoming a shepherd. He must know great Alpine routes and passes, together with all the tracks, paths, watering places and shelters from the wind. The shepherd must be able intuitively to foretell changes in temperature, know the diseases and sicknesses of his charges, and know how to choose good grasses for grazing. Besides their staffs, which "know the feel of the grass," they carry whistles or flutes, and in Corsica seashells are also used to signal to the flocks.

The animals' obedience to their masters is most surprising. In the north of the Aubrac Massif three shepherdesses sound horns at the crack of dawn, and immediately all the sheep, horses and cattle leave their stalls and gather for the departure. In the evening one more round on the horn is enough to make them leave the most remote pastures and return to the village.

The animals are also able to look after themselves well enough even when left alone. On mountain paths they never move in a disorderly manner, but follow one of their number whom they recognize as the leader. Among horses it is always a stallion, but among horned animals, though a male may lead, a cow or she-goat is more common. Even the fierce bulls of the Camargue meekly follow a cow when she is chosen as leader. (Pigs alone stand out by their lack of discipline and spirit of anarchy!)

The leading animal wears a bell, and the rest follow the sound without ever falling too far behind. The sound has an exciting and gladdening effect on them. In the early morning the beasts in their stalls become impatient to leave when they hear

Even in Paris, not all quarters are glamorous: but when two people are in love, they can find enchantment anywhere.

Cattle-grazing is an old industry in the high country of the French Pyrenees. The snow-capped peaks in the background are lower spurs of Vignemale Peak, the highest mountain in the French Pyrenees.

the tinkling of the bells that the shepherds are bringing to be attached to the animals.

After the brief and touching blessing ceremony the departure begins—with uproar and rejoicings. The cows carry fine collars of worked leather, wrought iron and wood, and there is a little yoke between their horns with a brightly colored pennant on it.

Often the flocks are so big that three or four shepherds must go with each. One of these is the leader, and just before setting off he says a prayer, which the others repeat after him. The leader then takes an oath, promising to show the way to all who have lost it, to offer them milk, fire and water, to let them use his cloak and his tent, and to place a stone on the graves of those that have died on the mountains.

The shepherds take no part in the choice of a leader of the flock or herd. The animals alone decide, and the choice is often made some hours before departure. The animals become greatly excited when they are let out of their stalls after the long winter, and the shepherds let them act as they please. They begin a furious struggle among themselves. At a certain moment a space is left around one of their number. This shows that it is the strongest or the most highly spirited, and that it will be obeyed by the others.

TENDING THE FLOCKS

The departure of the flocks of sheep is even more spectacular than the departure of the herds. A number of different owners bring their animals to one place and divide them up into groups of ten thousand, twelve thousand or even twenty-five thousand head. In all, there may be up to 400,000 animals setting off for the mountains in their *compagne,* as the huge flocks are called.

Obviously, a shepherd of exceptional ability is needed to lead this enormous number, and a kind of general staff is formed from among the most experienced. It is made up of heads of divisions—regents—who elect a regent-general. Other shepherds look after their particular flocks.

The regents do not lead the migration, but follow it on mules. They meet for consultations, and go off to inspect little-known or dangerous routes. They examine the damage the flocks have caused in the properties they pass through and pay the owners. The regents do not take advantage of their position, and enjoy no undue privileges. They are not men who travel comfortably themselves, while dispensing advice and wisdom to the lesser shepherds. They have all spent lifetimes among the flocks and herds and have exceptional experience.

During the march the animals have to be separated and classified according to sex, age and breed. Weaker animals must be placed at the head of the columns so that they will not fall behind. The strongest have to be put last. Newborn lambs must be kept with their mothers. All this work must be supervised by the regents. There is one sheepdog to every 400 head, and consequently a *compagne* of 400,000 head is accompanied by at least 1,000 large and powerful dogs, wearing sharp-spiked iron collars, each of which is capable of taking on a wolf alone.

The flocks do not all follow the same route, and it is one of the regents' duties to choose the routes before departure so that each flock will have enough grass and water. When the lay of the land makes it necessary for all to follow the same track, great distances are left between them. It is not as common as it once was to see these huge flocks of sheep on the march, even though it is only thirty or forty years since they began to be organized on such a scale.

Today, improved roads and means of transport make it easy for the sheep to be carried to their destination and there is no longer such a need for a general staff of experts. Nevertheless, *compagnes* may still be found on the move, in the valleys connecting Provence with the Alps, especially in May and June, when they are going up into the mountains, and in autumn, when they are coming down.

THEIR ENEMY—THE WOLF

The shepherds' greatest enemy, after storm and disease, is the wolf. Dogs are sent against them only as a last resort, when the wolves are actually making attacks, but it is obviously better to avoid such attacks and to spare the dogs.

A shepherd judges by certain signs whether they are near or not. The presence of flocks of cranes, especially if they circle over the sheep, is a sign of safety. In Charente when the shepherds see them they utter the following appeal: "Circle, crane, circle over my old ewe/ and complete a full circle/ like a windmill/ circle crane, circle/ over my old ewe./ If you make three circles/ my sheep will be fortunate."

On the other hand, it is dangerous for the flocks to approach snow-covered areas, because the wolves often shelter in caves nearby. When he sees such a place the shepherd halts the flock and sends his dogs to investigate. If a wolf is discovered it is quite possible that the dogs will have the better of the fight and either will kill him or put him to flight. But if the wolves make a surprise attack the terrified sheep scatter in all directions and are lost.

SHEPHERDS' SAINTS

The earliest patrons of shepherds were the Virgin Mary and St. John the Baptist, and a number of other saints, such as St. Anthony of Egypt

The cowherds and shepherds of the Landes, in southwestern France, not far from the foothills of the Pyrenees, often watch their flocks from stilts; but they only wear these colorful clothes on feast days.

The grotesque mask and headdress of this Basque folk dancer are believed to have come about as a result of Spanish influence. The Basques come of a different racial stock from their neighbors. Scholars are at a loss to explain where they originally came from. Their language is completely unrelated to any other language in Europe.

in the grass for the animals to eat on the saint's feast day. In Auvergne cheeses are taken to church and exchanged for St. Blaise's candles. These are taken to the cow stalls, where the head of the family traces a cross on the ceiling with the smoke and one under the belly of each cow. In the sheep pens a cross is traced in the air and a little wool from each sheep is burned. Finally, some drops of wax from the blessed candles are allowed to fall on the threshold.

St. Blaise's pastoral character is most marked in Burgundy, and in the 18th century there were very few parishes without a confraternity in his honor. Even today almost every village around Chalôn-sur-Saône has one.

ST. ELIGIUS' FESTIVALS

St. Eligius is both an agricultural and a pastoral saint. In Alsace and Brittany he is known as St. Aló, and is particularly concerned with horses. In the North many of the chapels dedicated to him were built by stable-owners and breeders. He receives great honor in the Catalan-speaking districts, especially in Roussillon, where the devout and enthusiastic people hold picturesque festivals for him.

At Arles-sur-Tech, after the mules have been blessed, they are galloped wildly through the streets of the town. And at Serralonga youths and girls execute a dance with a special counterpoint rhythm while standing in the saddle. Each rider makes his horse sway in time with this rhythm, giving expression to his own fancy. The result is a scene of great movement, excitement and beauty. When the dance is over, there is a wild

and St. Blaise. In Alsace, St. Anthony is honored by auction sales of hams, the proceeds of which go to decorate churches dedicated to him. As late as 1935, pig-owners touched the feet of his statue with pieces of bread, which they then gave to their pigs.

In Sare his statue is found in all cow stalls and he is also the patron of horses and sheep in that town. In Dauphiné the shepherds have adopted him as their patron because he was a hermit—like them. They carry his image on the top of their staffs when they go up to the mountains. Colored images of the saint may be found all over the French countryside, surrounded by figures of all kinds of animals.

St. Blaise is regarded by French shepherds as the patron and physician of sheep. In a 16th-century hymn his aid is invoked against wolves, wars, usurers, rabies and fire. Many Alsatian shepherds give their beasts St. Blaise's holy water to drink before setting out for the high pastures, and take little loaves with them to hide

Donkeys are still commonly used for transportation and for field work on the rugged French island of Corsica in the Mediterranean.

Like everything else the Basques do, the "seven jumps" dance is unique. It is unlike any other folk dance in France. When the dancers jump, they are said to be "flying."

race for more than a mile to Font-del-Mas, where everyone drinks, sings and dances until midday. Then the riders gallop back to the village. In the evening the girls dance a spectacular *farandole* through the town.

St. John the Baptist was once the chief patron of shepherds, but his cult has noticeably diminished in recent times. His medal is still to be found on shepherds' staffs, but there are few public ceremonies in his honor.

St. Agatha is regarded as a protector of flocks because of her ability to ward off storms, hail and fire. In addition, she protects houses, both in town and country, and also stables and cow stalls.

THE FRENCH AT PLAY

As everywhere else in the world, there are many different forms of recreation in France, but perhaps no other people has such a gift for abandoning itself completely to simple joys. To see this it is enough to walk through a park or garden in a French city or watch the people in the squares of some popular section.

Children, for example, can spend a whole morning skipping rope, endlessly repeating a refrain that varies only in details: *Alexandre le Grand/ Roi de Macédoine/ avait un cheval/ nommé Bucéphal* (Alexander the Great, King of Macedonia, had a horse called Bucephalus); or *Alexandre le Petit/ Roi de Sibérie/ avait une souris/ nommée Biribi* (Alexander the Little, King of Siberia, had a mouse called Biribi); or *Alexandre le Gros/ Roi de Montecarlo/ avait un chameau/ nommé Calicot* (Alexander the Big, King of Monte Carlo, had a camel called Calico).

A longer refrain goes as follows: *V'la c'qui vient d'paraît'/ un enfant j'té par la fenêt'/ D'mandez Le Petit Journal/ Cinq centimes, un sou/ Demandez le journal/ Le Petit National/ Cinq centimes, un sou/ Dix centimes, deux sous/ Quinz centimes, trois sous...* (Look what has just happened—a baby thrown out of a window. Ask for the *Petit Journal*, five centimes, one sou. Ask for the *Petit National*, five centimes, one sou. Ten centimes, two sous. Fifteen centimes, three sous...). This goes on till the skipper makes a mistake and trips over the rope.

THE PRIEST OF YOUTH

Many country festivals that used to have a religious character are now completely secular in France. This is a result of the powerful anticlerical movements which have existed in the country since the Revolution.

In a village of Isère, for example, the organizer of festivals is called the *abbé de la jeunesse* (priest of youth), which shows the origin of the office. Today, any youth may have the job, but before the Revolution the duty of organizing the feasts clearly fell to priests. The organizer, in order to make the festival a success, must invite as many girls as possible. He goes from house to house and undertakes to assume responsibility for their safety.

In the Ancre Valley the feast in honor of the patron saint is organized by a young man who goes about with a violinist and collects ribbons, ties, handkerchiefs, sashes, earrings and garters from the girls in order to put them up for auction. At the sale, prices go up as the girls vie with their wooers to get the articles back again. The proceeds pay for the ball and banquet in the evening.

The youth leader is not always known as the *abbé*, for in many places the title itself has been changed to eliminate its former connection with religion. In Arras, he is called the Prince of Love, and in Reims the King of Fools. In still other places, however, instead of being secularized the office has been raised in rank, and in Abbeville the youth is called the Bishop of the Innocents. Amiens has its Pope of the Fools. The office of youth leader is frequently conferred for life, or it may revolve among members of youth associations. It also sometimes happens that the girls have their own societies, and elect their Queen or Leader.

DRAFTEE'S FESTIVITIES

The departure of young men for military service—which marks their passage from youth to manhood—is celebrated by various kinds of festivities. There is dancing and drinking, and sometimes also a procession, during which money is collected to cover the expenses of the feast. The procession is headed by a standard-bearer carrying the draftees' emblem, which in the Theys region is a laurel with snowflakes, and live hens in Burgundy and Savoy.

In winegrowing regions the young men gather in an inn, and bottles of wine are hung from the ceiling together with humorous mottoes and patriotic slogans. When the soldiers return from the army the bottles are taken down and everyone drinks toasts.

In Yonne the recruits are accompanied on their way by their younger friends till a certain elm is reached.

In the town of Les Baux in southern France, midnight mass on Christmas Eve is marked by the ceremony of the presentation of the lamb.

Dressed in the white garb of pilgrims, a group of girls walk in solemn procession at the shrine of St. Bernadette in Lourdes. Thousands of sick people travel to this Catholic shrine hoping to be healed.

Here they halt, and each man hammers a nail inscribed with his name into the tree. They drink a last toast, and are gone.

When they return from their service they go back to the tree. If the nailhead has rusted away the young man concludes that he will not succeed in life. Perhaps this custom is the origin of a phrase frequently heard in France: *Attendez-moi sous l'orme* (Wait for me under the elm), which means, "You will have to wait a long time."

Many different kinds of songs are sung at these festivities. Some are almost incomprehensible to outsiders because they refer largely to local events. Generally, the conscript sings of his hopeless sorrow at having to leave his parents, his home, and his sweetheart, perhaps never to return. Their tone is due to the fact that they arose during the Napoleonic period, when conscription was universal, service prolonged, and wars almost continuous. Today, the songs have been modified in many places to suit the times.

UNIVERSITY CUSTOMS

In France the universities have very special forms of entertainment. One of the most celebrated is the Bal des *Quat-Arts* in Paris, which is held once at the time of matriculation and again when degrees are bestowed. The Paris Polytechnic celebrates the *Séance des Cotes*, during which new students are given traditional names. The tallest is called Mega (Greek for "big") and the shortest Epsilon (the smallest Greek letter), and so on.

At the military school of Saint-Cyr the new students are initiated by the seniors, who make them put on full dress and get on their knees at their bedsides. In contrast, the end of the academic year is celebrated by the *Pékin de Pompe*. In this ceremony an effigy is violently ill-treated and then burned in a bonfire in the middle of the school courtyard.

In 1939 the students of the Faculty of Pharmacy in Paris celebrated the end of the academic year with a procession through the streets of the Latin Quarter. "Miss Pharmacie," represented by a huge devil, came first, and was followed by Julius Caesar escorted by two guards armed with the bayonet-like sabers used by gendarmes. A band followed, which accompanied students singing old songs.

Two notable pharmacists were in medieval dress, on motorcycles. A bier was carried by students on which lay pharmaceutical supplies destined for a bonfire. After other floats came crowds of students dressed in medical gowns which were either torn or painted and decorated. After the procession ended a bonfire was lit in the courtyard of the Faculty, and there was singing and dancing.

At the Agricultural School in Grignon new students take an oath upon a rock that is said to have been used by the Druids.

All universities have their own characteristic festivals, but in Paris the greatest and most spectacular are the celebrations of the Ecole des Beaux-Arts, which are especially enjoyed by the foreign colonies in the city and by the thousands of tourists.

Parisians have a saying, *Paris, c'est la France* (Paris is France); but, in fact, from the point of view of traditional life and folklore, Paris seems to have declined more than other places in France. This is partly due to the presence of so many foreign influences, but mainly to the requirements of living in a great capital city.

The instinctive elements in life, which create diversity of customs in the provinces, cannot survive to the same extent in the city. If the machinery of the city is to run smoothly, rational considerations must take first place. The instincts are thus suppressed to a considerable degree. However, Paris provides more than ample opportunity for merriment, relaxation and entertainment.

Paris, City of Light

Paris leads all of France in entertainments and diversions and it has held this position for three centuries.

The most splendid century of Parisian life was no doubt the 18th, when the nobles and aristocrats lived lives of ceremony, pleasure and amusement centered around the great balls and banquets at Versailles.

These diversions added to the resentment in the hearts of the people

Sick patients at the shrine of St. Bernadette in Lourdes wait in wheelchairs to be carried into the grotto to pray for help. Like many of those who tend the sick at Lourdes, the man at the left is a volunteer.

and helped to bring on the Revolution. The people were largely excluded from the gay life of the 18th century, and so the most characteristic Parisian era came not in the 18th but at the end of the 19th and the beginning of the 20th century.

Today Paris tries to prolong that tradition with the help of tourists, who fill her celebrated places of entertainment—her daring shows and her night clubs, cellars and bars. The attempt is only partly successful, because modern organized tourism vulgarizes the romantic spirit that was the secret of the gay life of the 1880's—called the *Belle Époque*.

This is not to say that there is no glamorous night life in Paris—the difficulty is that it is hard to find. It would take a month to discover its secrets, but the tourist agencies take their clients to an obvious kind of Parisian night life in one evening. Or they take them to one celebrated show, such as the *Folies-Bergère* or the *Lido*.

THE CHAMPS-ÉLYSÉES

To discover an aspect of Parisian night life that no tour would ever reveal one can begin with the tree-lined Champs-Élysées. This is a city within a city. Behind those trees are some of the most celebrated theaters of Paris: the *Marigny*, the *Ambassadeurs*, the *Théâtre des Champs-Élysées*, the *Comédie*, the *Studio*. There are also some very chic cabarets, some fashionable restaurants, cinemas, cafés and luxury hotels.

The Champs-Élysées is the place where Parisian exhibitionism reaches its peak. Even in the time of the kings noblemen raced in their carriages along the Cours la Reine, which is the part of the avenue near the Seine. Today, a young man who wishes to show off his custom-built sports car chooses the same road. This great broad avenue, leading from the Place de la Concorde to the Arch of Triumph, is always full of beautiful automobiles—and the cars contain beautiful women.

In general, the entertainment offered in the Champs-Élysées is of a rather special kind. One can enjoy the finest French cooking, old wines and orchestras in the restaurants, as well as outstanding entertainers, whose numbers are very refined, in the *cabarets*. The most interesting spectacle in these places is often the people who go there. Elegant women and celebrities from the worlds of art, cinema, politics and international finance are all to be seen.

The two "Monts"—Montmartre and Montparnasse—are two famous hills of Paris. Both have lost much of their former glory. Montparnasse has long contested Montmartre's claim to be the center of the city's artistic life and entertainment, and the battle still goes on. Both "Monts," which lie on opposite sides of the city, have been the home of famous artists of every nationality. Each has its crowd of well-known restaurants, bars and cabarets.

MONTPARNASSE

On Montparnasse the diversions are apt to be more showy than solid.

Just as the theaters of the Avenue Montaigne were included with the Champs-Élysées, and the *Folies-Bergère* will be included with Montmartre, so the cabarets of St. Germain-des-Près will be included with Montparnasse, and also the cellars and other clubs that are, or were, meeting places of the Existentialist philosophers.

The *Rose Rouge* and the *Tabou* are famous because Juliette Greco sang there. The *Café de Flore* and the *Deux Magots* are also famous, and have been for very many years—recently because Jean Paul Sartre, the Existentialist, used to frequent them.

Today neither of these celebrities will be found in these places. Instead, bearded students and girls in jeans with long unkempt hair sit there with their solitary Pernod or Martini. Strangers and tourists watch these young people with curiosity and sometimes ridicule them. But they began a fashion that has spread throughout the world, and their clothes and behavior are a Parisian invention, which was copied by the beatniks of America and Britain.

The Place de Rennes now has nothing of particular interest except the crowded *Café Dupont*. It is surrounded with hotels, cafés and restaurants that are frequented more by tourists than by Parisians. In Montparnasse's better days many artists used to come here, especially to the *Café de Versailles*.

The Boulevard Montparnasse leads out of the Place de Rennes, and on it are the principal sights of the area: big cafés, restaurants, dance halls and bars, and famous bookshops which have celebrated collections of reproductions. There are a few antique shops, and shops selling artists' materials, a flower shop or two, but, strangely enough, no art dealers. On this street is the only architectural monument in Montparnasse—the church of Notre-Dame-des-Champs.

Not far away is the Carrefour Vavin, a crossroads that is the heart of Montparnasse. This corner was once a meeting place for the civilized world. The celebrated international cafés, the *Dôme*, the *Coupole* and the *Rotonde*, are here.

HOME OF ARTISTS

Until 1914 Montparnasse had a very individual character, and it seemed to have a great future before it. Many artists had emigrated there from Montmartre. The *Rotonde* was already well known and Lenin and Trotsky could both be seen there. Modigliani, who had abandoned Montmartre for Montparnasse, greeted Utrillo with cries of joy when he came down from the other "Mont" to visit him. The two would go on a spree. Each introduced the other as the better drinker, and their night out always ended in the police station.

The *Dôme* was a quiet little bar where German artists met. The delegation that went to greet Pascin on his arrival from Munich at the Gare de l'Est in 1907 left from there. Canudo, with an ivy leaf in his lapel, was also a faithful customer.

When Van Dongen returned from his first visit to Egypt he settled at Montparnasse in a strange studio made of ferroconcrete. He painted the floor and the ceiling red and green, and received his guests bare to the waist with his beard adorned with little blue and red spangles.

In 1914, on July 14 (Bastille Day), a great ball was organized at the Carrefour Vavin, which was illuminated with Chinese lanterns. Many famous artists and poets were present. World War I broke out only a few weeks later, but as soon as peace came the life of Montparnasse was resumed at a higher pitch than ever before.

The Carrefour Vavin then became the meeting place for artists from all over the world, who came to Paris to breathe its air of freedom. They found new meaning in the soft light of the Île-de-France, and in views of the Louvre, and Notre-Dame. Foreign artists, such as Picasso, Chagall, Zadkine, Van Dongen and Fujita, flourished alongside French painters, such as Matisse, Rouault, Derain, Vlaminck, Dunoyer de Segonzac and Utrillo. It was the Golden Age.

OTHER FAMOUS CAFÉS

One afternoon in December 1923 the *Rotonde* was solemnly opened as if it were a public monument. Gustave Kahn, the poet and art critic, made a speech, and everyone was invited to eat free of charge. This ceremony was more important than was thought at the time, for not only was a new *Rotonde* opened, but soon a new Montparnasse arose.

The owner had turned the bar into an art gallery; there were pictures hanging on all the walls and above the stairs. As well as its bar the *Rotonde* had a jazz band on the first floor. There were dancing, expensive drinks, little tables, and customers wearing evening dress.

The *Dôme* was also renovated, and it opened to reveal that its only decorative feature was flowered wallpaper. The *Dôme* had never followed the fashions of the other cafés, and a little later it was extended into the next building, where a bar and red leather armchairs were installed.

Then another great event occurred—a third big café, the *Coupole*, was opened in December 1927. It was decorated by local artists, and its bar soon became a very brilliant meeting place. Its barman, Bob, became a well-known character.

The name Montparnasse was known all over the world in the same way as the *Moulin Rouge* and the *Folies-Bergère*. All kinds of groups gathered about the café tables: fat clowns, penniless professors, revolutionary pharmacists. They chattered so loudly that they drowned the clatter of plates and cutlery, the clinking of glasses, and the waiters' voices.

Montparnasse's distinctive character did not last long, however, for the place soon became fashionable. Clients from the elegant quarters of the city, as well as many strangely dressed young men and women, came there. Both the *Coupole* and the *Rotonde* had a room where fashionable women came to take tea and to dance. The lower middle classes began to frequent Montparnasse, and on Saturday evenings shopgirls and clerks mingled with the crowds on the pavements.

The grotto in which Bernadette Soubirous, a French peasant girl, had a vision of the Virgin Mary in 1858 is today lined with the crutches and pious offerings of those who have been cured.

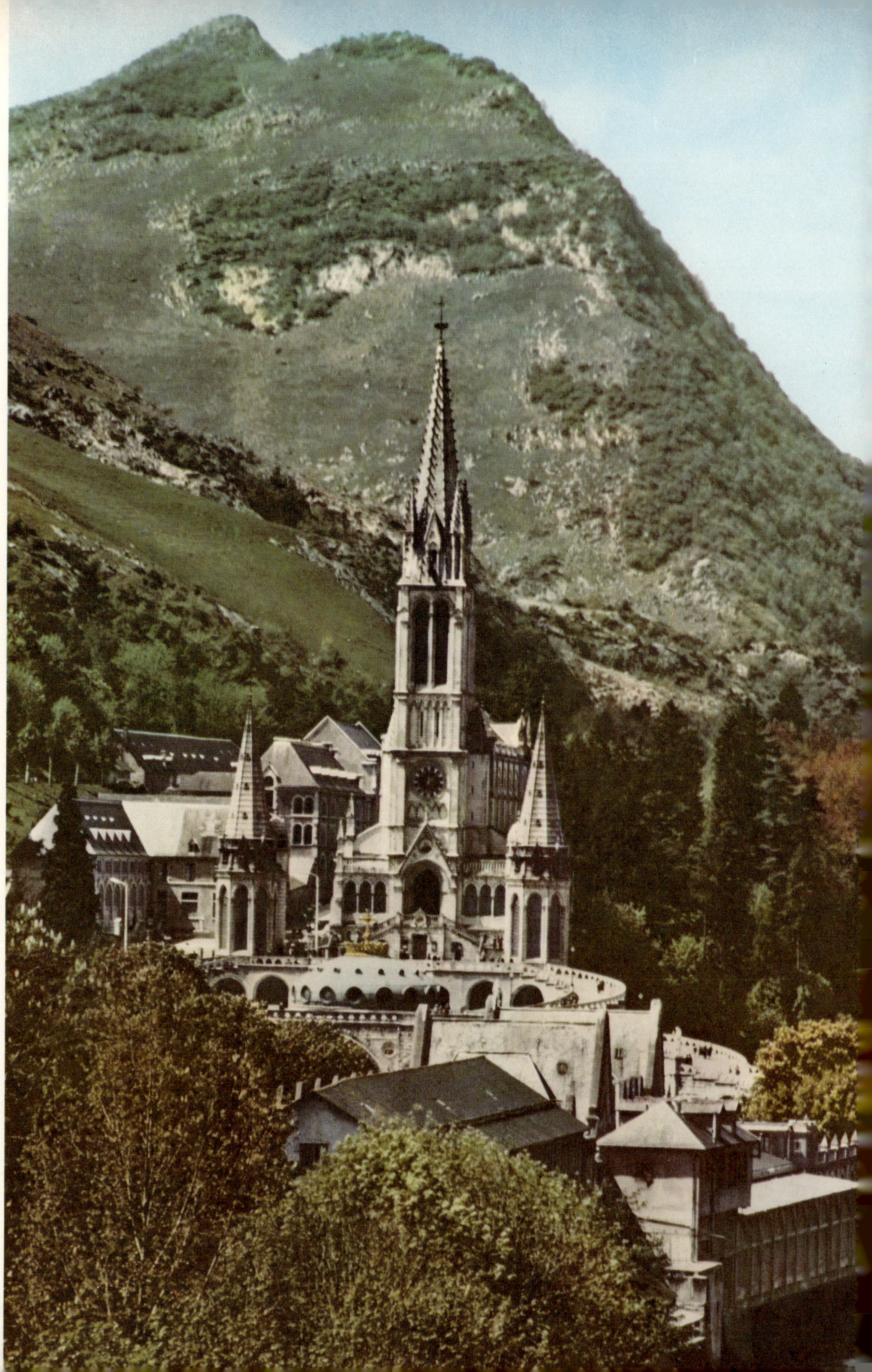

FRANCE • *The People* / 163

The artists, however, were always kings there. Fujita drove about in a gray-striped car with a chauffeur in white livery. He had a town house and Braque designed a country house for him. Utrillo bought a château near Lyon, and other artists had yachts. Every Saturday, Van Dongen invited half of Paris to his villa in Rue Juliette-Lambert. Pascin took hundreds of people, many of whom he did not know, to the night clubs in the Place Pigalle at his own expense.

A week never passed without a dance or a masked ball at *Bullier's,* the *Maison Watteau* or the *Moulin de la Galette.* The most insignificant anniversary served as a pretext for celebrations lasting till dawn.

Then came the Depression. Money ran out, and no one would buy pictures. Pascin killed himself; Fujita went back to Japan to avoid his creditors. Several heroes of those Bacchic years went to prison. Lent followed Carnival.

THE JOCKEY NIGHT CLUB

Close to Carrefour Vavin on the Boulevard Montparnasse is the restaurant *Au Bon Coin,* which used to be known simply as *Chez Baty.* Its cellar was famous. Guillaume Apollinaire and André Billy often went there.

Further on, a plaque indicates the house where Jongkind lived. The ground floor is occupied by the *Jockey* night club. When Bob from the *Coupole* ran it, it was a French interpretation of a bar in the American West.

Its closed door and windows gave it a sinister look. Inside it was a human caldron. A cowboy thumped a piano, Hawaiians played banjos, and a few couples tried to dance through the throng. Some looked for places to sit, and others shouted. There were clouds of smoke and the room was decorated with brightly colored stills from Western films. Near the door was a wooden bar. The tables had paper covers and anyone who found half a chair to sit on was lucky. The *Jockey* set the tone for the night life of Montparnasse.

Rue Delambre was the place where the flower of Montparnasse and Parisian journalists used to meet at dawn. Bars stayed open all night throughout the section. The *Select* was always crowded, especially in the early morning. Chauffeurs met at the *Kosmos,* opposite, which was very popular.

The *Bal Nègre* in Rue Blomet owed its success to its handsome *doudous* who performed West Indian dances in native dress. There are numerous bars and restaurants of all kinds in this part of the city: the *Poisson d'Or* in Rue Vavin, the *Schubert* in Boulevard Montparnasse, *Jimmy's* in Rue Huygens.

THE 'CLOSERIE DES LILAS'

The *Closerie des Lilas* really belongs more to the Latin Quarter than to Montparnasse. It is a frontier post, but it lost its gaiety before World War I, when Paul Fort stopped holding his Tuesday gatherings for poets and writers there. Paul Fort led the poets of the time, and Hans Ryner was a leading novelist.

It was Hans Ryner who brought about the outbreak of a "war" in which the patrons of the *Closerie des Lilas* fought those of the *Napolitain.* Though the Tuesday meetings had stopped, after World War I banquets were still held at the *Closerie* to honor various poets.

This custom received a mortal blow from a Surrealist offensive during a dinner given in honor of Saint-Pol-Roux. Surrealists staged an invasion of the *Closerie* in force, and after this encounter the banquets ceased.

At this point the wanderer in Paris must make a choice. He can either go along the Boulevard de l'Observatoire as far as the Place Denfert-Rochereau—near Rue Boulard, where André Lothe lived. Or he can go to the Parc Montsouris where Fujita, Derain and Braque have lived.

A third route goes toward the Porte de Versailles and the Place Desnouettes, where Antoine Villard settled and made a collection of Douanier Rousseau's works. This route takes one to Rue Vercingétorix, where Gauguin lived.

Finally, the wanderer can remain in the heart of the Latin Quarter by taking the Boulevard Edgar Quinet, going along by the cemetery and reaching the Rue de la Gaîté. This street has been called Rue de la Joie by its inhabitants because for many years it was a street of cabarets and places of entertainment. The

The cathedral and hospital at Lourdes are set in the green foothills of the Pyrenees. The town reflects the inner serenity of those who work there to help the sick.

In some regions, when the head of a peasant family dies, members of his family go barefoot and place lighted candles on the threshold of the house as a sign of mourning.

tradition is not entirely dead. Cinemas, bars, neon lights and jukeboxes all preserve the atmosphere of an everlasting fete.

THE THEÂTRE MONTPARNASSE

In 1819, when Seveste built the *Théâtre Montparnasse,* Rue de la Gaîté was lined with acacias and had an attractive rural appearance. Cheap wine from Argenteuil drew workers and their families there on Sundays and Mondays, and Seveste's theater was an added attraction. At first, only local people attended it, and two melodramas and a revue were often put on the same evening. The curtain went up at six and fell for the last time at midnight.

In the middle of the theater was a large stove where the spectators could warm the food they had brought with them. Entire families would eat cabbage soup during the interval. No one imagined that a century later Gaston Baty would turn this same theater into a rendezvous for high society, artists and poets, and that first-class plays would be presented on its stage.

Rue de la Joie offered many other entertainments during the 19th century. There were café-concerts, dances and restaurants. Dance halls such as the *Veau qui tette* and the *Éléphante* were frequented by rather questionable characters.

In 1833 the *Mille Colonnes* was opened and had a brilliant success. A restaurant was added to it later. After a time it became a cinema and later a music hall called *Bobino.*

Agnès Capri transformed the *Gaîté-Montparnasse* into a hall for "high-class" entertainment, but the *Casino Montparnasse* has kept its popular character. However, many other places of amusement have been turned into movie theaters.

In the evening the streets are lined with cars, and the cafés and bars are overflowing with customers. Today the stars of the *Théâtre Montparnasse* have cars, and will not be seen strolling in the street, but the *Bobino* performers may sometimes be seen dining at the *Iles-Marquises,* an old restaurant famous for its oysters and rich wines.

ART SCHOOLS

Though the life of Montparnasse is less spectacular than formerly, artists still find it a good place to live in. The art schools are always full of French and foreign students. Many amateur and professional artists go to the drawing classes held late every afternoon. Every Monday morning models go to Rue de la Grande Chaumière to wait to be hired. This "model market" is a picturesque sight. Some of the more important private art schools are also in this street.

MONTMARTRE

They say that Montmartre is dying—that it is already dead. "If only you had known old Montmartre, when Degas, Toulouse-Lautrec and Renoir were there!" In fact, Montmartre's most important period was the one following Impressionism—a period which came to an end in 1914. At that time, Fredé, Dorgelès, Carco, Picasso and Max Jacob all lived there.

Montmartre is one of the tourist's chief goals in Paris. Its appearance and atmosphere have not changed much; the lanes and alleys are still there, and so is the air of friendliness and familiarity, which is more common on the Mediterranean than in Paris.

Montmartre is a city within a city, although it is usually known as a village. Its melancholy gardens with their broken walls have bunches of thistles in them, but one can still see a few lilies, a cherry tree or a pergola.

The streets are narrow, and there are long flights of steps flanked by little houses, hotels and hovels. The great white dome of Sacré-Cœur dominates everything. Along with the Place du Tertre and its immediate surroundings, it forms a kind of acropolis.

The upper part of the district, the so-called Old Montmartre, has the best-known restaurants, night clubs, bars and cafés, such as the *Moulin de la Galette* and the *Lapin Agile.* Here, also, are the antique shops and artists' studios.

Below Old Montmartre a network of brightly lit streets stretches out from the Place Pigalle, the Place Blanche and the Place de Clichy. Here the Belle Époque had its real flowering. This kind of life passed away before World War I, but its memory and traces of it still remain.

The *Dix-Heures* is a celebrated *théâtre de chansonniers* (music hall), where many famous singers began their careers; the *Lune Rousse* is an outstanding musical cabaret, and the *Tabarin* has inherited the tradition of the cancan from the *Moulin Rouge.* Thousands of tourists crowd into these places every night. The con-

The religious emotions of devout Frenchmen have often been expressed in carvings of wood and stone. With his hammer and chisel, Job, the image-maker of the small fishing village of Locronan in Finistère, works like a man of another century for the greater glory of God.

ducted tour, *Paris by Night*, has made the skills and arts of chefs, headwaiters and maîtres d'hôtel somewhat superfluous. The bus goes around quickly, making prearranged stops, and the tourists are told what to enjoy. Should anyone prefer to take his pleasures alone, he may join the nightbirds for whom dinner at Montmartre has traditional importance. Among them reigns an atmosphere of liberty without license, mild intoxication, and the pleasure of being a little silly among one's friends.

Chez Florence was founded in 1928, and has maintained its reputation ever since. It has the atmosphere of an elegant salon. The atmosphere at *Eve* is completely different. There is an excellent swing band, and the laughing animation of the place can make you forget your regrets about the past and your worries about the future. In spite of its decline between 1910 and 1920 the *Moulin Rouge* has kept its world reputation and is still an important tourist attraction.

A well-known group of writers used to meet at night in a very strange place called *La Potinière*, between Rue Blanche and Rue Coustou. The woman behind the bar wore a monocle, and the pianist, by the name of Wolf, played anything he was asked. The diners had to be patient and wait their turn to be served.

Through the smoky atmosphere of the room, with its permanent smell of fried potatoes, one could discern the faces of Francis Carco, André Derain, Michel Georges and André Warnod. Henri Béraud would turn up at three in the morning. Song writers, such as Noël-Noël, did not have to be asked twice to recite something from their repertoires. When they rested, students and soldiers began their own songs.

Rue Lepic, which twists and turns about the hill up to the *Moulin de la Galette*, has a hundred different appearances during the day. People get up late, after the butchers have

For the inhabitants of Montmartre, the artists' quarter in Paris, any holiday, however obscure, is a good reason to throw a party. A few balls of crêpe paper, some musicians, and there you have it—the makings of a fine party. Those who are lucky enough to have dates dance. The rest watch.

hung up their sausages and hams in their shops. A procession of street traders then begins, and the smell of coffee rises into the air. The barmen, in blue jackets with their sleeves rolled up, arrange rows of glasses on the shelves and fill them with white wine. At midday people come in for an aperitif or a Vittel-menthe.

Rue Lepic has neither public transportation nor noisy traffic, and at this hour everyone begins to take his meal in peace. Life begins again in the street toward evening, and noise and familiarity reign. At night, however, it is quiet once more. A long American car may glide silently, like a shining shadow, up the street toward the Place du Tertre—and then the cats come out.

PLACE PIGALLE

Once Place Pigalle was the last stop for many screeching trolleys. Artists' models waited around the fountain. The Cirque Médrano, with its many memories of Degas and Toulouse-Lautrec, has hardly changed since 1860. At that time Montmartre was a pleasant suburb just beyond the walls of the city. It still looked like a village, with its windmills, little cottages and lanes, and its background of farms and vineyards.

Montmartre was annexed to Paris in 1860, and bore the invasion of the artists that followed with a resigned, rather sly air. Artists in search of spacious rooms for studios invaded Rue Berthe, Rue Gabrielle, Rue des Martyrs and Rue des Abbesses before finding courage to tackle the heights.

In Rue Dancourt is the attractive little *Théâtre de l'Atelier,* which is the last surviving example of the kind of theater in which popular melodramas were staged outside the city limits. Parisians used to come there to applaud the heroes and sigh for the wronged heroines.

Nearby are streets that have hardly changed at all over the years—Rue Berthe and Rue Gabrielle. Then, there are the steps leading to the *Butte* (hill), and the Place du Tertre which, with its rustic wineshops and its sunshades, is like a toy village. The renowned *Mère Catherine* has not changed its appearance or style or its pretty little garden as big as a handkerchief. Its greatest rival is *Madame Patachou*, which has a tradition of cutting off its clients' ties.

First Nights at the Theater

A première is a typically Parisian institution. Every new show must be "launched" with one. Instead of a bottle of champagne, all Parisian society (*Le Tout-Paris*) is used at the "launching."

Le Tout-Paris is a mixture of people who, from the time the first leaves fall in the autumn until summer comes again, feel themselves obliged to attend the birth of every new show in the capital and to bring to it the aura of their own fame. They are like royal or public personages laying the first stone of a new building. *Le Tout-Paris* is present so that both they and the show will be talked about on the day after.

Those who are invited are obliged to wear evening dress. They are allowed no time to read the critics' reviews the next day, like common mortals, before giving an opinion on the play, but must decide then and there. For this reason alone they are very cautious and applaud with the tips of their fingers. They begin to form their opinions of the work during the first intermission, basing their positions on what they hear others say as they move about.

The French Academy, the Goncourt Academy, the General Staff, ambassadors, government ministers, stage and movie actors, leading painters, dress designers, editors, aristocrats and journalists make up the ranks of this select band.

Sometimes, two "launchings" can occur on the same night. *Le Tout-Paris* then divides. But by means of strategic withdrawals during one performance and transfers to the other, it is possible for the two halves to exchange theaters during the evening.

Incidents like the one that took place when Hugo's *Hernani* opened in 1830 occur only once in a century, in the ordinary course of events. But this is no reason for running the risk of missing anything. The evening of Feb. 25, 1830, was a dramatic one, for the champions of Romanticism and those of Classicism transformed Hugo's play into a field of battle.

Another famous evening was the one at the *Théâtre Ambigu* when, during a performance, Marie Duplessis, *la Dame aux Camélias*, first cast her eyes on Liszt. The ghostlike pianist felt her warm look, and asked the critic Jules Janin, with whom he was discussing the play, "Who is that beautiful woman watching me?" "Don't you know her?" asked Janin. "She is Mademoiselle Duplessis, or better, Countess du Plessis, the queen of our first nights!"

The next day, when Dr. Koreff came to see Marie Duplessis, she asked him if he knew Liszt. "I do indeed," he replied. As she continued to ask for information about him, he added, smiling, "Since he has had the good fortune to attract you, I will put him on my prescription."

The last love affair of the Lady with the Camellias thus began during the first night at a theater. In such matters, Paris is like a provincial city: many people must have gone about claiming to have witnessed the little scene.

A BATTLE OF JEWELS

Another famous incident took place at a first night at the *Folies-Bergère*. The beautiful Otero was at the height of her career and she wished to deal a mortal blow to her rival, Liane de Pougy. In order to do this, she appeared in her box covered with every piece of jewelry she had.

Liane de Pougy was warned by a friend about what Otero was going to do. When, therefore, the former appeared in her box on the other side of the theater from Otero there was stunned silence. She wore not even one piece of jewelry—not a single stone, not even a ring. Behind her stood her maid, covered with brilliant pendants, tiaras, rings, necklaces and brooches.

PARISIAN LOVE OF THE THEATER

The Parisians have always had a great love for the theater, for it allows them to indulge their taste

When the Eiffel Tower was finished in 1889 it was the highlight of the Paris Exhibition. Structural engineers and architects marveled at the ingenious design of the tower and the graceful use of iron. Gustave Alexandre Eiffel, the engineer who built it, used 7000 tons of iron in its girders. Today the 984-foot tower has become a symbol for the entire country. Each year thousands of visitors take the bus trip to the base of the tower, where elevators take them up and up and up. The observation platforms at different levels of the tower offer unmatched views of the capital.

The trees and the ripples in the water lend a deceptive air of tranquillity to this quiet fishing scene. The river is the Seine. Less than a mile away, across the Pont des Arts, lies downtown Paris. In the background are the towers of the cathedral of Nôtre Dame, which is built on Île de la Cité, a small island in the middle of the Seine.

FRANCE • *The People* / 169

for the spectacular and gives them inexhaustible topics of conversation.

Even during the Revolution, *le Tout-Paris* was at its post at the premières, in spite of general poverty and misery and the threat of prison the next day for many of the participants. Even the threat of the scaffold—a stage upon which any of them might yet be called to play the chief part—did not stop them from attending.

During the long and humiliating German occupation—when the theaters had to be reached in the blackout, performances started early and there were many German uniforms in the stalls—the tradition was not broken.

On the evening of April 21, 1958, the *Théâtre des Champs-Élysées* was filled with the usual first-night crowd. The celebrated Ballet of the Marquis de Cuevas was giving a performance.

Just before the curtain should have risen the seventy-three-year-old marquis appeared on the stage to announce that he had received a court order not to put on one of the ballets on the program, but that he had decided to go ahead. "I thought," he said, "that in France everything was free and clear of obstacles. But I was wrong. But it is not France's fault. It is the fault of one man."

He was referring to Serge Lifar, the ballet dancer. Their boxes were side by side. During the intermission they met and exchanged some sharp words. Lifar had no gloves with him to throw down in challenge, but used his lace handkerchief instead. The marquis replied with a slap on the cheek, as if to a naughty child.

The photographers were not present during almost the whole of this scene—this unrehearsed offstage ballet. They now rushed in, and cried, "Another. Give him another!" to the marquis, in order to take photographs.

The next day all Paris was buzzing with the story. The affair continued, to everyone's ironic delight, until a duel was fought at a villa near Paris. The ballet dancer was scratched by the marquis' sword—and the marquis fainted. Later a touching reconciliation took place.

A NEW PROFESSION

In order to prepare the seats for a first night it is necessary to be a specialist on the affairs of society. A new profession, that of organizing gala evenings, has been created. These experts study the theater seating diagrams like members of a general staff. They refer to the strategy adopted in past evenings in the way that Napoleon's colonels must have referred to his tactics at Austerlitz.

Colors must be blended (masculine black and white with feminine tulle, silk and crinolines), and in all the great theaters run by the State, such as the Opera, the two theaters of the *Comédie Française* and the *Opéra Comique,* a brilliant scene must be created in the theater as well as on the stage. This is one reason for inviting students from the various Academies, for they wear their dress uniforms.

The important people in the stalls, the circles and the boxes must be placed so as to prevent the formation of parties and groups and to avoid social errors. Recently a theatrical strategist had the idea of telling each ticket holder not only the number of his seat but also the name of the person next to whom he would be seated. The reasons are obvious. In a city like Paris everyone has enemies, and the strategist, aware of his inability to know everything, was wise to act as he did. The men can prepare what they are going to say, and their wives will know better what to wear if they know with whom they will be sitting.

GUARDS FOR FIRST NIGHTS

For more important first nights a velvet canopy is erected at the theater entrance. A very important première is indicated by the presence of two

The Luxembourg Gardens is only one of the beautiful parks in Paris. Others include the Tuileries Gardens and the Jardin des Plantes. For Parisians a park is not just a place covered with grass. Flowers, statuary, fountains, pools and tables for board games, a box lunch or quiet conversations are all part of the parks of Paris.

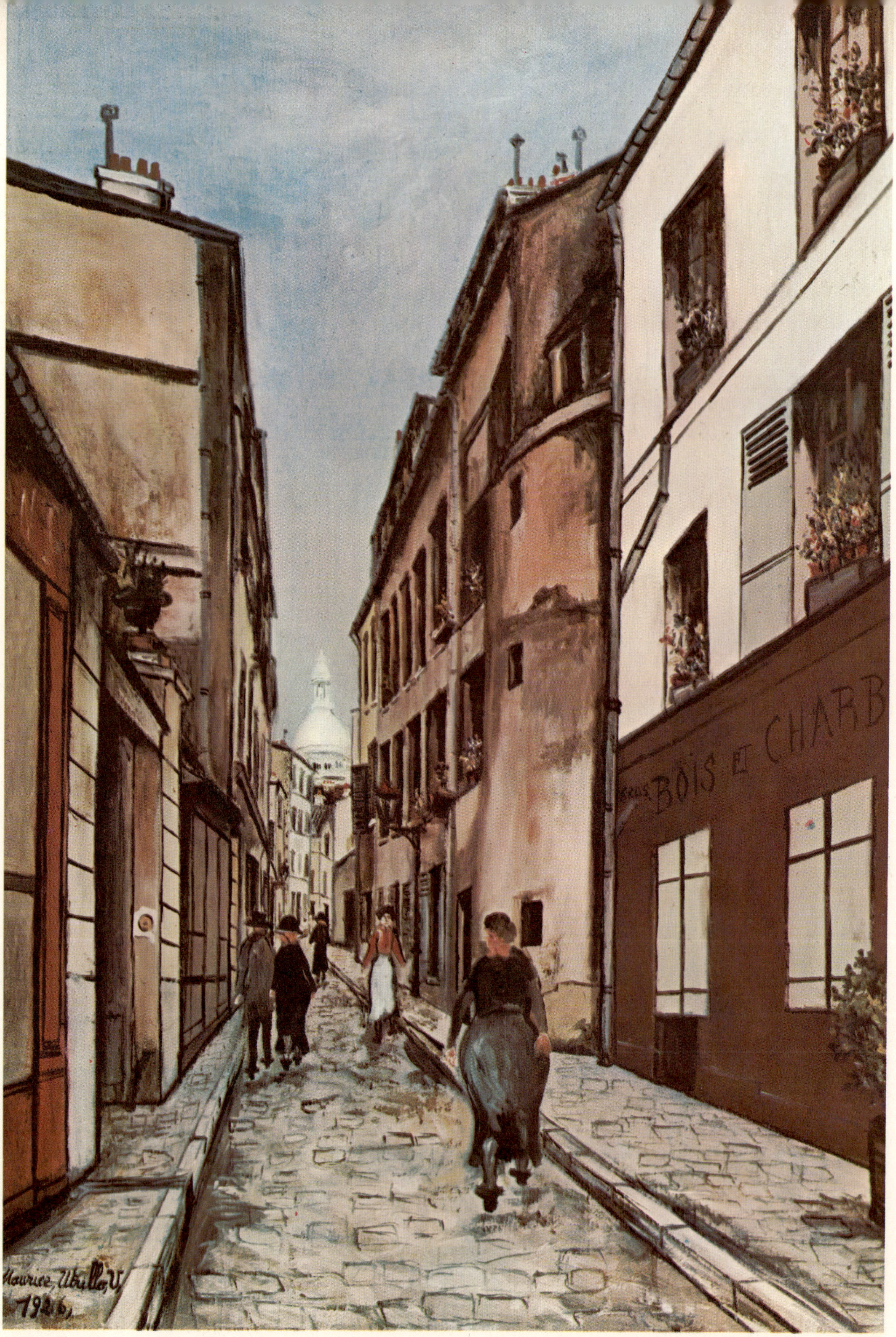
GROS BOIS ET CHARB
Maurice, Utrillo, V.
1926,

Artists have flocked to Montmartre since 1860, when it was incorporated with Paris. The old houses and quiet streets have inspired hundreds of paintings by artists who have become famous. This one, by Maurice Utrillo, is of Rue Saint Rustique. The white dome in the background is the church of Sacré Cœur, which dominates the hill of Montmartre.

ranks of Republican Guards in full-dress uniform (silver helmet with horsetail, black jacket with scarlet lining, and white doeskin breeches). These Guards are hired out by a special department of the Army on condition that one minister at least attends the theater.

Fashionable society remains in the lobby for a long time before taking its seats. Most *généraleux* (as frequenters of *générales,* or first nights, are called) want to have the pleasure of entering between the two ranks of soldiers with drawn swords. When the guards present arms for some person of importance the men before and behind him feel that it is being done for them. The women try to be in range of the cameras at exactly the right moment, so that ordinary people may see their furs on television.

The ritual of first nights provides employment for many people, apart from those depending on the entertainment industry. Dressmakers profit from them, and sometimes, to get publicity, models are sent to first nights wearing the house's best gowns. The women hate to wear the same clothes every time, for they worry about what their friends and acquaintances are thinking—so they need new gowns.

The men are more conservative. A tuxedo or full evening dress can be made to last ten years, in spite of the pounds that accumulate on the body and the ever-increasing strain imposed on the buttons. But tailors keep on launching new fashions for men too.

Hairdressers are always at work.

Turtleneck sweaters, windblown hair and love are the perfect combination for the Left Bank in Paris. The students who live in the Latin Quarter on this side of the Seine give the place an intensely intellectual and Bohemian atmosphere. The name of the Quarter, which is the educational center of Paris, dates back to medieval times, when all scholars used Latin.

Paris is an inexhaustible treasure hoard for the antique lover. A 19th-century tea kettle for a few francs or an exquisitely worked Renaissance candlestick for thousands—the antique dealers are prepared to sell both.

Someone introduces the fashion of women wearing wigs. Other women adopt the fashion, and send their maids off to get one too. The secret is to find a maid with the same size head as yourself.

The printers of the luxurious and costly programs, seamstresses, jewelers, photographers, florists and many other tradespeople and craftsmen profit directly or indirectly from these gala evenings. Barbers benefit from them, as it is fairly common for men to have their hair either permanently or semipermanently waved. All barbers in fashionable districts have the necessary equipment. It is surprising to see how many fair-haired men there are in Paris from time to time.

Luxury restaurants also play their part in first nights. The habitués, at least those who can afford it, like to finish the evening at a well-laid table in an expensive restaurant. The women want to make the fullest use of their evening dress.

ONE-NIGHT PERFORMANCES

The most brilliant first nights are those that are also last nights—that is, special performances for one night only. The important thing is to be able to say that you were one of the few who were there. In this way the pleasure is vastly increased, even though the admission price is also far greater. On these evenings no invitations are issued, for the performance is usually for some charity.

Every year actors who happen to be in Paris at a certain time appear in a gala production at the *Cirque d'Hiver* given by the Artists' Union for the benefit of the old-actors' homes. Outstanding stars put on special circus acts, and the show lasts all night.

The little theaters also follow the tradition. The first night has the same purpose as in the big theaters, but it is conducted in an entirely different way. They manage to do without Republican Guards. There would be nowhere to put them.

The *Théâtre de la Huchette*, for example, is in a basement and it is not unusual in the middle of a performance to hear the tenant on the first floor turn on his water faucet. It has seventy seats and, as in many Paris theaters, the audience has to go into the street to smoke during the intermission.

The *Théâtre de Poche* has eighty seats, and the actors often have to go on stage directly from the orchestra. The *Studio des Champs Élysées* can hold, at most, 150 spectators. The *Théâtre du Tertre* is in

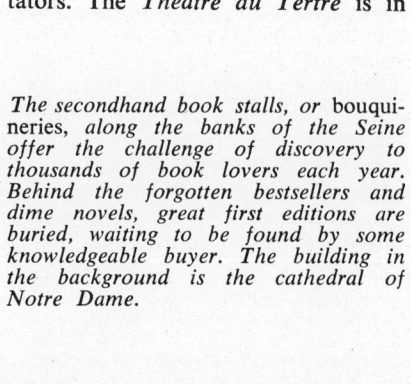

The secondhand book stalls, or bouquineries, *along the banks of the Seine offer the challenge of discovery to thousands of book lovers each year. Behind the forgotten bestsellers and dime novels, great first editions are buried, waiting to be found by some knowledgeable buyer. The building in the background is the cathedral of Notre Dame.*

a tower near the *Moulin de la Galette*. Many others just escape being pocket size, but are not much bigger than large rooms.

For first nights in these places evening dress is not required.

These little theaters are often the strongholds of the avant-garde. In the recent past, many critics have made mistakes in criticizing plays which later were praised. Therefore, today few will risk expressing dislike of or opposition to the new styles. Any avant-garde playwright can depend on having an audience that will be ready to applaud anything he puts on and to shout down the slightest protests of "reactionaries."

Finally, there are other premières which do not take place in theaters. Fashion shows are an example. The great ones take place twice a year, in summer and in winter, when *haute couture* (high fashion) carries out full-scale maneuvers.

Dior's two salons are flooded with people anxious to give triumphal honors to the successor of the great man, and Marc Bohan appears in regal fashion on the balcony of the shop in Avenue Montaigne. Yves Saint Laurent, who left Dior to open his own salon, Balenciaga and Chanel also are centers of excitement when new lines are introduced.

New stores, new mineral waters, new records, new books—all are launched with first nights.

THE CRAFTS

LIKE ALL INDUSTRIOUS AND IMAGINATIVE people the French can boast of crafts of the highest order. The most obvious successes of French craftsmanship are in majolica (glazed, richly colored pottery), porcelain, jewelry, furniture and tapestry. All these have illustrious traditions and great names among the individuals and firms that have produced the work over the centuries.

From the time of Louis XIV French furniture makers have been in the front rank. Sèvres and Limoges porcelain are famous the world over, and the word Gobelins has become synonymous with tapestry.

Beginning in the 11th century, bricks and varnished bricks were manufactured everywhere. However, the art of ceramics did not develop until the 16th century. The role of Bernard Palissy in this development is well known. His terra cotta plates, on which are depicted plants, serpents

Cabarets in the Latin Quarter and in Montmartre are often as informal as clubrooms. The patrons of Le Chat qui Pêche *(The Fishing Cat) will spend the evening over a bottle of wine, deciding the nature of the Good, the True and the Beautiful.*

The cobblestone streets, the warm wood paneling of the old houses and the dozens of little restaurants and cabarets make the old Montmartre section of Paris a favorite tourist spot.

and lizards in brilliant colors, are famous. The Louvre, the Cluny Museum and the Sèvres factory all possess very fine examples of his work. The different kinds of majolica work developed rapidly—especially the celebrated majolica of Henry II and of Deux-Sèvres, also known as Saint-Porchaire. These factories soon became famous for their saltcellars, sugar bowls, cups, and candlesticks, all in architectural forms. The Dutuit collection in the Petit-Palais in Paris has some very beautiful examples.

The 17th century was a brilliant period, especially in Rouen. In 1646 Nicolas Porel obtained the privilege of making majolica ware for fifty years, but he did not use it, and soon transferred it to Edmo Poterat, of Saint-Sever. His were the first splendid examples of majolica, decorated with lace and festoon effects in blue, which formed frames for the crests of the noble families of Normandy.

Louis Poterat, son of Edmo, improved upon his father's work, and also discovered how to produce a very fine transparent ware. This discovery enabled him to obtain the privilege of building a factory anywhere in France for the purpose of

FRANCE · *The People* / 175

making plates and vases.

Majolica with Chinese decoration is not found before the first years of the 18th century. Guillebeaux, the maker of the great dinner service presented by the city of Rouen to Charles Francis II, Duke of Luxembourg, seems to have been the first to produce it. Porel, Poterat and Guillebeaux are the three great names associated with the majolica of Rouen. Nevers also acquired importance as a majolica center during the 18th century, with the introduction of the Chinese style.

But enameled majolica began to

On an outing to Montmartre, it's hard to decide which way to look first. The sister is trying to herd her schoolchildren into a wax museum next door to the Auberge de la Bohème, *a sidewalk café. That a waxworks should be located on a quiet street is typical of the peculiar, extravagant quality of Montmartre.*

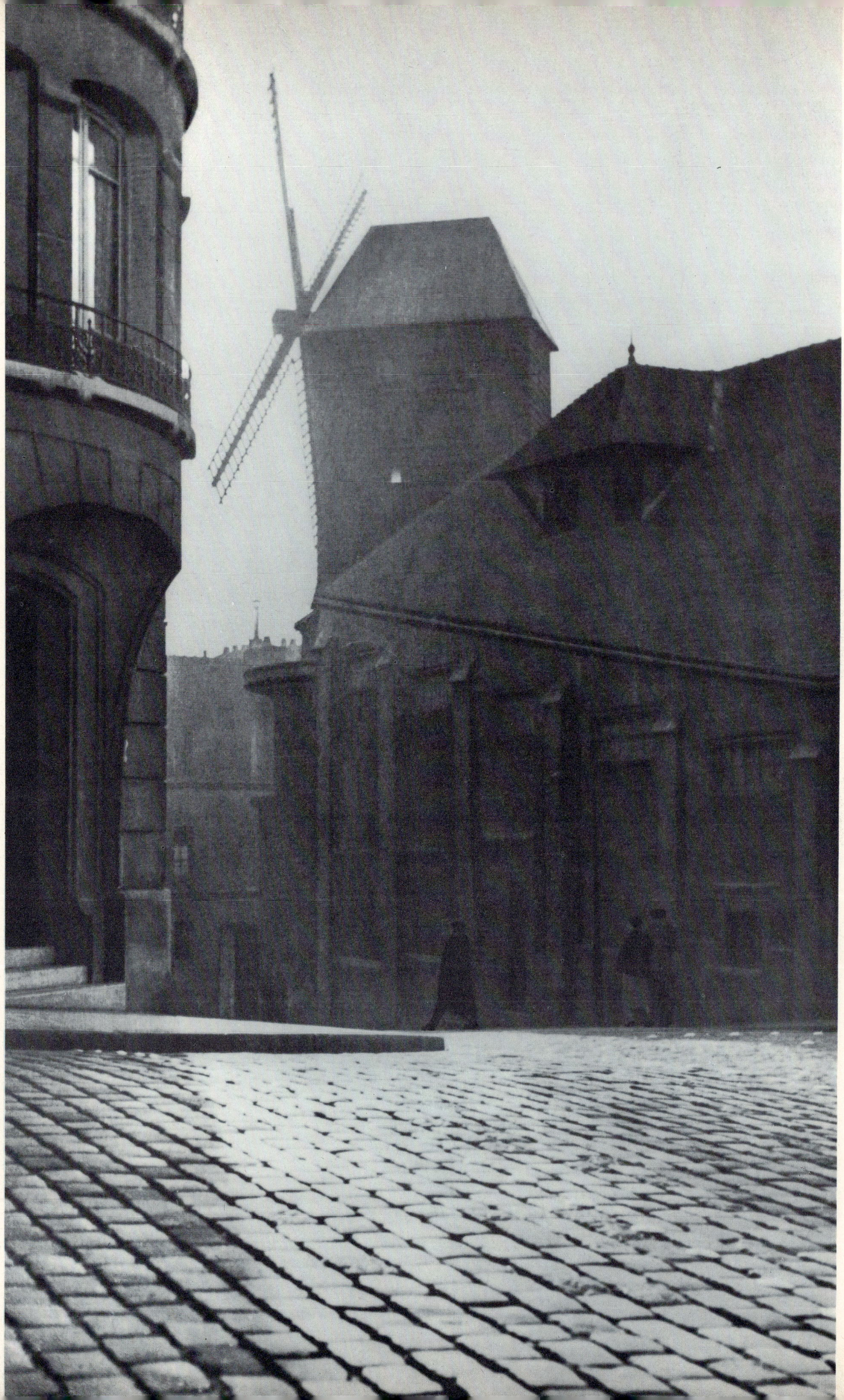

The Moulin de la Galette (the Money Mill) at the top of the hill on the Rue Lepic in Montmartre is one of the famous old restaurants of the artists' quarter. The narrow cobblestone streets in this section may be alive with people until late at night, but in the early morning, when the rest of Paris is already bustling, the blinds are still drawn along the Rue Lepic.

decline during the same century, because of the popularity of porcelain —ware made of transparent white paste.

PRODUCTION OF PORCELAIN

The manufacture of porcelain began in France when the majolica makers saw that their trade was being threatened by the rise of imports of Chinese porcelain. The principal raw material needed to produce porcelain is kaolin (a pure, white clay). In Europe, it was first discovered in Saxony, and a new and important period in the making of porcelain began. The marvelous Saxon ware spread throughout Europe and met with the greatest success. But the secret of manufacture was so closely and jealously kept that it did not become known in France until fifty years later.

Kaolin was discovered in France in 1768 in Saint-Yrieux near Limoges, and great French porcelain factories then reached the summit of their success.

"The Royal Porcelain Factory of Sèvres" began in Vincennes and was transferred to Sèvres in 1756. The products of both places are usually described as Sèvres ware. From 1756 until 1768 Sèvres made only soft ware, but after 1768 (the year kaolin was accidentally found) the secret of making hard paste was discovered. Both kinds of ware were made until the beginning of the 19th century, when soft paste was no longer used.

The best and most fashionable artists of the time worked at Sèvres. The factory owed its greatest development to Madame de Pompadour, for it was she who arranged for it to be named a Royal Factory. Several colors used at Sèvres have contributed to her fame. These were the cobalt-blue known as *bleu de roi* (royal blue), the sky-blue known as turquoise, and the flesh-colored rose known as "Pompadour rose." There were also "pansy blue," pale yellow, yellow-green and field-green.

From the beginning, Sèvres made flowers in relief and colored garlands for mirrors and other pieces of furniture. Some famous Sèvres pieces are the *Bather* by Falconet, the doors of the Academy, the Cupid Vase known as the *Garde-à-vous*, the portrait of La Rue supported by two tritons, and the *Bachelier* vase.

Limoges was famous in the Middle Ages for its so-called *champlevé* enamels, and during the Renaissance for its painted enamels—jewel-like works of art. Today the manufacture of porcelain is one of its principal industries. There are thirty factories employing more than 9000 workers. Half of its production is exported to the United States.

TAPESTRY

The art of tapestry-making is highly appreciated in France. The oldest factory was founded in 985 at Saumur, and the oldest example that exists is the Bayeux Tapestry (really an embroidery), which dates from the 11th century.

From the 12th, and especially from the 13th century, tapestry began to be very widely used in the interiors of houses and castles. Its use in this

In the casual atmosphere of Montparnasse, passersby assume the right to discuss aesthetics with the artists who are out painting scenes of the quarter. Montparnasse, on the left bank of the Seine, was originally an independent township. It was not included within the city limits of Paris until after 1848, when the tolls on the bridges crossing the Seine River were abolished.

178 / France • *The People*

The Moulin Rouge (the Red Mill), one of the landmarks of Montmartre, has retained its reputation, if not its flavor, from the 1880s. At that time the cabaret was a favorite rendezvous for the struggling young artists who were developing the style of painting now known as Impressionism. Auguste Renoir and Edgar Degas were both patrons of the Moulin Rouge at one time or another. The can-can entertainments offered at the cabaret were depicted many times by Henri Toulouse-Lautrec.

Place Pigalle in Montmartre was once the last stop on the trolley line. Trolleys don't run there any more, but Place Pigalle has done quite well without them. The night life of the area is famous, and activity in the plaza reaches its peak around midnight.

way reached a peak in the 14th and 15th centuries. At that time the leading factories were at Paris, Arras, Valenciennes and Lille.

Besides tapestries depicting numerous persons, there were also *verdures*, in which vegetation and floral decoration were most important. In the Middle Ages tapestries with persons on them were also called *draps à images*. Those from Arras rapidly took first place and the word "arras" became synonymous with tapestry in English and other languages.

The art of tapestry-making took an important step forward in the middle of the 16th century when workshops were opened at Fontainebleau—these were later transferred to Paris. In the 17th century, Louis XIV's minister, Fouquet, installed a workshop at Maincy and placed Charles Le Brun, the painter, in charge.

When Fouquet was disgraced, the king confiscated the works and transferred them to the Gobelins' factory. This factory took its name from its founders: Jean Gobelin, who came to Paris from Reims at the end of the 15th century, and his son Filibert.

Toward the end of the 18th century tapestry imitated painting in many ways. Today the so-called *au point* style is favored. This is a kind of embroidery on a large scale executed on linen or cotton with Algerian or Chinese silk.

THE GREAT FURNITURE MAKERS

One of the most celebrated names in the great tradition of French furniture making is that of André Boulle, who was in the service of Louis XIV.

His cupboards and commodes (chests of drawers) have more strength than elegance. They are rectangular, and are supported by massive legs because of their weight. The inlay of colored wood depicts vases or bunches of flowers, which wholly cover the panels.

Philippe Caffieri belongs to the same century, and was an excellent woodcarver and bronze worker. He worked at the Tuileries, the Louvre and Versailles.

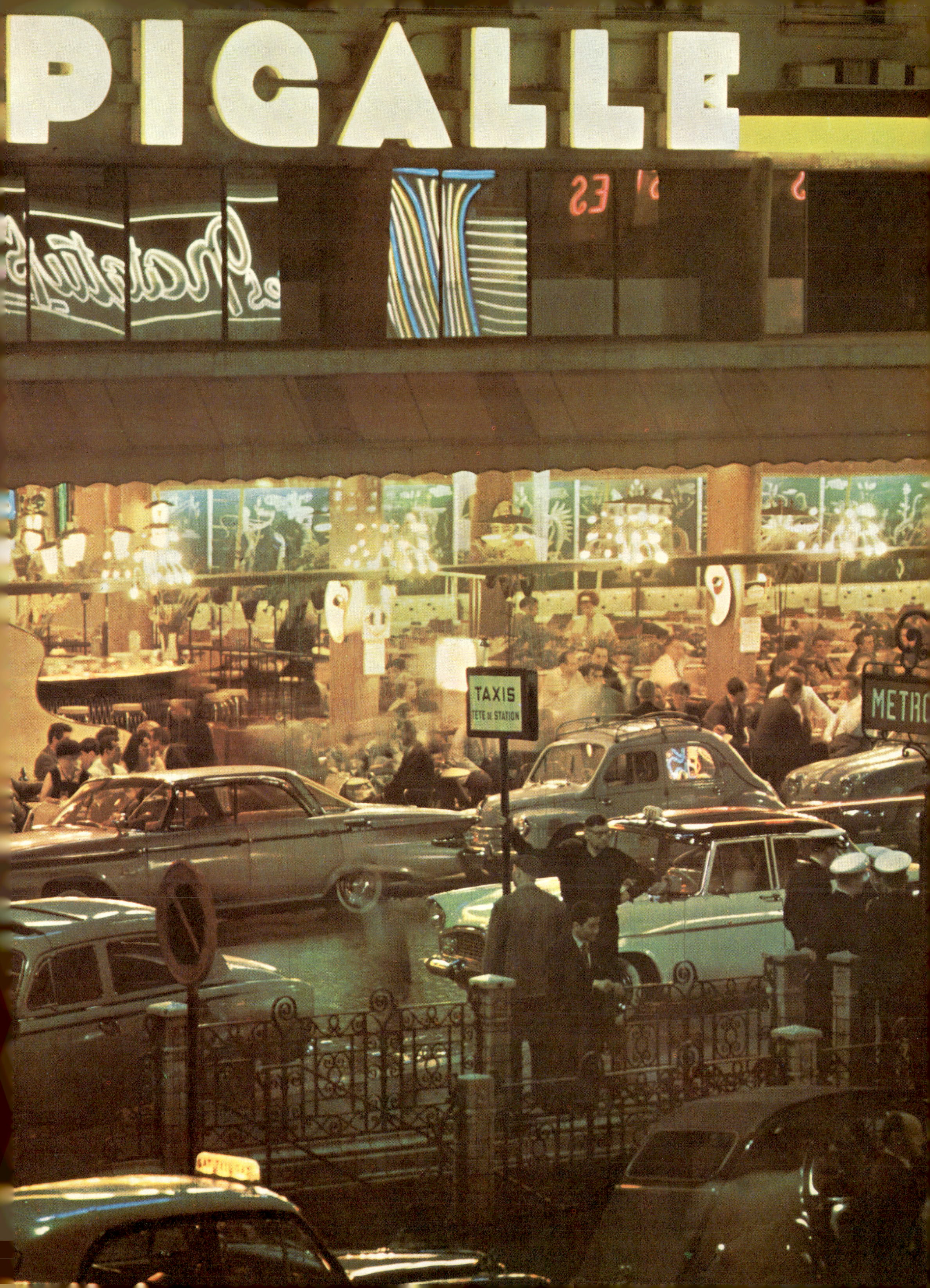
PIGALLE
TAXIS
TÊTE DE STATION
METRO

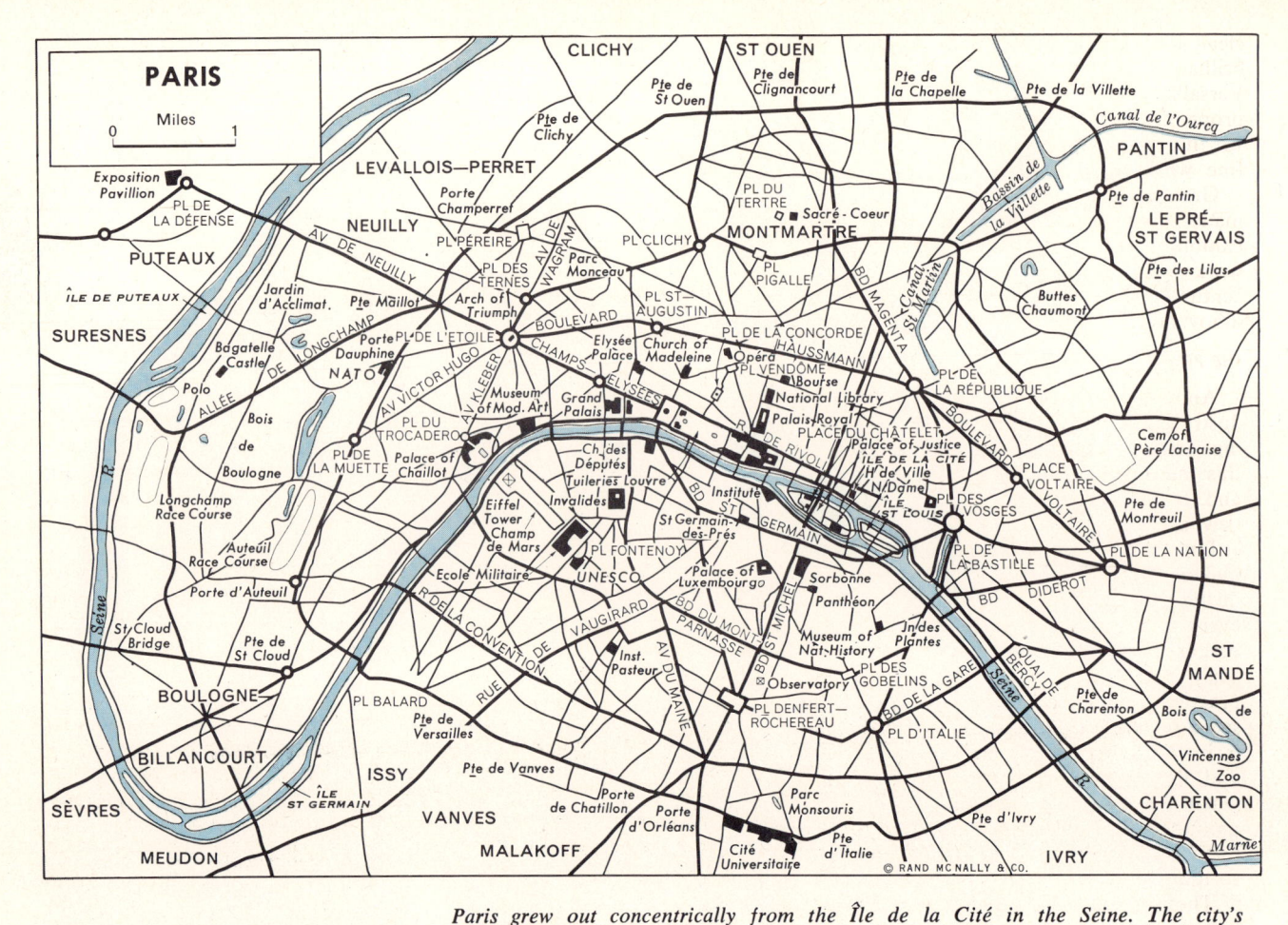

Paris grew out concentrically from the Île de la Cité in the Seine. The city's expansion can be traced on the map, where the ever-widening circles of boulevards that replaced the old city walls show up like the rings of a tree.

In the 18th century the Louis XV style arose, the first period of which may be said to extend from 1700 to 1740, and should more accurately be called the Regency style. The forms favored under Louis XIV were softened and lightened.

Carlin was a leading exponent of the Louis XV style, and Marie Antoinette commissioned him to make desks and chests of drawers for herself and her friends. Most of these little masterpieces have been preserved.

François Hache produced a great deal of furniture of admirable perfection, and Georges Jacobs, the founder of the workshop called after him, was also outstanding. He made particularly fine beds, chairs, armchairs and sofas. His family produced furniture from the reign of Louis XV until that of Charles X.

The Louis XVI style began about 1750 with the work of François Leuleu, who furnished the royal residences and part of a pavilion at Luciennes.

The most notable furniture maker of the reign of Louis XVI, and possibly the greatest furniture maker of all time, was undoubtedly Heinrich Riesner, who came to Paris from Germany. A study of his genius is a study of the entire Louis XVI style in its most elegant and refined form. This style was a neoclassical one; it was simple and plainly decorated with trophies, cornucopias and tripods.

The tradition of French cabinetmakers has been preserved down to

The owner of this delicacy shop in Paris is putting out the specialty for the day —decorated spiced bread shaped like pork chops.

our day. But unfortunately in France, as in every other country of Europe, craftsmanship has declined. Many old families of cabinetmakers have died out or have abandoned their craft.

METALWORK

The jewelers and goldsmiths of Paris have been famous for more than fifteen centuries. Illustrious jewelers and metalworkers also lived at Limoges, Toulouse and Montpellier.

Until the 13th century the craft was mainly concerned with sacred objects, produced for use by the Church. But in the 14th century such magnificent works all but disappeared and the art was applied to secular uses. Great table pieces and saltcellars were made. Many were of gold and were decorated with colored enamel, pearls and precious stones.

The reign of Louis XIV was a period of splendor. Vases, candelabra, mirrors, candlesticks and other objects made at this time give us a clear idea of the magnificence and brilliance of life at the Court of Versailles and of what was considered proper for the greatness of the king. In the 18th century other equally fine work was done.

Great efforts have recently been made to modernize the craft. Every exhibition of jewelry and fine metalwork held in France during this century has reflected efforts at innovation.

THE PERFUME INDUSTRY

Another flourishing modern industry is the perfume industry. Leading fashion designers take part in this industry by lending their names, and, from time to time, by launching new scents.

But the real French perfume makers are obscure people who live in the provinces and know intimately every secret of their craft. The very best are found in Grasse, in Provence. They are not theoreticians but practical men, with an extremely fine sense of smell. When a new mixture is in the process of formation, they, and they alone, know by the odor when it has reached the right moment. The chemists then begin their analysis and write down the formula.

These men, who might well be called "master craftsmen," are in fact known as "noses." It is well worthwhile to visit them and see them work.

Off the right bank of the Seine is Les Halles, which for centuries has been the wholesale food market of the entire city of Paris. Today, Les Halles is no longer able to cope with the vast quantities of food the city needs to feed itself. The government has drawn up plans to replace Les Halles with a number of smaller markets in different parts of the city that will process food much more efficiently and hygienically, but traditionalists have protested violently against the abandonment of the old market.

FOOD AND DRINK

FRENCH COOKING HAS AN ILLUSTRIOUS history, but it is not as old as might be expected, especially in comparison with the history of French politics, warfare and social life. The Gauls, even after the arrival of the Romans, do not seem to have been particularly good cooks. Their banquets were abundant but simple: roast meat, boiled meat, a little fish, a little honey.

Charlemagne encouraged the cultivation of vines and fruit trees, and he may be given some of the credit for founding the vineyards of France. Whaling began in the 9th century, and whale's flesh appeared more and more often on the tables of French lords. The tongue was considered a great delicacy.

In those days guests brought their own knives. Only spoons were supplied by the host. Forks had not yet been invented. Before plates were introduced meat was served on thick slices of bread, which were thrown to the dogs when the meal was over. The diners used the tablecloth to wipe their lips.

The now famous refinement of French cooking is due to a woman —Catherine de Medici, the queen of Henry II, whom she married in 1533. She brought with her from Florence the cuisine and customs of Italy. Turkey, peacock, swan, turtle, eel, beaver and green beans were all served for the first time in France on her initiative.

In the late 16th century the feasts became enormous. At a certain wedding nine oxen were roasted, as well as eighteen calves, eight sheep, eighty suckling pigs, 100 goats, 150 capons, 200 chickens and 120 other birds of various kinds. In addition, there were eighty geese, sixty pheasants and about 150 brace of game birds. As many as 200 different dishes would be served at one meal in rich and highly varied forms. A celebrated pie was made to contain a complete orchestra.

In the 17th century tables were decorated with fountains, flowers and birds which were released when the toasts were drunk. The richness of Louis XIV's banquets is well

The wealthiest and most distinguished members of French society spend their evenings attending gala theatrical and musical performances. This one is at the Opéra. The presence of the uniformed Republican Guards flanking the guests along the balustrades indicates that the occasion is indeed a special one. The Guard, an elite corps of the French Army, is only assigned to social events if a person of at least ministerial rank is scheduled to attend.

known. The king was a great eater, and at his feasts six dishes of different game meat were usually served, as well as ten turtles, four dishes of fish and eight of other meat, in addition to the hors d'œuvres and pastry. It was in the reign of Louis XIV that the celebrated Parmentier introduced the idea of eating potatoes as a main vegetable—and this habit has been adopted by all Western peoples since.

The Revolution brought austerity back to the kitchen, and the gross overeating of the past did not return. Nevertheless, within the limits imposed by modern conditions and modern energy the French are still distinguished for the richness and variety of their cooking. This is due to the notable differences in taste in the various regions of the country.

REGIONAL SPECIALTIES

The Île-de-France is the historical heart of France, and its capital is Paris. Among its more delicate dishes are lark pie, Paris mushrooms (from Carrière-sous-Bois), chicken paté baked under a layer of béchamel sauce, the well-known onion soup *(soupe à l'oignon)* and the *entrecôte Bercy,* a thick steak with a butter and white wine sauce.

Along the banks of the Seine fish are served in wine sauce, and in the more modest Parisian restaurants one can always find a steak *Châteaubriand aux pommes*.

Pommes soufflées were served for the first time in 1857 in a restaurant on the terrace of Saint-Germain-en-Laye. This way of cooking potatoes was the result of an accident. The railway from Paris to Saint-Germain-en-Laye was being opened, but the official guests were late for the banquet because the first train was late. The cook was obliged to take the already fried potatoes out of the pans. He put them back in the fat to warm when the guests arrived, and had the pleasant surprise of seeing them swell up. Having a gift for happy improvisation, he called them *pommes soufflées* (swelled-up potatoes), served them as a specialty, and delighted the diners.

NORMAN RECIPES

Norman specialties are based on milk, butter, fish and eggs. Norman tripe is also exquisite, and is cooked in various ways. The little lobsters of Cherbourg are renowned, and are known as *demoiselles*. The omelettes of Mont-Saint-Michel are also famous. Fish and meat specialties are to be found also at Caudebec, Dieppe, Duclair, Falaise, Rouen, Lisieux and Vimoutiers.

The trout of Arques and Gisors and the biscuits of Le Havre are also remarkable. Norman recipes are very tasty, especially the stuffed rabbit decorated with yolks of eggs. There are twenty-one kinds of Norman cheese. Apples are often used in desserts (unlike elsewhere in France). The apples are baked in the oven, served with or without béchamel sauce, and are eaten with liqueurs and with cream. Wine, but more often Calvados—a spirit made from cider—is drunk. There are many kinds of Calvados, all with different aromas. The Jeannetonne smells of violets, the Fenouillets of aniseed and the Binet Doré of honey.

FISH OF BRITTANY

Brittany is a paradise for fish lovers because three quarters of its boundaries are seacoasts. Excellent oysters, lobsters, lampreys, eels, umber, dentex and gilt-heads are to be had. Fish is served in béchamel, or in white sauce. It also may be steeped in vinegar, fried and covered with cheese, or grilled and covered with mushroom sauce.

Fried fish are very good along the Loire, and there is excellent salmon at Nantes. Sardines fried in batter at Saint-Jacques and little fried eels at Saint-Nazaire are both excellent dishes. Fish soup, made in many different ways, is a specialty everywhere. A dry white wine, Muscadet, goes perfectly with fish, lobsters and shellfish.

But Brittany has other specialties besides fish. Because of its mild climate its vegetables are very good. The peas and cabbages of Nantes, the potatoes of Dinan, Pont-Abbé and Redon, the cauliflowers, artichokes, and onions of Guerande and Quimperlé and the beans of Roscoff are all sought after and often exported.

The local hams of Brittany, cured in a rough country way, with their

Whether in a peasant cottage or the plushest Parisian restaurant, the subtle blending of ingredients that characterizes French cooking can transform the most ordinary meats and vegetables into culinary masterpieces.

This picture, The Peasants' Meal, *painted by Louis le Nain in 1630, illustrates the honorable history of the French tradition of wine with dinner. According to an old French proverb, "A meal without wine is like a day without sunshine."*

own fragrance, are very good. Strawberries are cultivated in Plougastel, and almond paste is made at Pont-l'Abbé and is sold under the name of *Bigoudens*.

FOOD AND DRINK IN CHAMPAGNE

The province of Champagne makes us think of wine, but though they drink well in Champagne, they eat better. Due to the nearness of the forest of the Ardennes there are many excellent recipes for cooking game, especially wild boar. Boar and pork are cooked in white wine and then covered with aromatic herbs and grilled. Galantines, pâtés, and the celebrated hams of Troyes are other specialties.

Fish is common in the province of Champagne: trout in Aube, grilled eels with champagne, little fried fish dipped in champagne. The meat is excellent. Sainte-Menehould has particularly good recipes for cooking mutton, sauté of kidneys in champagne, and calf's head and tail boiled

184 / FRANCE · *The People*

A winery's reputation often depends on the judgment of a single man, who determines the quality and maturity of the finished liquor. This man is testing the maturity of a vat of cognac, the finest brandy produced in France. He uses a long tube to extract a sample without disturbing the rest of the liquid in the distilling vat. His glass is bulb-shaped, so that he can also test the bouquet of the maturing brandy. The wide bottom of the brandy snifter allows a large surface for the brandy, so that the fumes can rise. The narrow neck collects them for the drinker to savor. Sniffing a brandy while contemplating the world at one's leisure is a philosophical pastime enjoyed by many Frenchmen.

with bacon, spread with warm butter, and cooked on a slow grill.

Also noteworthy are the roast kid of Château-Thierry, the wild boar of Argonne, the white pudding of Rethal and the red cabbage soup of Mourmelon. Well-known cheeses are those of Coulommiers, the Marne, Langres and Suippes. The cookies and spiced bread of Reims are famous. In this region the cookies are generally very rich—some literally drip with butter.

The most characteristic northern dish is the *garniture à la flamande*, made of carrots, lettuce and cabbage with roast lamb and veal. Another Flemish specialty is the use of beer in sauces—as in eel cooked in beer —and in some soups.

BURGUNDIAN WINES AND RECIPES

Burgundy is often said to be "of purple and gold," the reference being to the colors of her wines. These are among the best in France. The French speak with great respect of Romanée-Conti, Clos Vougeot, Montrachet, Musigny, Volnay, Chambertin and Nuits-Saint-Georges.

Wine is used on a large scale in Burgundian cooking, and, because of its excellent quality, produces very good sauces. Burgundy has at least 140 regional dishes, and many of the best French recipes come from there.

Burgundian vegetables are fragrant, and the fruit is delicious. Game abounds; fresh-water fish are very tasty; the meat is superb; the poultry is fat. In addition, the hams of Dijon, one of the culinary capitals of France, are among the best in the world.

Burgundy also has recipes for a great number of lark and woodcock pies. Its mustard is very fine and tasty, and so are its spiced breads and liqueurs. Saint-Jean-de-Losne, Auxerre, Meursault, Chablis and Flavigny have delicious candies. Beaune has big fish and fillets of beef. Charolles, famous for its beef, also offers fish cooked in red wine as well as stewed chicken.

Châlon-sur-Saône has blue trout and eels; Chablis has meringues and Chagny cheese brioches. Burgundian cheeses are famous, especially those from Avallon, Soumaintrain, the Abbey of Cîteaux, and Epoisses. The snails of Burgundy are celebrated.

Franche-Comté and the Jura are well known for their cheeses, and fondues (cheese melted with white wine, salt and pepper) are very popular. Another specialty, *ramequin de fromage*, made of cheese melted in water, butter, onion, salt and pepper, is similar to Welsh rabbit.

The regional dish of Franche-Comté is the so-called *Gaude,* a sort of porridge made of corn flour. The *potée franc-comtoise* is also rather common, and is made of beef, bacon, smoked sausages, leg of mutton, cabbage and potatoes. Noteworthy wines are Château-Chalon, which is very dry, and also white and golden Arbois.

The Vosges are well known for their mountain trout, aniseed bread and marzipan pastries. Vosges cheeses are rather strong. Chocolate with cherry flavoring is made similar to that of Switzerland. The beer is excellent.

DISHES OF THE LOIRE VALLEY

Clemenceau said that the Loire valley is "one of the corners of France, where France is most itself." It is also one of the places where one can eat best.

The inhabitants of the region are proud of their butter sauce made over a slow fire and never brought to a boil. Stuffed fish, fricasseed chicken, stuffed artichokes, salads, sausages, white and black blood puddings, pea soup, and buttered cauliflower purée with vinegar are the traditional dishes of Anjou. The wines of the Layon valley, the Loire coteaux and Saumur are all well regarded.

In Tours, Vouvray wine is used in cooking many foods including tripe, eggs and beef, which are done in this way as specialties. There are few striking specialties at Orléans. Its lark and hare pies are much like those to be found elsewhere. There are many different kinds of pastries, however, including apple tarts and almond cakes.

The cooking of Auvergne is not as well known as that of the other provinces, but it is exquisite. *Tourte à la viande* is a pie made with pork and veal forcemeat and the local potée is a fine peasants' soup made in copper pots with little pieces of salt pork. Salmon pies in Brioude and kid cooked in wine are two other specialties of Auvergne.

Like Auvergne, Limousin is not very well known for its cooking, but here is the recipe for the best-known dish of the province, called *le clafoutis*. Take three eggs, three spoonfuls each of flour and sugar, a little salt, and three cups of milk.

Break the eggs one after the other into the flour and salt. Mix them well; pour in the milk little by little; then add the sugar. Pour the flour-and-egg mixture over a pound of pitted cherries and bake for ten or fifteen minutes. When it is ready spread sugar over the top.

Fat beef, fat chickens stuffed with cabbage, stuffed goose neck, goose liver, turkey, salad with nut oil, hares *à la royale,* goat-milk cheese, and fresh pork are all specialties of this province.

FISH OF LA VENDÉE

The coasts of La Vendée abound with fish, which are cooked with great skill and originality. An example of this is the use of red wine in the fish soup made in Sables-d'Olonne. The soups of this region are of the peasant type called *louche debout* (which means that they are so thick that the spoon stands up in them by itself). They usually have bases of cabbage, smoked ham, potatoes and a little garlic.

Other specialties are the *moyettes* (beans cooked in cream) of Fontenay-le-Comte and the cookies shaped like mermaids, called *melusines de Lusignan.* There is also a flour-and-corn soup. The oysters and shellfish are famous.

Equally famous is the tasty *présalé* mutton, so called because the sheep feed on pastures along the coast where the salt air gets into the grass and flavors their flesh. Oysters are raised along the coasts, and they are usually eaten raw, sometimes accompanied by little hot sausages and local black mustard.

The Charente is famous for sardines. The local custom is to eat them uncooked after they have been marinated for two or three days, together with butter and a local wine.

Cognac is made by distilling certain wines of Charente. The liquid that is distilled is originally white. It receives its golden color from the Limousin casks in which it is stored. The special wood with which the casks are made becomes impregnated with brandy and adds to the special flavor.

THE WINES OF BORDEAUX

The region of Bordeaux is an important winegrowing area. It is said that Bordeaux has two notable things: good wines and beautiful women. But its cooking is also very good. It does not have a great number of regional specialties, but the ones it has are very refined.

The tender lamb of Pauillac, the plums of Agen, the oysters and fish soups of Arcachon, the *pâtés de foie gras,* woodcock, geese, tripe, snails, noodles, and almond pastries delight lovers of food. The traditional soup of Bordeaux is made with pork fat, onions and egg yolks. The *entrecôte à la Bordelaise* is justly famous, and

French cooks are always interested in new ways to prepare food. The woman in the picture is picking up a few pointers from the chef in the restaurant as he prepares a chicken for the pot.

has been poorly imitated at Paris.

Marmande brandy, Bordeaux anisette, and the Vieille Cure liqueur made by the monks of Cenon are outstanding products of the region. The Duke of Richelieu, when he was governor of French Guiana, used to drink Bordeaux wines to recover from the tropical diseases he incurred. He died at the age of eighty-four. The Bordelais therefore feel that they have some reason for calling their wine *eau-de-vie* (water of life).

Once the duke heard an old bishop rebuking some heavy drinkers on the grounds that they were displeasing God. Richelieu tasted the wine and exclaimed, "Why would God make such good wine, if it is displeasing to him?" Among the vineyards in this region are Médoc, Graves and Sauternes.

Château-Yquem, Château-Margaux, Château Mouton-Rothschild, Château-Lafite and Château-Latour are the best wines of Bordeaux.

BASQUE EELS AND OYSTERS

Béarn and the Basque country probably have the most singular kind of cooking in France. In winter, for example, cold fresh oysters and hot boiled sausages are eaten in alternate mouthfuls in the Basque country and the contrast is said to be very pleasant.

The Bidassoa River forms part of the frontier between France and Spain and divides the Basque country into two parts. From it come the tasty eels of La Hendaye, which are served with different kinds of garnishing and stuffing. Oysters and a great many other kinds of shellfish come from Saint-Jean-de-Luz, which is on the coast near Biarritz.

The hot hors d'œuvre known as *sanguete* is unique, but it is not to everyone's taste. It consists of chicken blood cooked with fat, onions and garlic.

In the Basque country everything has a violent character—food, language, the windy climate, the highly colored costumes, and the landscape. Pepper, green and red peppers, and

Because cooking is considered a high art in France, merchants who sell good food are extremely proud of their work and their wares. A butcher is not just a man who slaughters animals and sells meat. He is the cook's trusted advisor. He alone can tell madame whether the veal is perhaps a bit dry today, or when the roast beef is particularly succulent. As a result, he feels that he is an important partner in every successful dinner his customers cook.

The French housewife, for her part, is a careful shopper. To get the choicest fruits and vegetables she does her marketing very early in the morning, soon after the fruit man returns from Les Halles with the day's produce.

spices and herbs of all kinds are much used. The wines and liqueurs are very strong, dry and harsh. A well-known Basque liqueur is *izarra*, and the best-known wines are *Madiran*, *Portet* and *Juraçon*.

Geographically, Armagnac does not belong to Béarn and the Basque country, but in regard to wine it does. It is a very important wine-growing area, and its highly refined liqueurs compete with the products of Cognac. The high quality is due not only to the special processes and treatments used but also to the alluvial soils in which the vines grow.

THE LAND OF COCKAIGNE

The French say: *Gascogne, pays de Cocagne* (Gascony is the Land of Cockaigne—where anything could, and does, happen). This also applies to the manner in which the Gascons prepare food.

When they describe their dishes they do so with such brilliance and ingenuity that the listener feels he has already tasted them. Like the Gascon temperament, the Gascon cuisine is full of contrasts. Their

The judges of the annual tripe contest in Caen receive encouragement from the sidelines as they set to work. The city, which considers itself to be the tripe capital of the world, sponsors the contest. Every year at a banquet, twenty gourmets from the Tripière d'Or (the Golden Tripe-dealer, a professional association) decide which dealer in the city has the best tripe.

dishes can be strong and delicate at the same time, just as the Gascons can be tough and mild at the same time.

They serve woodock with a sauce to which Armagnac brandy has been added. Veal is served together with wild boar. They cook beans with hardly any water, adding a few drops at a time, as the liquid evaporates, in order to bring out the flavor.

In Roussillon the vegetables are excellent: peas, lettuces, potatoes, beans, mushrooms, artichokes, asparagus. These, together with the good mutton from the pastures of the Corbières hills, game and ham, are all specialties of Gascon cooking. The wines are dry and "sincere," like everything in these provinces, and the white, red and rosé wines of Banyuls are outstanding.

Languedoc has several outstanding gastronomic specialties. The fish dishes, snails, and the pâtés to be had in Nîmes, Montpellier, Toulouse, Narbonne and Perpignan are considered incomparable by many.

The pastries containing sheep's milk, cheese made in Lodève, the tripe stew of Bédarieux, the snails of Narbonne and the chicken sauté of Quillan, are, however, real specialties.

Languedoc, however, produces more wine than any other part of France, and on account of the diversity of the terrain the wines are quite varied. There are delicate, dry, aromatic, sparkling and bubbling wines, and good red and white table wine. The muscat from Frontignan is very good, and was praised by the Duke of Richelieu and Voltaire. The French sometimes use the bubbling wines of Languedoc as substitutes for champagne.

FISH FROM THE RHONE

The Rhone valley is a long, broad strip stretching out on both sides of the river and containing some of the most fertile regions of France.

For a gourmet, a visit to Lyon is an unforgettable event. Carp taken from the Saône and the Rhone is so well cooked there that many travelers cannot believe that these are the same kind of fish that they tasted elsewhere. Even the modest restaurants in the city serve all the specialties of the whole Rhone valley.

Silk merchants who came to Lyon from all over Europe centuries ago returned full of praise for its cooking. However, no particular dish may be pointed out as the best.

Chicken is cooked in innumerable ways, and ordinary vegetables are transformed into unusual dishes with sauces made from secret recipes. Veal and beef are roasted, minced, stuffed, made into sausages and blood puddings, and served with artichokes full of *foie gras*. The wine is the famous Beaujolais.

Bresse, which supplies Lyon with food, is the homeland of Brillat-Savarin, the noted gourmet, who wrote *The Physiology of Taste*.

SAVOY AND PROVENCE

In Savoy cooking is simple and basic. Peasant soups and fondues predominate, as in all Alpine countries. The *gratins* (dishes covered with a cheese or bread-crumb crust) of Dauphiné are famous, as is the liqueur of the Grande Chartreuse.

The Alpine regions do not have a particular cuisine of their own. There are several curious dishes, however, such as the nettle salad made with a pepper dressing in Chamonix, the jugged hare of Mégève, and the Alpine cheeses of Pelvoux.

Provençal cooking has been praised by famous men, such as Mirabeau,

Alphonse Daudet, Mistral and Paul Arène. Two of its outstanding dishes are fresh sardines and the *gratins*. *Rayolles* are a kind of ravioli, but they are stuffed with vegetables instead of meat, and eaten especially at Christmas. Chicken is cooked with tomatoes, snails *à l'Arlésienne*, tripe *à la mode de Marseille*, while tomatoes are stuffed with garlic and parsley.

FOOD OF THE CÔTE D'AZUR

The Côte d'Azur is divided, gastronomically, into two distinct sectors: luxury restaurants and hotels, and modest ones. In the former, specialties from Dijon, Lyon and even Béarn, and all the dishes belonging to the standardized international cuisine, are available. In the latter are found the tasty dishes that derive from Provençal and Italian traditions.

In Nice and the surrounding countryside an excellent salad of nettles with a dressing of anchovy sauce and garlic is made. The nettles are dipped by each diner into a bowl containing the sauce (which is set on a little stove in the middle of the table), and eaten like asparagus.

The *ratatouille* of Nice is a mixture of tomatoes and other vegetables with garlic and peppers. *Fassum*, a specialty of Grasse, is cabbage stuffed with rice and peas. In Grasse also, *fougassettes*—hearth cakes—are made of flour mixed with oil and orange essence. Omelettes are made with acacia blossoms, and with rum *flambé*. Another specialty of the Mediterranean coast is the *pissaladiera*, a pizza covered with chopped onions cooked in black olives and anchovies.

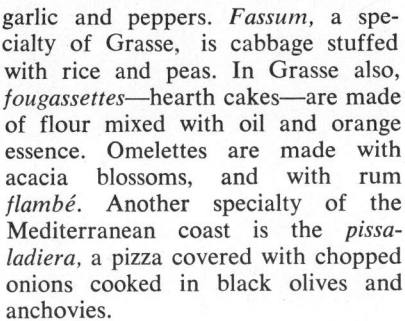

Corsica is famous for its smoked sausages. Ham is known there as *prisuttu* and is excellent. Corsican pork chops and pig's liver are very tasty. The outstanding Corsican wines are Forcino, Bianchetti, Pariglia, Vin du Cap, and Patrimonio.

ALSACE AND LORRAINE

The cooking in Alsace and Lorraine is of a high quality. Cutlets, liver, sausages, smoked shoulder of veal and mutton, and hot sauces with a great deal of pepper, are all favorites. Pheasant with sausages, and brains with steamed potatoes are special dishes, as well as goose stuffed with meat, sausages and minced onions cooked in butter.

Besides these dishes for those with strong stomachs, there are the delicate fish of the mountain streams of the Vosges, trout with mushrooms, sole with white wine and sauté potatoes, artichokes and little mushrooms, and chicken and steak *à la crème,* with egg and butter.

There are many other tasty, popular dishes, such as *bakenote*, made with meat, onions and potatoes; Strasbourg onion soup; and *pâté de foie gras*, a Strasbourg specialty.

Finally, there are the candies and pastries. Those of Alsace and Lorraine are more German than French. The Strasbourg apple tart has a caramel flavor and is covered with cream. *Boutemousse* is a fruit tart. And there are many more pastries and cakes, some of which are served with flaming cherry brandy.

Kirsch, or cherry brandy, from Alsace is of the finest quality. Also, among the wines, Riesling, Traminer and Muscat are well known.

Trade organizations set professional standards for members' products and are important as social groups. They also sponsor trade festivals. The annual procession of the cooks of Ribeauville includes floats shaped like different dishes. The one in the foreground is a savarin, *an elegant, rum-flavored French cake.*

PAGE	THE HISTORY
190	CAESAR TO THE CAROLINGIANS *Roman Conquest and Rule ... Barbarian Invasions ... The Franks ... The Merovingians ... The Carolingians ... Charlemagne*
196	MEDIEVAL FRANCE *Capetians ... Albigensian Crusade ... Louis IX ... Philip the Fair and the Papacy ... Fourteenth-Century Crisis ... Hundred Years' War ... English Victories ... Joan of Arc ... Louis XI*
204	RENAISSANCE AND REFORMATION *Italian Wars ... Francis I ... Reformation ... Wars of Religion*
207	HENRY IV TO LOUIS XVI *Henry IV ... Edict of Nantes ... Louis XIII ... Richelieu ... The Fronde ... Louis XIV ... The War of the Spanish Succession ... The Seven Years' War ... The Enlightenment*
215	THE REVOLUTION, THE EMPIRE AND THE RESTORATION *The Revolution ... Fall of the Bastille ... Execution of Louis XVI ... The Terror ... Fall of the Jacobins ... The Napoleonic Period ... Retreat from Moscow ... The Restoration*
224	LOUIS PHILIPPE TO NAPOLEON III *1830 Revolution ... Second Republic ... Second Empire ... Napoleon III ... Franco-Prussian War ... Paris Commune*
227	THE THIRD REPUBLIC *Foundation ... Colonial Expansion ... World War I ... Between the Wars ... The Totalitarian Challenge*
231	WORLD WAR II AND THE FOURTH REPUBLIC *The Fall of France ... The Vichy Regime ... The Fourth Republic ... Early Postwar Period ... France and the United States*
234	THE FIFTH REPUBLIC *De Gaulle Comes to Power ... Domestic Policy ... End of Algerian War ... France, Europe and the World*

CAESAR TO THE CAROLINGIANS

IN HIS BOOK *Gallic Wars (De Bello Gallico)* Julius Caesar described Gaul as the territory bounded by the Atlantic Ocean, the Pyrenees, the Alps and the Rhine. In the 1st century B.C. this area was occupied by different peoples with a common Celtic origin.

Originally, the social and political organization of the Gauls was barbaric and primitive, being based on a nomadic way of life characterized by warfare. Agriculture and settled political life soon developed, however, and were at first based on the clan system. Next, commerce developed, especially along the great rivers, and the first examples of Gallic money date from the 3rd century B.C. They were modeled on Greek coins from Marseille.

At the time of the Roman conquest, however, Celtic society was far from being unified. The various

Southern Gaul fell to the Romans in 121 B.C., but the rest of Gallic territory—which included most of modern France—was not taken until almost seventy years later, between 58 and 52 B.C., when Julius Caesar's legions finally conquered it. The Romans' influence was particularly strong in southern Gaul, as the many monuments they built show. Among them is this triumphal arch at Saint-Rémy.

peoples were strangers and often enemies to each other, and while the priests—the Druids—were a unifying force, this seems to have affected only the aristocratic elements of Gaul. There was not even unity within the tribes, because the aristocratic groups were sharply divided from the rest of the population.

THE ROMAN CONQUEST

The Romans benefited from this double antagonism—rivalry between the tribes and internal social divisions. The Roman Conquest was at first limited to that part of Gaul in the Rhône valley between the Alps and the Mediterranean. This area made up the province of *Gallia Narbonensis,* with its capital at Narbonne, and was usually known as *Provincia,* "The Province," from which comes the name "Provence."

It was Julius Caesar (100 B.C.-44 B.C.) who extended Roman rule to the whole of Gaul. He took advantage of the quarrels that the pressure of the German peoples advancing from the Rhine was causing among the tribes and the pro-Roman feelings of the aristocrats to subdue the whole country between 58 B.C. and 52 B.C.

Vercingetorix, the chieftain of Auvergne, tried to bring about a general uprising to overthrow the Roman power. But his effort failed, after a long and bitterly contested struggle that culminated in the siege of Alesia by Caesar in 52 B.C. This event completed the Roman Conquest, but many uprisings occurred later, and it was not until the time of the Emperor Vespasian in A.D. 70 that Gaul could be considered to have been fully subdued.

Under Roman rule Gaul enjoyed a long period of economic and social development. Large areas of land were opened up to cultivation and new crops were introduced. Wine-growing, which has acquired such importance in France, was also introduced. Cities grew up and expanded, especially in the Province (for instance, Narbonne and Lyon). Commerce, which remained largely in the hands of Greeks and Syrians, who had settled in that region some centuries before the Roman conquest, also expanded.

ROMAN RULE

Essential to the establishment of Roman rule in Gaul, apart from the question of military power, was the support received from the local aristocrats, who willingly accepted Romanization and promoted it among their peoples. These aristocrats sought a Latin education, adopted Roman customs, dress and language, and tried to win the conquerors' trust and to gain positions of responsibility.

Roman culture spread gradually to all classes and Latin slowly took the place of the Celtic languages in daily affairs. Place names and personal names were Latinized, and there are many French place names today that evidently derive from Roman family names—for instance, Savignac, Savigné, and Savigny are all from *Sabinus.*

In the long run, the Roman domination of Gaul had a disruptive effect. The double burden on the common people imposed by the local aristocrats and Roman taxes brought about the same kind of decadence that occurred throughout the rest of the Western Empire.

The countryside lost population on a large scale, the commercial life of the cities declined and peasant uprisings became frequent. Measures such as those binding the peasants to the soil, controlling trade in the towns and the industrial guilds, and reinvigorating the army by introducing barbarian mercenaries were tried, but with little effect. They only tended to aggravate the problems.

As the country grew weak in this way, the pressure of the Germanic barbarians on the eastern frontier increased. This pressure was contained during the whole of the 4th century A.D. by means of a system called *foederatio,* by which the barbarian tribes were received as guests on Roman territory. They were given land on condition that they defended the frontiers against newcomers. The efforts of energetic emperors like Julian and Valentinian also helped to hold back the pressure of the barbarians.

BARBARIAN INVASIONS

By the 5th century, however, the whole defense system of Roman Gaul rapidly collapsed. In 406 a wave of Germanic Vandal invaders opened the way to the Franks and Burgundians, who settled on the western bank of the Rhine. The capital of Gaul therefore had to be moved from Trier on the Rhine to Arles.

In 412 the Visigoths settled in *Gallia Narbonensis* as *foederati* (allies) and founded a flourishing kingdom with its capital at Toulouse. The Roman general Aetius was able to check further inroads by the barbarians and was famous for having driven back the Huns under their leader Attila in 451. But Aetius died in 454 and the barbarians again advanced.

The Visigoths reached the Loire, and the Burgundians settled on the lower courses of the Rhone and the Durance. The Franks occupied modern Brabant in the north and the western banks of the Rhine and the Moselle. In the first half of the 6th century Celtic peoples fleeing from Britain occupied the Armorican peninsula, modern Britanny. The Gallo-Roman territories between the Loire and the Somme that were still unoccupied were thus cut off from the rest of the Empire, and soon fell to the invaders.

The Franks—The Merovingian Dynasty

The Salian Franks were among the least numerous and least advanced of the peoples settled within the Roman frontiers at the time of the fall of the Empire. They lived in a marshy and somewhat inaccessible

About 475 A.D., when the Roman Empire in the west was disintegrating most of Gaul was already divided up among Romanized Germanic tribes. The Franks were in the north, the Visigoths in the south, and the Burgundians in the east. Among the cities, Argentoratum is modern Strasbourg, Burdigala is Bordeaux, Massilia is Marseille and Mediolanum is Milan.

area and had been only slightly influenced by Roman civilization. But it was this people who accomplished the task of reunifying Gaul and who gave it their own name—*Francia*.

The rise of the Franks to power occurred during a relatively brief period and was the work of King Clovis (465-511). He destroyed the kingdom of Syagrius, the last relic of the Roman occupation, in 486, defeated the Alamanni in the battle of Tolbiacum in 496, and in 507 attacked the Visigothic kingdom in the south and won a brilliant victory.

In this way most of Roman Gaul, with the exception of outlying areas such as Britanny and Gascony, fell to the Franks and to their Merovingian dynasty. Clovis' successors conquered the kingdoms of Burgundy, Provence and Languedoc.

There were many reasons why this small nation of Franks, who are estimated to have numbered only about 30,000, and who were backward in comparison with their neighbors, should have had such success.

One reason is that they were the only barbarian people who had adopted the Christian religion at an early date. The Church had great influence in Roman Gaul, and it had been spreading since the 4th century.

Many new dioceses were formed. As the power of the civil authorities in these regions was reduced, or given up, the bishops and clergy took on greater prestige and exercised the effective power. The Franks sought the support of the bishops, and assured them of those privileges that the Visigoths refused to give.

Under the Merovingians the social crisis that had been increasing since the last centuries of the empire intensified. But the new social forms and organization that were to result in French feudal society also began to appear.

CITIES WITHER AWAY

The fall of the Roman Empire and the arrival of the Arabs in the Mediterranean area restricted commercial and urban life still more. Under these circumstances, the Gallo-Roman cities withered away within the confines of walls that had become too extensive for them.

These developments were all symptoms of a progressive decline of the economy and weakening of the social

Above: The Frankish King Charlemagne, or Charles the Great, was crowned emperor on Christmas Day, 800 A.D., by Pope Leo III. This act was symbolic of the attempt to revive the unity of the Roman Empire in the west after the disruption of the barbarian invasions. Charlemagne, as the map on this page shows, had brought much of what is now France, Germany and Italy under his control. This mosaic in the Lateran in Rome shows St. Peter, center, with Charlemagne and Pope Leo III, left.

Right: Charlemagne ruled from 768 to 814, but the empire he created did not hold together after his death. In 843 the Treaty of Verdun divided the lands called the Carolingian Empire after Charlemagne's Latin name, Carolus, among three of Charlemagne's grandchildren. Charles of Aquitaine received the Frankish lands in the west, Neustria and Aquitania. Lothar retained the empty title of Emperor. He was also King of Italy and of the Middle Kingdom, later called Lotharingia (from which the modern word Lorraine comes). This Middle Kingdom, between the Franks on the west and the Saxons and Bavarians on the east, ran from the Mediterranean to the North Sea. Louis of Bavaria ruled the eastern lands.

system. The administrative, commercial and financial system of the Empire broke up into a number of self-sufficient economic and social units. These units were the *villae*—estates—of individual landowners and the possessions of the dioceses and abbeys.

Since the State was based on this loose and broken state of affairs it was not able to develop a solid structure. Nothing was more unlike a modern state than the Merovingian kingdom, for it was considered as the private property of the king and was divided among his heirs.

The highest officers of the kingdom were nothing more than servants of the king and his court, as their names—Majordomo (butler) and Constable (head groom)—indicate. The financial and administrative machinery was very primitive, and the only regional rulers were the counts *(comites)* who had very elementary functions. The court had no fixed seat, and justice was administered in a crude fashion.

The patriarchal nature of the Merovingian kingdom and the loose form of society within its borders explain its history. After Clovis, the record of the dynasty became a series of violent struggles among various heirs and revolts on the part of the great landowners.

From time to time a strong personality, such as Dagobert (629-639), succeeded in imposing his rule over all contestants. But at Dagobert's death the kingdom was again divided and the struggles were resumed.

During the entire 7th century the House of Neustria (western France north of the Loire) and the House of Austrasia (from the Rhine to Brie and Champagne) were in continual conflict, and Aquitaine lived its own life. At first it seemed as if Neustria would prevail, but the situation changed completely when Pepin of Héristal, the Majordomo of Austrasia, gained control of both regions by the Battle of Tertry in 687. The Merovingian dynasty continued to exist, but it was deprived of power.

When Pepin died, in 715, the Neustrian aristocracy challenged his successor's authority. But one of his bastard sons, Charles, later surnamed Martel (the Hammer), managed to regain full control after five years of fierce struggle. Charles Martel's victory over the invading Arabs at Poitiers in 732 brought him great prestige and he assumed the title of sole Majordomo for Austrasia and Neustria.

Pepin the Short followed him, and succeeded in subduing the great lords who had revolted. In order to make his actual power legitimate, he had himself crowned King in 751 by Pope Zachary, and became the founder of the Carolingian dynasty. The Merovingian family, long in the background, died out.

Charlemagne set up a Palace School to improve education. Heading it was Alcuin of York, who later became Abbot of Tours. Scholars from many lands were gathered together and considerable effort was put into copying books. We owe many of our oldest copies of Latin authors to the work of Charlemagne's Palace School. In addition, the school and the men who graduated from it, helped to dispel the ignorance that had spread over much of Europe with the barbarian invasions.

Around the 11th century there grew up in several parts of Europe a popular demand for reforms in the morals and liturgy of the church. Many of the reformers, like the founders of the Cistercian Order and Pope Gregory VII, worked within the framework of organized religion, and from their efforts a revitalized Christianity arose. But some of those who agitated for reform felt that the church as a whole had become too wealthy and too powerful to be the true teacher of salvation. These people, who were called Catharists (from the Greek word for pure), believed that earthly things had only evil in them, and that to achieve salvation one had to deny the body absolutely. One group of Catharists sprang up in southern France, in the old county of Toulouse. They came to be known as the Albigenses, from the town of Albi, even though Albi was not the center of the religious movement. At first the Albigenses were concerned mainly with living up to their religious beliefs, but several powerful feudal lords of southern France saw in the movement an excellent opportunity to take over the church lands. In the early 13th century, the movement had become so strong that Pope Innocent III declared a crusade against it, and land-hungry barons from northern France, eager to move in on the heretical Albigensian lords, invaded the territory. In the troubled centuries that followed, castles and keeps were put up all over the countryside. Even the churches took on the appearance of fortresses. The 13th-century cathedral of St. Cecilia in Albi still looks as if it could withstand a siege.

The Carolingians

When the Carolingians came to power they ruled a territory extending much further than modern France. Ethnically, however, a clearly defined France did not exist in the early Carolingian period.

The Carolingian family's own domains were on the Moselle, and this circumstance caused it to look beyond the natural frontiers of the kingdom, to Germany. Pepin and Charles the Great—Charlemagne— (768-814) waged war against Saxon, Bavarian and Avar tribes in Germany.

Furthermore, the coronation of Pepin by the Pope, and the role of protector of the Church which the Carolingian kings were assuming more and more, led them to intervene in Italy against the Lombards. Eventually they controlled all the north and center of the peninsula.

CHARLEMAGNE

From these conquests and the alliance with the Papacy the Holy Roman Empire was born. Charlemagne was crowned Emperor in Rome on Christmas of the year 800. In his person Roman Imperial dignity was reincarnated and sanctified by the blessing of the Pope.

The ideals that inspired the recreated Holy Roman Empire also inspired Charlemagne's successor Louis the Pious and the advisers of both emperors, who included the best scholars of the age. To them was due the resumption of classical studies in what is known as the Carolingian Renaissance.

This Empire was soon revealed to be artificial and temporary, for distinct ethnical and territorial regions kept on taking shape within it. The famous Strasbourg Oath is the first surviving document we have showing the existence of an ethnic and linguistic difference between Germans and French.

In Strasbourg, Louis of Bavaria and Charles of Aquitaine swore before their troops in different languages, German and a low Latin which was in the process of becoming French. They promised not to make a separate peace with their brother Lothar, the eldest son of Louis the Pious, who claimed supreme power.

The Treaty of Verdun, which in 843 put an end to differences between the heirs of Louis the Pious, confirms the evidence of the Strasbourg Oath. By this treaty, Charles of Aquitaine received Aquitaine, Neustria and Burgundy, territories making up a large part of modern France, while Louis of Bavaria received the territories across the Rhine which correspond roughly to modern Germany. As for Lothar, he was awarded the imperial title and lands between the Rhine and the Saône.

Lothar's territories were called Lotharingia after him—a name from which comes the modern Lorraine. And for many centuries these territories were the cause of contention between France and Germany.

FRANCE AND GERMANY

There is no reason to think that France and Germany were individual nations in the modern sense at the time of the Treaty of Verdun. However, that treaty was the origin of 1000 years of division between the two regions.

After the Treaty of Verdun the Frankish Kingdom went through difficult times. Charles the Bald (840-877) and his successors had to cope with great difficulties created for them by the insubordinate aristocracy and by invaders.

In the south, Saracens made incursions into Languedoc and Provence, and the Norsemen began to raid the northern provinces. In the 9th century the latter devastated the French countryside several times and besieged Paris.

They were repulsed only after long struggles, and settled in the northwestern part of the country, which was called Normandy after them, and became a duchy. They rapidly merged with the Frankish population and adopted French and Latin culture.

THE END OF THE CAROLINGIANS

The Carolingian dynasty came to its end in conditions of anarchy and intrigue. After a series of disputed successions and hostilities, the crown went in 987 to Hugh Capet, Count of Paris and Duke of France, the founder of the Capetian dynasty that is identified with the history of medieval France.

During the Carolingian age a state in the modern sense did not exist, and whatever remained of Roman organization was weakened still further. The king's authority over his vassals and his own officials was limited. The officials were not so much the king's servants as feudal lords who owed allegiance to him. Their loyalty was bought at the price of allowing them to hold

It was at Aigues-Mortes in southern France that Louis IX embarked for the Seventh and Eighth Crusades. The port which he constructed outside this seagate of the medieval fortified town is now silted up.

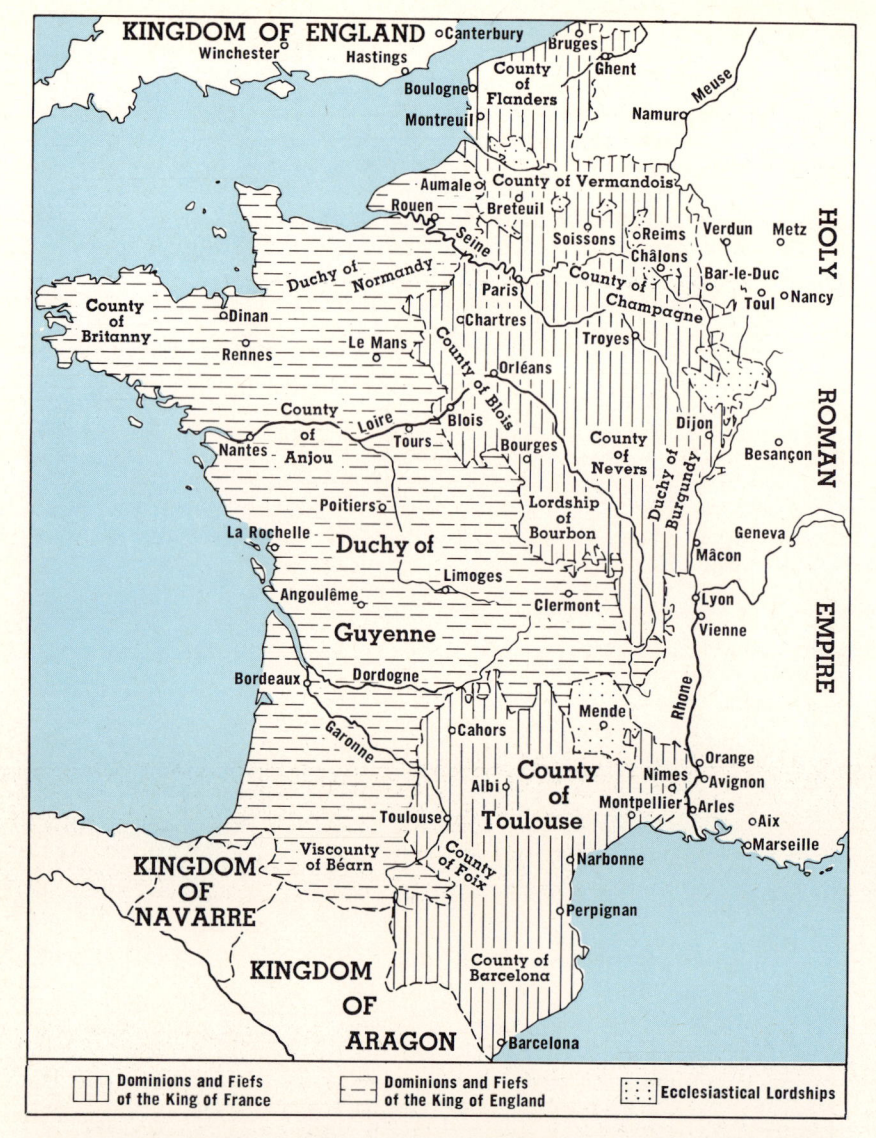

In 1154 more than half of France was in English hands, partly as a result of Eleanor of Aquitaine's marriage to Henry II. The domains of the King of France were insecure because of frequent rebellions by his powerful vassals.

extensive estates that weakened the treasury and the royal domains.

Attempts to make up for these losses by seizures of Church property, as under Charles Martel, were in vain; the Church's position in the Holy Roman Empire and her spiritual and political authority did not allow such a solution to endure.

Social and economic life remained based on the lords' estates under the Carolingians, as it was under the Merovingians. These lands were divided into two parts. One was the *réserve*, cultivated directly by the lord by means of the unpaid labor of his serfs or "men." The other was the *tenures*, which the serfs cultivated on their own account after a payment —generally of labor or of crops—to the lord. Lord and man thus had a contractual relation: the former gave his serfs protection and the latter supported him by their work on the *réserve*.

Such contractual relations tended to spread from the lower toward the higher ranks of society. The lesser lords sought the protection of the greater, and became their vassals. In his turn, the greater lord became a vassal of one greater than he—a bishop or a count. The king stood at the summit of this pyramid of social and contractual relations, and he was considered sovereign liege lord (*souverain fief-fé*).

MEDIEVAL FRANCE

The Capetians

THE BEGINNINGS OF THE CAPETIAN dynasty can hardly be distinguished

In 1137, Louis VI, King of France, married his son Louis to Eleanor of Aquitaine. As her father's heiress, she was to inherit the large southern counties of Guienne and Gascony. But Eleanor did not provide her husband with a male heir, and he had his marriage with her annulled in 1152 after he had become King as Louis VII. She at once married Henry Plantagenet, the future Henry II of England. Thus the Kings of England added Eleanor's huge inheritance to their extensive possessions in France. Eleanor, who is shown here with members of her Court, was known for her patronage of the arts, and helped to bring the brilliant culture of her homeland in Provence to both Paris and London.

historically from the end of the Carolingian. The history of the French monarchy throughout the 10th and 11th centuries is a history of continual struggles against the great vassals and of complicated conflicts over the succession to the throne. The monarchy therefore failed to increase its authority. The royal domain remained tiny, and in general it may be said that under the first Capetians the monarchy barely managed to survive.

The most important events of the period, however, were not the activities of the royal house but the first foundations of a new social and political organization. These developments were already visible during the last Carolingian century. Beginning in the 11th century, the population, which had remained stationary for centuries, began to increase.

This increase was accompanied by a strong move to bring new lands under cultivation and to found new towns. Great tracts of forest or wasteland were cultivated, and on them were built the numerous *Villesneuves* (new towns), which appeared everywhere on the map of France.

This great mass movement toward new lands—which a modern historian has likened to the race for land in the American West—naturally tended to weaken the bonds of servitude holding the serfs in subjection to their lords. A serf bearing the weight of too much forced labor had the alternative of fleeing and settling in the new territories. The great work of clearing land undertaken by the monks, especially the Cistercians, hastened this tendency. The movement was irresistible, and the feudal lords themselves felt its force. Sometimes they anticipated the general desire of society and freed the serfs of whole provinces.

Many technical innovations brought about a great improvement in agriculture and a consequent advance in trade. The little market close to the lord's castle was no longer enough, and larger market towns grew up to handle more goods and to receive superfluous labor from the countryside.

The ancient Roman cities began to regain population and became the seats of new crafts and centers of new communications and commerce. In the south this urban renaissance was greatly stimulated by the resumption of trade in the Mediterranean basin as a result of the Crusades, in which so many southern French lords fought.

In the north the growing cities were more decisively antifeudal than in the south. In such towns as Laon, Beauvais, Noyon, Soissons, Cambrai and Saint-Quentin, the burghers—citizens free of feudal obligations—soon became conscious of their power in society. They demanded constitutions from the bishops and counts, their overlords, with whom they now entered into conflict.

CULTURE AND ART FLOURISH

This general development of social life is reflected in the rich culture and art of the time. The *Chanson de Roland* and the poems of Chrétien de Troyes were written; Romanesque art flowered; and famous episcopal schools were set up in Chartres and Paris, where the great and restless intellect of Abelard shone. There was a rebirth of philosophical and theological studies; Aristotle's works were rediscovered and translated; and the desire for religious reform gave rise to the Cluniac movement.

The Capetian monarchy itself took on a new character and function. It became a dynamic institution capable of solving the tensions and problems of the transformed society all around it, to organize it and unify it.

In fact the great historical achievement of the Capetians was to unify the various independent feudal territories that had arisen during the Carolingian age. Louis VI, the Fat (1108-1137), succeeded in reducing the feudal rebels of the Île-de-France. Furthermore, by marrying his son Louis to Eleanor of Aquitaine he paved the way for France eventually to annex the territories south of the Loire.

However, soon after he ascended the throne, Louis VII (1137-80) made haste to repudiate Eleanor, and she married Henry Plantagenet, Count of Anjou, the future Henry II of England. France and England there-

Louis IX reigned from 1226 to 1270. During his reign the French monarchy was powerful and the country was prosperous. He kept the feudal lords under control and repulsed an English invasion. A most chivalrous knight and an idealistic ruler, Louis IX was also a devout Christian and was canonized a saint in 1297. He led the Seventh Crusade in 1248. This attempt to recapture Jerusalem failed. In 1270 he led the futile Eighth Crusade to Tunis, where he and most of his army perished from disease.

fore came into conflict over the lands to the south and west of the Loire.

This conflict eventually gave rise to the Hundred Years' War. That struggle was already foreshadowed in the reign of Louis VII and those of his successors, Philip Augustus (1181-1223), Louis VIII (1223-1226) and Louis IX (1226-1270).

Under Philip Augustus the struggle for Aquitaine and Normandy was settled in favor of France. Poitou and Anjou were acquired next, through the great victory of Bouvines, won by Philip over King John of England. Under Louis VIII French territory reached to the Dordogne, but much was given up by Louis IX in 1259, when he made peace with England and renounced French claims to Périgord, Limousin, Saintogne to the north of the Dordogne, and part of the Agenais and Quercy.

CRUSADE AGAINST THE ALBIGENSES

In addition to extending its territory to the west and southwest, the French monarchy also moved toward the county of Toulouse in the southeast, which at the beginning of the 13th century was ruled by Count Raymond. The movement was begun by Philip Augustus from territory in Auvergne acquired by his predecessors.

In its drive to the south, the French Monarchy utilized as an excuse for intervention the rise of the Albigensian heresy in the southeast, and the protection of the heretics by Raymond VII of Toulouse.

The expedition was commanded by Simon de Montfort, and became a real Crusade, approved and blessed by the Church. The population of Languedoc and Provence put up a long and fierce resistance, which led to severe reprisals and religious persecution at the hands of the Dominicans and the Inquisition.

However, the struggle ended with the French monarchy victorious. On the death of Raymond in 1249, a large part of his dominions passed to Alphonse of Poitiers, a younger brother of Louis IX. The Capetians had established a base in Languedoc.

LOUIS IX, SAINT AND CRUSADER

The Capetians reached the summit of their power under Louis IX. The royal domains had been broadened and consolidated; the rebellious feudal lords of Central France had been subdued, the power of the dukes of Aquitaine and the counts of Toulouse had been reduced.

The lands ruled by Louis IX occupied a large part of the area of modern France. But the territories to the south of the Dordogne, the Cerdagne, and also the territories to the east of the Meuse and the Rhone were still independent.

Louis IX, the King who became a Saint, devoted a large part of his reign to crusades in Africa. He was admired by all Europe, and he was looked upon as a kind of mediator between Christian rulers. That the Church supported him is illustrated by the Pope's crowning of his brother, Charles of Anjou, King of Sicily.

The power of the Capetian monarchy was not due solely to its military and political successes, but also to the economic well-being that France enjoyed at this period. The Fairs of Champagne, visited by merchants from all over Europe, were the economic heart of Europe, and reached their height at the end of the 13th century. At these Fairs, tapestries made in the rich cities of Flanders were exchanged for spices from the Far East, while Hanseatic and English merchants met bankers from Florence and Sienna.

In the 13th century Notre-Dame cathedral at Paris was completed, and Chartres cathedral and the Sainte-Chapelle at Paris were also built. Gothic art and sculpture flourished. The romance, the *Roman de la Rose*, was begun, and Villehardouin and Joinville wrote their histories.

Paris became a huge workshop, besides being the residence of the court. In addition, it had one of the most important universities in existence, where famous philosophers such as Robert of Hales, Bonaventure, Albertus Magnus and Thomas Aquinas taught.

After the reign of Philip III, the

About 1438, Johann Gutenberg, a German metalworker, invented a means of printing from movable metal type. His invention was to change the history of Western Europe. By 1500 there were over a thousand printing shops in Europe. Books were no longer the expensive luxuries of the very rich. A man who could get his ideas printed could have them discussed by hundreds and thousands of people. The great religious books of Christianity were no longer the prized possessions of churches and monasteries only. The ordinary citizen could afford to have a Bible of his own. The printing press was crucial in helping to spread the thoughts of men like John Calvin, the outstanding French figure of the Reformation.

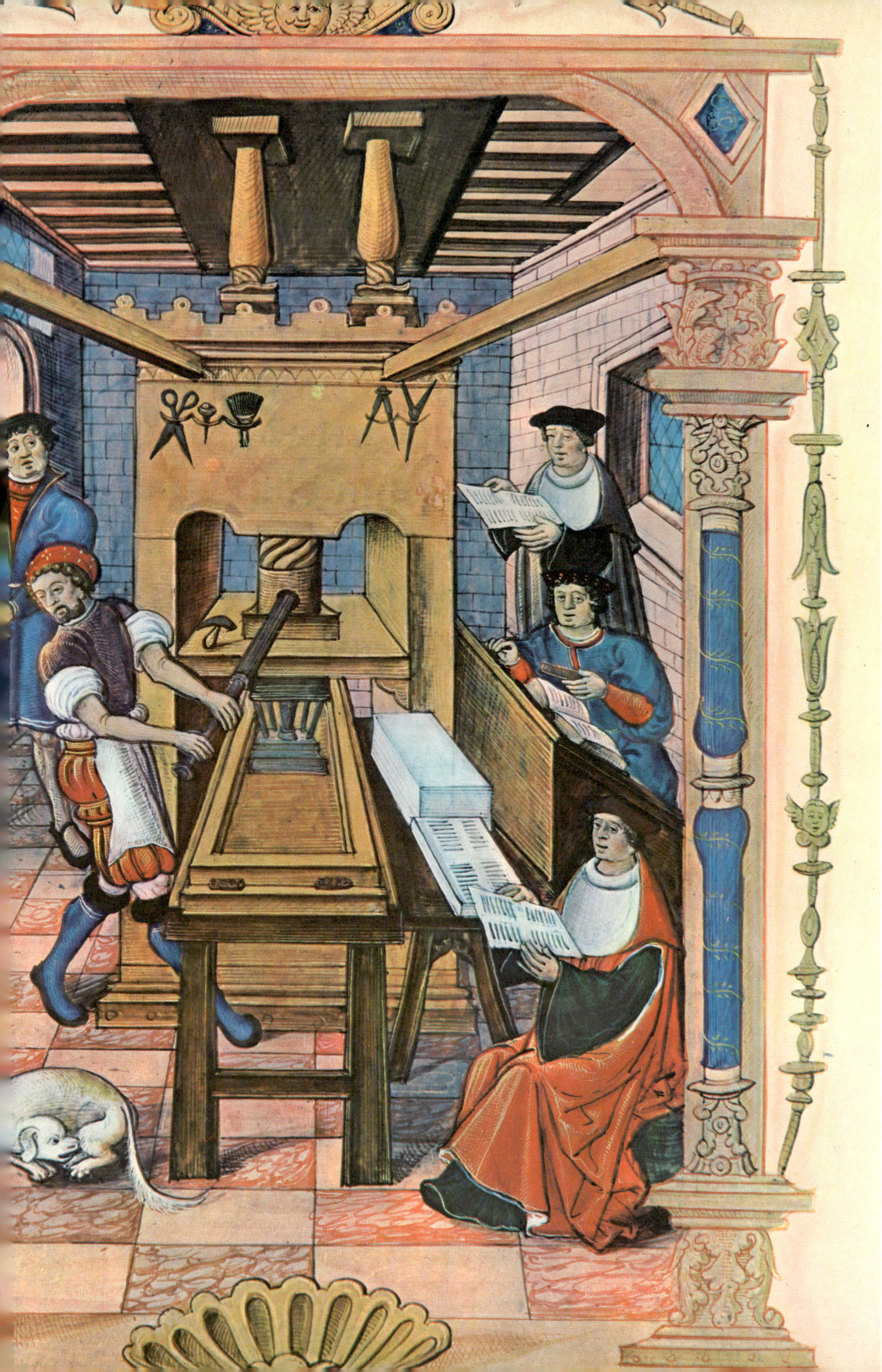

Bold, in which no events of great historical importance occurred, the next brilliant and powerful reign was that of Philip the Fair (1285-1314). Philip continued the policy of territorial expansion. The Count of Hainaut and the bishops of Mende, Le Puy and the Lyon region all recognized the sovereignty of the King of France. And royal marriages gave the Crown of France a claim on the duchy of Burgundy.

PHILIP THE FAIR AND THE PAPACY

But the name of Philip the Fair is linked above all with his victorious struggle against the Papacy. The questions at issue were important. One was recognition of the French Crown's right to tax the French clergy. Another was the limitation of the export of money to Rome through Italian bankers for various ends, such as crusades and the general upkeep of the Papacy. Still another question was the upholding of French sovereignty against the claim of the Pope's universal sovereignty, first made by Pope Boniface VIII.

The struggle reached a climax in the celebrated rebuff given by the king's representative to the Pope at Anagni in 1303—an event which shook Europe. Boniface VIII died of the shock. After the brief reign of Benedict XI, French agents succeeded in having a French cardinal, Bertrand du Got, elected Pope. Philip the Fair increased his pressure on the new Pope. In 1307 the king had the Knights of the Order of the Temple (the Templars) arrested and condemned to death on charges of immorality. In this way he was able to be rid of a formidable financial opponent, and seize its property.

The Pope was unable to do anything to protect the Templars and this defeat marked the beginning of the decline of Papal claims to universal sovereignty. On Bertrand du Got's death, a majority of French cardinals elected Jacques Duèse from Cahors in the county of Toulouse as Pope. He reigned as John XXII, and went to reside in Avignon, where the popes remained until 1378.

THE KINGS' POWER INCREASES

At the same time, the French monarchy continued to perfect the institutions founded by Louis IX to increase its control and influence over the life of society. Appeals from the decisions of the various local and feudal courts to the *Parlement* of Paris, which was the High Court of Justice, became more frequent.

The Exchequer—the king's treasury—was declared by a decree made in 1320 to be the sole administrator of the revenues from the king's domains; formerly they had been in the care of the Templars. The king's control over his representatives in outlying districts became stronger and more effective. And his advisers were more and more chosen from among the legal experts of the University of Montpellier.

THE ESTATES GENERAL

In connection with his quarrel with the Pope, Philip the Fair wished to be sure of the backing of the French people. Therefore, instead of relying on the advice of the clergy and nobility only, he called a meeting of all three "estates"—the clergy, the nobility, and the "third estate." This was the origin of the tricameral body known as the Estates General, somewhat similar to the English Parliament, but destined to have a much less successful history.

All these changes caused the nobles to lose influence at court. But Philip the Fair was by no means an absolute ruler over his country. Many of the means and instruments of rule considered essential for a modern state were lacking or present only in an elementary form.

In spite of the fact that mercenary

Saint-Flour, like many towns of southern France, was built on the top of a steep hill and later grew down the hillside. Villages were usually founded in such inaccessible places only for reasons of defense. During the 14th and 15th centuries, when Saint-Flour was established, France was in the turmoil of the Hundred Years' War.

soldiers were used more and more from the 14th century on, the king still depended largely on the good will of his great vassals for an army. Both nobles and towns strongly opposed the king's desire to exact taxes, forced gifts, loans and other contributions to his treasury demanded on all kinds of pretexts.

Sometimes the resistance broke into open revolt, as when the rich Flemish cities defeated the king's army at Courtrai in 1302, and when the nobles of various provinces revolted in 1314 and 1315.

In spite of these limitations, the French monarchy was strong and vital in the first decades of the 14th century. This was proved when the succession crisis caused by the death of Louis X in 1316 was fairly easily surmounted and came to an end with the beginning of the new dynasty of Valois in 1328.

The limits of the authority and power of the central government were revealed later when the whole of French society was subjected to a bitter trial by an extremely dangerous situation provoked by internal as well as external causes.

The Fourteenth-Century Crisis

From the beginning of the 14th century many of the circumstances that had favored the prosperity of French society under Louis IX and Philip the Fair began to disappear.

Flemish clothmaking went through a critical time in the early years of the century. The Fairs of Champagne declined as new routes from Italy to Germany were opened up both through the Gothard Pass and the Rhine valley and also by sea when Genoese merchants sailed around through the Atlantic. A number of bad harvests had a ruinous effect on the rural economy.

All these factors helped to bring about the 14th-century depression. It became necessary for the first time to devalue the currency. After 1343 Philip VI frequently had recourse to this measure.

Finally, a terrible plague, the Black Death, raged in France in the summer of 1348. This disaster killed an estimated one-third of the population and led to panic and hoarding.

The Flemish cities that had lost their cloth trade yearned to be free of French domination. The nobility, which had come near to ruin because of the plague and the devaluations, sought an answer to its problems in revolt. And the peasants and the people of the cities, both rich and poor, were aroused by their troubles.

THE HUNDRED YEARS' WAR

It was at this point that France found herself plunged into the longest war in her history, the Hundred Years' War. Her great internal weakness was an invitation to an enemy such as Edward III of England to attack, and he *did* attack.

The war soon became a struggle for existence on both sides. The original question was whether Guyenne should belong to France or England. But it became of secondary importance when, in 1340, Edward, with the support of many allies and the Flemish cities, claimed the throne of France.

Philip VI was soon in great danger, for he was defeated in the battle of Crécy in 1346. His son, John the Good, who succeeded him in 1350, was abandoned by a large part of the nobility, led by Charles the Bad, King of Navarre, and was defeated and captured at the battle of Maupertuis in 1356.

This defeat threw France into a very grave crisis. Charles, the young Dauphin (the title of the heir to the throne), had to face the combined opposition of the nobility led by Charles the Bad and the citizens of Paris who were in revolt. Under the leadership of Etienne Marcel, a leading merchant, the Parisians sought to force the monarchy to give the right of control over its actions to the Estates General.

In March 1358 a rising stirred up by Etienne Marcel caused the Dauphin to leave Paris. In May the countryside also rose against him. However, Etienne Marcel's plan of combining the revolting citizen and peasant forces failed because Charles the Bad quickly repressed the peasant rising. The Dauphin was able to regain control of the situation by exploiting the differences among his enemies.

In the meantime, at London, Edward III succeeded in forcing John the Good to sign a very harsh peace treaty. The Estates and the Dauphin refused to ratify it, and Edward resumed the war on French territory, but without much success. The Peace of Brétigny was then made in 1360, by which France renounced all rights to the lands between the Loire and the Pyrenees. The first phase of the Hundred Years' War had ended with a serious French defeat.

After John the Good died in prison in England in 1364, the Dauphin ascended the throne as Charles V. He began his reign by repressing a new revolt by Charles the Bad. Charles V also tried to calm the chronic dissatisfaction of the Flemish cities by arranging a marriage between his brother Philip, Duke of Burgundy, and Margaret of Flanders.

Moreover, improvements in the taxation system allowed the troops to be paid more regularly. Thus, in 1368, it became possible to reopen hostilities against the English and to reconquer much of the territory ceded at Brétigny.

STRUGGLE TO CONTROL THE KING

The progress that had been made under Charles, surnamed the Wise, was thrown into jeopardy on his death in 1380. He was succeeded by his son, Charles VI, who was a minor at the time of his accession. For twelve years, from 1380 to 1392, Charles VI tried to rule and hold the ambitions of the great nobles in check by depending on the help of his father's advisers.

As he grew older he showed clearer signs of madness. Consequently, several groups of aristocrats used him, successively, to advance their ambitions. Soon two main parties emerged, led respectively by Philip the Bold, Duke of Burgundy, and by the House of Orleans.

Between 1392 and 1412 the royal power did not really exist in France, as the Burgundians and the Armagnacs—as the followers of the dukes of Orleans were known—fought for power and for control over the king.

In 1413, Henry V came to the throne of England, and was soon making war on France. The French whom he defeated at Agincourt in 1415 were Armagnacs. They held Paris at the time, and the Burgundians soon took advantage of the disastrous situation. John the Fearless, who had succeeded Philip the Bold as Duke of Burgundy, entered Paris and declared himself king. The King and the Dauphin had to retire south of the Loire.

ENGLISH VICTORIES

In the meantime Henry V had taken Rouen and was threatening Paris. Negotiations for a reconciliation between Burgundians and Armagnacs failed when John the Fearless was assassinated by Armagnacs.

From 1309 to 1378 seven popes made their official residence at Avignon. Violent civil disorders in Rome and in much of Italy made the popes prefer the safety of the town on the Rhone. During the papal residence Avignon became a magnificent court. The wealth of all of Christendom contributed to the tapestries, paintings and defenses of the fortified castle there. Benedict XII began building the castle in the 1330s and it was completed under his successor, Clement VI.

But even Avignon was not spared the shock of the Hundred Years' War, then crippling France. More than once the great stone walls of the castle repelled bands of armed looters. When the papacy returned to Rome at last, Avignon declined, although the papal palace remained as a symbol of the days when the city was the capital of Christendom.

John's son, Philip the Good, immediately went over to the English and signed the Treaty of Troyes in 1420. By this treaty the Dauphin was declared banned from France and Henry V of England, who had married Charles VI's daughter Catherine, assumed the title of Regent of France.

When Charles VI and Henry V died in 1422 France was divided into three parts. England ruled Normandy, part of Guyenne, Picardy, Ile-de-France and Champagne. Philip the Good ruled Flanders, Hainaut, Artois and Burgundy. The Dauphin, Charles, who called himself King of France, but who was called by his enemies King of Bourges, still had the central provinces, Languedoc, Dauphiné and the Lyon region.

As time went on the Dauphin's position seemed to be becoming weaker and weaker. In 1428 the English besieged Orleans, and the city seemed about to fall.

JOAN OF ARC

At this point Joan of Arc entered French history. She was a peasant girl from the borders of Champagne and Lorraine, who declared that she had had visions in which the rightness of the Dauphin's cause was revealed to her by heavenly voices.

Joan was examined by a commission of theologians and lawyers at Poitiers and was allowed to go to Orleans. There she gave new heart to the defenders and forced the enemy to raise the siege. Then she persuaded the Dauphin to go to Reims and to be crowned there as Charles VII, a ceremony traditionally performed in that cathedral.

This plan seemed to be extremely dangerous, but the king accomplished the venture successfully, and his prestige grew enormously. A little later, in 1430, Joan fell into the hands of the English. Under the pretext that she was a heretic, after an unjust trial, they burned her at the stake in the market place at Rouen on May 30, 1431.

But Joan's brief and glorious life and her successes enabled the French to pass the critical point in the struggle. After the third decade of the century they began to reap the benefit of the long resistance that Joan and her message had done so much to strengthen.

Revival in France

The essential condition for a French revival was peace between the Armagnacs and the Burgundians. This was brought about by the Treaty of Arras in 1435, by which Charles VII promised to recognize all the conquests and possessions of the Duke of Burgundy.

Charles was then able to take the initiative. In 1436 he entered Paris, and in 1453 the English gave up all attempts to conquer France. Between 1450 and 1460 Charles devoted his energies to repairing the machinery of the state after the long period of anarchy. The Parlement and the Exchequer began to function again; new Parlements were established at Toulouse and Bordeaux; the country was divided into regions for tax purposes, and better means of collecting taxes were introduced.

Charles' work of restoration and renewal made it easier for the French to complete their last remaining task—to drive the English out of France. Between 1448 and 1452 the King of England was deprived of almost all his remaining territories on the continent—Normandy in the north and Guyenne in the south. Only Calais remained in English hands.

The Hundred Years' War between England and France started in 1338 and only ended in 1453. When Charles VII came to the throne of France in 1422, England ruled large parts of France and Charles' territory was restricted to the central provinces. Though he called himself King of France, his enemies called him King of Bourges. His misfortunes seemed to be overwhelming him when Joan of Arc appeared, put new spirit into the King's armies, raised the siege of Orléans, turned the tide of the Hundred Years' War, and had Charles crowned at Reims in 1429. Charles reigned until 1461, and before he died the English were driven out of France, retaining only a foothold at Calais. This portrait of Charles VII was painted by the most important French painter of the 15th century, Jean Fouquet, and is now in the Louvre in Paris.

THE REIGN OF LOUIS XI

In 1461, Charles VII was succeeded by his son Louis XI, one of the strongest personalities in the history of France. He was a scholar, an admirer of the political skill of the Italian cities, and an able diplomat.

His achievement was to complete Charles VII's restoration of the crown's territories and administration.

Louis XI's great opponent was Charles the Bold, who had succeeded Philip the Bold as Duke of Burgundy. Charles' character was almost the exact opposite of that of the realistic Louis. He was bold and chivalrous, and lacking in forethought as a politician.

However, in the beginning, Charles obtained certain advantages from the so-called War of the Public Good. Louis XI was obliged to yield Champagne to him. This meant that Charles' duchy stretched without interruption from Burgundy to Flanders.

But Louis soon raised up enemies against Charles on the latter's eastern frontiers, isolated him, and made sure of the neutrality of Edward IV of England. Charles tried to assert his sovereignty over Alsace and Breisgau, but was repeatedly defeated by the Swiss and fell in the battle of Nancy in 1477.

Until then, Louis had remained a spectator of the conflict, but he now intervened. He obliged Charles' heir, Mary of Burgundy, to recognize French sovereignty over Burgundy, Picardy, Artois and Franche-Comté by the Treaty of Arras in 1482.

Mary sought the help of the Hapsburg rulers of Austria and married the future Emperor Maximilian. She was also able to retain her Flemish dominions. In this way the House of Hapsburg came to rule the Netherlands.

OTHER FRENCH CONQUESTS

Louis' wars of conquest in the south were less fortunate, though after a long struggle with John II of Aragon he was able to annex Roussillon and Cerdagne in 1475. He also carried out a policy of progressively lessening the power of nobles by confiscating land whenever possible and increasing the authority of his central government.

Meanwhile the kingdom continued to recover from the devastations and impoverishment suffered during the Hundred Years' War. The countryside was repopulated. Trade increased and Louis tried to direct its expansion by royal action. He regulated the production of the city guilds. Silk-weaving was introduced in Lyon and Tours. His reign saw the beginning of the Lyon Fairs, which flourished in the 16th century.

These economic ventures brought profits mainly to a few speculators and merchants, not to the king's treasury. And the increased taxation that came with the new policy weighed heavily on the common people.

This was clearly seen in 1484 after the death of Louis XI in the previous year. His daughter Anne and her husband, the Regents for his infant son Charles VIII, summoned a meeting of the Estates General in Tours. This was the first general meeting of an assembly from all parts of the country—formerly the meetings had representatives from varying numbers of provinces. There was a universal desire for a reduction of the tax burden and a return to the wise policies and sound money of Charles VII.

These requests were met in part only. Young Charles VIII was not satisfied by the acquisition of Brittany through his marriage with its last duchess, Anne. He looked to Italy, where the warfare going on between the various states and cities

A statue of Joan of Arc, the national heroine of France, stands in the Place des Pyramides in Paris. The daughter of a farmer of Domrémy, a village on the borders of Champagne and Lorraine, Joan heard "voices" which urged her to aid Charles VII, then known as the Dauphin. Overcoming great difficulties, she managed to meet the Dauphin. She persuaded him to grant her troops and with them she raised the siege of Orléans in 1429. At this time she was about seventeen years old. It was largely at her insistence that Charles was crowned at Reims in 1429. Soon after, in 1430, she was captured at Compiègne by the Burgundians, who were then allies of the English. Charles made no effort to save her, and, after being tried and condemned for witchcraft, she was burned as a lapsed heretic at Rouen, which was then English territory, in 1431. She was rehabilitated in a new trial in 1456 and canonized in 1920.

offered him great opportunities for his ambitions. The expense of his expeditions to Italy canceled the partial tax relief granted to the country at Tours.

RENAISSANCE AND REFORMATION

The Italian Wars

In 1494, Charles VIII assumed the title of King of Naples and of Jerusalem. He made sure of the neutrality of the Hapsburg Emperor by returning Franche-Comté and Artois to Burgundy, and that of the Spanish King by restoring Roussillon and Cerdagne. Charles then marched into Italy, reached Milan, and went on to Florence, Rome and Naples against virtually no resistance.

It seemed that he was already master of the peninsula. But a league was soon formed among the Italian states against him and he was forced to withdraw to France, fighting the Battle of Fornovo, in 1496.

Louis XII, Charles VIII's successor, continued the latter's Italian policy. In 1499 he occupied the territory of Milan and arranged with Spain for a joint occupation of the Kingdom of Naples.

But Louis, like Charles, was unable to establish himself in Italy. The French became entangled in the complicated diplomacy of the country. Not only were they faced by attacks at different times from Spain and the Empire, but they also had to take part in the League of Cambrai against Venice.

Finally, the French gave way before the Holy League, formed against them by all their enemies and former allies. The Battle of Ravenna in 1512 forced them to retire from Italy.

FRANCIS I

Francis I had better success with the third attempt, made in 1513. He won a great victory at Melegnano and the gates of Milan were opened to him. The city became part of his kingdom by the Treaty of Noyon the next year.

The problem of making a definitive agreement about the relations between Church and State in France had to be solved, for it had remained constantly in the fore since the time of Philip the Fair at the beginning of the 14th century.

Louis XII seemed at first to base his policy toward the Papacy on asserting the superiority of General Councils of the Church over the Pope. But when the Council called by the king at Pisa in 1511 failed, he returned to a policy of seeking a Concordat—similar to a treaty—with the Papacy. He also ceased to cast doubts upon the Pope's spiritual authority.

By the Concordat of Bologna in 1516, Francis I recognized the Pope's superiority to the General Councils and obtained advantages for the French monarchy. The kings of France were now able to control ecclesiastical life in France because of their privilege of choosing bishops and abbots.

A miniature by Jean Fouquet shows Louis XI founding the Order of St. Michael. Louis XI succeeded Charles VII in 1461 and reigned until 1483. Learning from the English victories over the French in the Hundred Years' War, he improved his standing army, especially its artillery. This enabled him to bring the feudal lords under control and wipe out private warfare, for their castles could not withstand artillery fire. A brilliant and unscrupulous statesman, Louis broke the power of the Duchy of Burgundy, which then included large areas of what is now eastern France. Under Louis' wise economic policies France prospered, recovering from the ravages of the Hundred Years' War. Louis was a very religious man and spent large sums of money to acquire holy relics, but his religion was tinged with a large dose of superstition. He wore amulets of all kinds about his person to prevent this disease and that misfortune. His hat was often covered with miraculous medals and stones said to drive away poisons. Vials of holy water from various places of pilgrimage hung from his neck. Like most people of his time, he was addicted to astrology and numerology.

In his later years Louis apparently suffered from some disfiguring skin disease and kept to his own rooms, rarely making public appearances. This and his far-reaching political strategies earned him the nickname "The Spider King," and gave him a sinister reputation among his contemporaries.

The Italian wars also freed the kings of France once and for all from the dependence on Italian bankers which had weighed so heavily on them during the 14th and 15th centuries. Many of these bankers emigrated to France, where they contributed to the success of the Lyon Fairs in the first half of the 16th century and became the king's financiers in his own dominions.

FRANCE ENCIRCLED

A few years after the Treaty of Noyon, Charles of Hapsburg, as a grandson of Ferdinand and Isabella, succeeded to the throne of Spain. As a grandson of Maximilian and Mary, he already ruled all the family's Flemish, Burgundian and Austrian dominions. In 1519, in spite of the opposition of Francis I of France, he was elected Emperor. France was thus encircled by the possessions of Charles V and war was inevitable.

The hostilities continued for many years and spread to every part of Europe. Fighting went on in Italy, Flanders, Provence and on the Pyrenees frontier. At first Francis I suffered disastrous defeats. He went to Italy to regain Milan, which Charles had occupied, but was defeated at Pavia and made a prisoner in 1525.

By the Treaty of Madrid in 1526, Francis recognized Charles' right to Burgundy, and abandoned all his ambitions in Italy. But he repudiated this treaty as soon as he was released; the war was resumed until, by the Treaty of Cambrai in 1529, France's claim to Burgundy was recognized by Charles. Neither ruler was satisfied, and it was clear that fighting would begin again.

Francis sought allies among the German Protestant princes, and the war recommenced in 1536. It was marked by alternating successes and defeats. There were several truces, but it lasted for all the rest of the king's reign, and that of his successor, Henry II.

Both sides showed greater and greater signs of weariness as the struggle went on. France had to make a financial effort from which a few benefited while the great mass of the population suffered. Sometimes dissatisfaction broke out into open revolt, as in the Guyenne rising in 1548.

The value of money declined continuously, and the rise in the cost of living, hastened by the inflow of silver from the Spanish possessions in America, made the economic situation worse.

In the meantime the fundamental political objectives of the contending monarchs altered. The Emperor abdicated in 1556 and divided his dominions between his son, Philip II of Spain, and his brother, Ferdinand of Austria. This diminished French fears of a universal Hapsburg Empire overcoming France.

As for the French, they now wished to free themselves from the maze of Italian politics, especially since Italy had declined in ecomonic importance. The opening of the sea route to the East and the discovery of the Americas were causing Italy to take a secondary place in European affairs. The center of European power was shifting towards the north and toward the Atlantic.

The Reformation and France

Another reason for the lessening of the rivalry between Spain and France was the spread of the Protestant Reformation in Europe. In France the Reformation gave rise to hopes of political as well as religious changes, and the monarchy was obliged more and more to turn its forces against the internal threat.

Learned circles that had absorbed the humanist culture of the Renaissance at first favored the new form of religion. Ideals of humanist and religious tolerance, such as Erasmus had spread through the whole of Christendom, made a deep impression. French 16th-century writers, such as Marot, Rabelais, Du Bellay, Bodin and Montaigne, show how strongly these concepts appealed to cultivated men, and also that they were at the heart of the Reformation in France.

The introduction of printing and the translation of the Bible into French helped these ideas to spread among the educated. (Le Fèvre d'Etaples, one of those who laid the foundations for the Reformation in France, published his translation of the New Testament in 1523 and the Bible in 1530.)

As these aspirations and ideas spread they took on a more radical form. In 1534 posters condemning the Mass appeared in several French cities and at Amboise on the door of the King's bedchamber. John Calvin's *Institutes of the Christian Religion* was published in Latin in 1536 and in French in 1541 and was an important expression of the new spirit.

Charles VIII reigned from 1483 to 1498 and acquired Brittany for the French crown by his marriage with its last duchess, Anne. In 1495 he led an expedition to Italy to claim the crown of Naples. He marched through the peninsula almost without meeting resistance, but a league of Italian states was formed against him, and he was forced to withdraw. The expedition, however, did much to bring the influence of the Italian Renaissance to France.

After this date, Calvinist preachers won numerous converts, especially among the lower nobility, the craftsmen in the cities and the peasants. In some parts of the southwest, in Normandy and Provence, the Reformation made particularly deep inroads; it came more and more into the open; its first churches were built; and the desire to extend reform from religious to political affairs became stronger and stronger.

The monarchy tried by even more drastic means to suppress this reform movement. In 1545 many Waldensians were massacred in Provence, and in, 1547, the *Chambre Ardente* was set up to investigate and judge cases of heresy.

In these circumstances those who, like the Constable Anne de Mont-

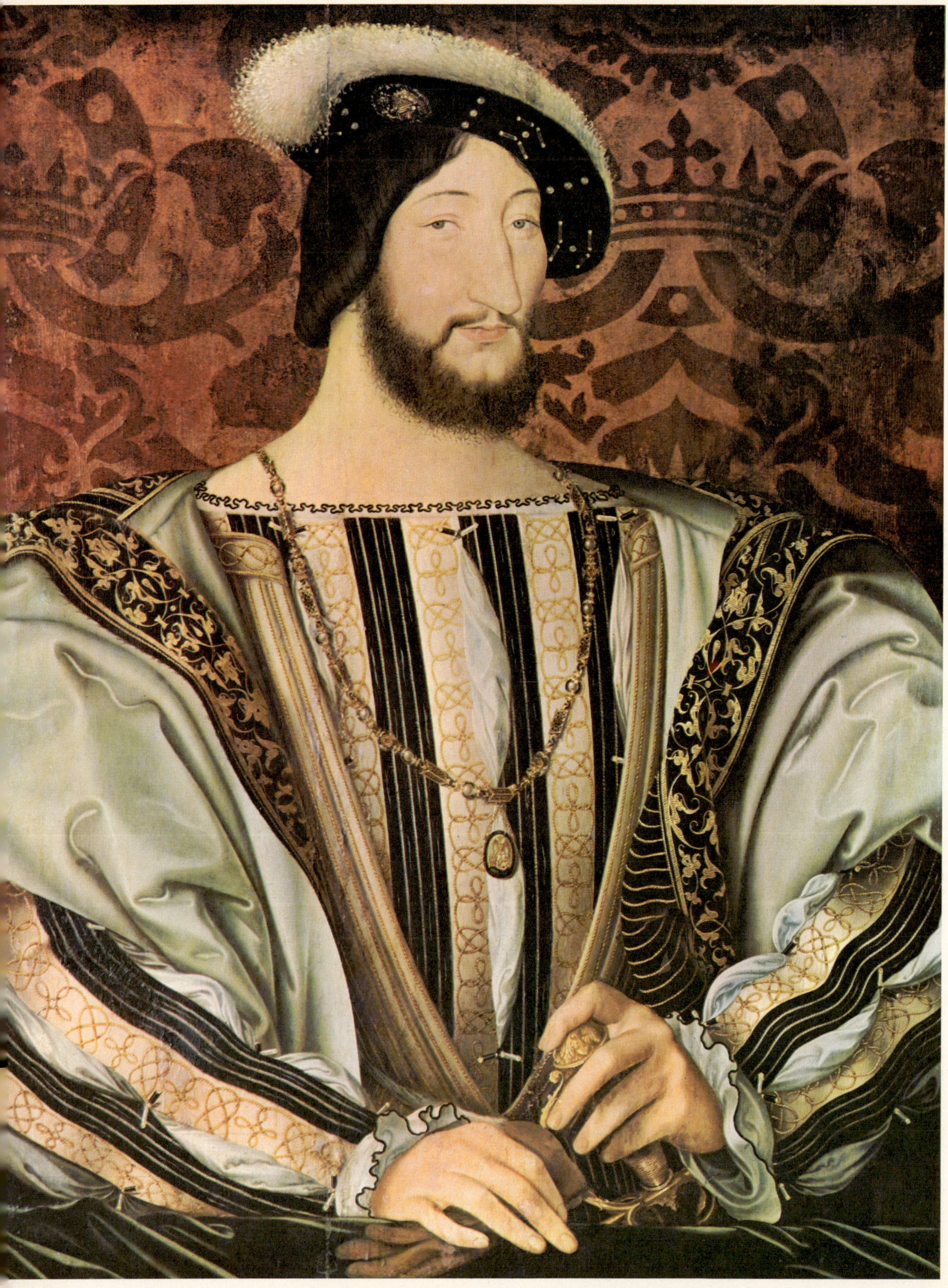

Francis I reigned from 1515 to 1547. He was a patron of the arts, and Leonardo da Vinci, Benvenuto Cellini and François Rabelais were among his protégés. France at this time was encircled by the possessions of Charles V, Holy Roman Emperor and King of Spain. Francis fought three wars against Charles, all of which were unsuccessful or inconclusive. In one of them Francis was captured at the Battle of Pavia in 1525. Imprisoned by Charles, he won his freedom only by signing the humiliating Treaty of Madrid in 1526. The portrait, attributed to Jean Clouet, brings to life Francis' magnificence and love of pomp.

morency, advocated putting an end to the conflict with the Empire, were more and more heeded at Court. The Duke of Guise opposed Montmorency's policy, and, with the support of the many Italians living in France, tried to have the policy of conquest in Italy continued.

During the reign of Henry II, the policies of these two parties were continually in conflict. During a period of Guise ascendancy, hostilities were resumed and the French were able to acquire the three important bishoprics of Metz, Toul and Verdun. When Montmorency returned to favor, the Truce of Vaucelles was negotiated in 1556.

The Guise policy of intervention against Spain in Italy received a serious setback from a defeat at Saint-Quentin in Flanders in 1557; in 1559, the Treaty of Cateau-Cambrésis ended the long struggle between France and Spain, and France gave up her Italian ambitions.

The three bishoprics remained under French control, however, and Calais was regained from England in the last period of the struggle. Soon after, Henry published the Edict of Ecouen, which was nothing less than a declaration of war on the French Reformation. The Wars of Religion had begun.

The Wars of Religion

In 1559, the year of Cateau-Cambrésis and the Edict of Ecouen, the first synod of the Reformed Churches of France met in Paris. The two sides in what was to be a long and violent struggle stood face to face: on the one hand the Catholic hierarchy and its supporters, and on the other the already numerous Reformed Churches. (According to Coligny, there were 2150 of them.)

It is difficult to be sure what social groups were represented by these two opposing ranks. All classes were represented among the Huguenots—the members of the Reformed Churches—as among the Catholics: the people, the nobility and the clergy.

Certainly, among the Huguenots there was a clearer awareness of the necessity for a general reform of religious and political abuses. This meant that the inhabitants of the cities, who were burdened by the monarchy's tax policy and indignant at the privileges of the clergy and the nobility, were more deeply attracted to the new ideas.

The monarchy made some attempts at conciliation between 1560 and 1562. The Edict of Amboise sanctioned the existence of two different forms of Christianity, and the Estates General was summoned in the hope that it would make the conflict less harsh or find a solution to the political and social problems that had become entwined with the religious one.

Catherine de' Medici, Regent for her son Charles IX, went further and brought Catholics and Huguenots together in the Conversations of Poissy, but without result.

The massacre of Huguenots at Vassy by Guise troops in 1562 began the first phase of the Wars of Religion, and the two sides found their natural leaders: the Catholics in the Duke of Guise, Anne de Montmorency and Saint-André; and the Huguenots in Admiral de Coligny, the Prince of Condé and the King of Navarre.

The hostilities, which went on for a long time, turned into a series of local encounters. During them, Montmorency, Antoine de Bourbon, Condé, Saint-André and the Duke of Guise all lost their lives. The war was interrupted in 1570 when Catherine and Coligny agreed on the Peace of Saint-Germain. This confirmed the Edict of Amboise that allowed the Reformed Churches to exist, and assigned the Huguenots certain strongholds or "places of security"—La Rochelle, Montauban and others.

But this peace turned out to be only a truce, for in 1572 Catherine suddenly reversed her policy. On St. Bartholomew's Day, Aug. 24, of that year massacres of Huguenots took place in Paris and all over France. (This was the celebrated Massacre of St. Bartholomew's Day.)

In spite of the terrible blow, the Huguenots did not lay down their arms, and several cities closed their gates to the royal troops. The necessity for a new peace was seen, and it was agreed upon in 1576—"The Peace of Monsieur"—after the death of Charles IX in 1574 and the accession of Henry III.

But many of the Catholic nobility did not accept the terms of the treaty, and formed themselves into a "League" under the leadership of Guise in order to continue the struggle against heresy and tolerance. Jean Bodin led a moderate party which tried to mediate between the two extremes of the League and the Huguenots, but the struggle grew fiercer.

The economic position of the country became worse and worse, and the Estates General summoned in 1576 was unable to remedy it. The League refused to compromise and forced Henry III to cancel the edicts of toleration already issued. It went so far as to provoke a rising in Paris in 1588.

Henry thought the best way to gain an advantage over the League was to have Guise assassinated. This was done in the castle of Blois on Dec. 23, 1588. Not long afterward he himself was slain by the fanatical Jacques Clément, a monk and member of the League.

HENRY IV TO LOUIS XVI

THE DEATHS OF BOTH THE KING and the head of the League made the situation even more difficult, for the heir to the throne was a Huguenot, Henry of Navarre. He was supported by most of the cities south of the Loire, while the League controlled entire provinces, such as Burgundy and Brittany, as well as Paris itself.

War broke out again. The League was supported by Philip II of Spain, who sent troops. After a struggle lasting several years, Henry decided to remove the greatest obstacle between him and the throne, and became a Catholic in 1593. In the next year he was crowned at Chartres, and in 1595 received formal absolution from the Pope. Strengthened in this way he was able to defeat the League and force Spain to make peace by the Treaty of Vervins in 1598.

THE EDICT OF NANTES

Henry IV issued the Edict of Nantes in 1598; it recognized the existence of two forms of worship and two religious organizations in France, and confirmed the possession by the Huguenots of their "places of security." Under Henry IV, Huguenots acquired great political importance and made a notable contribution to the new personal policy of the king. They also largely displaced the nobles of the League in positions of power.

Both the Duke of Sully and Olivier de Serres, two of Henry's chief ministers, were Huguenots. They were largely responsible for the work of restoration and economic recovery through tax relief to agriculture, land improvement, road building and the development of river navigation.

The French monarchy was losing the feudal characteristics it had retained even under Francis I, and was turning into a modern state. The king now carried on his government with the aid of trained and qualified men who served in the Council of State and the Council of Finances. Henry tried to make his administration modern and efficient.

The provinces were no longer ruled by governors, as in the past, who had often been hard to manage and tied to local interests. Instead of governors there were *Intendants*, usually middle-class administrators with special training, who were responsible directly to the king.

FINANCIAL REFORMS

This reorganization of the machinery of the state allowed Henry to undertake a financial reform, which was largely the work of Maximilien de Béthune, Duke of Sully. He made radical alterations in the system of recording revenue and expenditure and every year an *Etat Général*, resembling a modern budget, was produced.

Other aspects of the French administration still suffered from the piecemeal way it had developed in the past. The sale of offices continued to trouble the reformers, and caused much discontent.

Apart from the Treaty of Vervins that ended the war with Spain, Henry's reign contained little of note in the field of foreign affairs. Most important was the transaction by which the Dukes of Savoy gave Bresse and Bugey to France in return for a free hand on the other side of the Alps. In 1610, Henry considered reopening the struggle against Spain and Austria, but before he could begin it he was killed by a Catholic fanatic on May 14 of that year.

The Reign of Louis XIII

This sudden and unexpected disaster seemed likely to throw France back into the turmoil of the middle of the previous century. Maria de' Medici, Henry's widow, became Regent for her young son, Louis XIII. She was strongly under the influence of a number of Italians and the so-called Devout Party, all of whom were opposed to Henry's policies.

Religious troubles began again. The more militant Huguenots resented the increasing power, influence and activity of the Jesuits. Armed encounters occured. Maria de' Medici favored the Catholic side more and more, and the marriages of her son, Louis XIII, to the Spanish princess, Anne of Austria, and of her daughter, Elizabeth of France, to the son of Philip II of Spain showed where her sympathies lay.

In 1617, Louis XIII began to govern. At first he followed a policy similar to his mother's, and provoked Huguenot hostility by himself leading an expedition against Béarn and Navarre—traditional Calvinist strongholds. He integrated them with France and reintroduced Catholicism. But the Huguenots reacted so strongly that the king got into serious difficulties.

CARDINAL RICHELIEU

It was then that there appeared upon the stage one of the most important figures in the history of France, Armand du Plessis, Cardinal Richelieu. He was born in 1585 in a family of the lesser nobility of Poitou. He was made a cardinal in 1622 and a few years later became the King's principal minister. One central idea dominated his great political intellect; the absolute pre-eminence of the interests of the State over every private, individual or collective interest.

He was a devout Catholic and encouraged religious and charitable work, such as that of St. Vincent de Paul. But Richelieu never allowed French interests or policy to be identified with those of the Papacy or the traditional Catholic powers.

He fought the Huguenots because they were dangerous political opponents, and he deprived them of their strongholds. But once this victory was gained he observed to the letter the clauses of the Edict of Nantes which gave the Huguenots religious rights. In foreign affairs he had no hesitation in following the traditional French policy of aiding Protestant powers and causing them to fight Spain and Austria.

MOVES AGAINST THE HAPSBURGS

His political star rose high with the successful campaign against the Huguenots that ended with the seizure of their great stronghold, La Rochelle. When the internal situation was under control, Richelieu resumed the anti-Hapsburg policy that Henry IV had been contemplating at his death.

Great opposition to this course came from the groups about Maria de' Medici and the Queen, Anne of Austria, but Richelieu acted with prudence and cunning. He did not involve France in the first phase of the Thirty Years' War, which had

Cardinal Mazarin, a Sicilian, was a protégé of Richelieu, whom he succeeded as Chief Minister in 1642. The next year, when Louis XIII died, leaving as his heir nine-year-old Louis XIV, Mazarin rose to power. He dominated Louis XIV's mother, Anne of Austria, who was officially the Regent during Louis' long minority. For the rest of his life, the Cardinal was the most powerful man in France. His harsh policies led to a rebellion of the nobility called the Fronde, during which the King had to flee from Paris. After the Fronde outbreak had been crushed, Mazarin embarked in a successful war against Spain that enlarged France's territory in the south and in Flanders. Shortly after this triumph, in 1661, Mazarin died.

EMINENTISSIMO PRINCIPI CARDINALI
DVCI DE RICHELIEV
Sic ille ora gerit tacitum spirantia numen Richelius; terris, et metuendus aquis.

Armand du Plessis, Cardinal Duke of Richelieu was one of the great figures of French history. Born in 1585, he became chief minister to Louis XIII in 1624. Thereafter he was the real ruler of France until his death in 1642. Under Richelieu the powers of the crown were greatly increased. Many Huguenot strongholds, which made up a sort of state within the state, were forced to surrender their political privileges. Richelieu greatly increased the power of France in Europe, at the expense of Spain and the Holy Roman Empire, whose enemies he supported during the Thirty Years' War. He avoided direct French involvement in war as much as possible, but managed to gain considerable territory for his country. Richelieu was also a patron of the arts. He endowed several buildings of the Sorbonne and established the French Academy.

broken out in Germany in 1618. Instead, he restricted himself to creating difficulties for Spain and Austria by means of alliances.

He was largely responsible for the Valtelline and the Mantuan wars between 1624 and 1628—both were defeats for the Hapsburgs. Later, he arranged for King Gustavus Adolphus of Sweden to invade Germany.

France entered the war only after Gustavus died in the battle of Lützen in 1632. By 1642 French troops had reached the country's so-called "natural frontiers" on the Scheldt, Alps and Pyrenees. In 1643 the Prince de Condé defeated the Spanish infantry at Rocroi and in 1644 Viscount Turenne routed the Imperial troops at Nördlingen. Richelieu died in 1642 and Louis XIII in 1643.

CARDINAL MAZARIN

The new king, Louis XIV, was a child; his mother, Anne of Austria, Louis XIII's widow, entrusted the government to Cardinal Mazarin, a Sicilian. In spite of the poor state of the economy, a result of the war, and the steady opposition of the nobility and Parlement, Mazarin continued Richelieu's policies and brought them to a successful conclusion.

The Peace of Westphalia in 1648 ended the Thirty Years' War, and also confirmed France in her possession of most of Alsace, which she had invaded and seized. By balking the Hapsburgs' attempt to re-establish their leadership of the German princes, France founded the era of her own leadership of Europe. To make this an unchallenged leadership it was necessary to attack Spain, which had not signed the Peace of Westphalia.

The assault on Spain had to be postponed, however, for the internal situation of France had become very difficult. The interests harmed by Richelieu's great designs, and the nobility, which had been deprived of power, found expression for their resentment in the movement known as the Fronde.

THE FRONDE

The signal for the beginning of the Fronde was given by the Parlement of Paris when it opposed the levying of new taxes. Popular risings followed in the provinces, and finally the nobility rose under Condé, the victor of Rocroi. A propaganda campaign by means of pamphlets was undertaken against Mazarin and he was obliged to take refuge in Cologne. Louis XIV himself had to leave Paris and take refuge in Poitou.

The members of the Fronde disagreed among themselves, however, and the movement had contradictory aims. The king found an able supporter in Turenne, and the situation was brought under control.

The French were also soon able to begin their long-contemplated attack on Spain. After Mazarin's return to Paris in 1652 the war began in Flanders. Turenne's military skill and an alliance with Oliver Cromwell in England gave France the victory.

By the Treaty of the Pyrenees in 1659, France received Roussillon and Artois. Moreover, Louis XIV's marriage with Maria Theresa of Spain strengthened the foundations of a future claim to the throne of Spain, and assured France the leadership of Europe.

Louis XIV

Mazarin died in 1661 and the young King took sole and absolute control of the destinies of France. The phrase by which he is said to have expressed his sense of absolute power is well known: *"L'Etat c'est moi!"* (I am the State!). He insisted on respect for this power and his person from his courtiers and counselors. The identification of the state with the person of the sovereign was the continuation of a concept formed by Henry IV and strengthened by Richelieu.

Louis XIV pursued with great determination his aim of making France the dominant state in Europe. When Philip IV of Spain died, he called for the Spanish Netherlands to be "devolved"—handed down like a bequest—to his wife, Maria Theresa. In the war that resulted, he achieved brilliant military successes; only a coalition of England, Sweden and the United Provinces of the Netherlands induced him to negotiate a peace—which gave him part of Flanders.

LOUIS' POWERFUL FORCES

This War of Devolution showed Europe how powerful and efficient Louis' France was. He possessed an intelligent and experienced diplomatic service. His army came to number 400,000 and was, thanks to Louis' reforms, the first European army of a modern type. His navy already rivaled the Dutch and English fleets and enjoyed the use of newly built docks, arsenals and ports in Brest, Dunkirk and Toulon. France had, as well, an unprecedented system of fortifications built by the military architect, Vauban.

In 1672, Louis, after having isolated the United Provinces of the Netherlands by diplomacy, invaded them in great force. The Dutch were saved only because Spain and the Empire came to their aid, but the Spanish had to hand over Franche-Comté to Louis by the Treaty of Nimwegen in 1678. In 1681 the king seized the county of Montbéliard, the Saar and the German city of Strasbourg.

France now threatened Europe and had no rival. Her population at that time is estimated at 20,000,000, which was a very high figure in comparison with Spain's 6,000,000 and England's 8,000,000. Her power was increased by the extension of the colonial policy begun by Richelieu, and the French settlements in the West Indies and Canada flourished. Toward the end of the century Louisiana was acquired.

FRANCE'S ECONOMY BOOMS

In the meantime, France herself was enjoying a period of great economic development. Among the reasons for this were agricultural reforms and the gradual reduction of the authority of the nobility. Jean-Baptiste Colbert, Louis' principal minister, worked efficiently toward these goals. He made the tax system fairer; prepared a carefully balanced budget every year; and freed internal trade, as far as possible, from the numerous complicated taxes to which it had been subject.

Colbert also encouraged new economic ventures and new ideas. He built great public works, such as canals, and promoted the formation of great trading companies—the East Indies Company and the West Indies Company—which were like those existing in England and the Dutch Republic. He also set up manufacturing establishments run by the state—the Gobelins tapestry works and the Saint-Gobain glassworks—and encouraged other establishments protected and privileged by the state.

His policy of state intervention in economic affairs was based on an economic theory called mercantilism. According to this theory the wealth of a state was in direct relation to the amount of gold it possessed; and therefore its prosperity depended on exporting more than it imported. This led Colbert to promote and favor French exports and to impose taxes on imports.

Colbert's belief in mercantilism, then a new theory, was in line with the modernity of his other economic experiments and his general policy. Indeed, the achievements of Colbert showed French social progress and they deserve to be remembered along with the great intellectual and cultural achievements of the age.

A CREATIVE AGE

It was an age in which René Descartes' writings, among them, the *Discourse on Method,* opened new paths for philosophy. And the works of Pierre Corneille, Blaise Pascal, Molière and Jean Racine showed great sensitivity to psychological realities. Architecture passed through a Baroque period and then settled into the official classicism seen in the royal palace of Versailles.

The state for the first time felt a need to give more encouragement to cultural life than that traditionally afforded by the Court. Richelieu founded the French Academy in 1635, and this was followed by the Academy of Inscriptions and Belles-Lettres in 1663, by the Academy of Science in 1666 and by the Academy of Rome (for painting).

French culture produced some of its noblest works in this age: the tragedies of Jean Racine, Molière's comedies, Jean de la Fontaine's and Nicolas Boileau's verse, Jacques Bossuet's sermons. The Court of Versailles, which welcomed and fostered every aspect of cultural activity, symbolized French intellectual domination of Europe.

The King went to live permanently at Versailles in 1682, and this opened a new and very difficult period of his reign. Royal absolutism became more intolerant of every form of opposition or criticism. Violations of the Edict of Nantes and its repeal in 1685 forced thousands of highly skilled and industrious Huguenots to leave France to escape persecution. Their loss was a grave economic blow.

In 1688, William of Orange, who was Louis' cousin, and who hated him for what he had done to the Dutch, became King of England. He was now in a position to offer a serious threat to Louis' power. The forces in France that had suffered from Louis for either political or religious reasons turned to William. There were Protestant risings in the Cévennes that Louis suppressed bloodily.

As soon as he received the crown of England in 1688, William of Orange took England into the League of Augsburg, which had been formed between the Empire, Spain, the Dutch and Sweden to contain

Louis' aggression. France now had to fight all the great powers of Europe together, and the wars lasted for ten years.

In spite of brilliant victories, the French had to sign the Treaty of Ryswick in 1697 and give up all territories they had seized in the two decades since the Treaty of Nimwegen, except Strasbourg. The financial and military effort that France made during these years had caused great dissatisfaction among the people, and the unrest was increased by a series of bad harvests.

Taxes became heavier, and to raise money public offices were sold at greater and greater prices to the highest bidder. Speculation and financial adventures multiplied in Paris in the second decade of the 18th century, culminating in the failure of the Scotch banker, John Law. Such was the state of France when she found herself involved in the king's last great war—that of the Spanish Succession.

THE WAR OF THE SPANISH SUCCESSION

The Hapsburg line in Spain ended with Charles II, who willed his kingdoms to Philip, Duke of Anjou, a grandson of Louis XIV. The Emperor, who was of course a Hapsburg, opposed this choice and was supported by the Dutch and England. Only Bavaria and Savoy supported France, and the House of Savoy very soon went over to the other side.

The war was a harsh one for France. Things went against her at first, but she managed to retrieve her fortunes after defeat in the battle of Malplaquet in 1709 and at Denain in 1712. But when the Emperor Joseph died and it seemed likely that the Emperor Charles VI might succeed to the Spanish throne, England, now that William of Orange was dead, decided to negotiate.

The Treaties of Utrecht and Rastadt recognized Philip of Anjou as King of Spain, but the Spanish Netherlands and the Spanish possessions in Italy passed to Austria. France ceded North American territories, Acadia and Newfoundland, to England.

The Eighteenth Century

The War of the Spanish Succession brought England into the affairs of Europe as a power of the first rank. The rivalry between France and England was not confined to the question of dominating Europe, but extended to the two countries' colonies all over the world. These two new facts had much influence over

Louis XIV's reign from 1643 to 1715 was the longest of any French king. Under him the French monarchy attained its greatest glory. The remark Louis is supposed to have made—"L'état, c'est moi" (I am the state)—expresses perfectly his idea of his own importance. Until 1683 under the guidance of his great minister, Jean Baptiste Colbert, Louis initiated many important administrative and economic reforms. During this period France also acquired new territory through successful foreign wars and rose to an unrivaled position in Europe. From 1683 to 1715, however, a series of large-scale wars undid most of the good of the earlier years. Other European countries, fearful of Louis' ambition to dominate the continent, held France in check and exhausted her resources.

Louis lived and moved in an atmosphere of pomp and display, as shown by this picture of his arrival at the opening, in 1679, of the Invalides, a hospital which Louis had built for his veterans.

FRENCH KINGS OF THE HOUSES OF BOURBON AND BOURBON-ORLÉANS

Robert, d. 1317
Count of Clermont and Duke of Bourbon
Sixth son of Louis IX, King of France

founder of the house of Bourbon, from whom was descended in the seventh generation:

Anthony, d. 1562
King of Navarre

HENRY IV
1589-1610
(also King of Navarre, 1572-1610)

Louis XIII
1610-1643

- Louis XIV
  1643-1715

  Louis
  The Grand Dauphin, d. 1711

  - Louis, d. 1712
    Duke of Burgundy

  - Philip, Duke of Anjou
    King Philip V of Spain, 1700-1746
    from whom descended the Spanish Bourbons

  Louis XV
  1715-1774

  Louis
  Dauphin of France, d. 1765

  - Louis XVI
    1774-1792
  - Louis XVIII
    1814-1824
  - Charles X, d. 1836
    1824-1830

- Philip, Duke of Orléans
  d. 1701
  founder of the Orléans branch

  Philip, Duke of Orléans
  Regent of France, 1715-1723

  Louis, Duke of Orléans, d. 1752

  Louis Philippe, Duke of Orléans, d. 1785

  Louis Philippe, Duke of Orléans, d. 1793
  Member of the Convention
  Voted for the execution of Louis XVI, and himself was executed during the Terror

  Louis Philippe, d. 1850
  1830-1848

French policy after the death of Louis XIV in 1715.

Both Dubois, who directed French foreign policy under the Regency of the Duke of Orleans (1715-1723), and Cardinal Fleury, who directed it during the early part of Louis XV's reign, sought to come to an understanding with England. In 1720 the countries joined forces against Spain. The Anglo-French understanding helped France to succeed in the War of the Polish Succession (1733-1738), in which England took no part, and which resulted in France acquiring Lorraine.

At this time, French overseas possessions developed greatly. The French West Indies, in particular, produced a great quantity of sugar and were a rich market for the slave trade, which France practiced on a grand scale. The great French ports on the Atlantic, such as Bordeaux, prospered in consequence.

The policy of friendship with England did not last very long, for the War of the Austrian Succession (1740-1748) found France allied with Prussia against England, which supported Maria Theresa of Austria. On this occasion France came out of the conflict unharmed; the Treaty of Aix-la-Chapelle in 1748 provided for no changes in the ownership of territory involving France.

THE SEVEN YEARS' WAR

The next conflict, however, brought France a grave defeat. The Seven Years' War saw a total reversal of the traditional system of alliances: Prussia having become the strongest German state, France now lined up with her old enemy Austria, the Hapsburg domain, while England, which had defended Maria Theresa against the aggression of Prussia, changed sides.

The conflict begun in America in 1754, reached Europe in 1756. France entered the war tired and unprepared. Taxes, heavy already, had been increased. Public opinion was largely opposed to the war. The king's authority was lessened by court intrigues and by dissatisfaction with his favorites, and the persons in charge of the government lacked stability and skill.

All these negative factors affected the conduct of the war. Frederick II won victories over the Imperial armies, and England, under William Pitt, waged war against France and her colonies with great energy.

France was soon in a difficult position. Although Spain entered the war on the French side, this help had little effect.

By the Treaty of Paris, which put an end to the struggle in 1763, France lost many of her overseas possessions: New France in Canada, the islands of Tobago, St. Vincent and Dominica in the West Indies—all ceded to England; and Louisiana—ceded to Spain. In India, Dupleix' attempt to drive out the English had failed, and France agreed not to fortify Pondichéry, Chandernagor and the few other trading stations that were all that remained to her there.

France's domination of Europe was definitely over. The winning of Corsica from Genoa in 1768 was not enough to make up for these losses or to restore French prestige.

"THE ENLIGHTENMENT"

But France still led Europe intellectually and culturally. The names of Fontenelle, Montesquieu, Voltaire, Buffon, Rousseau and other great leaders of the new thought called "the Enlightenment" prove this. In 1751, Diderot and D'Alembert began their Encyclopedia, and a new school of economics was formed by the Physiocrats—Quesnay, Dupont de Nemours and others.

The famous portrait of Louis XIV by Hyacinthe Rigaud captures the spirit of the absolute monarchy, in which dignity and display almost obscure the man beneath the robes. Louis lived in public, even turning his dressing into a ceremony (the lever) *in which his bedroom was full of nobles.*

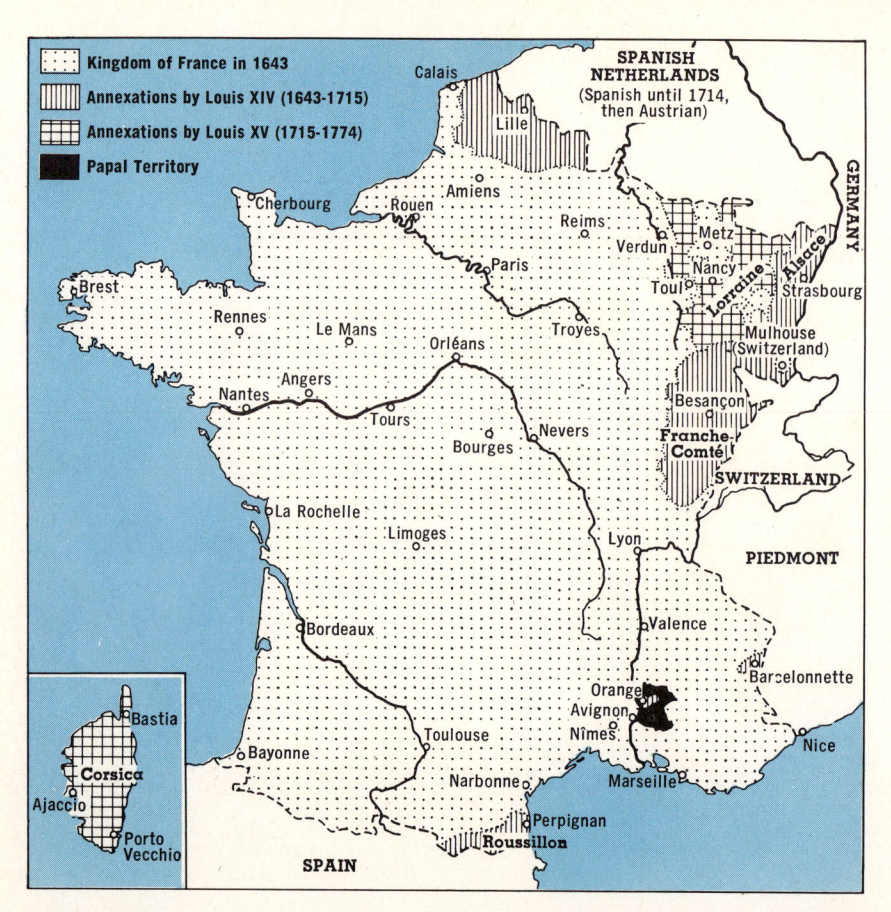

Left: During the reigns of Louis XIV and Louis XV France acquired new territory in the northeast, east and south and annexed the island of Corsica.

Below: Louis XIV began the construction of the Palace of Versailles in 1661. But it was only in 1682 that the enormous and magnificent edifice was sufficiently completed for him to move his Court there. It was so expensive to build that Louis did not allow its cost to become known. He used his Court to eliminate the independent power of the nobility. If a noble did not attend the Court, he had no chance of being given any administrative positions by the King, who gathered the power of the government in his own hands. If a noble fell from favor, he lost his positions. Thus Versailles became the symbol of absolute monarchy.

Since Louis' time, Versailles has had a very curious history. When it was built it was considered a wonder of the age. Other, poorer kings and princes all over Europe attempted to imitate its splendor for themselves. From 1682 to 1789, when the Revolution broke out, Versailles was the royal residence. During the revolutionary period it became a hated symbol of all the wastefulness of the monarchy, and afterward it was reduced to being a museum. But when the peace treaty ending World War I was signed in the Palace's Hall of Mirrors in 1919, Versailles resumed its honored place in French history.

France was already preparing the way for a new form of society. She was giving new ideas to the generation that was destined to bring about the French Revolution and the Napoleonic Empire.

Unlike the French culture of the century of Louis XIV, that of the century of Enlightenment was a rebellious and in some respects even a revolutionary one. It grew out of the struggle against superstition and religious intolerance and the criticism of the institutions and ideas of Louis XIV's time.

Among its great triumphs were the suppression of the Jesuit order in 1763 and Voltaire's long battle for tolerance against the Parlement of Toulouse with regard to the sentence imposed on Calas, a Protestant. The attraction of the Enlightenment lay in its rebellious nature, and the Revolution of 1789 was in fact a full expression of ideas that had been spreading and demanding expression in France for more than half a century.

THE REVOLUTION, THE EMPIRE AND THE RESTORATION

IN THE REIGN OF LOUIS XVI THE social and political rivalries that had been growing during the century became sharper. The structure of French society and the forces within it had become very complex over the years.

The nobility and the higher clergy had a privileged position. The middle classes with interests in farming and manufacturing were hampered by numerous feudal restrictions. The professional classes, however, were largely integrated into the existing system. But many of the rural and urban working class were extremely poor. All these classes had a *general* interest in France's being prosperous, but their *particular* interests were often in conflict.

The Revolution erupted because of the strains of the situation and also because of the miserable conditions under which large parts of the population lived. Most of all, the bourgeoisie—the middle class—had become rich, but had no political power or influence. It sought political power to match its wealth and size.

Attempts were made during the reign of Louis XVI to bring about a reform from above; but the changes made by Turgot, Necker and Calonne were balked by the opposition of various classes and interests that were harmed by them.

Jeanne Antoinette Poisson, Marquise de Pompadour (1721-64), was Louis XV's mistress from 1745 until her death. She is famous as a patron of artists and writers, including Boucher, Voltaire and Montesquieu. Through her influence over the King, she was the virtual ruler of France. Her foreign policy was responsible for the disaster of the Seven Years' War, which ended France's domination of Europe and cost France her colonies in Canada. Extraordinarily extravagant and rapacious, Mme. de Pompadour helped to bring the French monarchy into disrepute and thereby contributed to its overthrow at the end of the 18th century.

The victory won over England when France supported the American Revolution and the return of the West Indian islands lost in 1763 did not make up for the internal difficulties. The devotion to liberty and the spirit of revolt in America, and Benjamin Franklin's and George Washington's republicanism, had a strong effect on French opinion.

In 1789, a long conflict between the Crown and the Parlement of Paris, which was refusing to subscribe to more taxes, led to the summoning of the national body—the Estates General—for the first time since 1614. This move had been recommended by the nobility, who saw in it a return to the older state of affairs existing before the monarchy had become absolute; then the upper classes had dominated the Estates General.

The hopes of the nobility were not all realized, for the representatives of the Third Estate—the middle classes—requested that voting should be not by Estate but by individuals. If this were done the dominance of the nobility and clergy—the other two Estates—would come to an end.

When the nobles and clergy refused, the Third Estate proclaimed itself the National Assembly on June 17, 1789. The king was not able to persuade the members to go back on their declaration, and so, when they met on June 20, they found that their chamber in the palace at Versailles was closed to them. They met instead in the *Jeu de Paume* (the Tennis Court) and swore not to separate until the country had received a new constitution.

A few days later the nobility and clergy agreed to take part in the new National Assembly. But on July 11 the king, as a gesture against the bourgeoisie, dismissed his chief minister, the Swiss banker Necker

THE FALL OF THE BASTILLE

The people of Paris had so far been only spectators of the struggle between the Estates; but on July 14, led by members of the Third Estate, they seized the Bastille, a prison in Paris which was a symbol of the King's absolute power. Between July 19 and Aug. 6 there were many peasant uprisings all over the country.

This movement began as a wave of collective fear and hysteria, but soon turned into an attack on the nobility, many of whose châteaux were sacked or burned. In some provincial cities the bourgeoisie roused the people, the royal intendants were turned out, and municipal governments formed.

On Aug. 4 the National Assembly proclaimed the abolition of all feudal rights. And on Aug. 26 it published the Declaration of the Rights of Man and of the Citizen, which asserted the principles of liberty and equality of all citizens before the law.

The popular revolt had won—and had given the victory to the Third Estate. The people of Paris demonstrated their sense of victory on Oct. 7, when they marched to Versailles and forced the King and Queen to return with them to Paris.

All offices in the departments, the new administrative districts that replaced the provinces, were elective, including the judiciary. Torture was abolished, and every remnant of feudalism was cut out.

Highway tolls were done away with; weights and measures were made the same throughout the country. The possessions of the Church were confiscated and the clergy reduced to a body of persons with religious functions in the service of the State, to which they had to swear allegiance.

But even while the constitution was being drawn up, difficulties had arisen. Many of the nobility and some of the clergy put pressure on the Court, and there was already talk of an aristocratic plot aimed at overthrowing the Revolution with foreign help.

In the cities and countryside discontent was widespread. The "national property" obtained from the confiscation of the Church lands had been sold by auction, and this had benefited the richer members of the bourgeoisie to the disadvantage of the poor and less prosperous. The new paper money issued by the government—the *assignats*—which were backed by the sale of Church property, lost value.

RUMORS OF A PLOT

This was the situation when, in July 1791, the news came that the King had attempted to flee, and had been seized at Varennes near the northern frontier. The rumors of a Court plot seemed to have foundation, and a constitutional monarchy seemed no longer possible.

If the Revolution was to be saved a further step was needed—the monarchy must be abolished. This was being said in the revolutionary clubs that had grown up in Paris (the most important was the Jacobins' Club), and it was being repeated in the press, and in various quarters of the city.

The National Assembly continued until September 1791. A major part of its work was the preparation of a constitution incorporating many of the reforms of the past two years.

At this point the government under the new constitution took over. It reflected the political supremacy of the bourgeoisie. Sovereignty was vested in the Legislative Assembly.

The exquisite Petit Trianon in the park at Versailles was the favorite residence of Marie Antoinette, Queen of France and wife of Louis XVI. Louis, who came to the throne in 1774, was well-intentioned, but shy and stupid. Marie Antoinette, dissatisfied with her marriage threw herself into a life of pleasure. Diamond-collecting became her hobby. Bored with the dull routine and pompous etiquette of the Court, she would retire wtih her favorites to the Petit Trianon where she would throw "little" parties and costume balls costing thousands of francs each.